3

Hiro Mashima

Translated and adapted by William Flanagan
Lettered by North Market Street Graphics

Ballantine Books · New York

Fairy Tail volume 3 is a work of fiction. Names, characters, places, and incidents are the products of the author's imagination or are used fictitiously. Any resemblance to actual events, locales, or persons, living or dead, is entirely coincidental.

A Del Rey Manga/Kodansha Trade Paperback Original

Published in the United States by Del Rey Books, an imprint of The Random House Publishing Group, a division of Random House, Inc., New York.

Publication rights arranged through Kodansha Ltd.

First published in Japan in 2007 by Kodansha Ltd., Tokyo

ISBN 978-0-345-50556-9

Printed in the United States of America

www.delreymanga.com

9 8 7 6 5 4 3 2

Translator/Adapter—William Flanagan
Lettering—North Market Street Graphics

Contents

I love my guitar.
Of course, I'm terrible at it, but I
love strumming during breaks in
work...and when I'm stuck as to
what to draw on the Name*.
I just love strumming. Sometimes,
I strum while I work, and I get
the "Yeah, yeah" look from my
staff. You know the look. It's the
"Get back to work" look. Yeah...

—Hiro Mashima

*Name = A sketched first
draft of a manga.

Honorifics Explained

Throughout the Del Rey Manga books, you will find Japanese honorifics left intact in the translations. For those not familiar with how the Japanese use honorifics and, more important, how they differ from American honorifics, we present this brief overview.

Politeness has always been a critical facet of Japanese culture. Ever since the feudal era, when Japan was a highly stratified society, use of honorifics—which can be defined as polite speech that indicates relationship or status—has played an essential role in the Japanese language. When you address someone in Japanese, an honorific usually takes the form of a suffix attached to one's name (example: "Asuna-san"), is used as a title at the end of one's name, or appears in place of the name itself (example: "Negi-sensei," or simply "Sensei!").

Honorifics can be expressions of respect or endearment. In the context of manga and anime, honorifics give insight into the nature of the relationship between characters. Many English translations leave out these important honorifics and therefore distort the feel of the original Japanese. Because Japanese honorifics contain nuances that English honorifics lack, it is our policy at Del Rey not to translate them. Here, instead, is a guide to some of the honorifics you may encounter in Del Rey Manga.

-san: This is the most common honorific and is equivalent to Mr., Miss, Ms., or Mrs. It is the all-purpose honorific and can be used in any situation where politeness is required.

-sama: This is one level higher than "-san" and is used to confer great respect.

-dono: This comes from the word "tono," which means "lord." It is an even higher level than "-sama" and confers utmost respect.

-kun: This suffix is used at the end of boys' names to express familiarity or endearment. It is also sometimes used by men among friends, or when addressing someone younger or of a lower station.

-chan: This is used to express endearment, mostly toward girls. It is also used for little boys, pets, and even among lovers. It gives a sense of childish cuteness.

Bozu: This is an informal way to refer to a boy, similar to the English terms "kid" and "squirt."

Sempai/
Senpai: This title suggests that the addressee is one's senior in a group or organization. It is most often used in a school setting, where underclassmen refer to their upperclassmen as "sempai." It can also be used in the workplace, such as when a newer employee addresses an employee who has seniority in the company.

Kohai: This is the opposite of "sempai" and is used toward underclassmen in school or newcomers in the workplace. It connotes that the addressee is of a lower station.

Sensei: Literally meaning "one who has come before," this title is used for teachers, doctors, or masters of any profession or art.

-[blank]: This is usually forgotten in these lists, but it is perhaps the most significant difference between Japanese and English. The lack of honorific, known as *yobisute*, means that the speaker has permission to address the person in a very intimate way. Usually, only family, spouses, or very close friends have this kind of permission. It can be gratifying when someone who has earned the intimacy starts to call one by one's name without an honorific. But when that intimacy hasn't been earned, it can be very insulting.

FAIRY TAIL

3

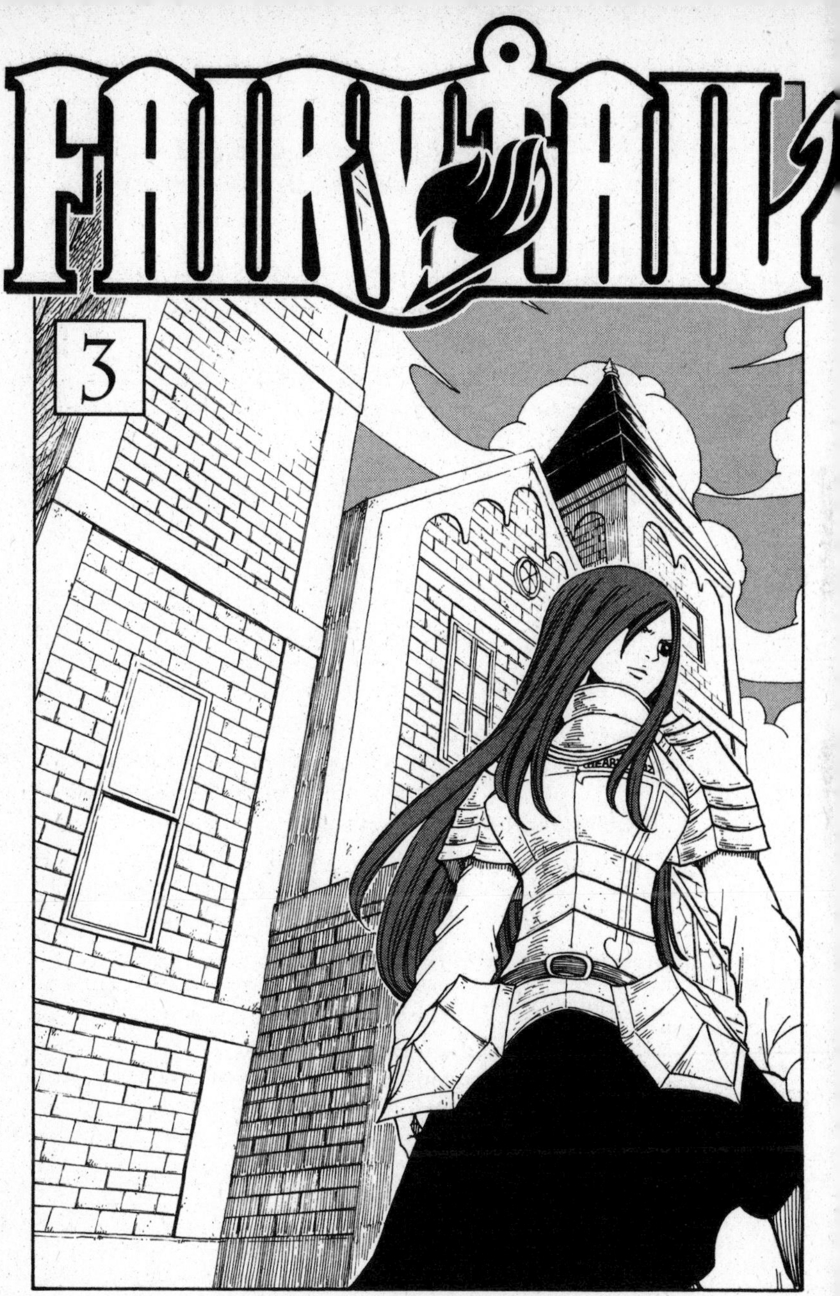

HIRO MASHIMA

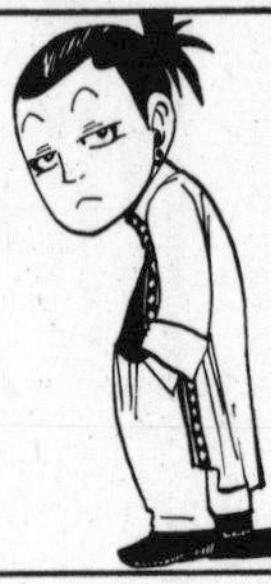

FAIRY TAIL

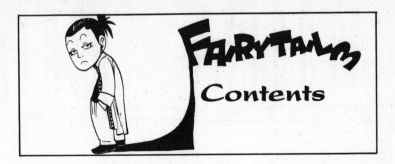

Contents

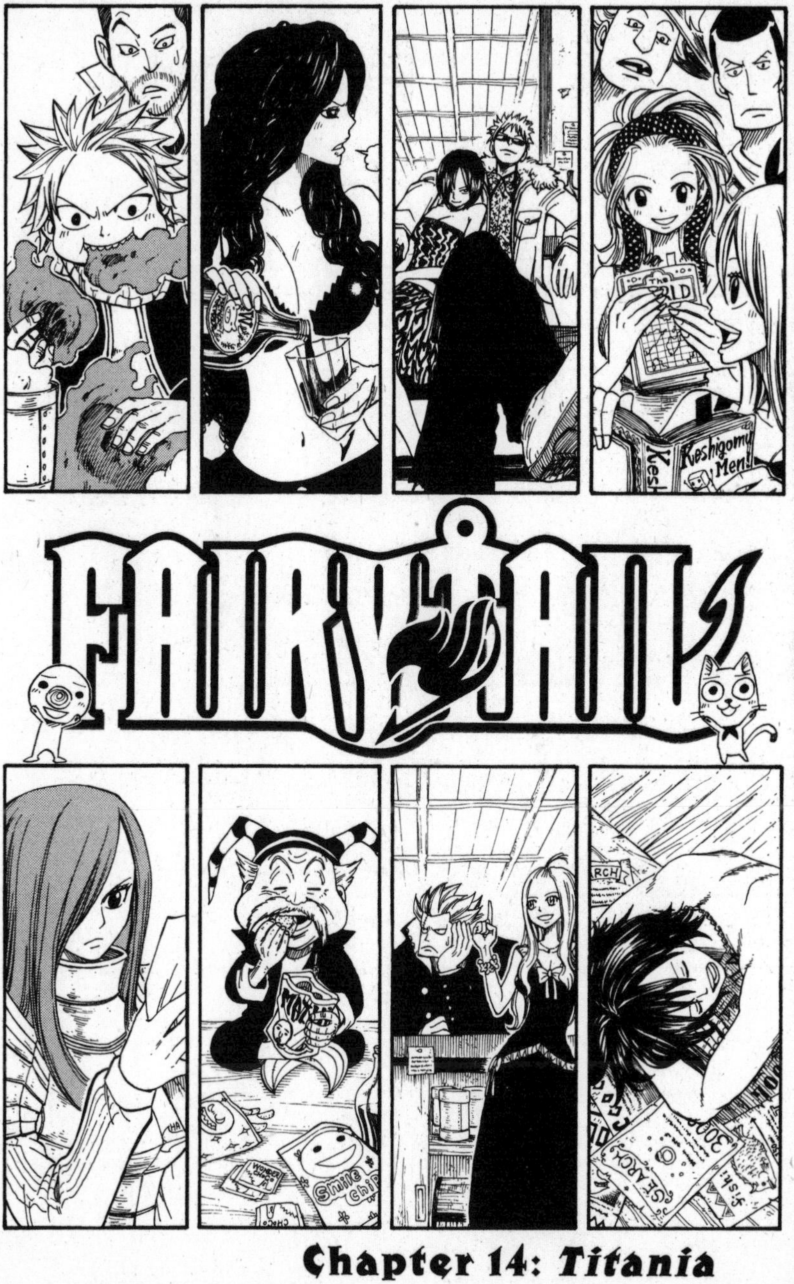
FAIRY TAIL
Keshigomu Men!
Smile chips

Chapter 14: *Titania*

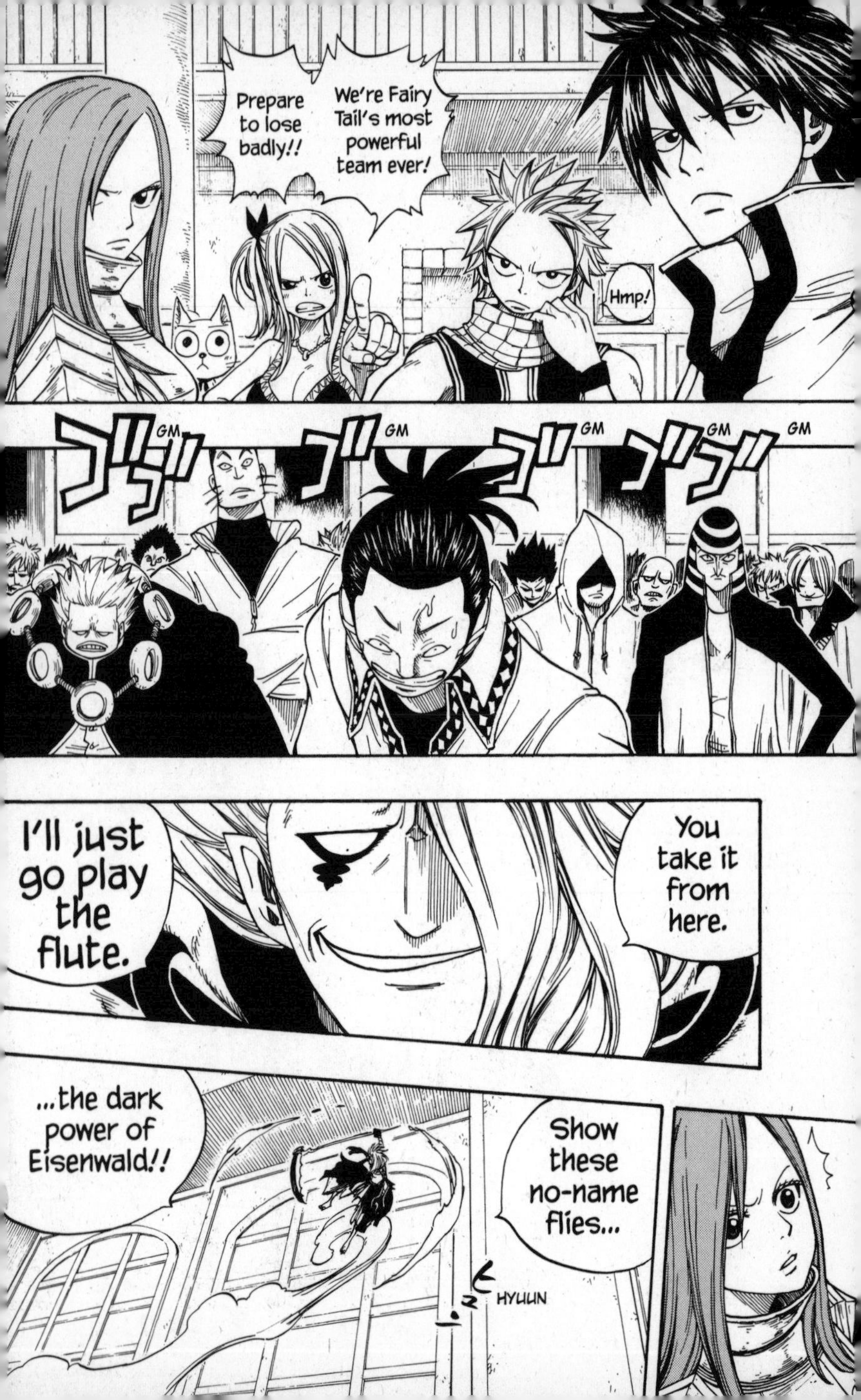
We're Fairy Tail's most powerful team ever!
Prepare to lose badly!!
Hmp!
GM
GM
GM
GM
GM
You take it from here.
I'll just go play the flute.
Show these no-name flies...
...the dark power of Eisenwald!!
HYUUN

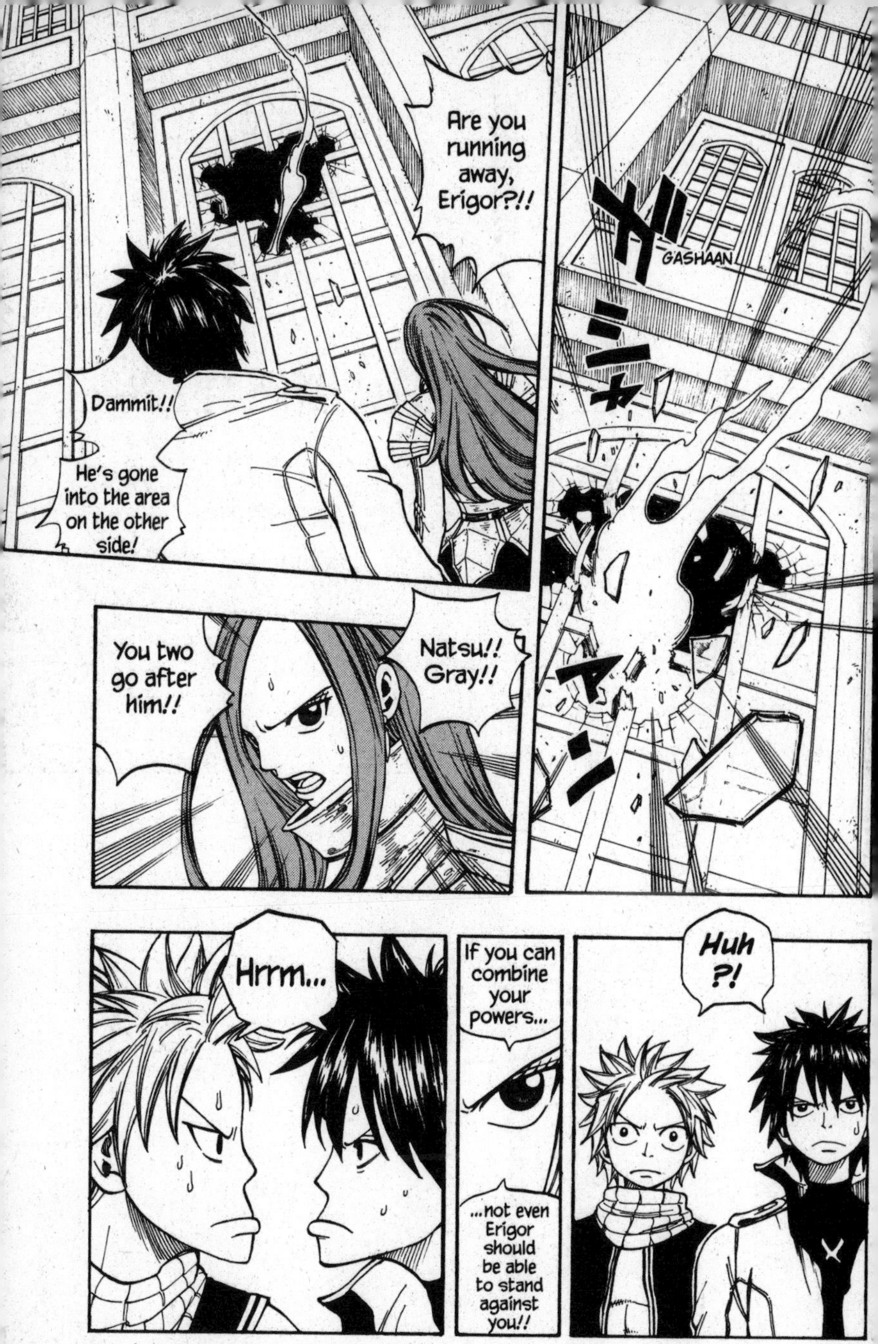
GASHAAN
Are you running away, Erigor?!!
Dammit!!
He's gone into the area on the other side!
Natsu!! Gray!!
You two go after him!!
Huh ?!
If you can combine your powers...
...not even Erigor should be able to stand against you!!
Hrrm...

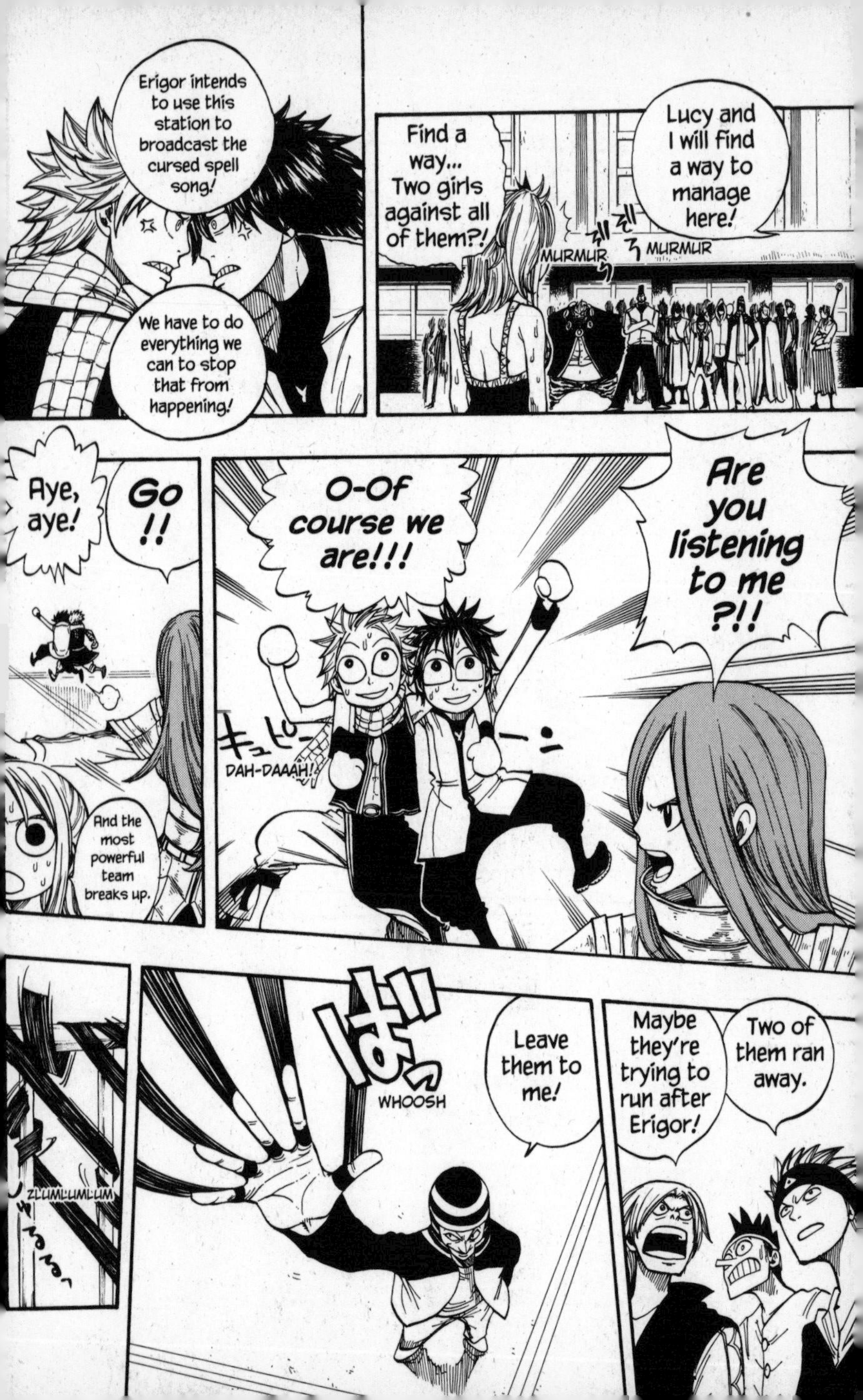
Lucy and I will find a way to manage here!
Find a way... Two girls against all of them?!
MURMUR
MURMUR
Erigor intends to use this station to broadcast the cursed spell song!
We have to do everything we can to stop that from happening!
Are you listening to me ?!!
O-Of course we are!!!
DAH-DAAAH!
Go !!
Aye, aye!
And the most powerful team breaks up.
Two of them ran away.
Maybe they're trying to run after Erigor!
Leave them to me!
ばっ
WHOOSH
ZLUMLUMLUM

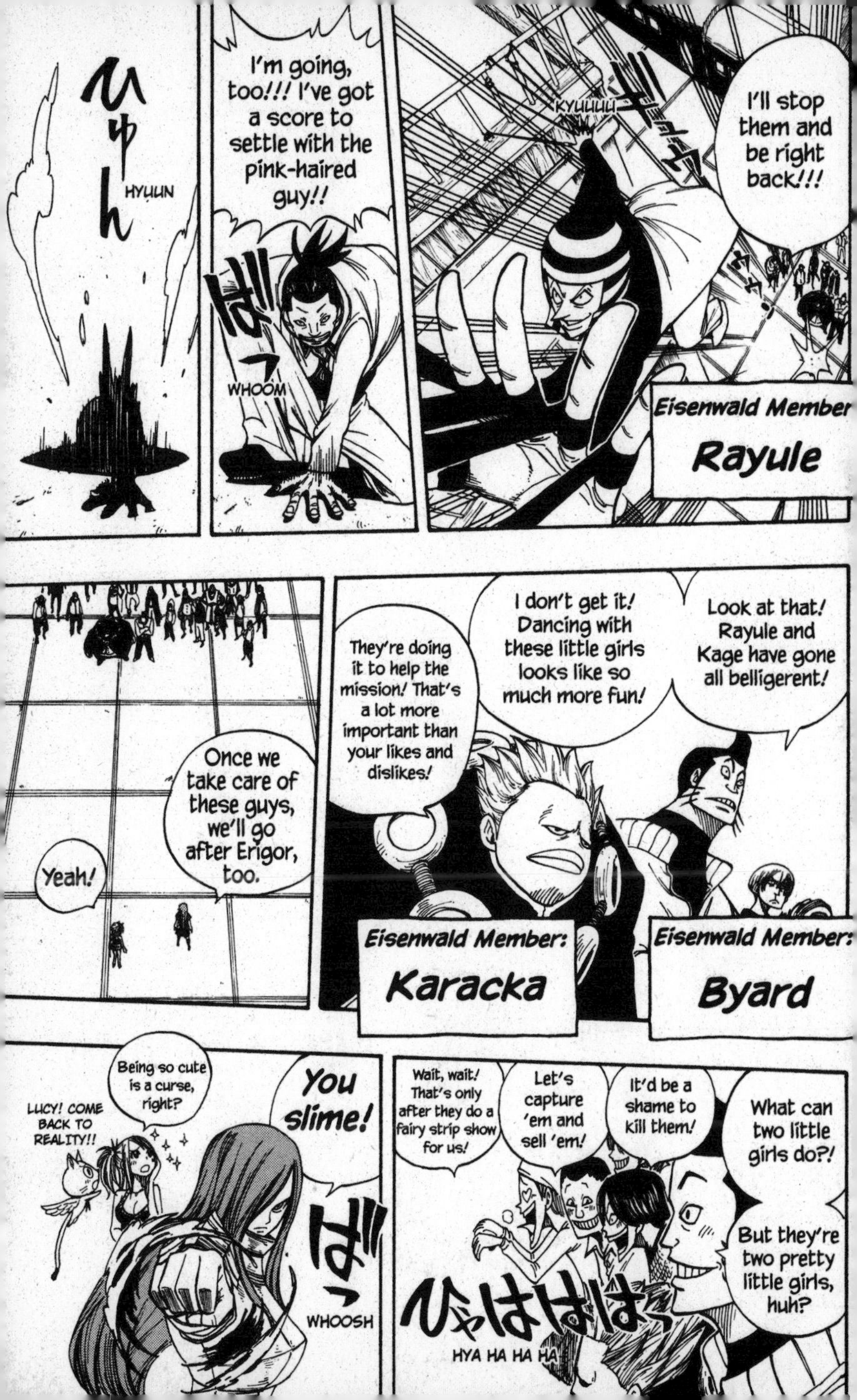
I'll stop them and be right back!!!
KYUUUU
Eisenwald Member
Rayule
I'm going, too!!! I've got a score to settle with the pink-haired guy!!
WHOOM
ひゅん
HYUUN
Look at that! Rayule and Kage have gone all belligerent!
I don't get it! Dancing with these little girls looks like so much more fun!
They're doing it to help the mission! That's a lot more important than your likes and dislikes!
Eisenwald Member:
Byard
Eisenwald Member:
Karacka
Once we take care of these guys, we'll go after Erigor, too.
Yeah!
What can two little girls do?!
But they're two pretty little girls, huh?
It'd be a shame to kill them!
Let's capture 'em and sell 'em!
Wait, wait! That's only after they do a fairy strip show for us!
ひゃははは
HYA HA HA HA
You slime!
WHOOSH
Being so cute is a curse, right?
LUCY! COME BACK TO REALITY!!

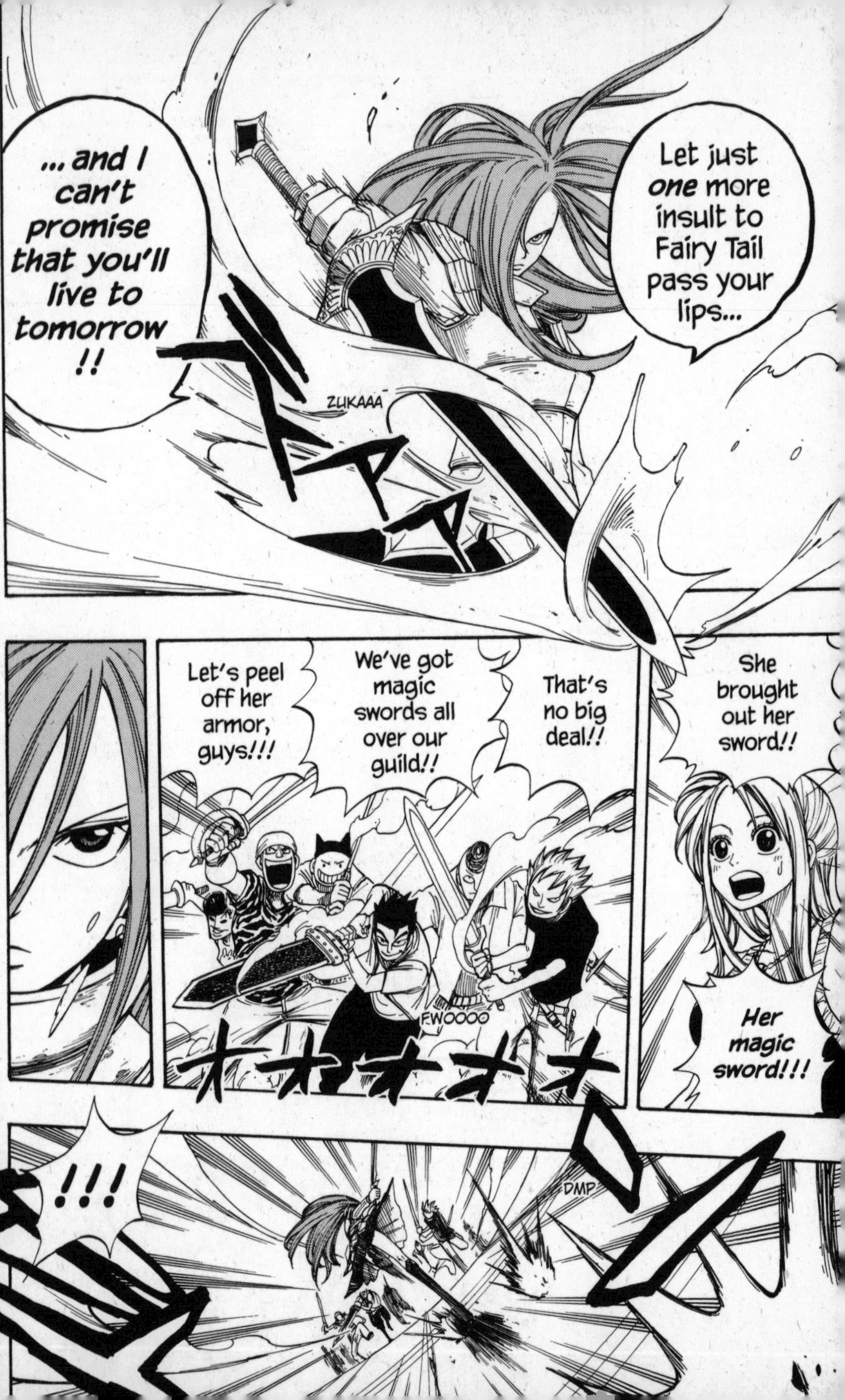
Let just *one* more insult to Fairy Tail pass your lips...
...and I can't promise that you'll live to tomorrow!!
ZUKAAA
She brought out her sword!!
Her magic sword!!!
That's no big deal!!
We've got magic swords all over our guild!!
Let's peel off her armor, guys!!!
FWOOOO
DMP
!!!

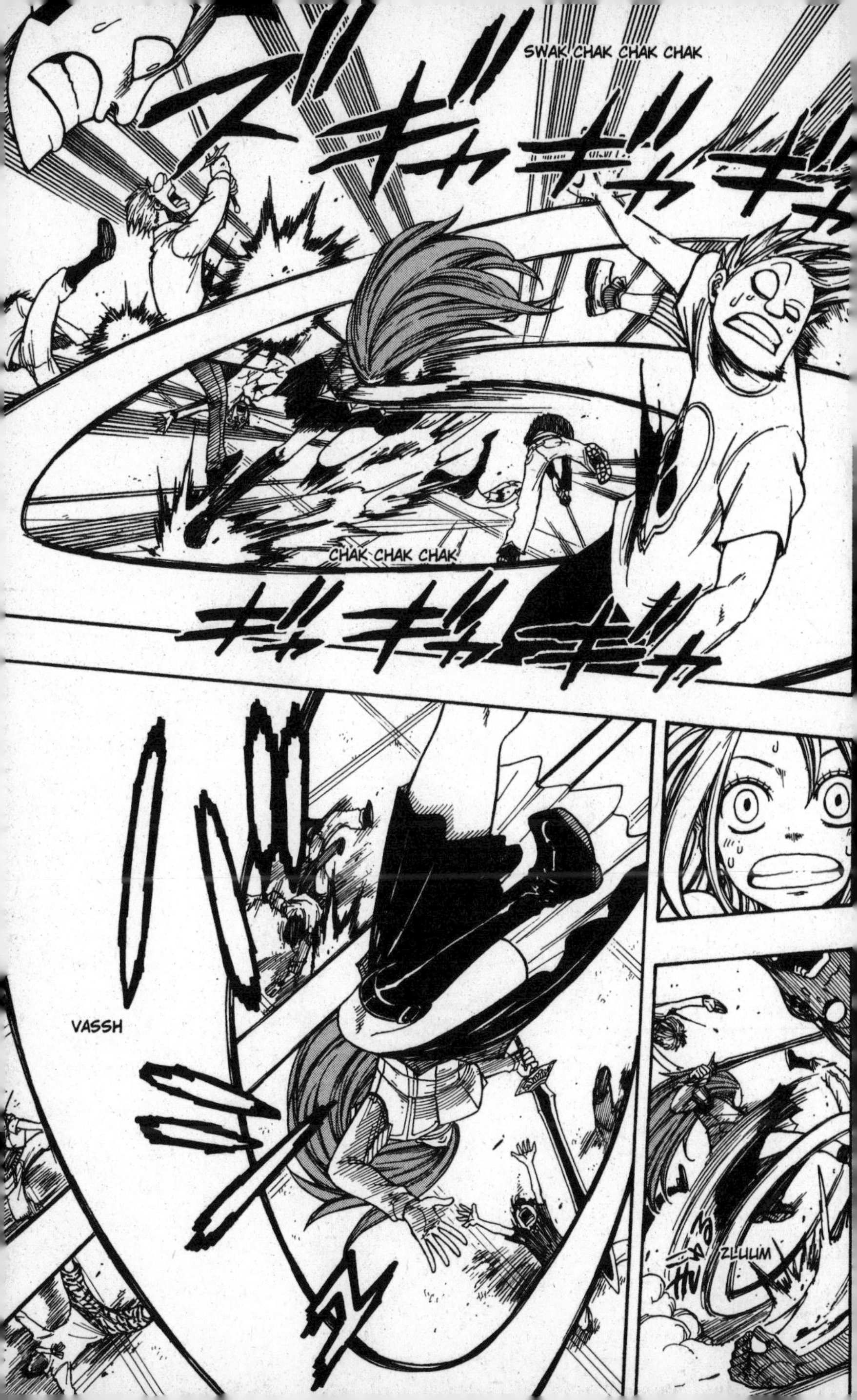
SWAK CHAK CHAK CHAK
CHAK CHAK CHAK
ZLUUM
VASSH

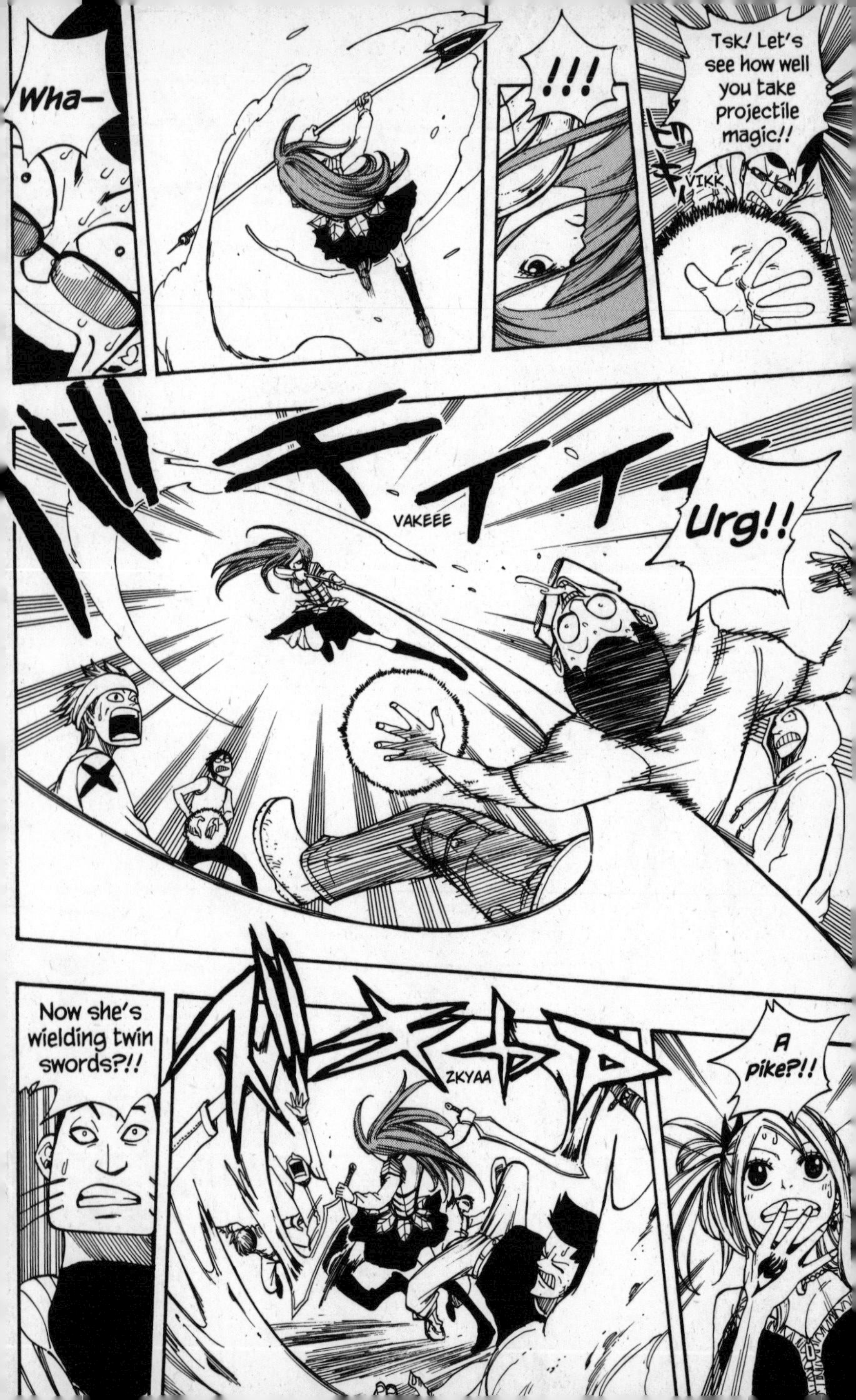
Tsk! Let's see how well you take projectile magic!!
VIKK
!!!
Wha–
Urg!!
VAKEEE
A pike?!!
ZKYAA
Now she's wielding twin swords?!!

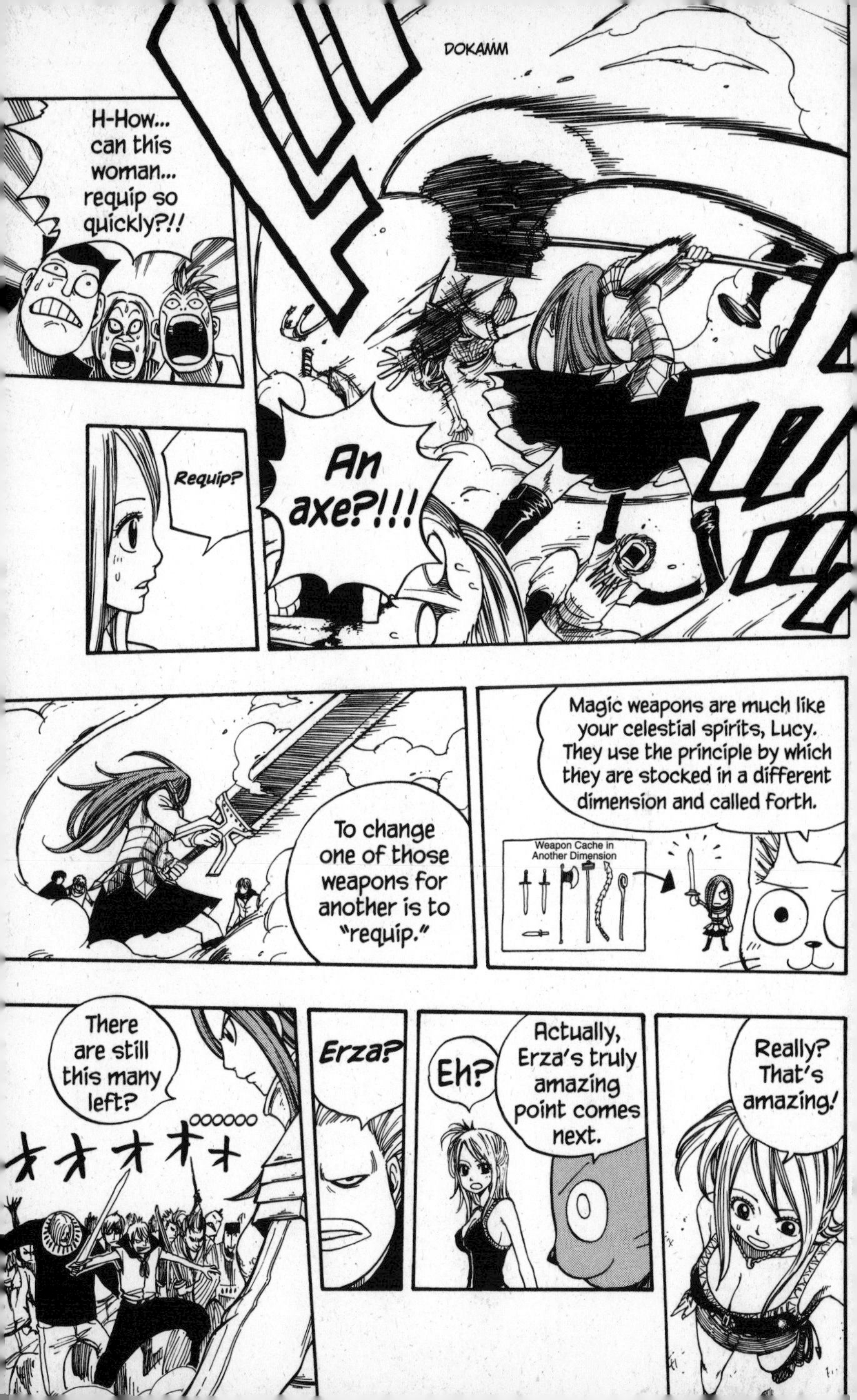
DOKAMM
An axe?!!!
H-How... can this woman... requip so quickly?!!
Requip?
Magic weapons are much like your celestial spirits, Lucy. They use the principle by which they are stocked in a different dimension and called forth.
Weapon Cache in Another Dimension
To change one of those weapons for another is to "requip."
Really? That's amazing!
Actually, Erza's truly amazing point comes next.
Eh?
Erza?
There are still this many left?
OOOOOO

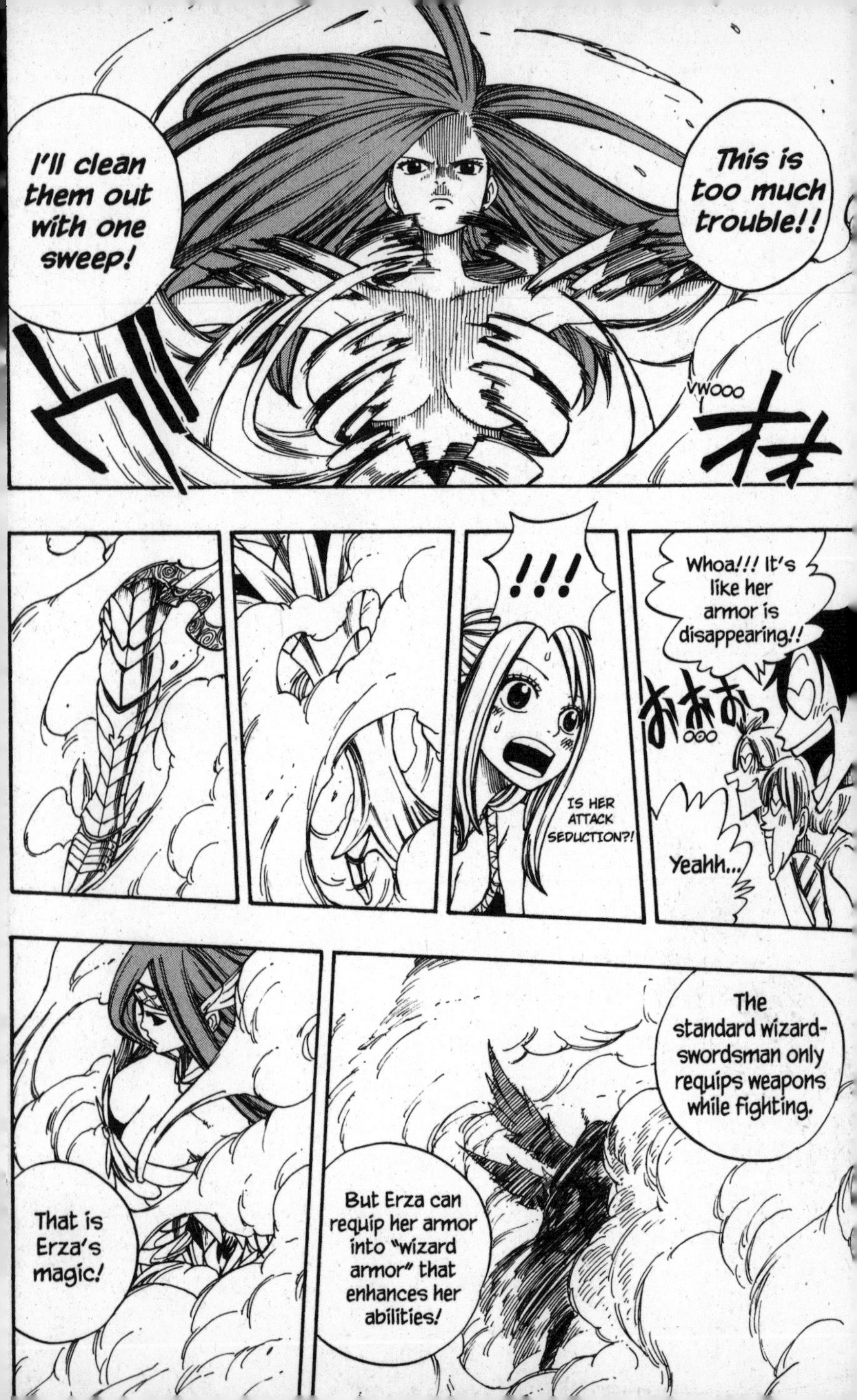
This is too much trouble!!
I'll clean them out with one sweep!
VWOOO
Whoa!!! It's like her armor is disappearing!!
OOO
Yeahh...
!!!
IS HER ATTACK SEDUCTION?!
The standard wizard-swordsman only requips weapons while fighting.
But Erza can requip her armor into "wizard armor" that enhances her abilities!
That is Erza's magic!

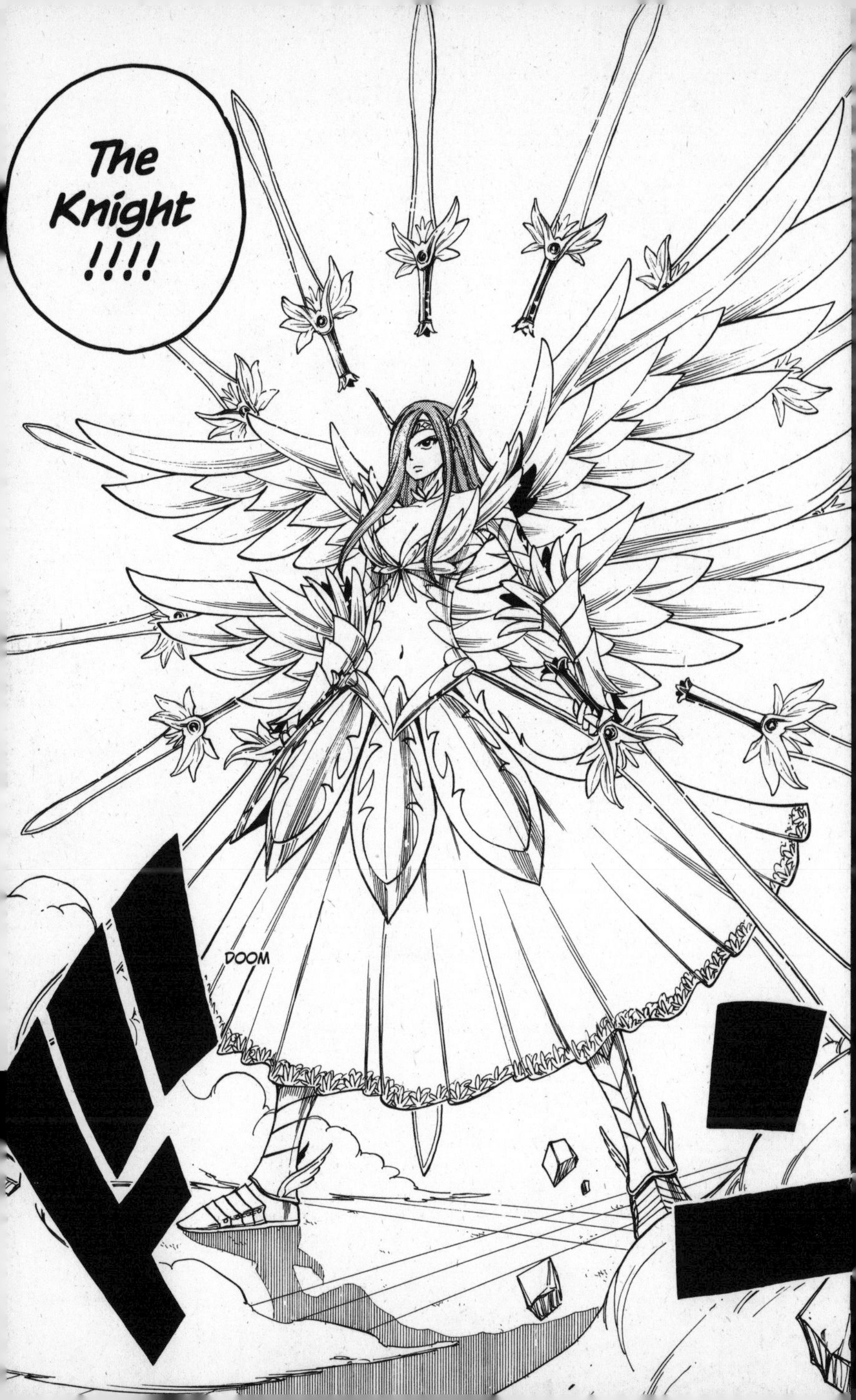
The Knight !!!!
DOOM

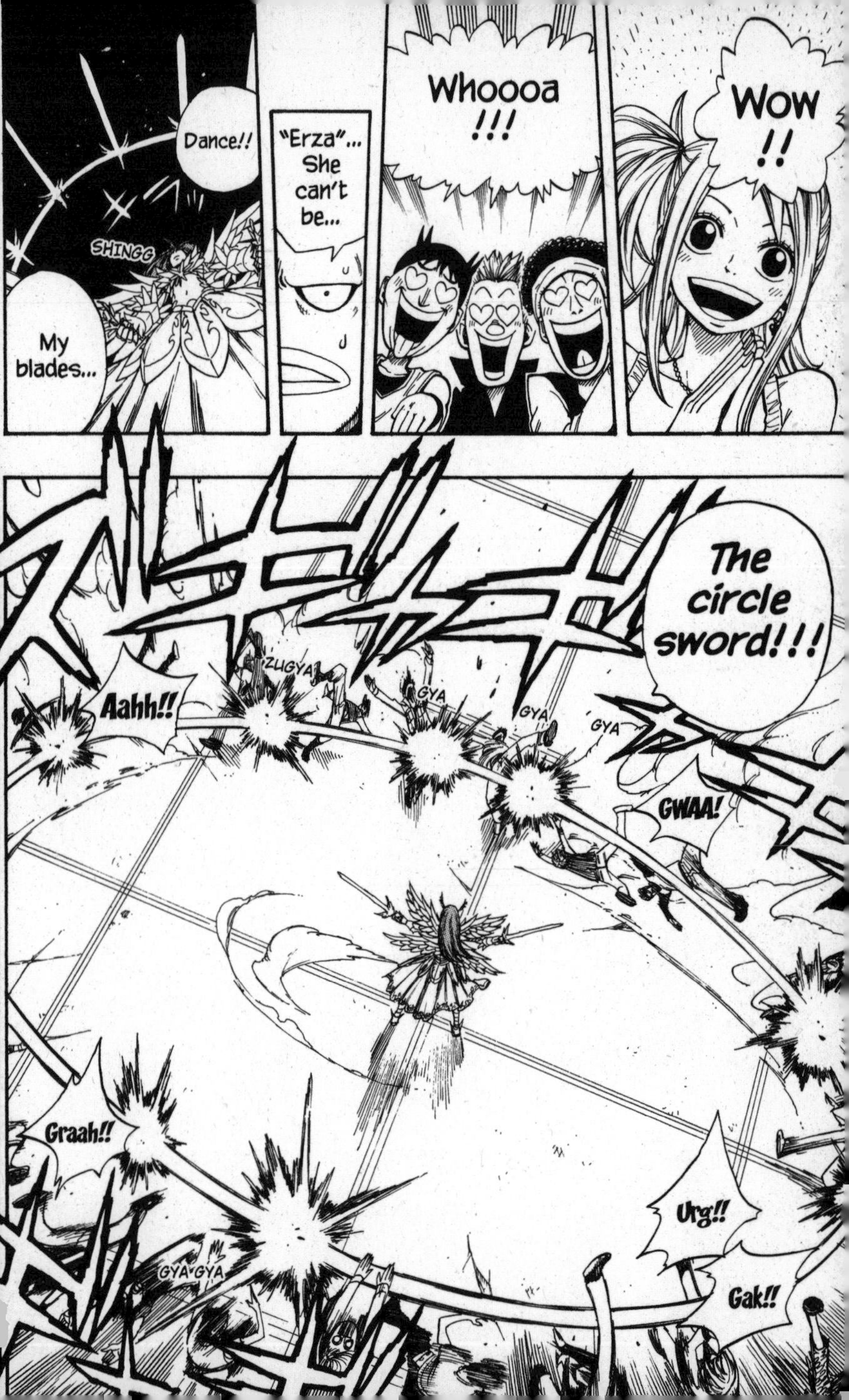
Wow !!
Whoooa !!!
"Erza"... She can't be...
Dance!!
SHINGG
My blades...
The circle sword!!!
GYA
GYA
GYA
ZUGYA
Aahh!!
GWAA!
Urg!!
Gak!!
Graah!!
GYA GYA

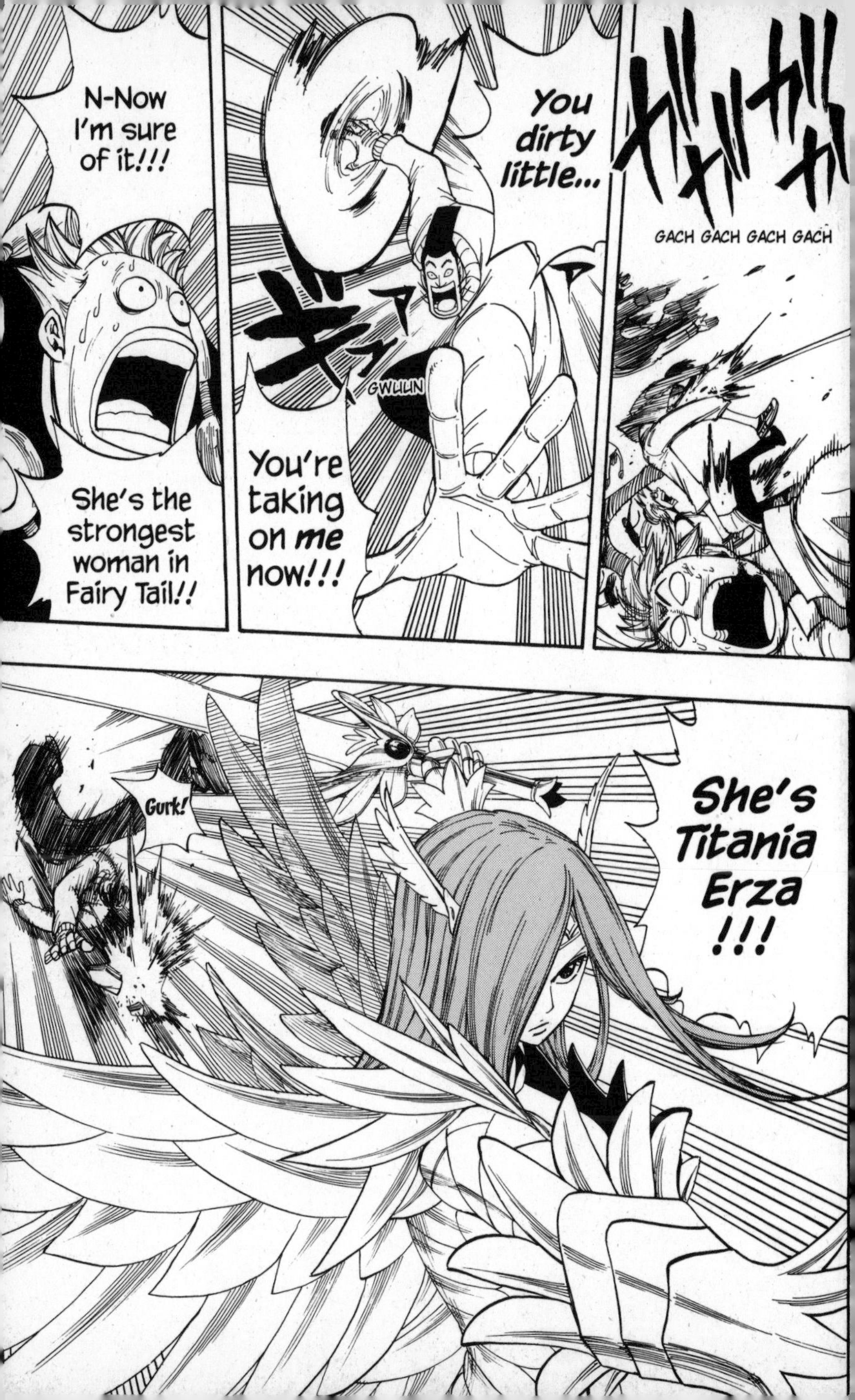
GACH GACH GACH GACH
You dirty little...
GWUUN
You're taking on *me* now!!!
N-Now I'm sure of it!!!
She's the strongest woman in Fairy Tail!!
She's Titania Erza!!!
Gurk!

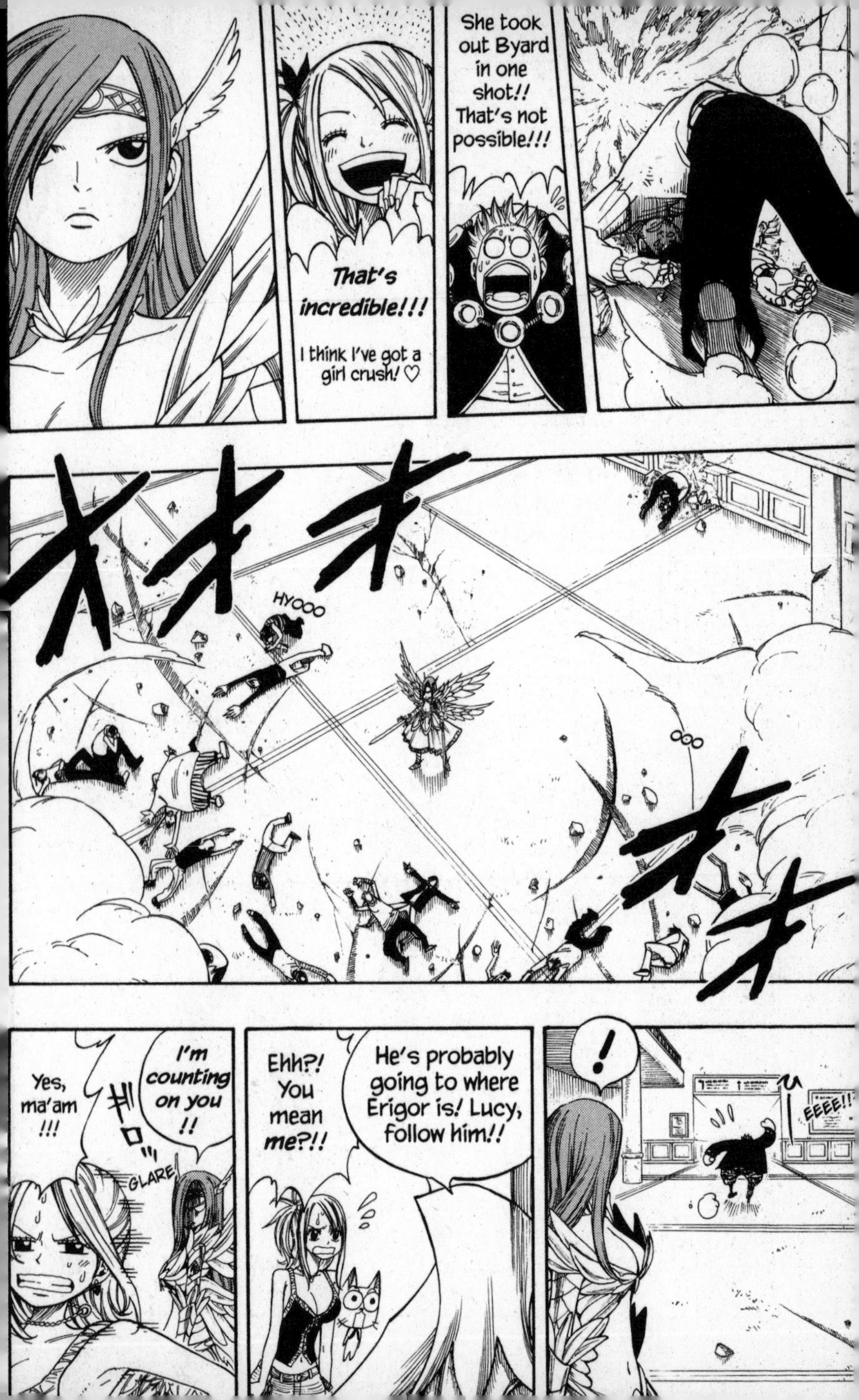
She took out Byard in one shot!! That's not possible!!!
That's incredible!!!
I think I've got a girl crush! ♡
HYOOO
OOO
!
EEEE!!
He's probably going to where Erigor is! Lucy, follow him!!
Ehh?! You mean me?!!
I'm counting on you!!
GLARE
Yes, ma'am!!!

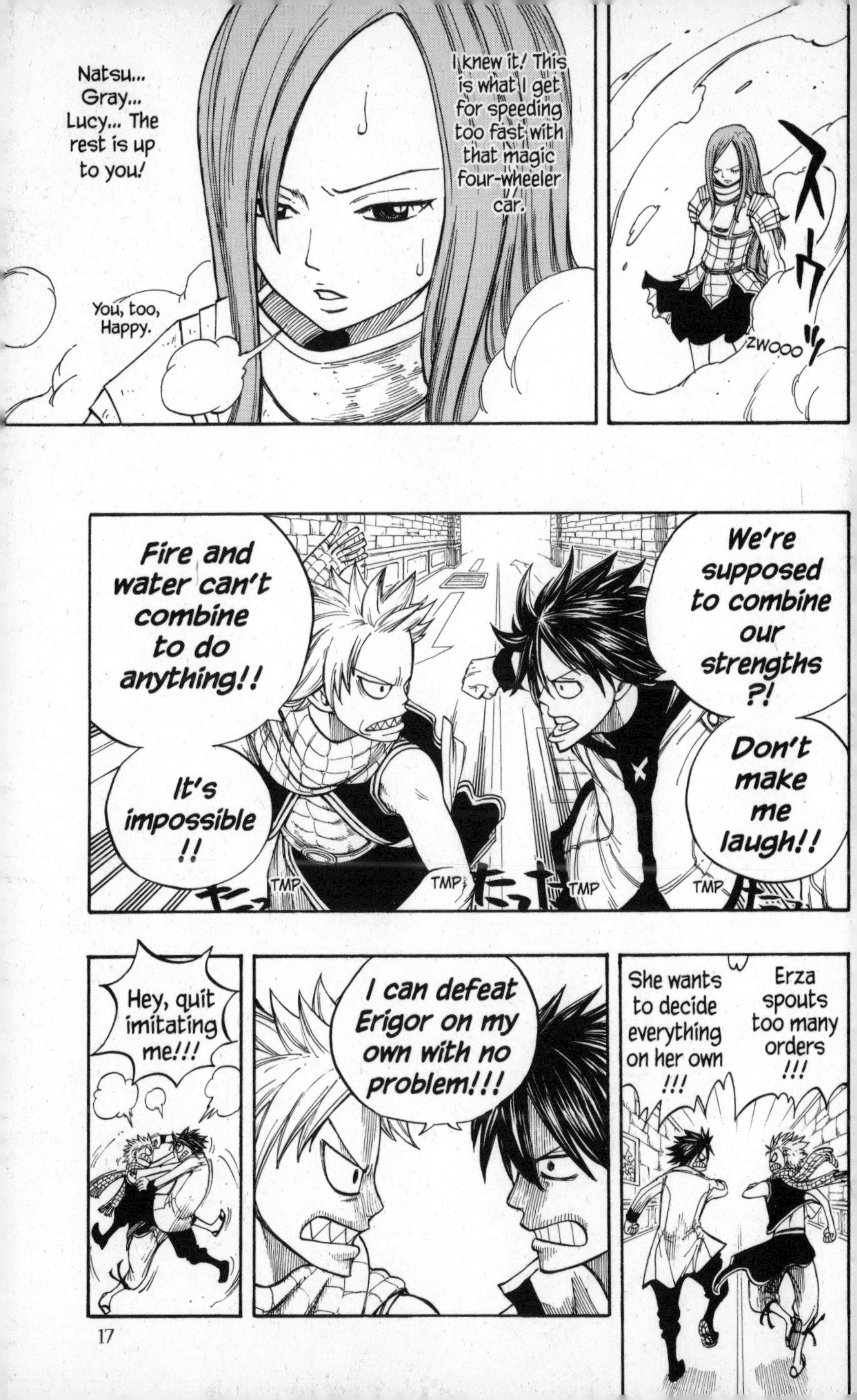

ZWOOO
I knew it! This is what I get for speeding too fast with that magic four-wheeler car.
Natsu... Gray... Lucy... The rest is up to you!
You, too, Happy.
We're supposed to combine our strengths?!
Don't make me laugh!!
Fire and water can't combine to do anything!!
It's impossible!!
TMP
TMP
TMP
TMP
Erza spouts too many orders!!!
She wants to decide everything on her own!!!
I can defeat Erigor on my own with no problem!!!
Hey, quit imitating me!!!

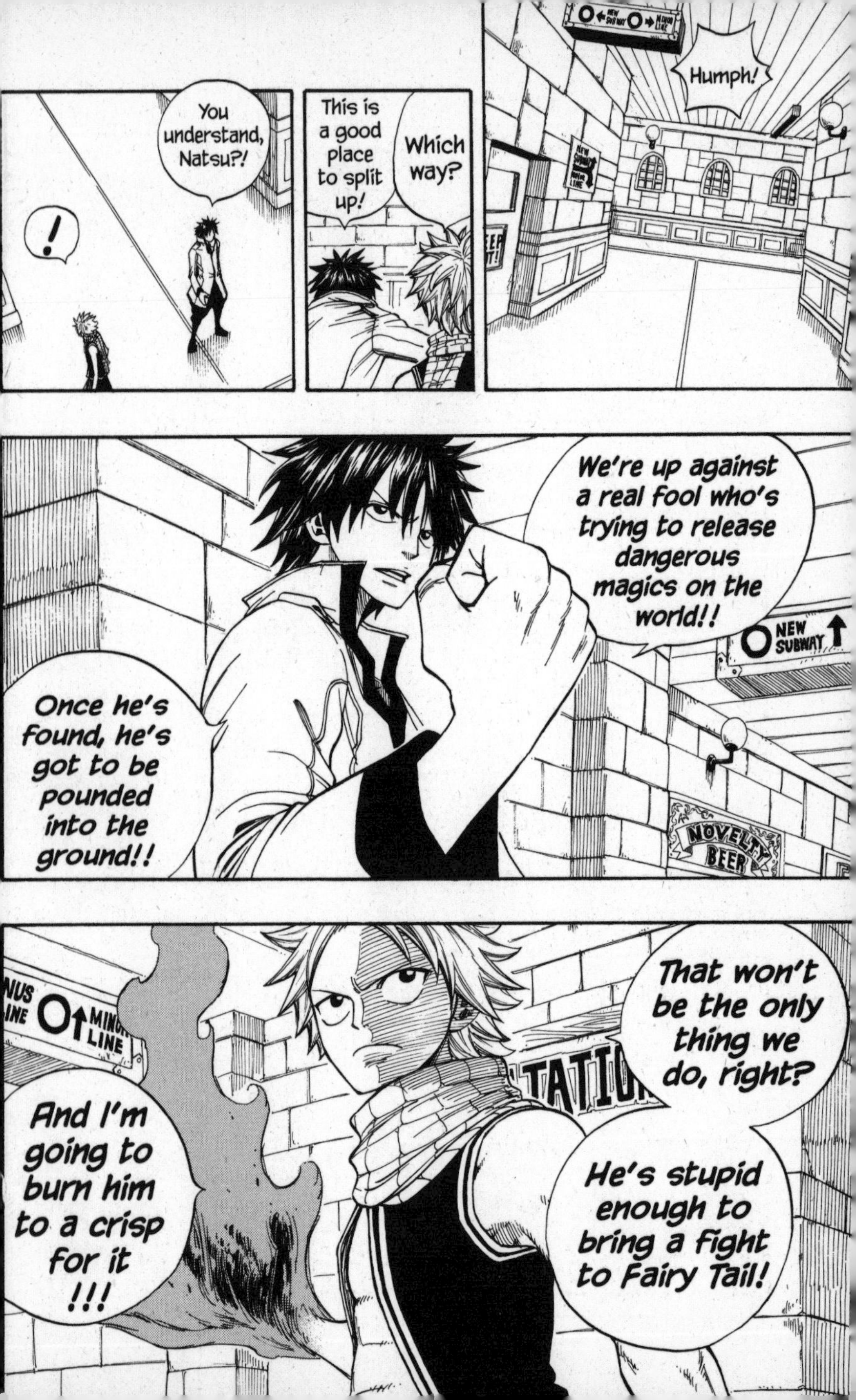
Humph!
Which way?
This is a good place to split up!
You understand, Natsu?!
!
We're up against a real fool who's trying to release dangerous magics on the world!!
NEW SUBWAY
Once he's found, he's got to be pounded into the ground!!
NOVELTY BEER
That won't be the only thing we do, right?
He's stupid enough to bring a fight to Fairy Tail!
And I'm going to burn him to a crisp for it!!!

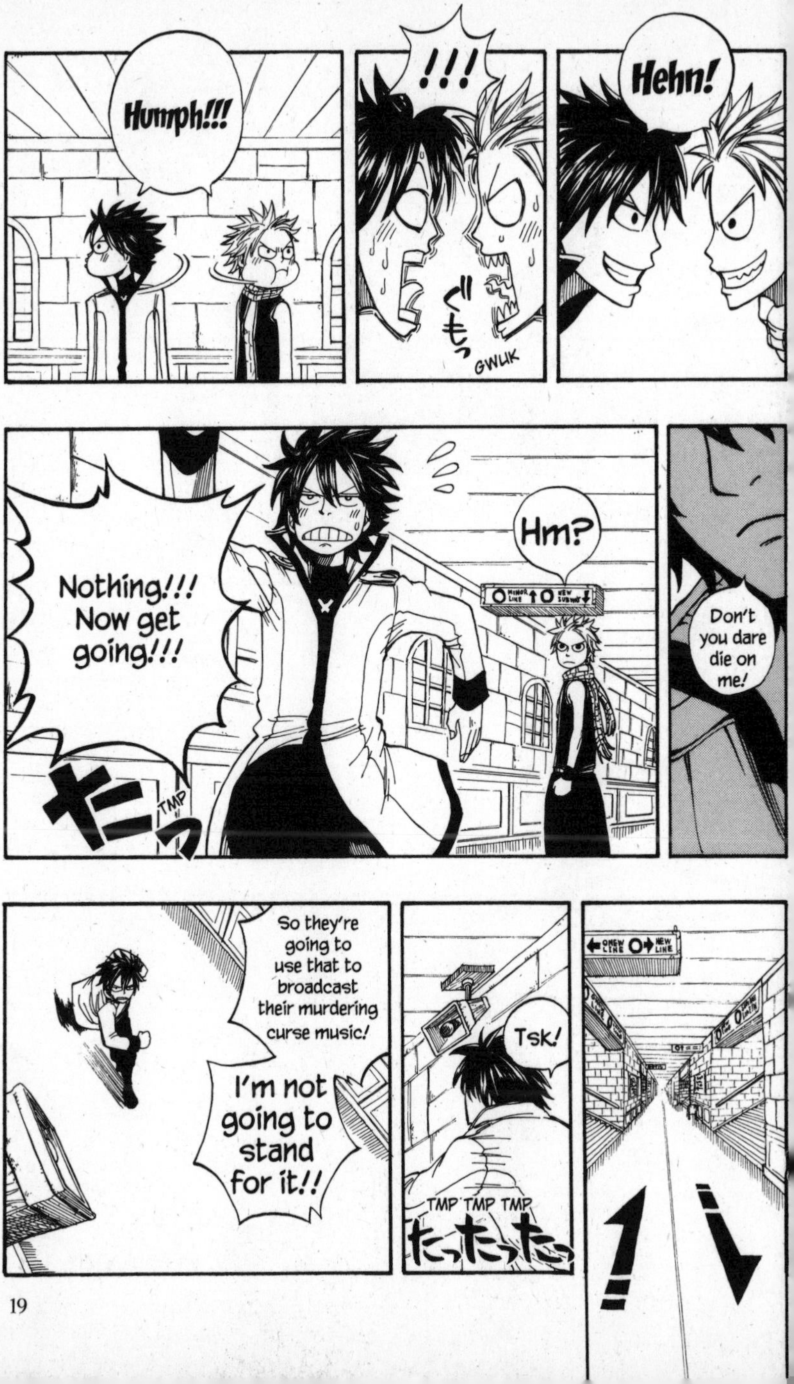
Hehn!
!!!
ぐもっ
GWUK
Humph!!!
Don't you dare die on me!
Hm?
Nothing!!! Now get going!!!
たっ
TMP
Tsk!
TMP TMP TMP
たったったっ
So they're going to use that to broadcast their murdering curse music!
I'm not going to stand for it!!

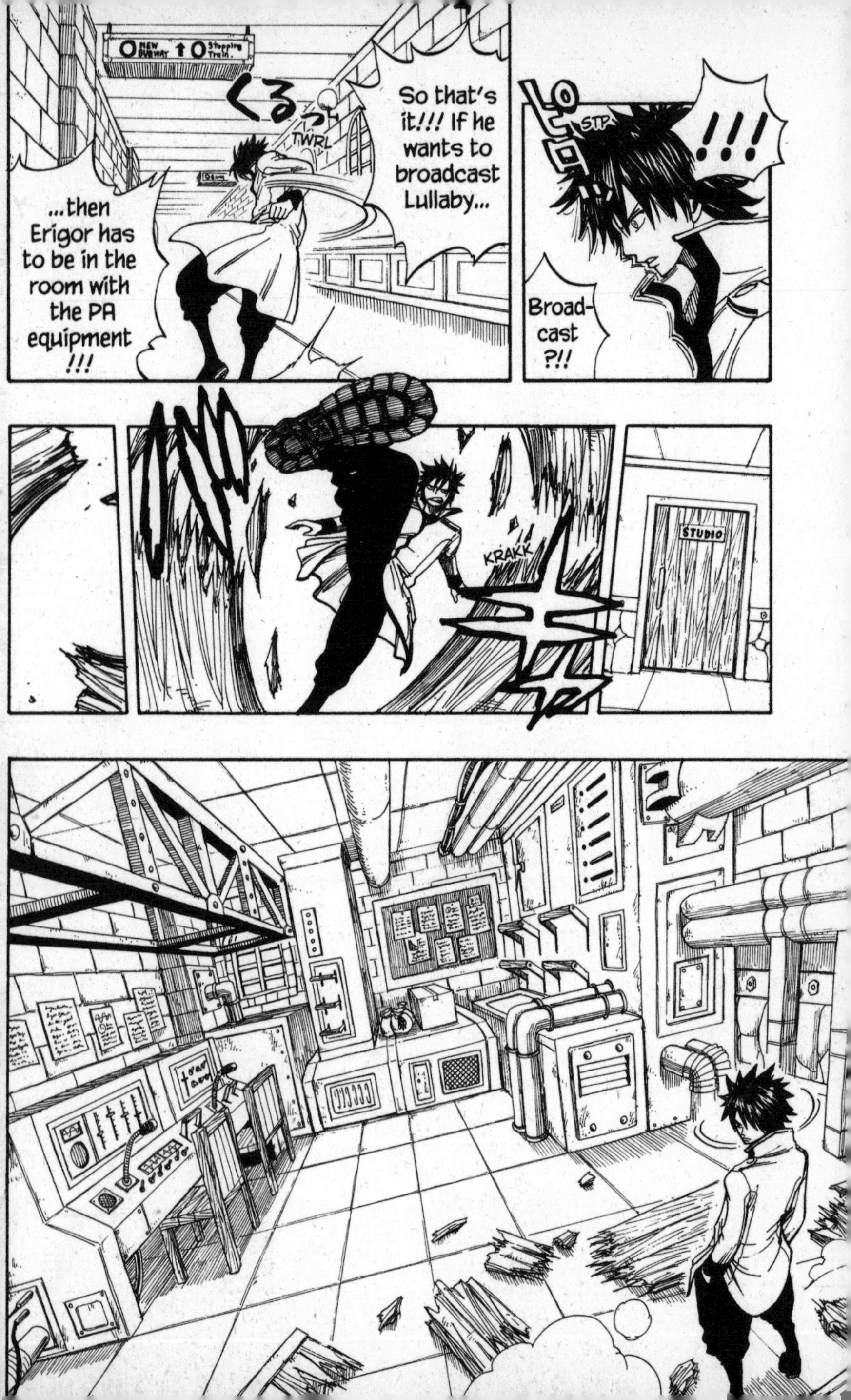
STP
!!!
Broad-cast?!!
NEW SUBWAY
Stopping Train.
くるっ
TWRL
So that's it!!! If he wants to broadcast Lullaby...
...then Erigor has to be in the room with the PA equipment!!!
STUDIO
KRAKK

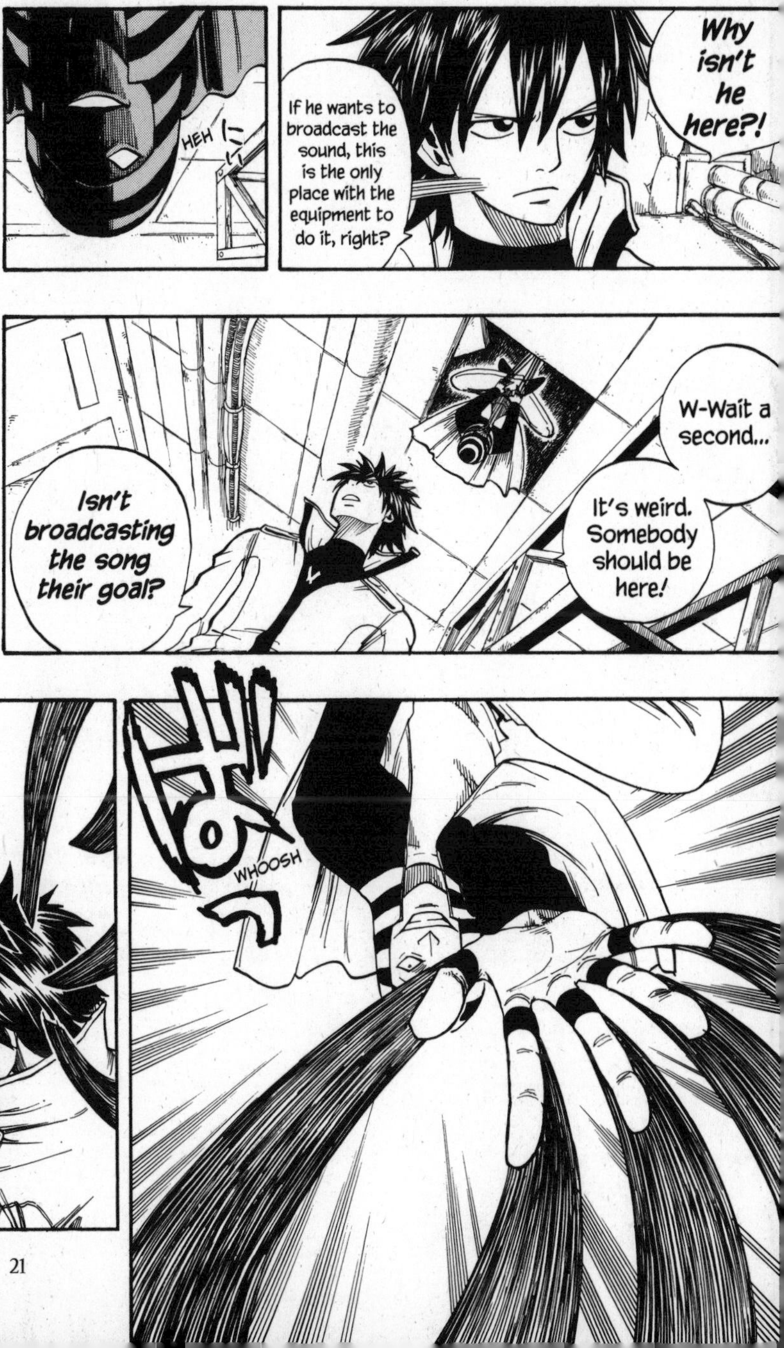
Why isn't he here?!
If he wants to broadcast the sound, this is the only place with the equipment to do it, right?
HEH
W-Wait a second...
It's weird. Somebody should be here!
Isn't broadcasting the song their goal?
WHOOSH

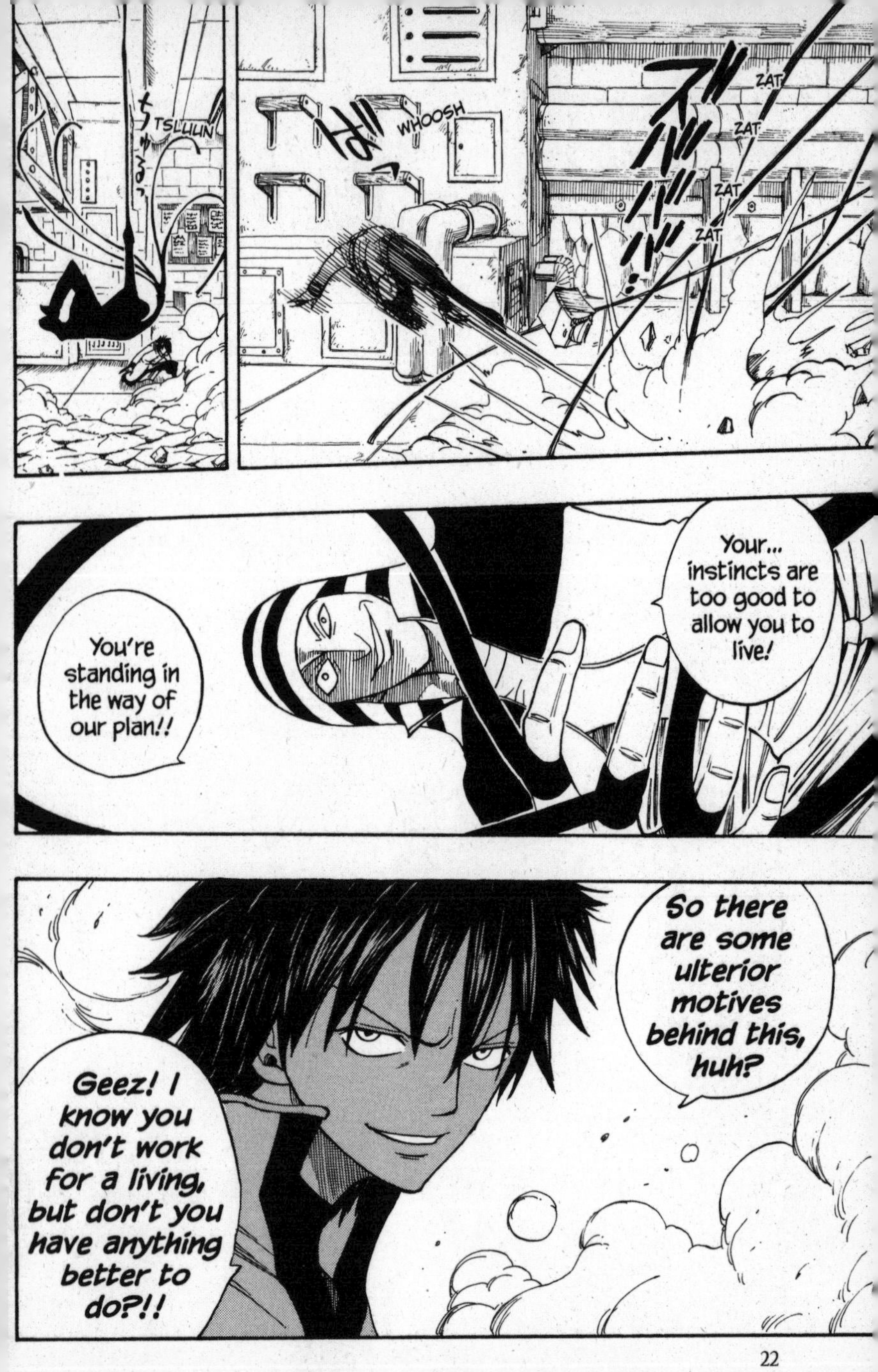
ZAT
ZAT
ZAT
ZAT
WHOOSH
TSLUUN
Your... instincts are too good to allow you to live!
You're standing in the way of our plan!!
So there are some ulterior motives behind this, huh?
Geez! I know you don't work for a living, but don't you have anything better to do?!!

Chapter 15:
Fairies in the Wind

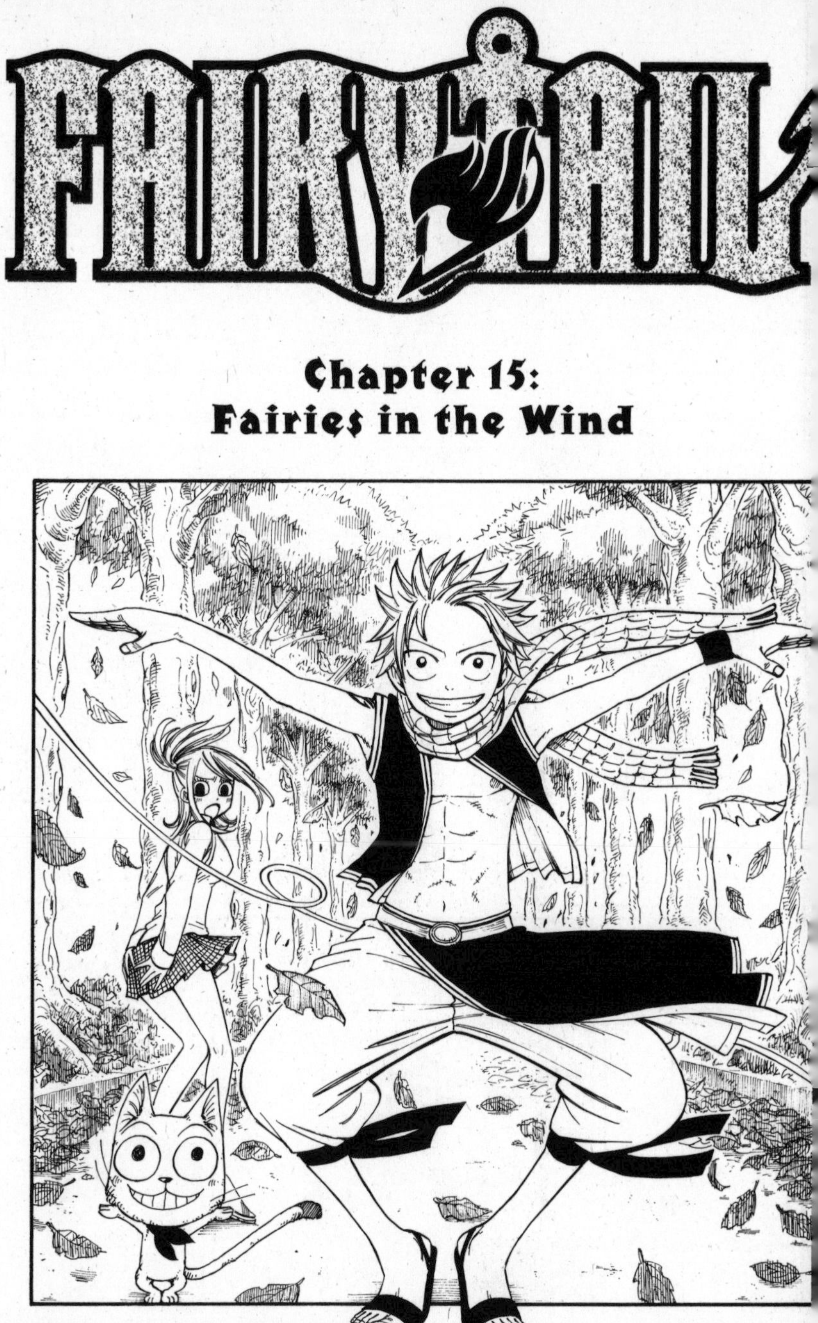

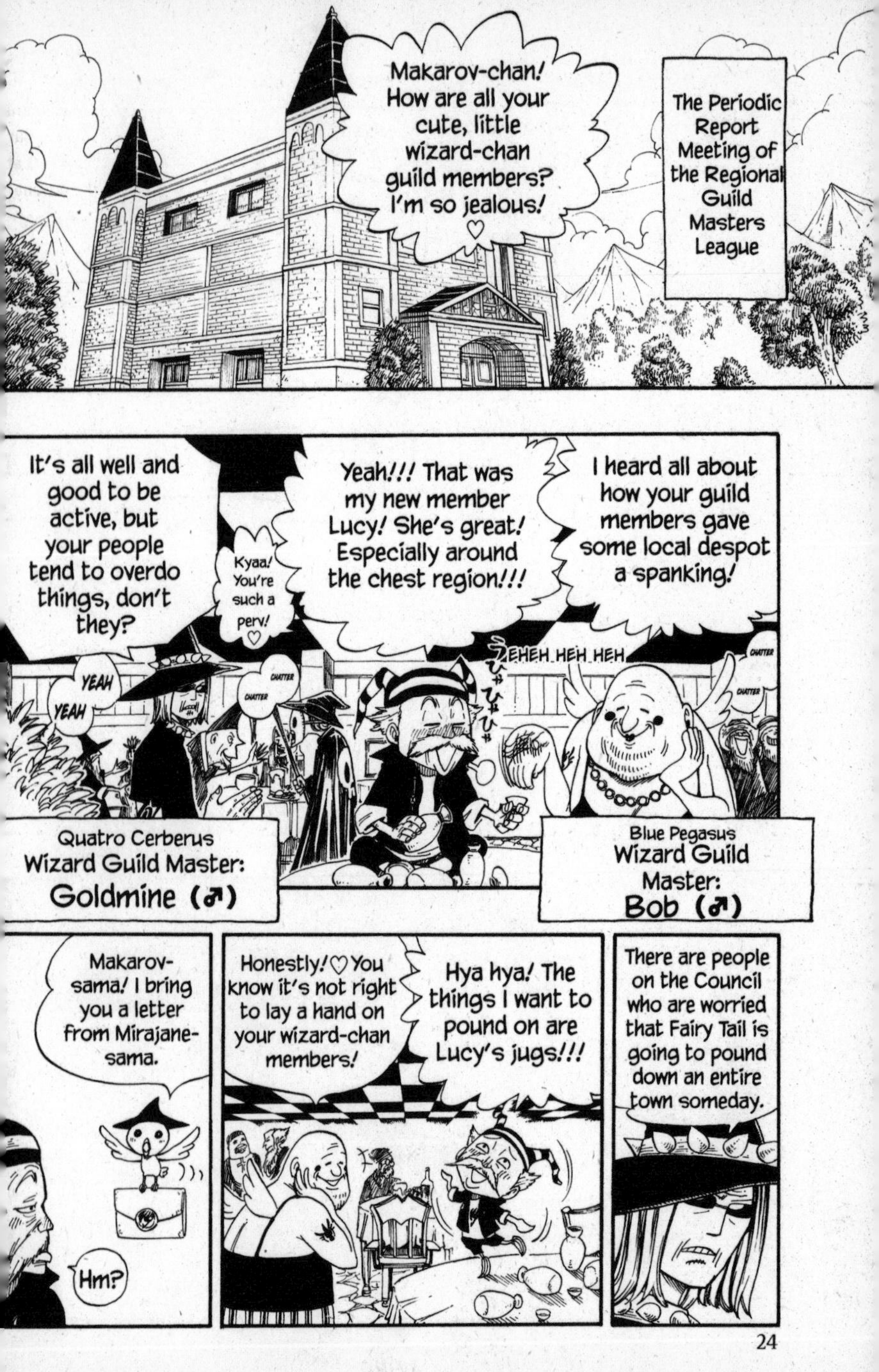
The Periodic Report Meeting of the Regional Guild Masters League
Makarov-chan! How are all your cute, little wizard-chan guild members? I'm so jealous! ♡
I heard all about how your guild members gave some local despot a spanking!
Yeah!!! That was my new member Lucy! She's great! Especially around the chest region!!!
Kyaa! You're such a perv! ♡
It's all well and good to be active, but your people tend to overdo things, don't they?
EHEH HEH HEH
CHATTER
CHATTER
CHATTER
CHATTER
YEAH
YEAH
Blue Pegasus Wizard Guild Master: Bob (♂)
Quatro Cerberus Wizard Guild Master: Goldmine (♂)
There are people on the Council who are worried that Fairy Tail is going to pound down an entire town someday.
Hya hya! The things I want to pound on are Lucy's jugs!!!
Honestly! ♡ You know it's not right to lay a hand on your wizard-chan members!
Makarov-sama! I bring you a letter from Mirajane-sama.
Hm?

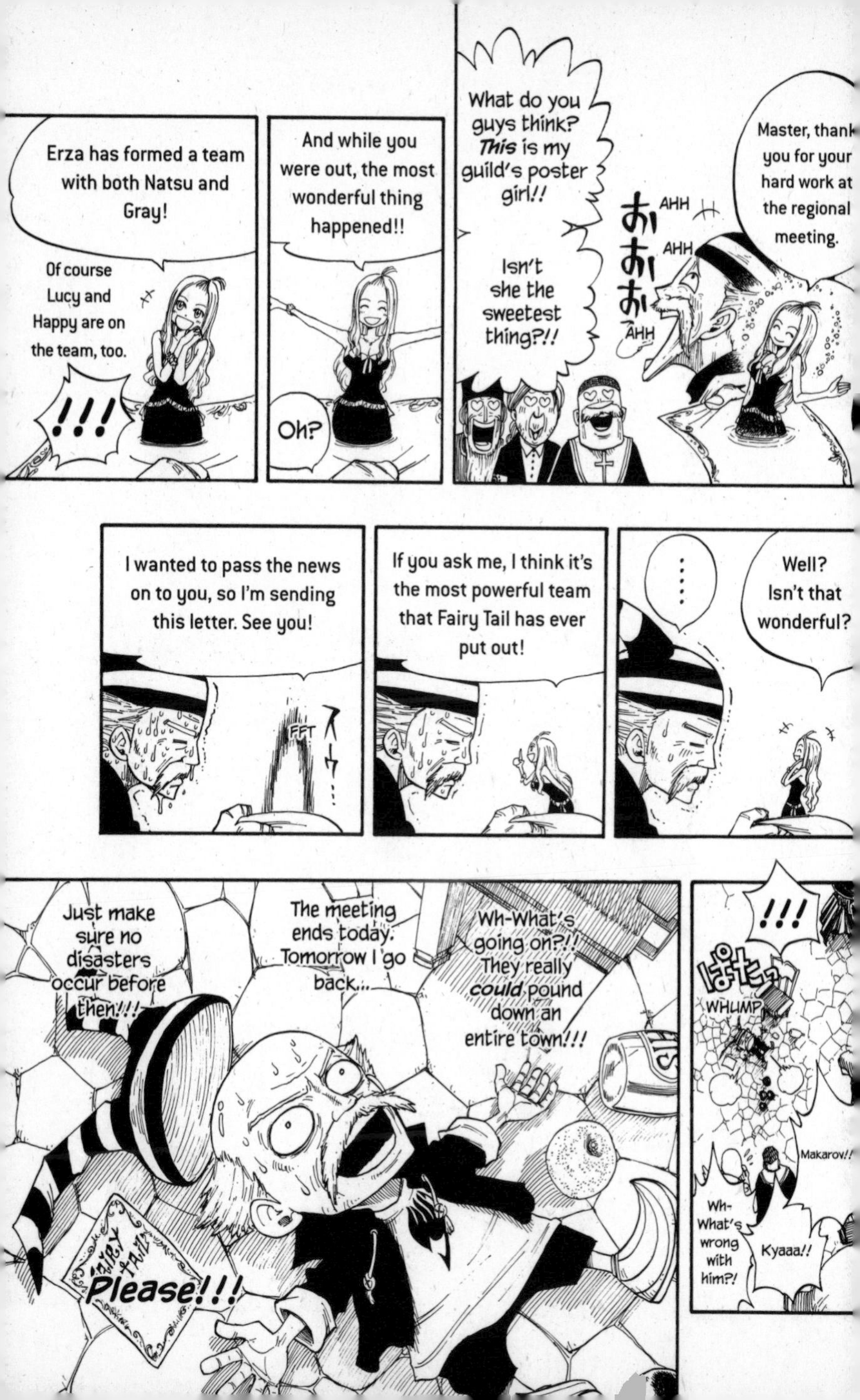
Master, thank you for your hard work at the regional meeting.
おおお
AHH AHH AHH
What do you guys think? *This* is my guild's poster girl!!
Isn't she the sweetest thing?!!
And while you were out, the most wonderful thing happened!!
Oh?
Erza has formed a team with both Natsu and Gray!
Of course Lucy and Happy are on the team, too.
!!!
Well? Isn't that wonderful?
......
If you ask me, I think it's the most powerful team that Fairy Tail has ever put out!
I wanted to pass the news on to you, so I'm sending this letter. See you!
スー…
FFT
!!!
ぱたっ
WHUMP
Makarov!!
Kyaaa!!
Wh-What's wrong with him?!
Wh-What's going on?!! They really *could* pound down an entire town!!!
The meeting ends today. Tomorrow I go back...
Just make sure no disasters occur before then!!!
Please!!!

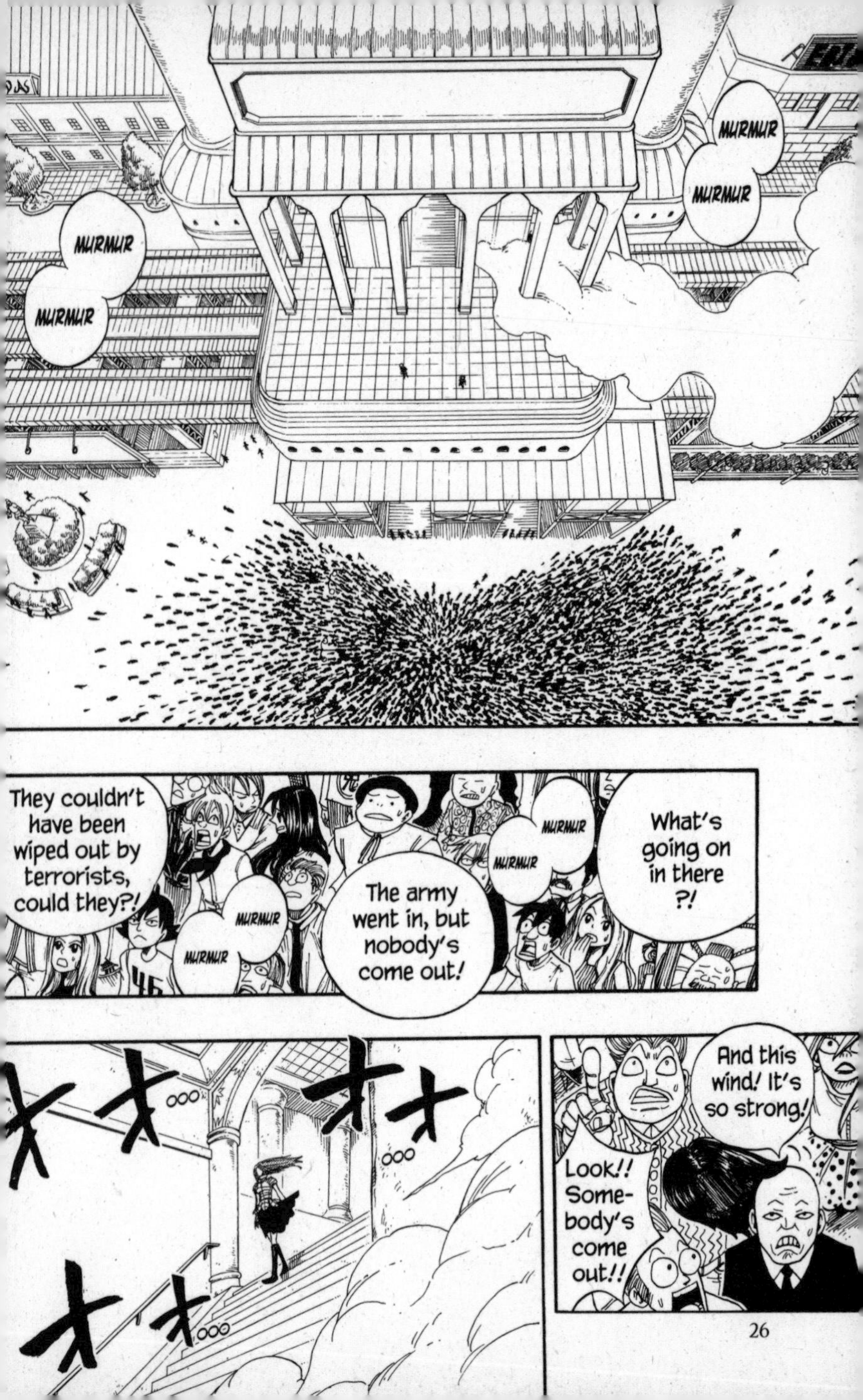
MURMUR
MURMUR
MURMUR
MURMUR
What's going on in there ?!
MURMUR
MURMUR
The army went in, but nobody's come out!
MURMUR
MURMUR
They couldn't have been wiped out by terrorists, could they?!
And this wind! It's so strong!
Look!! Somebody's come out!!
オォ ooo
オォ ooo
オォ ooo
オォ ooo

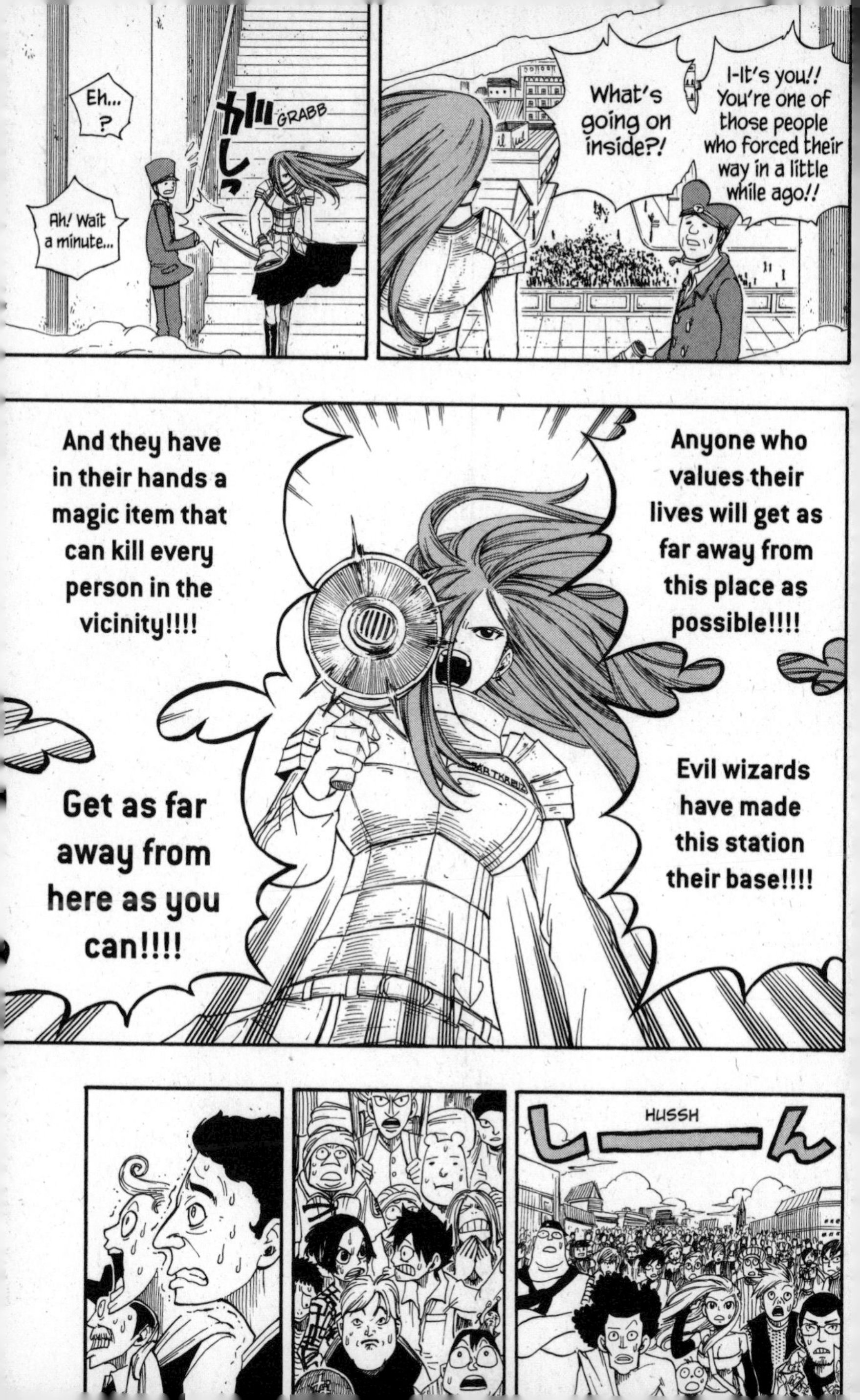
I-It's you!! You're one of those people who forced their way in a little while ago!!
What's going on inside?!
カシッ
GRABB
Eh... ?
Ah! Wait a minute...
Anyone who values their lives will get as far away from this place as possible!!!!
And they have in their hands a magic item that can kill every person in the vicinity!!!!
Evil wizards have made this station their base!!!!
Get as far away from here as you can!!!!
しーん
HUSSH

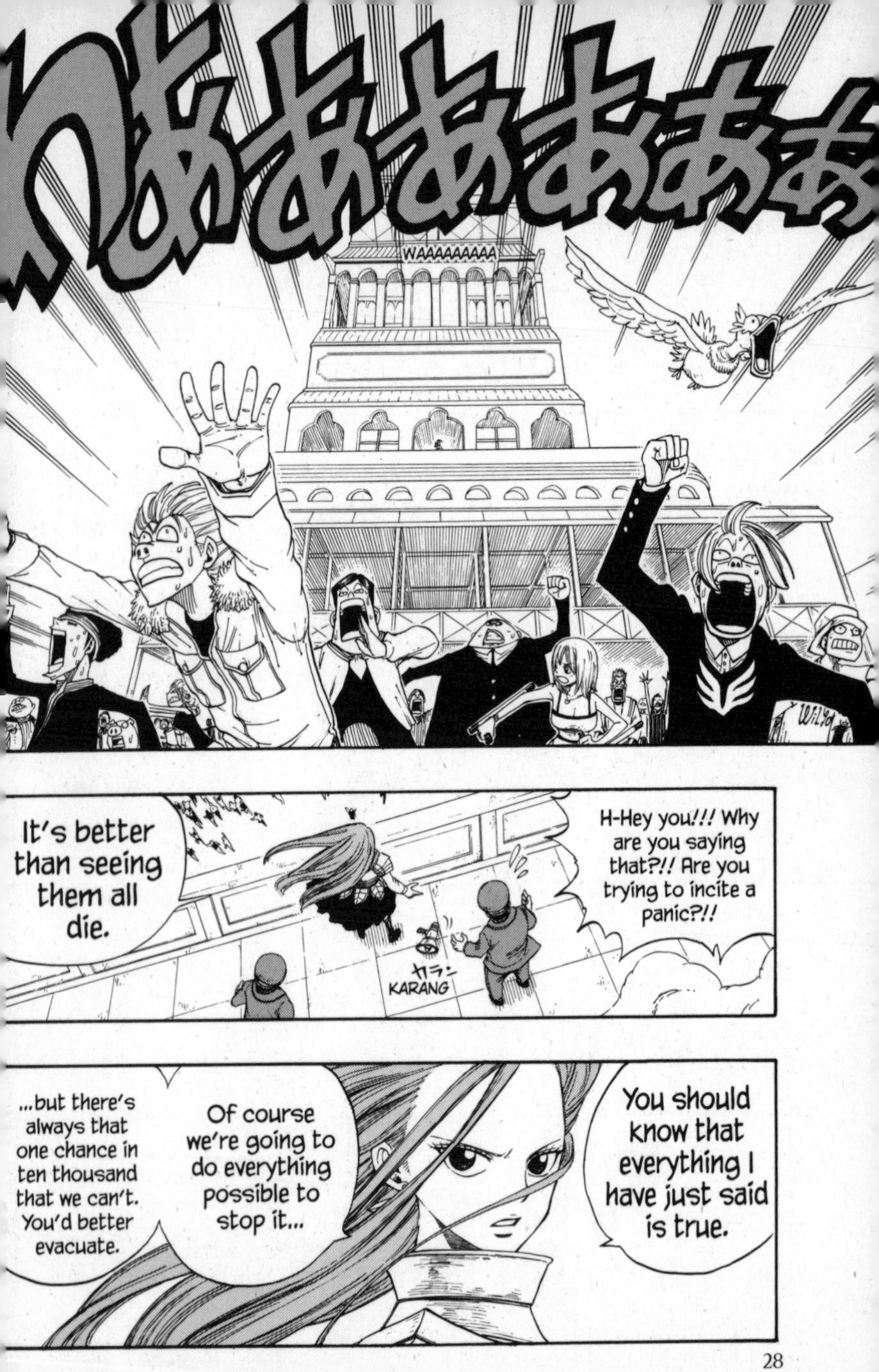
WAAAAAAAAA
H-Hey you!!! Why are you saying that?!! Are you trying to incite a panic?!!
It's better than seeing them all die.
カラン
KARANG
You should know that everything I have just said is true.
Of course we're going to do everything possible to stop it...
...but there's always that one chance in ten thousand that we can't. You'd better evacuate.

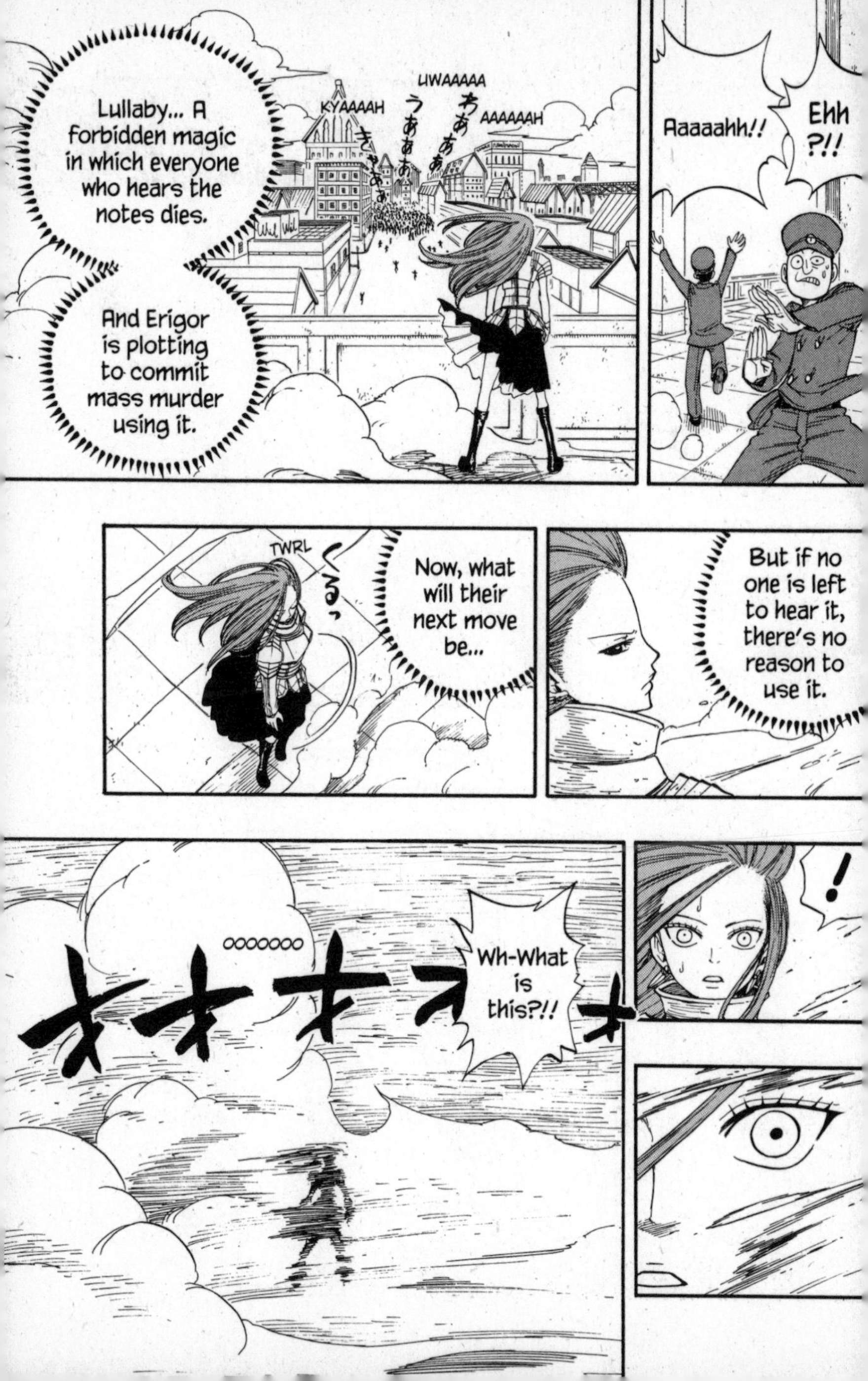
Ehh ?!!
Aaaaahh!!
UWAAAAA
AAAAAAH
KYAAAAH
Lullaby... A forbidden magic in which everyone who hears the notes dies.
And Erigor is plotting to commit mass murder using it.
But if no one is left to hear it, there's no reason to use it.
Now, what will their next move be...
TWRL
!
Wh-What is this?!!
OOOOOOO

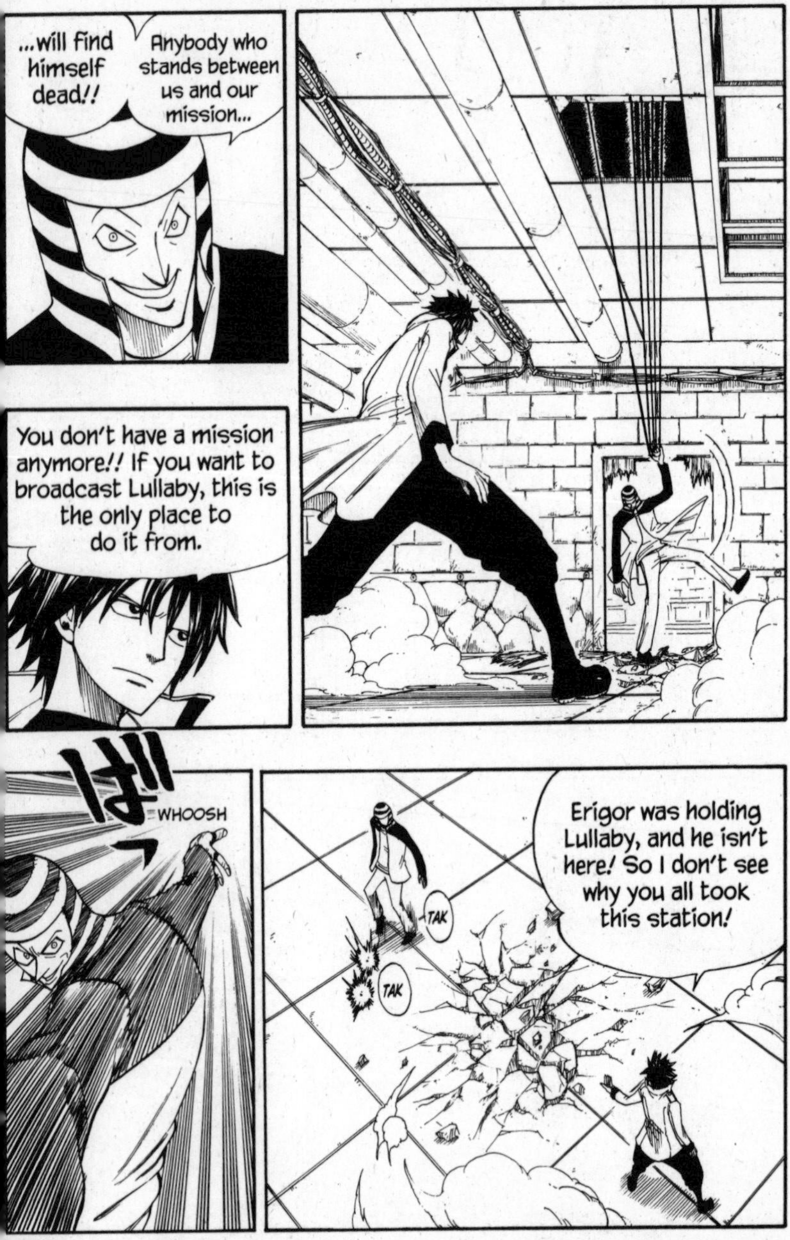

Anybody who stands between us and our mission...
...will find himself dead!!
You don't have a mission anymore!! If you want to broadcast Lullaby, this is the only place to do it from.
Erigor was holding Lullaby, and he isn't here! So I don't see why you all took this station!
TAK
TAK
WHOOSH

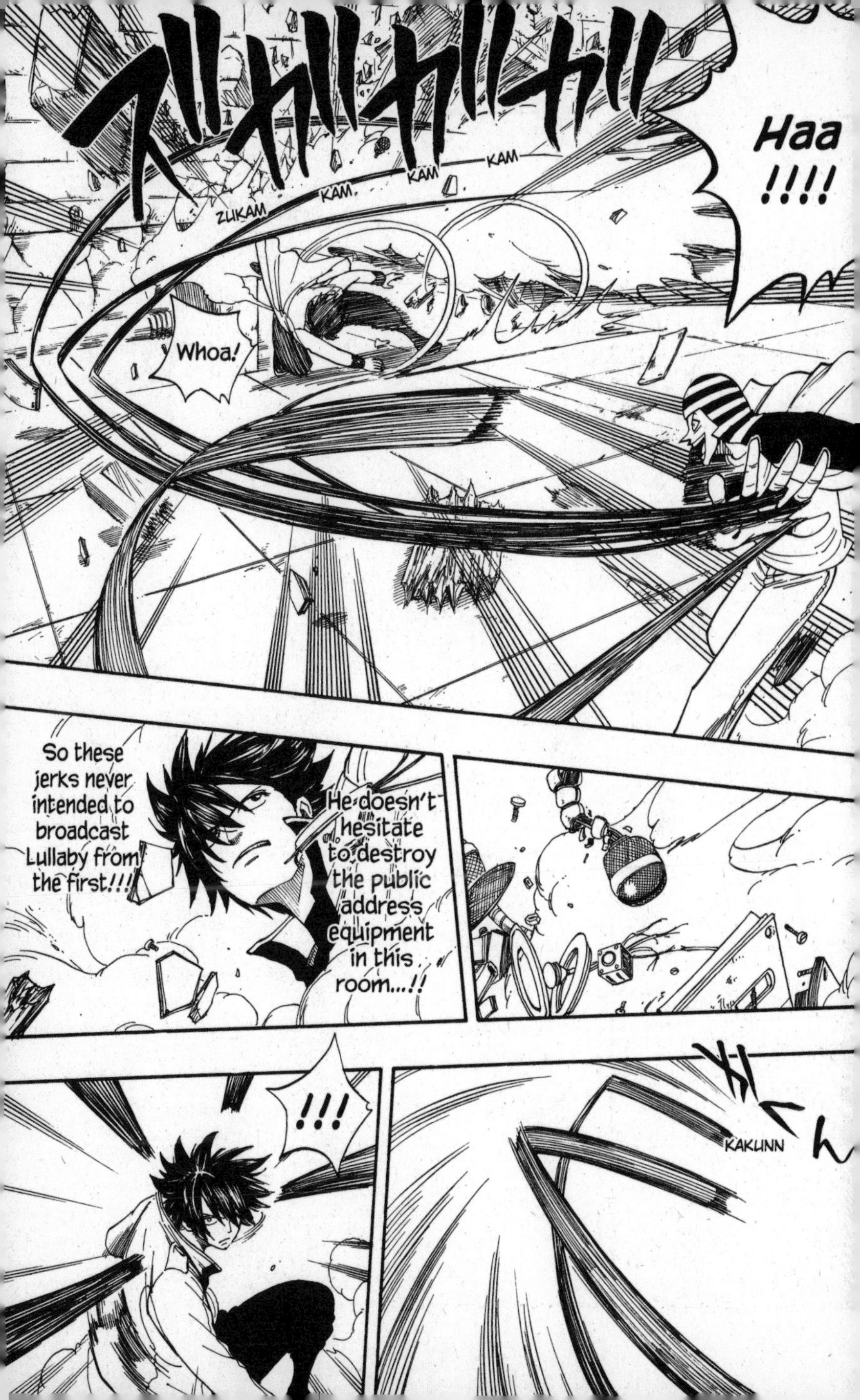
Haa !!!!
ZUKAM KAM KAM KAM
Whoa!
He doesn't hesitate to destroy the public address equipment in this room...!!
So these jerks never intended to broadcast Lullaby from the first!!!
KAKUNN
!!!

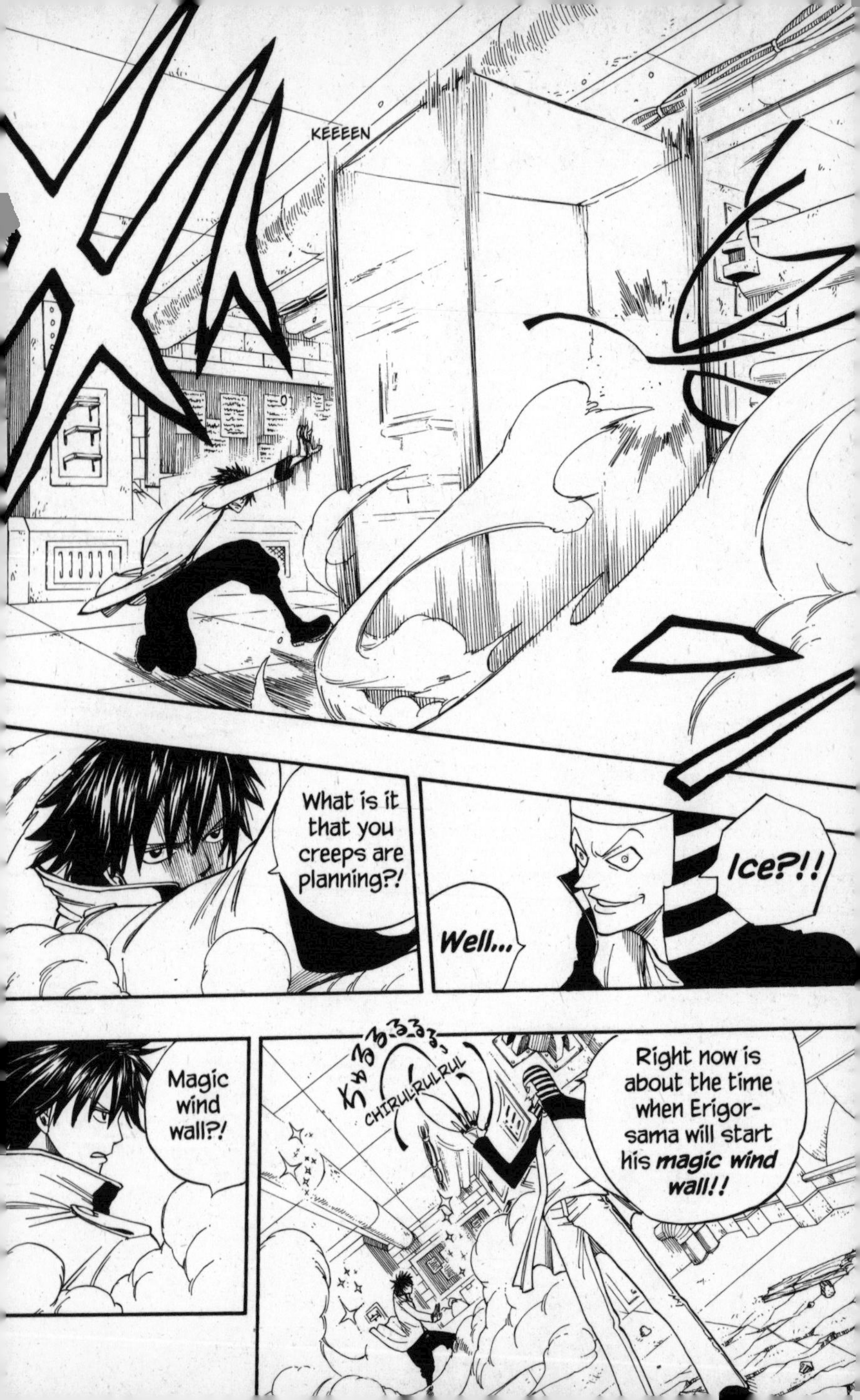
KEEEEN
Ice?!!
Well...
What is it that you creeps are planning?!
Right now is about the time when Erigor-sama will start his *magic wind wall!!*
ちゅるるるるる
CHIRU-RU-RU-RU
!!
Magic wind wall?!

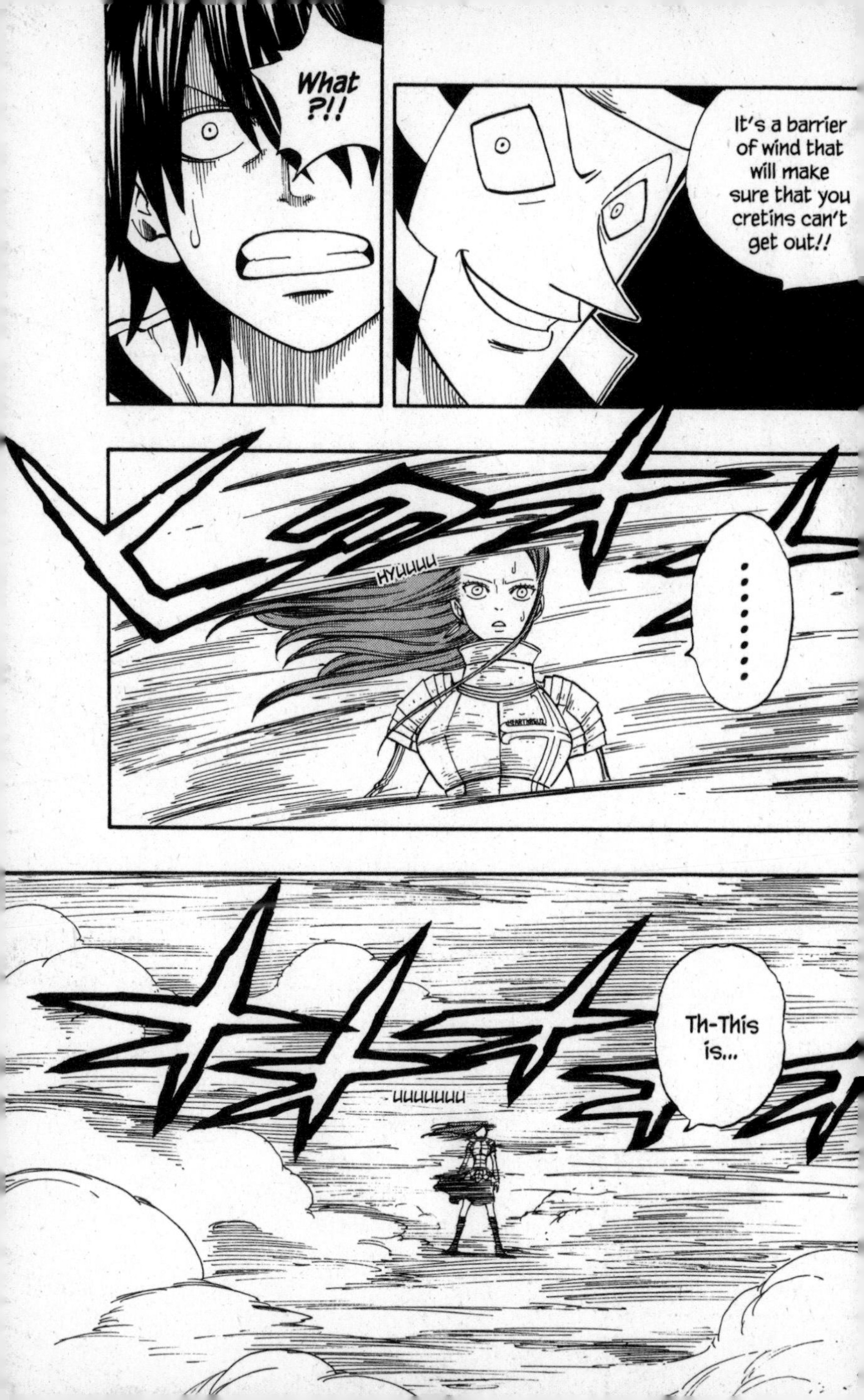
It's a barrier of wind that will make sure that you cretins can't get out!!
What?!!
....
HYUUUU
Th-This is...
UUUUUUU

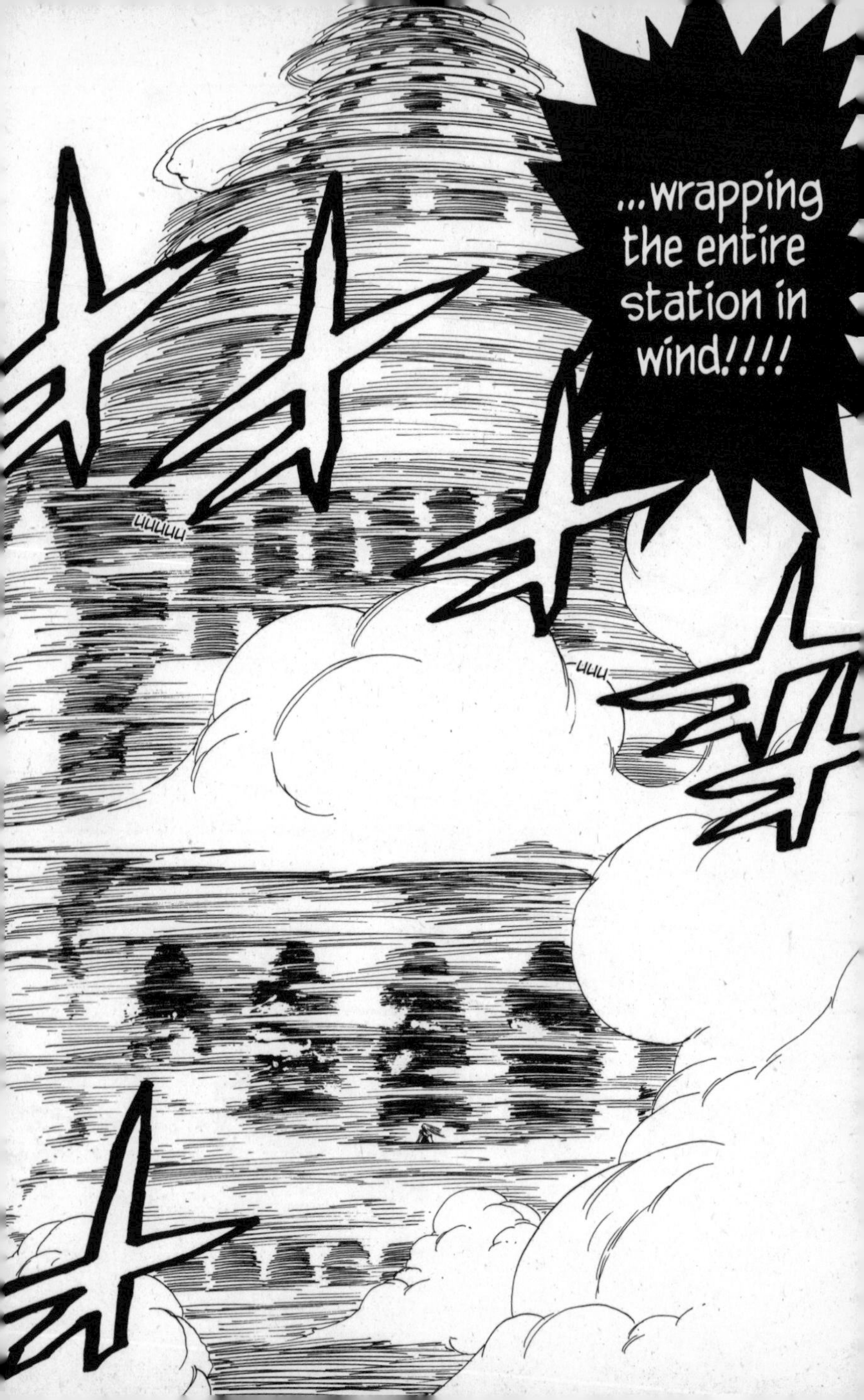
...wrapping the entire station in wind!!!!
UUUUU
UUU

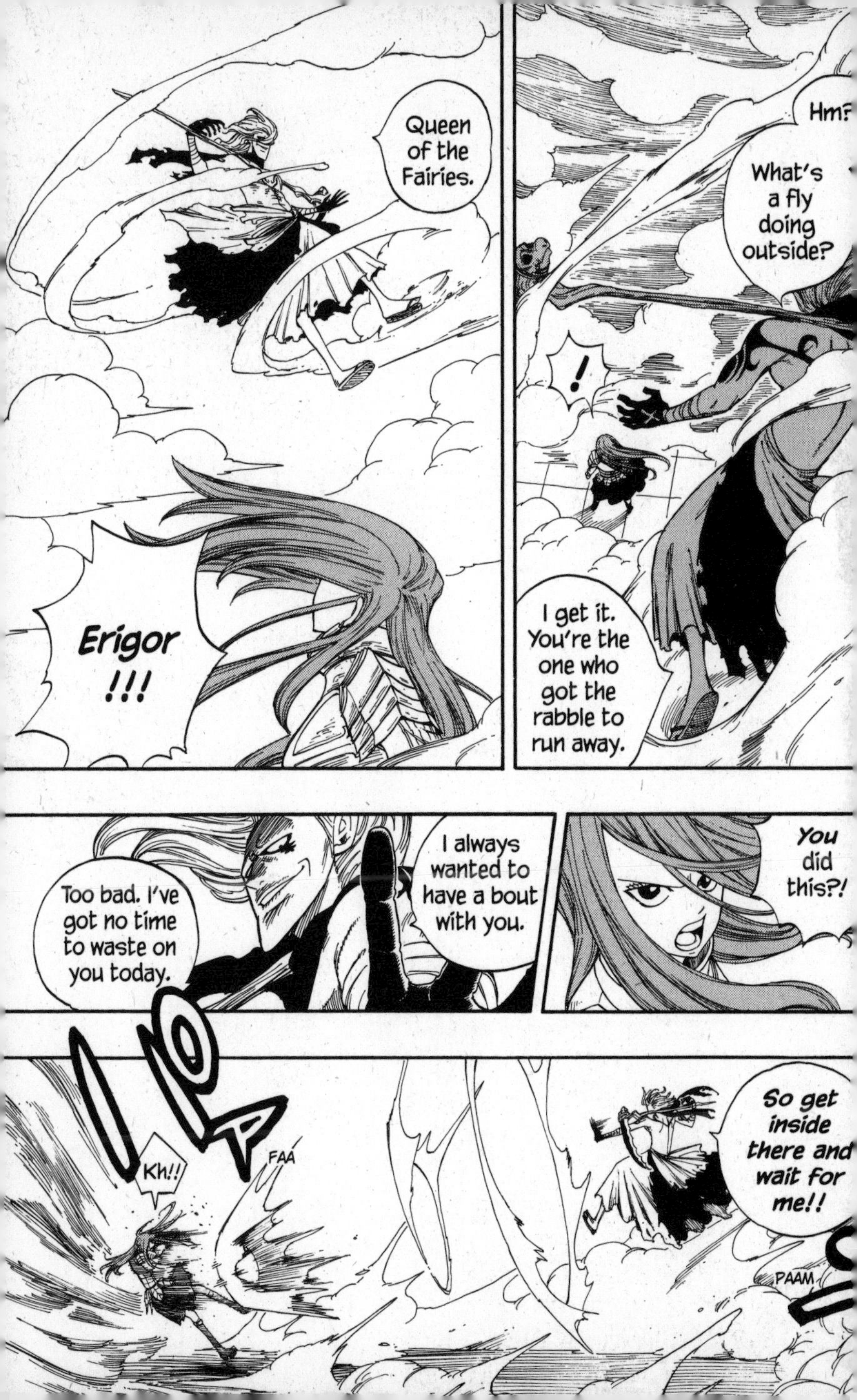
Hm?
What's a fly doing outside?
!
I get it. You're the one who got the rabble to run away.
Queen of the Fairies.
Erigor !!!
You did this?!
I always wanted to have a bout with you.
Too bad. I've got no time to waste on you today.
So get inside there and wait for me!!
PAAM
FAA
Kh!!

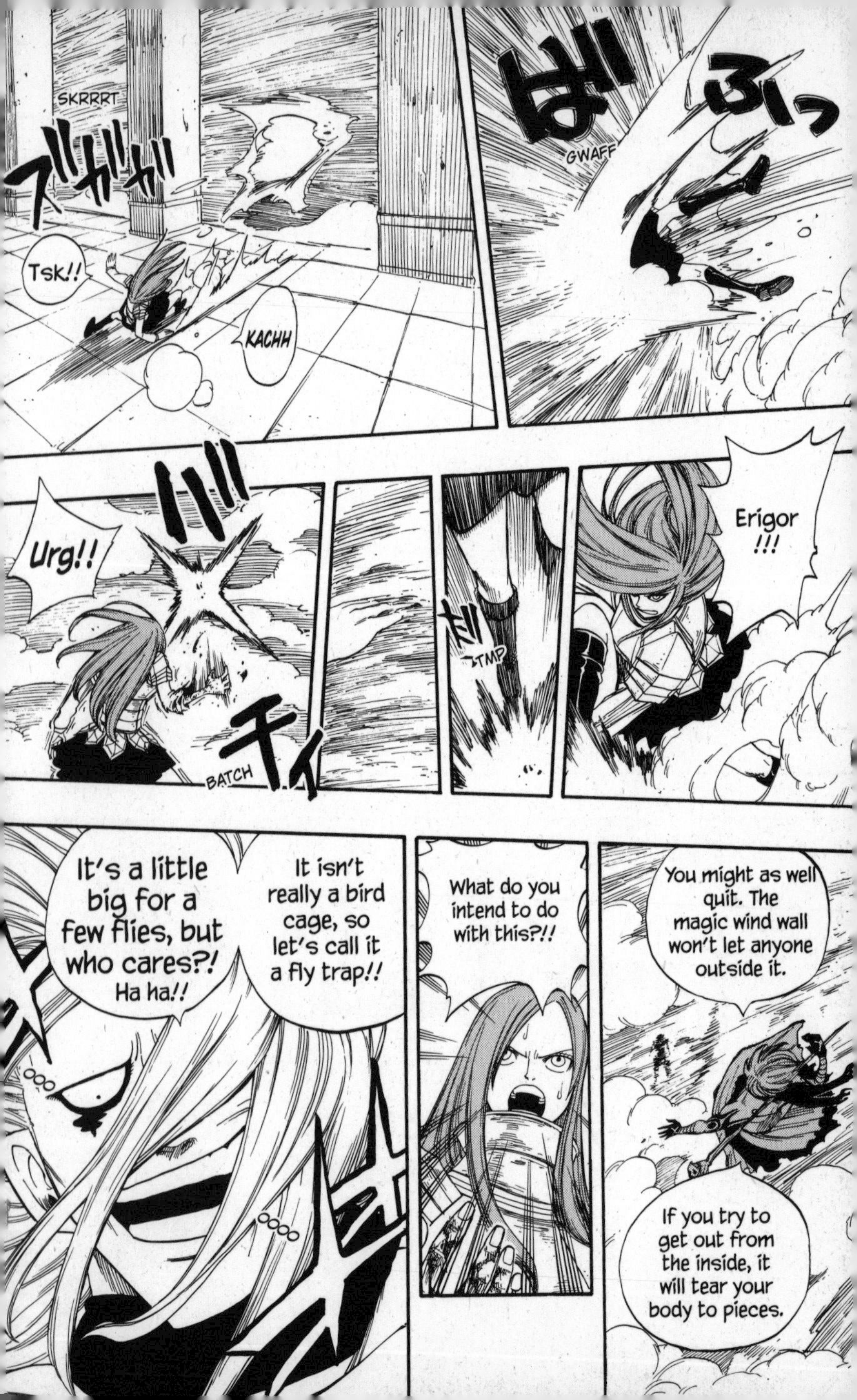
GWAFF
SKRRRT
Tsk!!
KACHH
Erigor !!!
TMP
Urg!!
BATCH
You might as well quit. The magic wind wall won't let anyone outside it.
If you try to get out from the inside, it will tear your body to pieces.
What do you intend to do with this?!!
It isn't really a bird cage, so let's call it a fly trap!!
It's a little big for a few flies, but who cares?! Ha ha!!

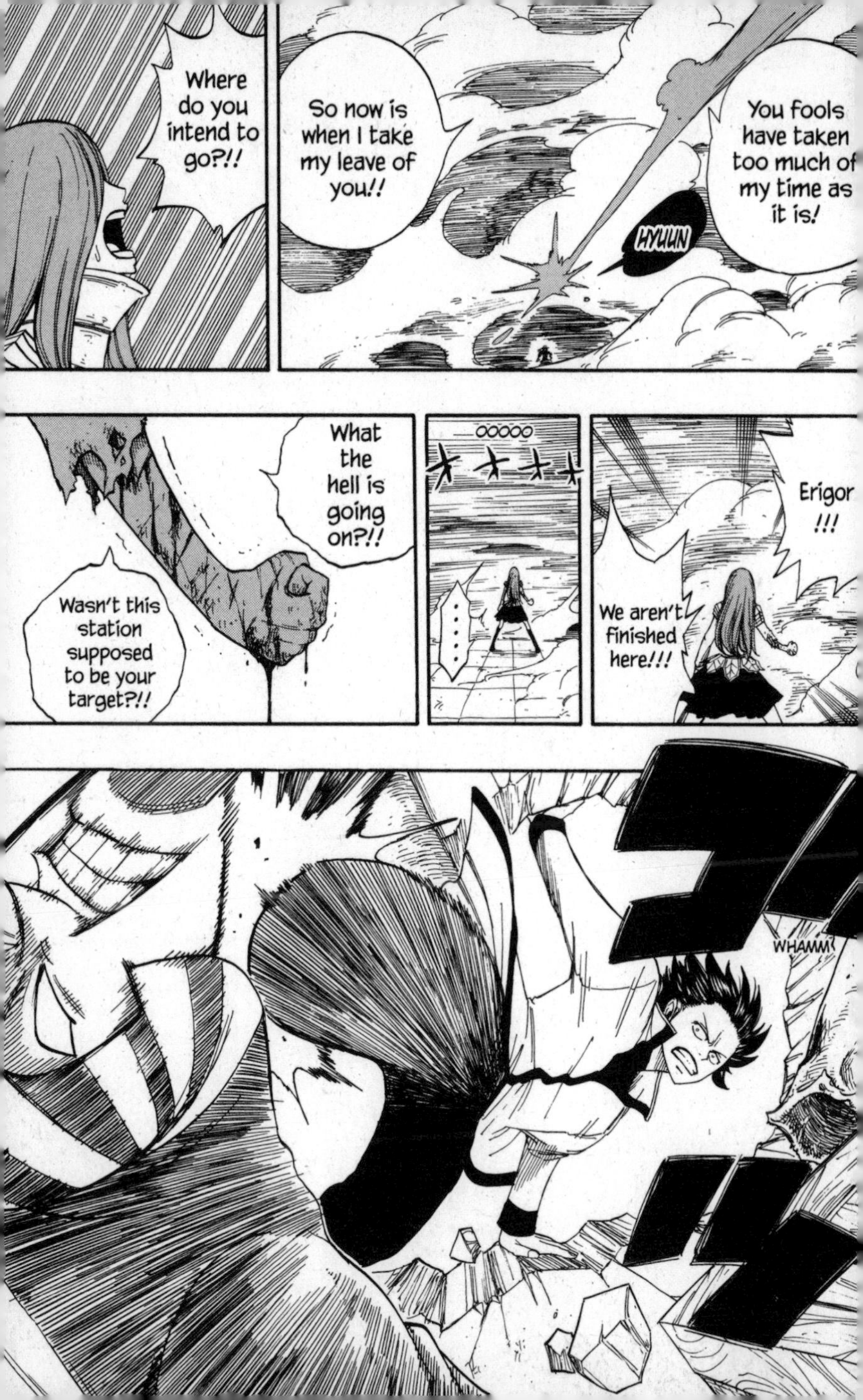
You fools have taken too much of my time as it is!
So now is when I take my leave of you!!
HYUUN
Where do you intend to go?!!
Erigor !!!
We aren't finished here!!!
—OOOOO
What the hell is going on?!!
Wasn't this station supposed to be your target?!!
WHAMM!

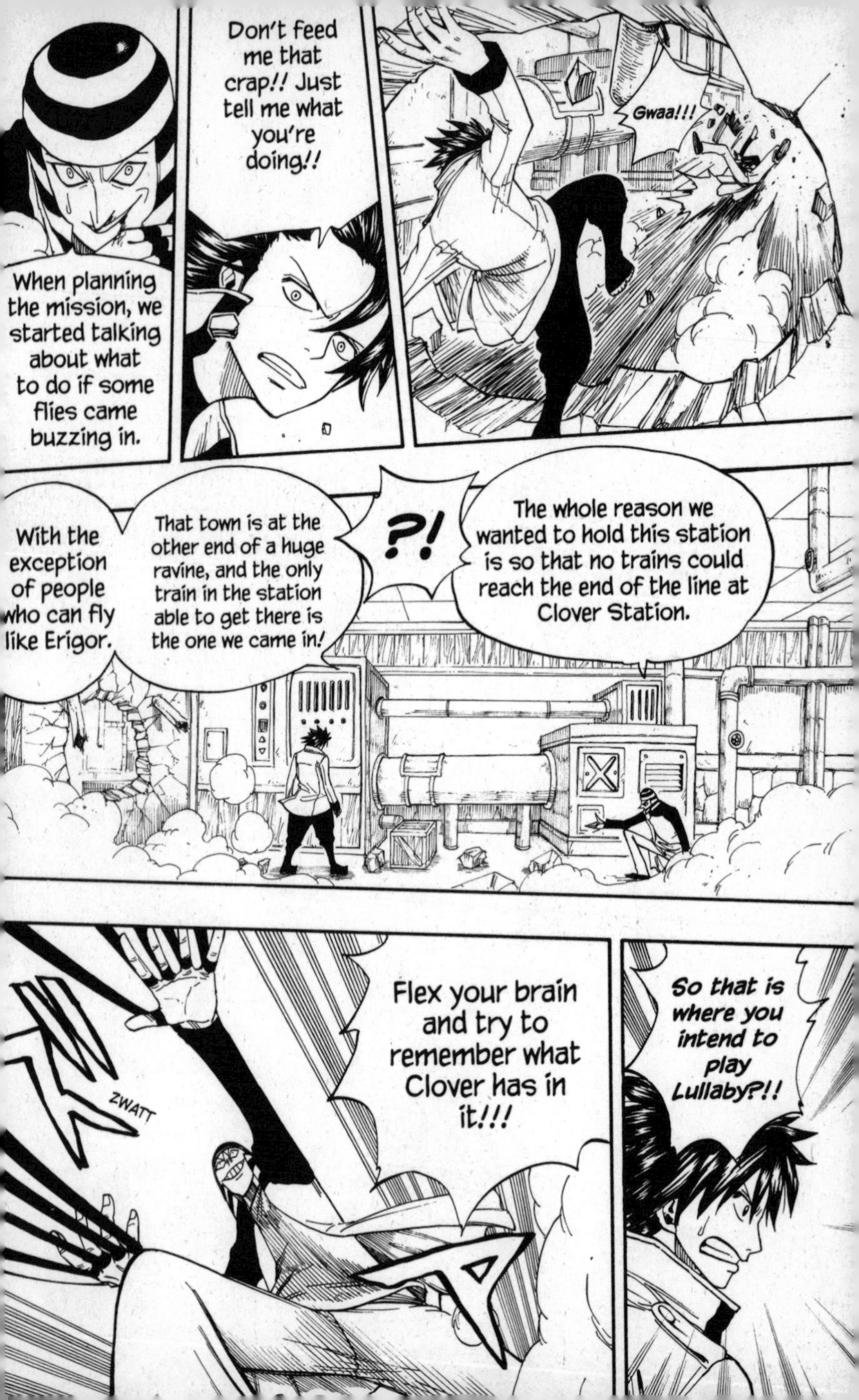
Gwaa!!!
Don't feed me that crap!! Just tell me what you're doing!!
When planning the mission, we started talking about what to do if some flies came buzzing in.
The whole reason we wanted to hold this station is so that no trains could reach the end of the line at Clover Station.
?!
That town is at the other end of a huge ravine, and the only train in the station able to get there is the one we came in!
With the exception of people who can fly like Erigor.
So that is where you intend to play Lullaby?!!
Flex your brain and try to remember what Clover has in it!!!
ZWATT

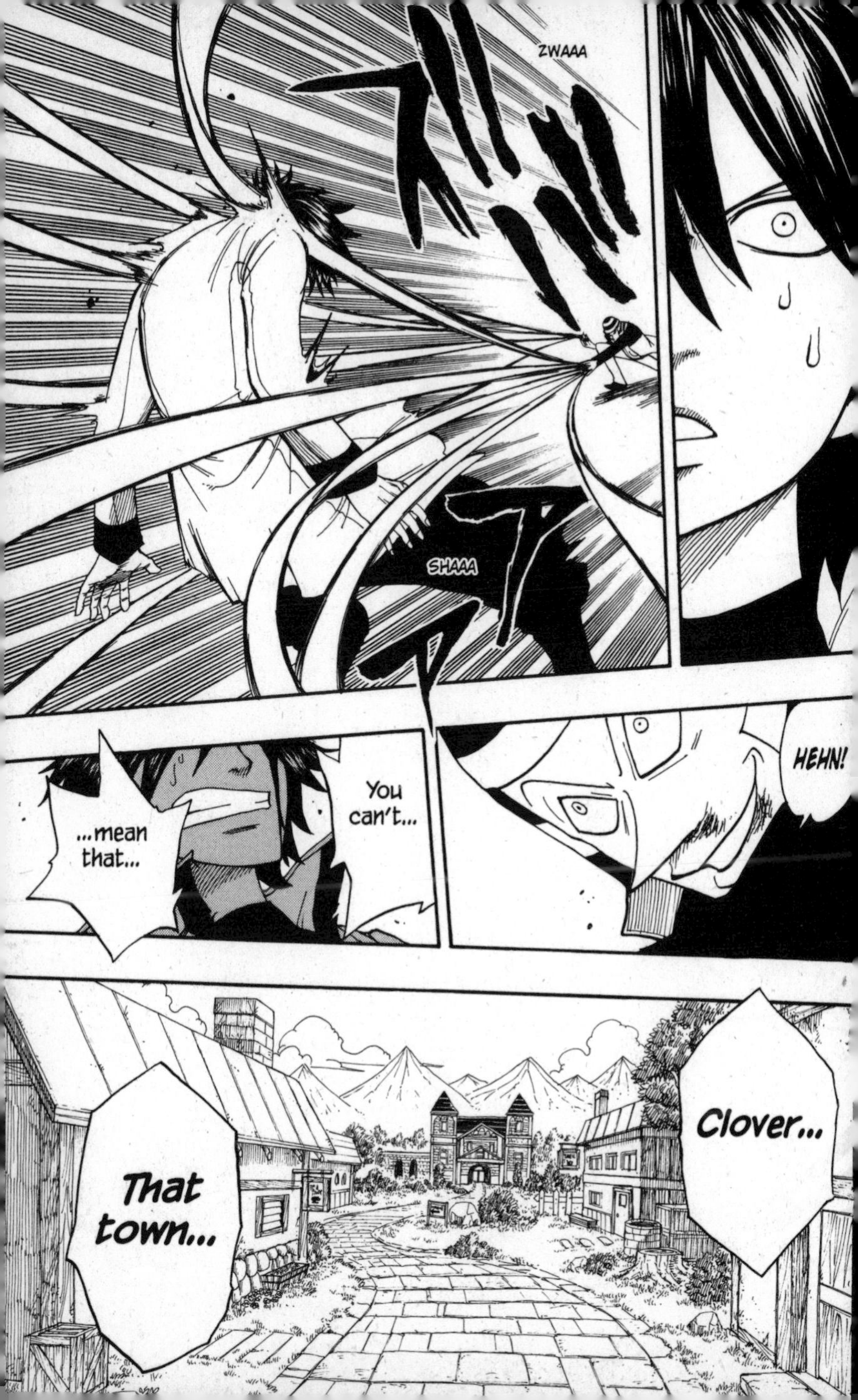
ZWAAA
SHAAA
HEHN!
You can't...
...mean that...
Clover...
That town...

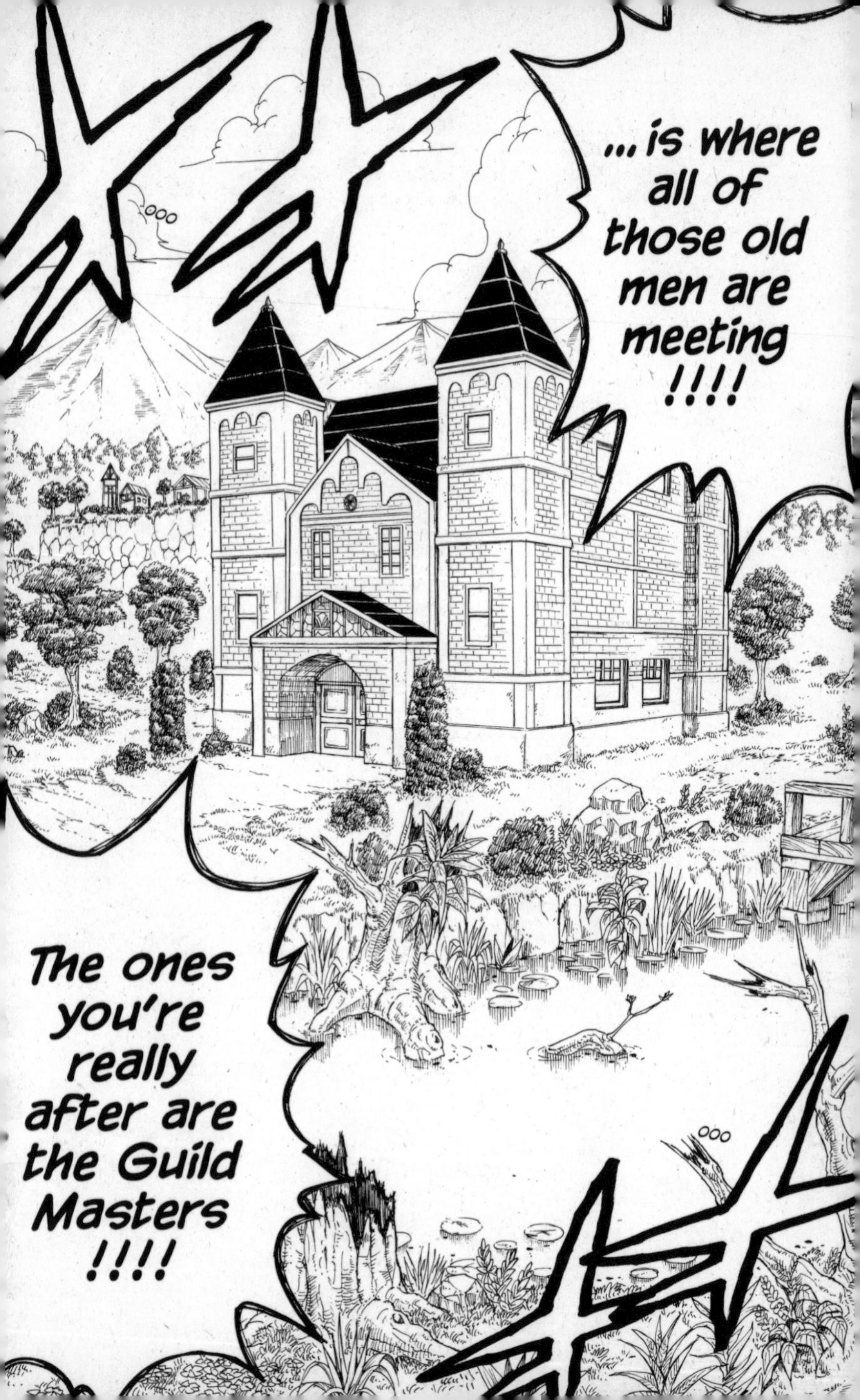
...is where all of those old men are meeting !!!!
The ones you're really after are the Guild Masters !!!!

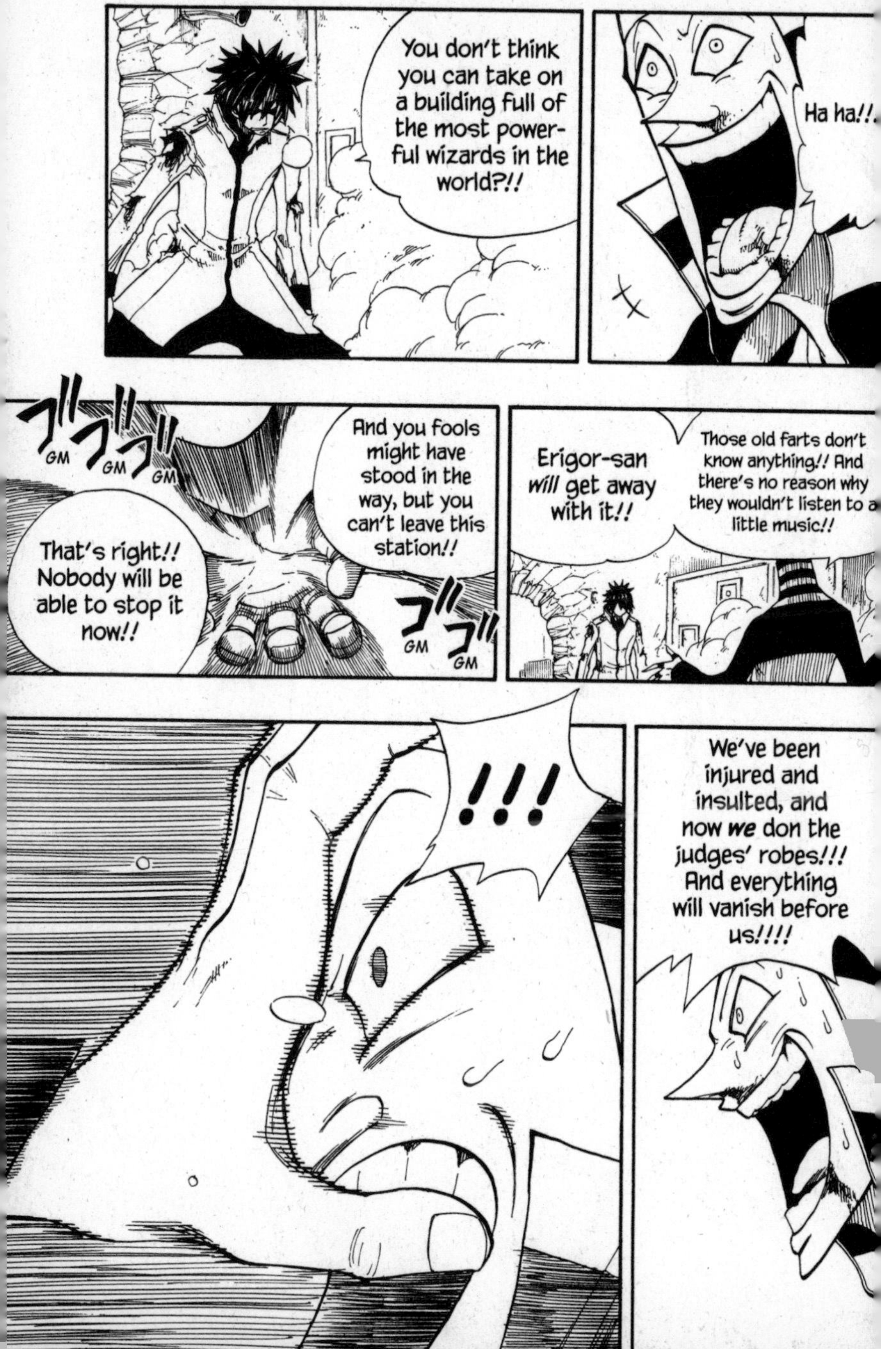
Ha ha!!
You don't think you can take on a building full of the most power-ful wizards in the world?!!
Those old farts don't know anything!! And there's no reason why they wouldn't listen to a little music!!
Erigor-san *will* get away with it!!
And you fools might have stood in the way, but you can't leave this station!!
ゴゴ GM GM
ゴゴゴ GM GM GM
That's right!! Nobody will be able to stop it now!!
We've been injured and insulted, and now *we* don the judges' robes!!! And everything will vanish before us!!!!
!!!

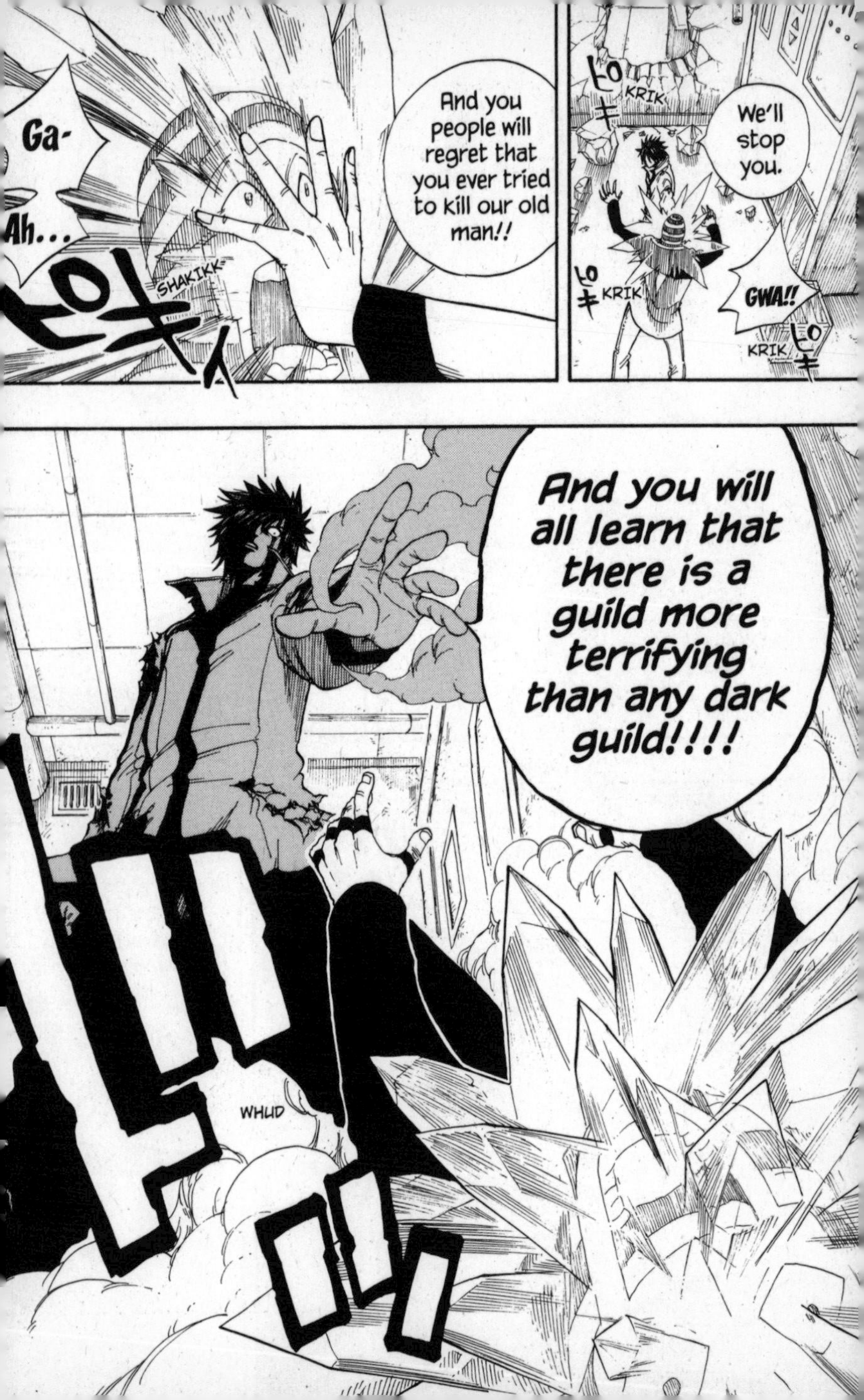
KRIK
We'll stop you.
GWA!!
KRIK
KRIK
And you people will regret that you ever tried to kill our old man!!
Ga- Ah...
SHAKIKK
And you will all learn that there is a guild more terrifying than any dark guild!!!!
WHUD

FAIRY TAIL

Chapter 16: Capture Kageyama!!

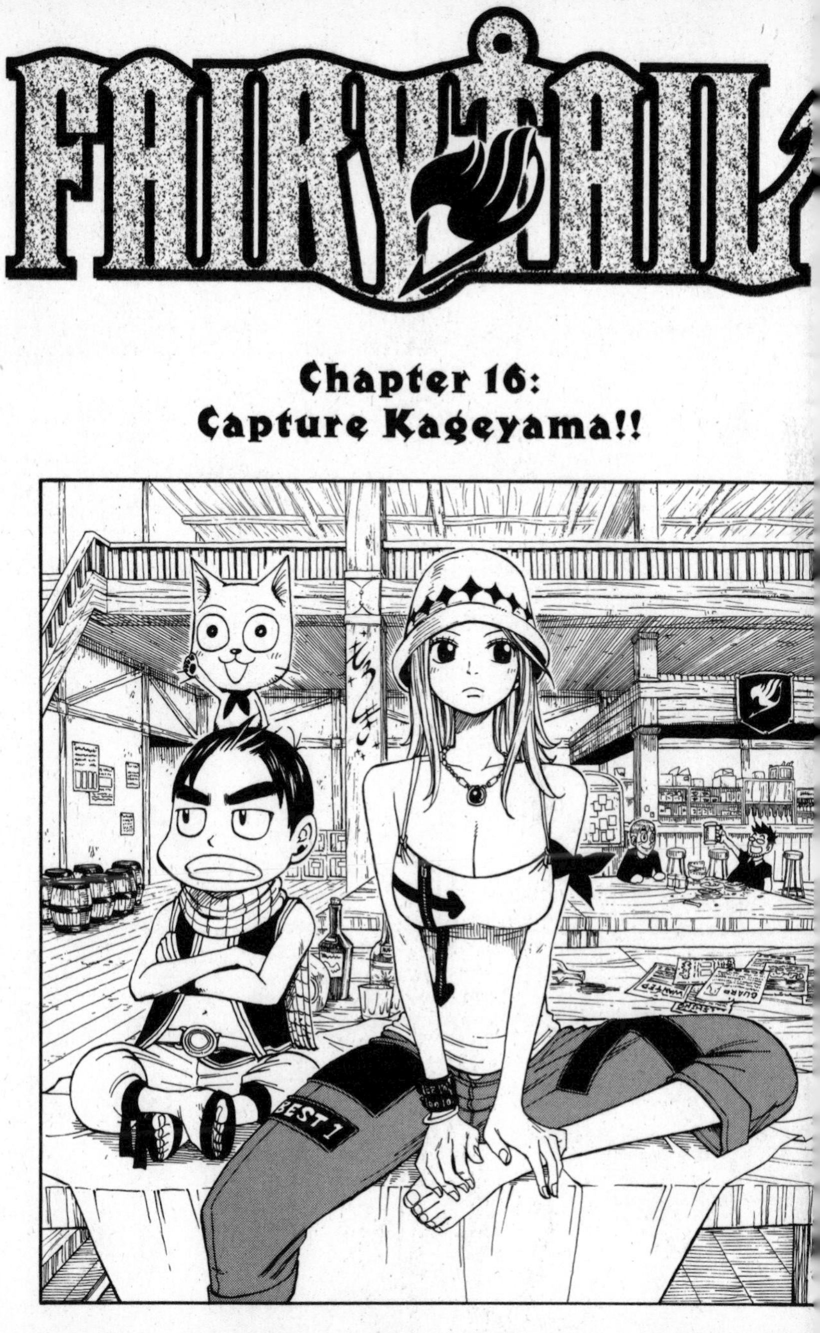
BEST 1

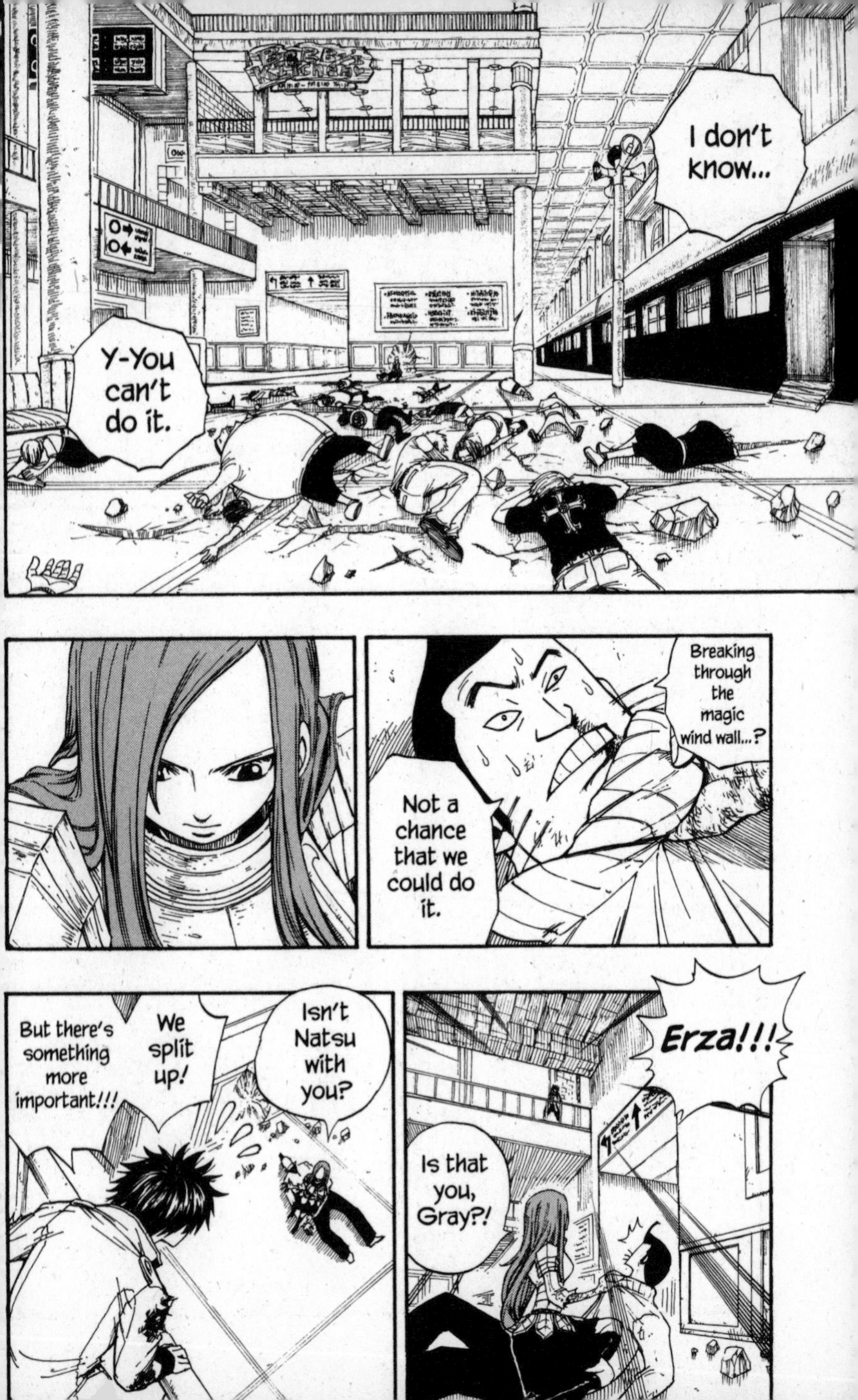
I don't know...
Y-You can't do it.
Breaking through the magic wind wall...?
Not a chance that we could do it.
Erza!!!
Is that you, Gray?!
Isn't Natsu with you?
We split up!
But there's something more important!!!

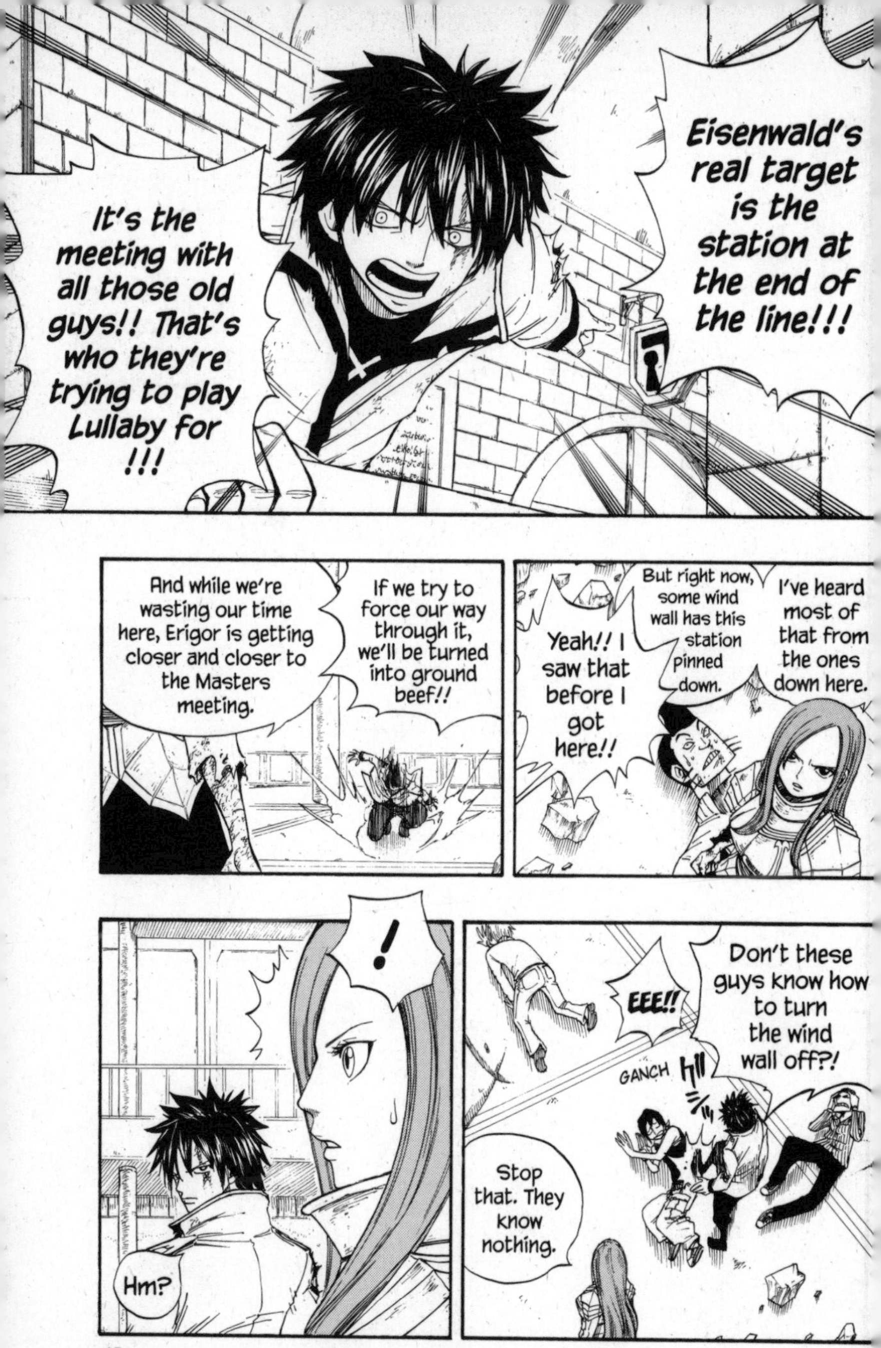
Eisenwald's real target is the station at the end of the line!!!
It's the meeting with all those old guys!! That's who they're trying to play Lullaby for !!!
I've heard most of that from the ones down here.
But right now, some wind wall has this station pinned down.
Yeah!! I saw that before I got here!!
If we try to force our way through it, we'll be turned into ground beef!!
And while we're wasting our time here, Erigor is getting closer and closer to the Masters meeting.
Don't these guys know how to turn the wind wall off?!
EEE!!
GANCH
Stop that. They know nothing.
!
Hm?

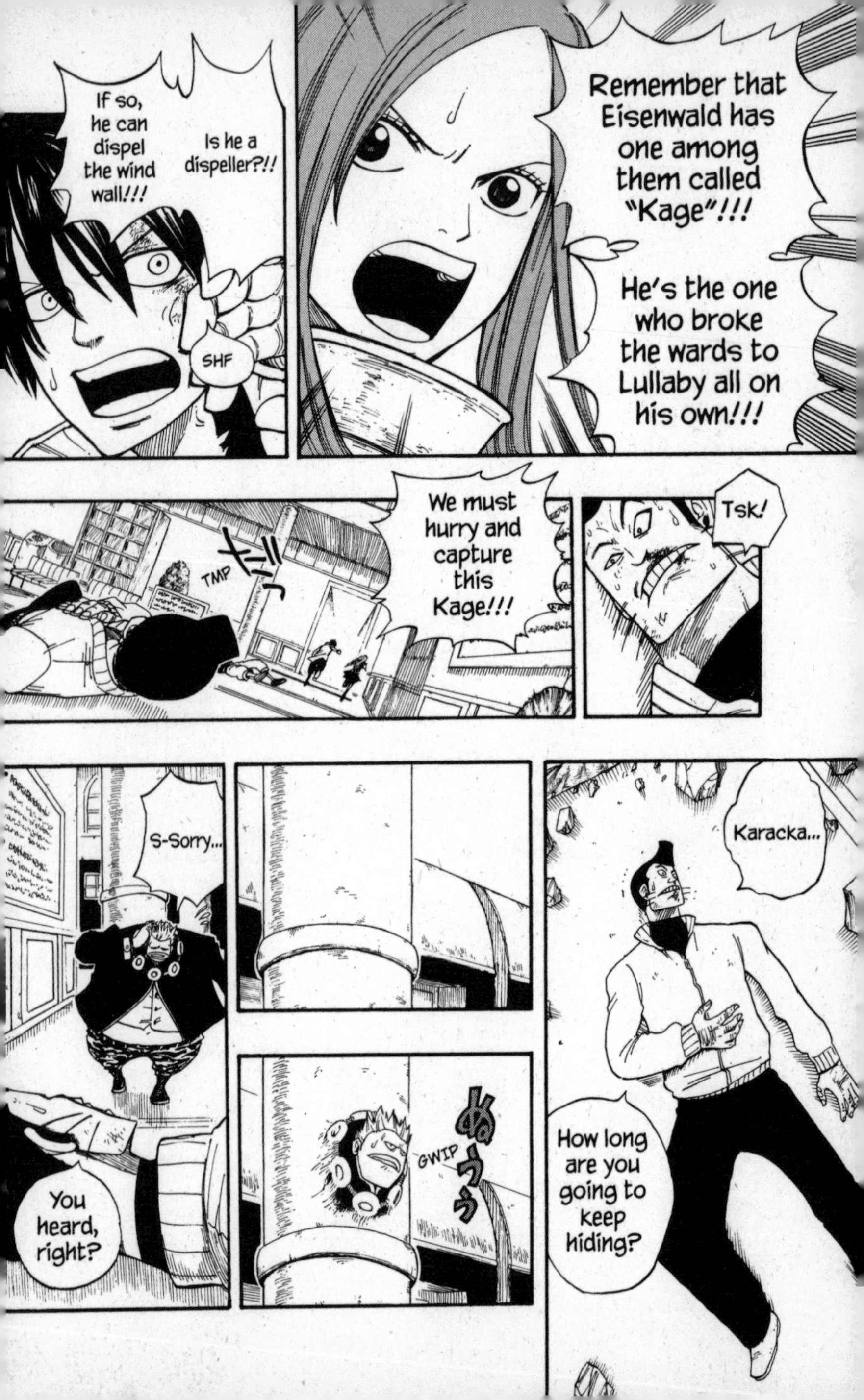
Remember that Eisenwald has one among them called "Kage"!!!
He's the one who broke the wards to Lullaby all on his own!!!
Is he a dispeller?!!
If so, he can dispel the wind wall!!!
SHF
Tsk!
We must hurry and capture this Kage!!!
TMP
Karacka...
How long are you going to keep hiding?
GWIP
S-Sorry...
You heard, right?

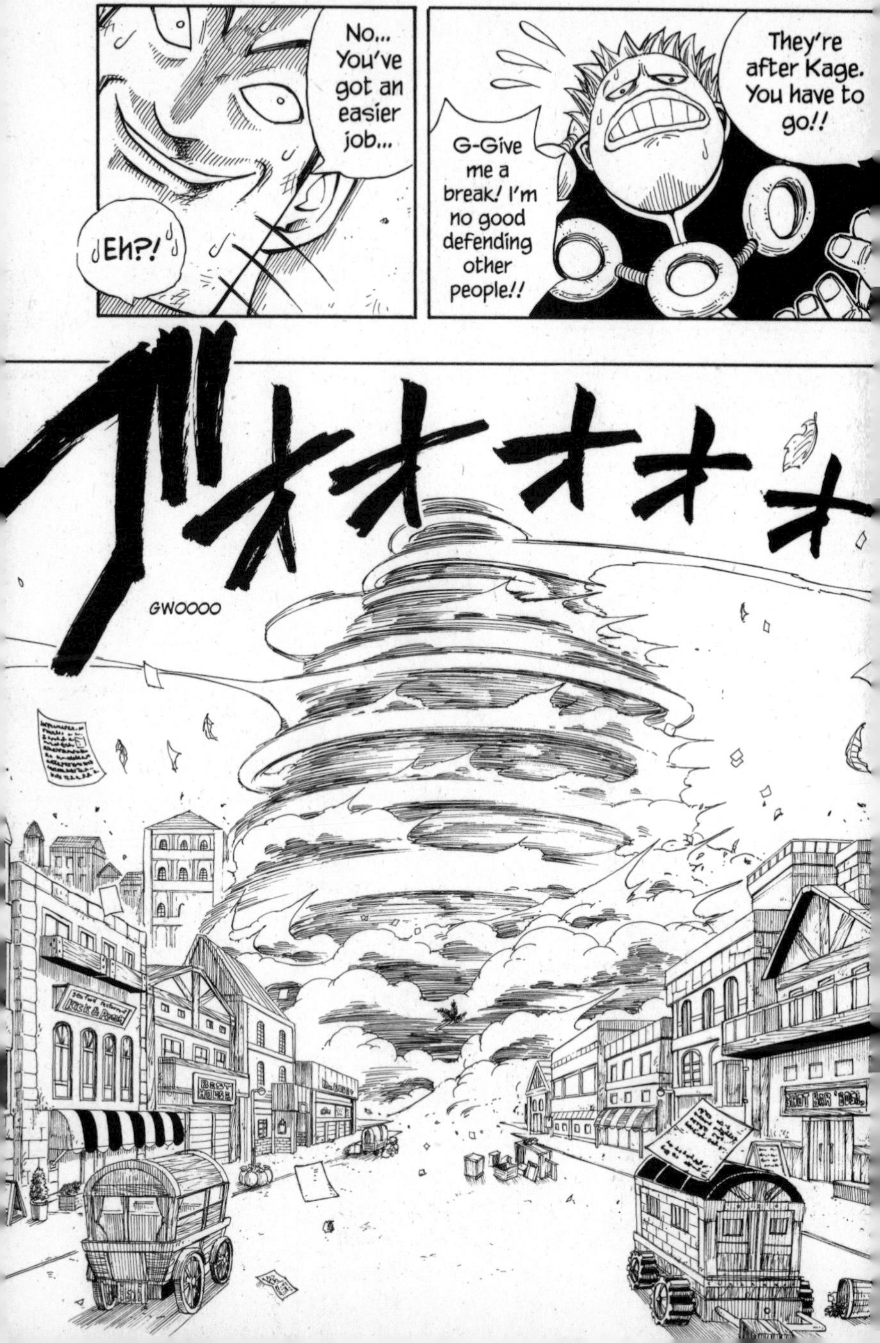
They're after Kage. You have to go!!
G-Give me a break! I'm no good defending other people!!
No... You've got an easier job...
Eh?!
GWOOOO

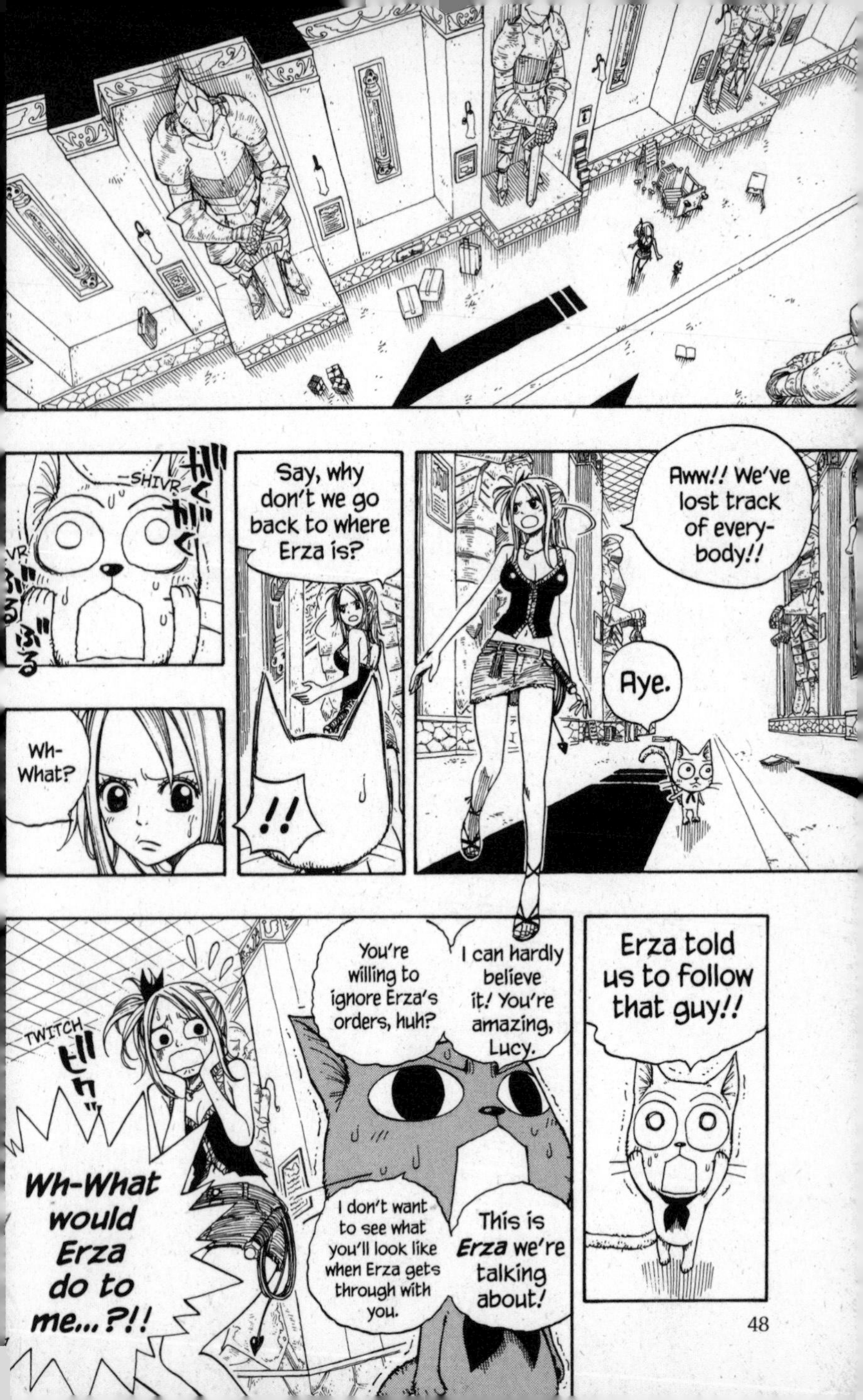
Aww!! We've lost track of every-body!!
Aye.
Say, why don't we go back to where Erza is?
!!
SHIVR
Wh- What?
Erza told us to follow that guy!!
I can hardly believe it! You're amazing, Lucy.
You're willing to ignore Erza's orders, huh?
This is Erza we're talking about!
I don't want to see what you'll look like when Erza gets through with you.
TWITCH
Wh-What would Erza do to me...?!!

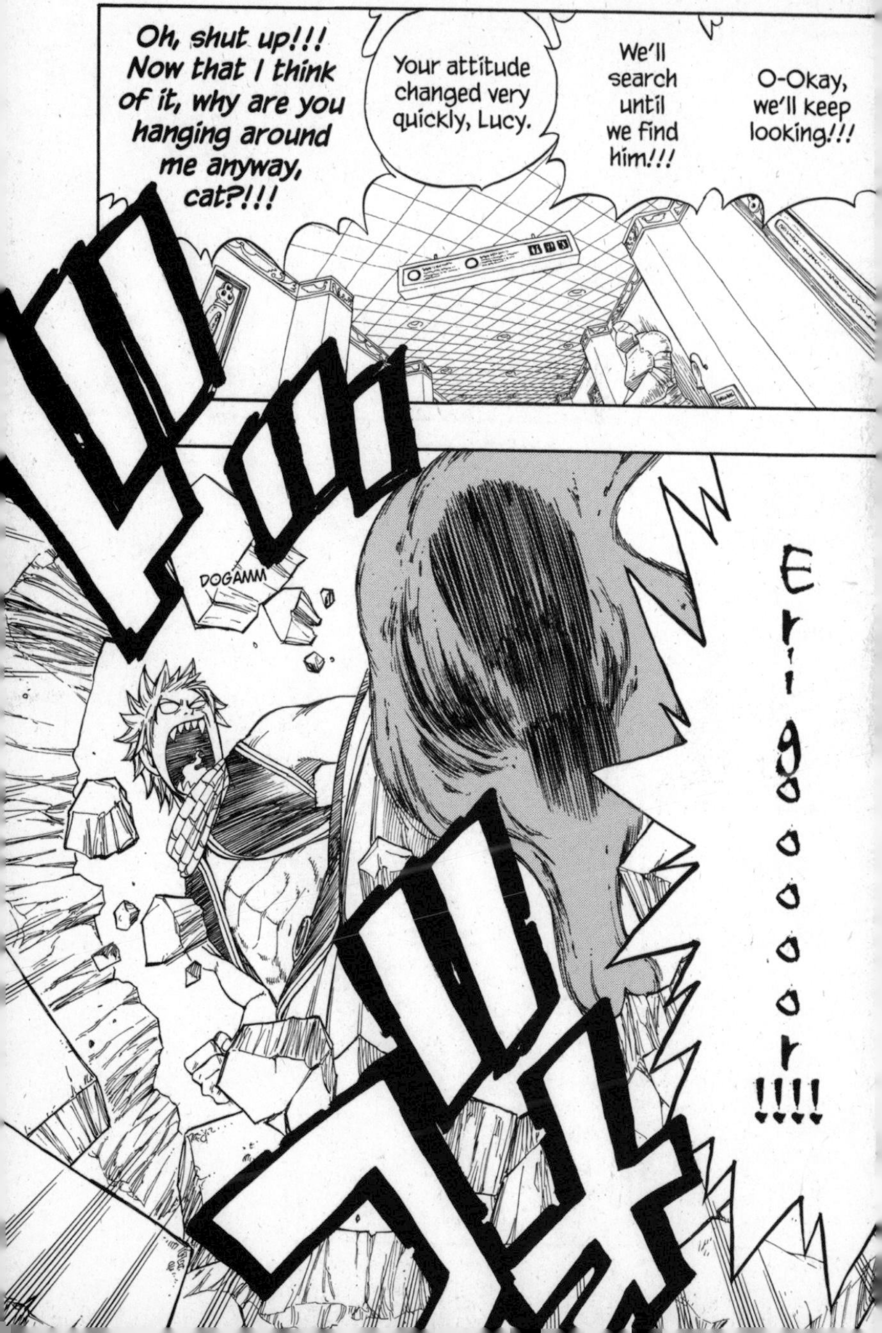
O-Okay, we'll keep looking!!!
We'll search until we find him!!!
Your attitude changed very quickly, Lucy.
Oh, shut up!!! Now that I think of it, why are you hanging around me anyway, cat?!!!
Errgooooor!!!!
DOGAMM

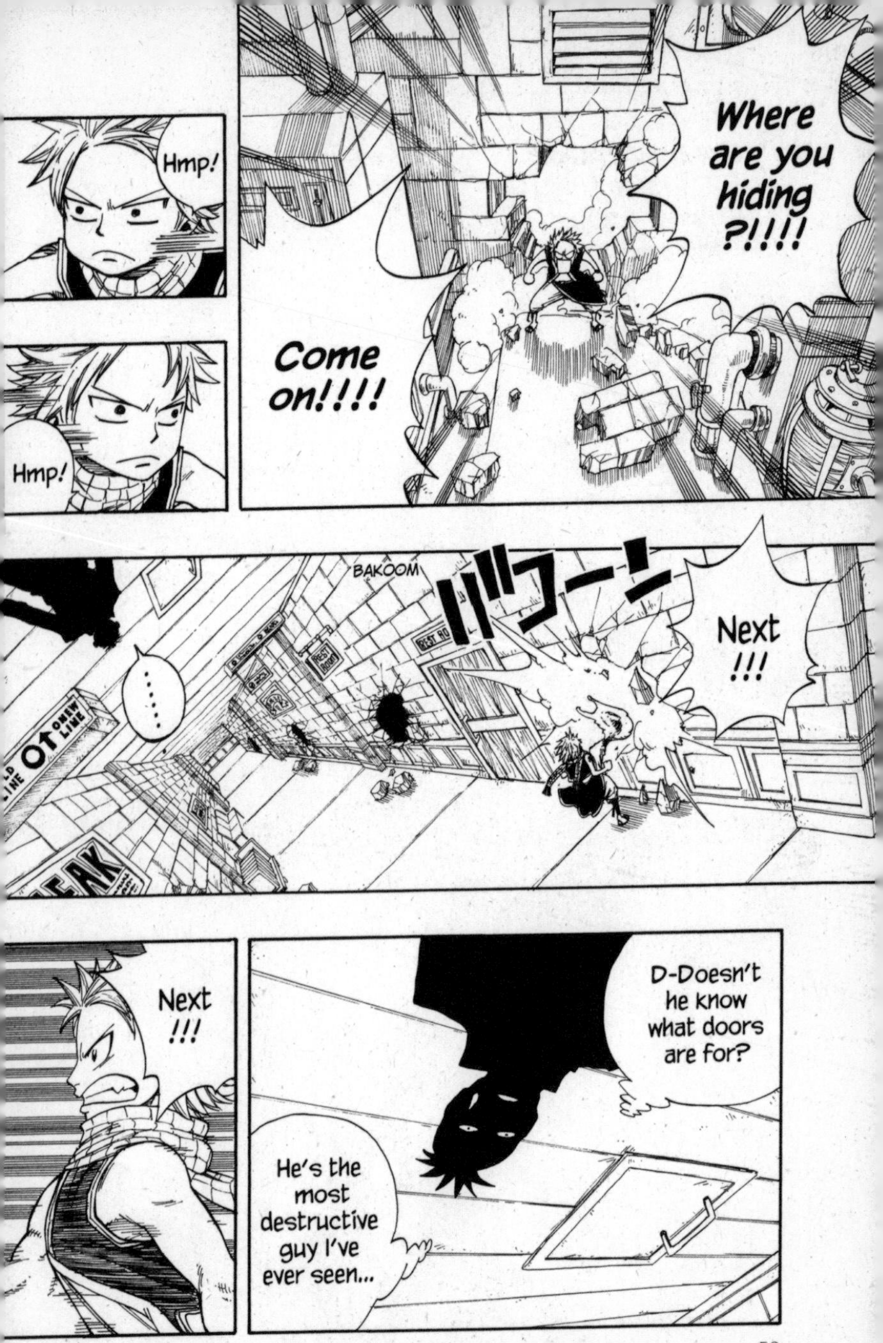
Where are you hiding?!!!!
Come on!!!!
Hmp!
Hmp!
Next!!!
BAKOOM
......
D-Doesn't he know what doors are for?
He's the most destructive guy I've ever seen...
Next!!!

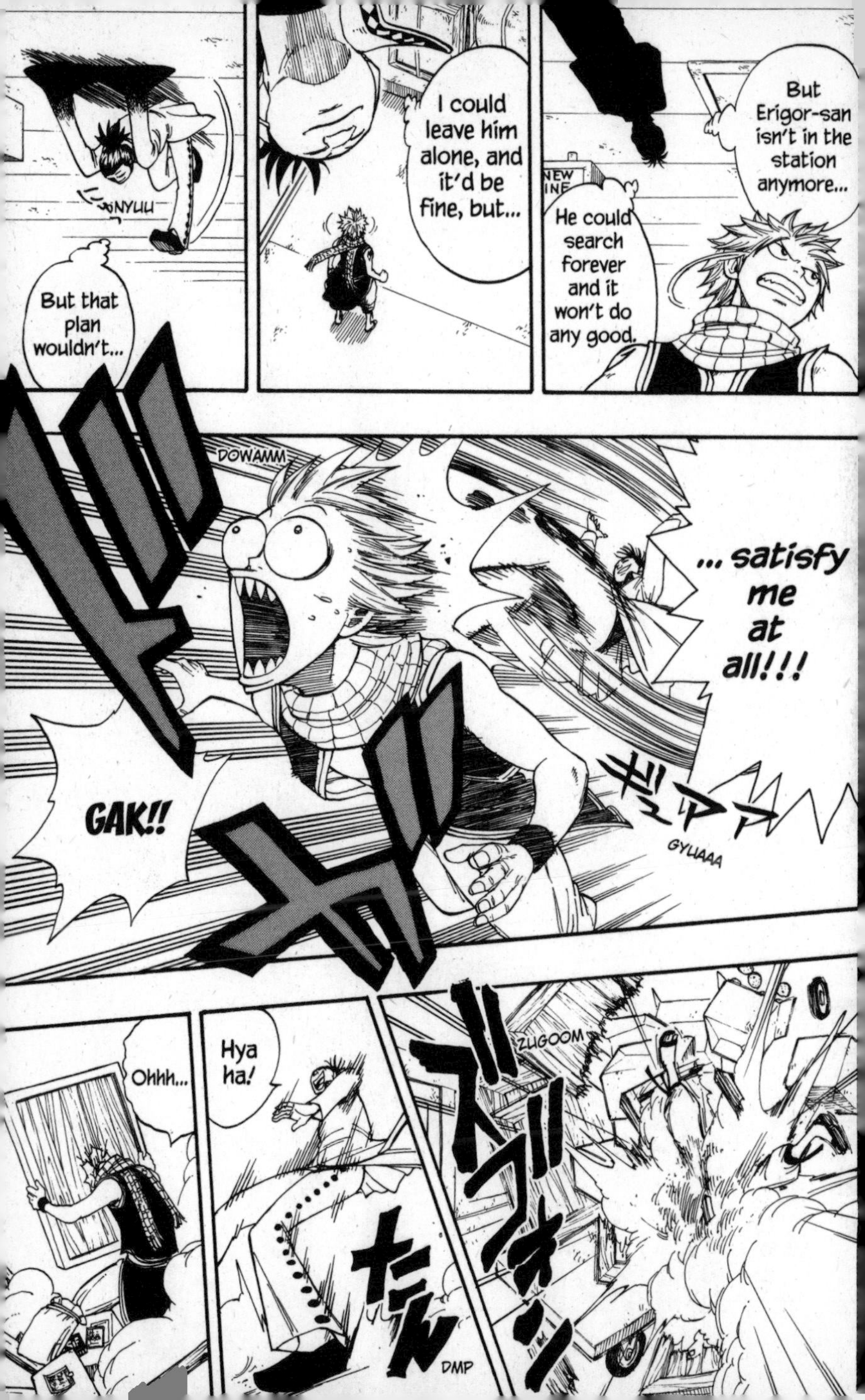
But Erigor-san isn't in the station anymore...
He could search forever and it won't do any good.
I could leave him alone, and it'd be fine, but...
NYUU
But that plan wouldn't...
... satisfy me at all!!!
GYUAAA
DOWAMM
GAK!!
ZUGOOM
Hya ha!
DMP
Ohhh...

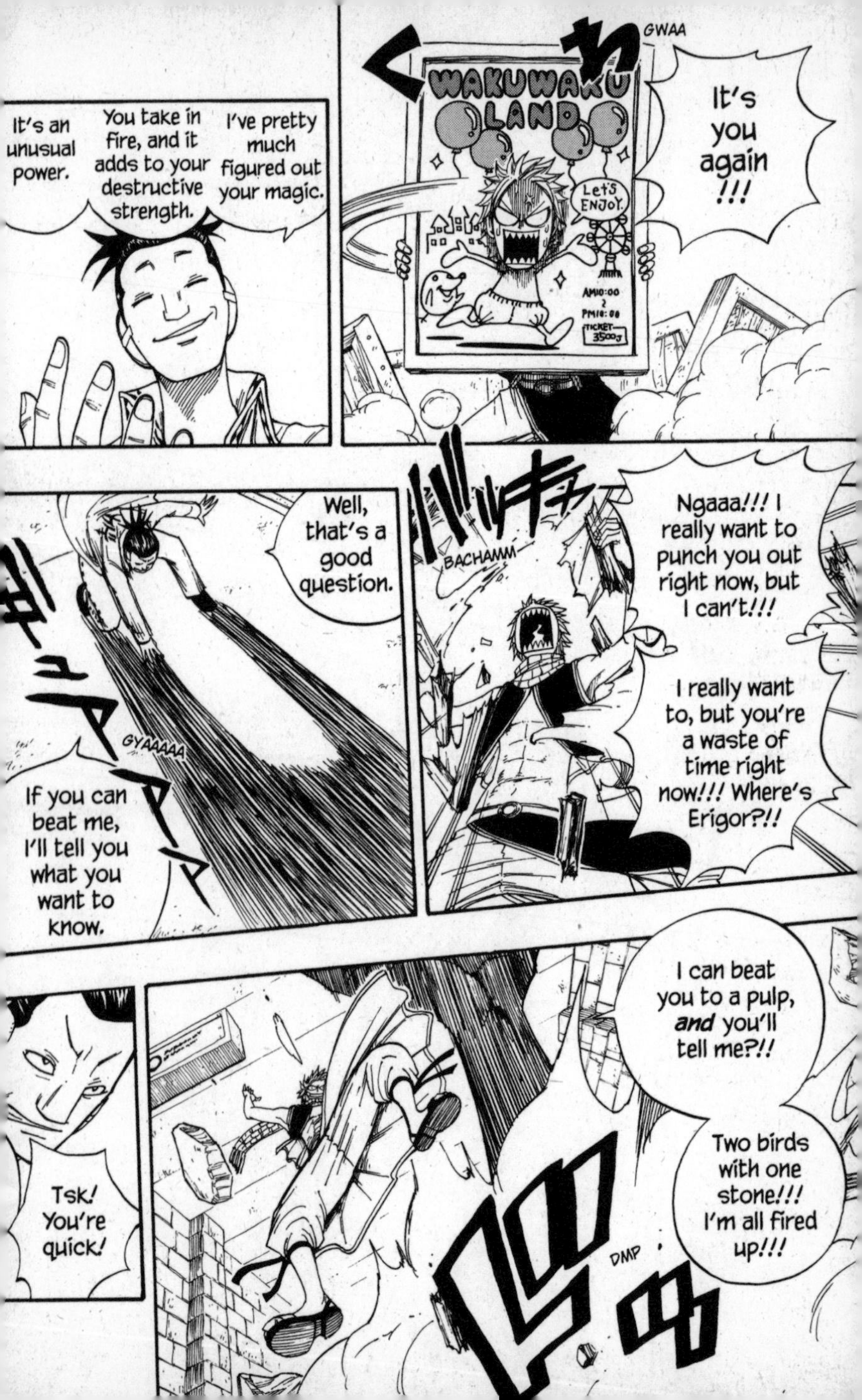
GWAA
WAKUWAKU LAND
Let's ENJOY.
AM10:00 ~ PM10:00
TICKET 3500J
It's you again!!!
I've pretty much figured out your magic.
You take in fire, and it adds to your destructive strength.
It's an unusual power.
BACHAMM
Ngaaa!!! I really want to punch you out right now, but I can't!!!
I really want to, but you're a waste of time right now!!! Where's Erigor?!!
Well, that's a good question.
GYAAAAA
If you can beat me, I'll tell you what you want to know.
I can beat you to a pulp, *and* you'll tell me?!!
Two birds with one stone!!! I'm all fired up!!!
DMP
Tsk! You're quick!

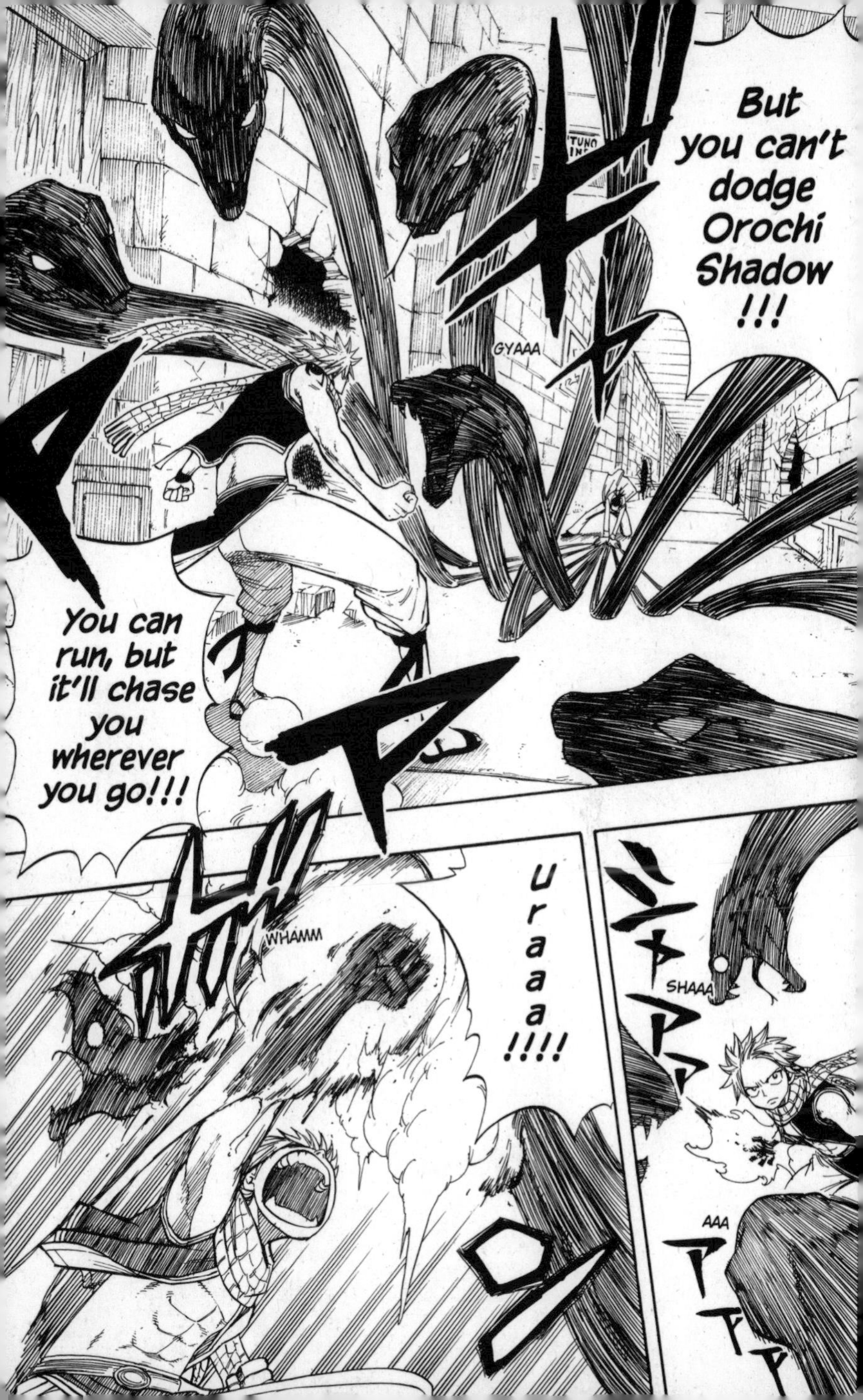
But you can't dodge Orochi Shadow!!!
GYAAA
You can run, but it'll chase you wherever you go!!!
SHAAA
AAA
Uraaa!!!!
WHAMM

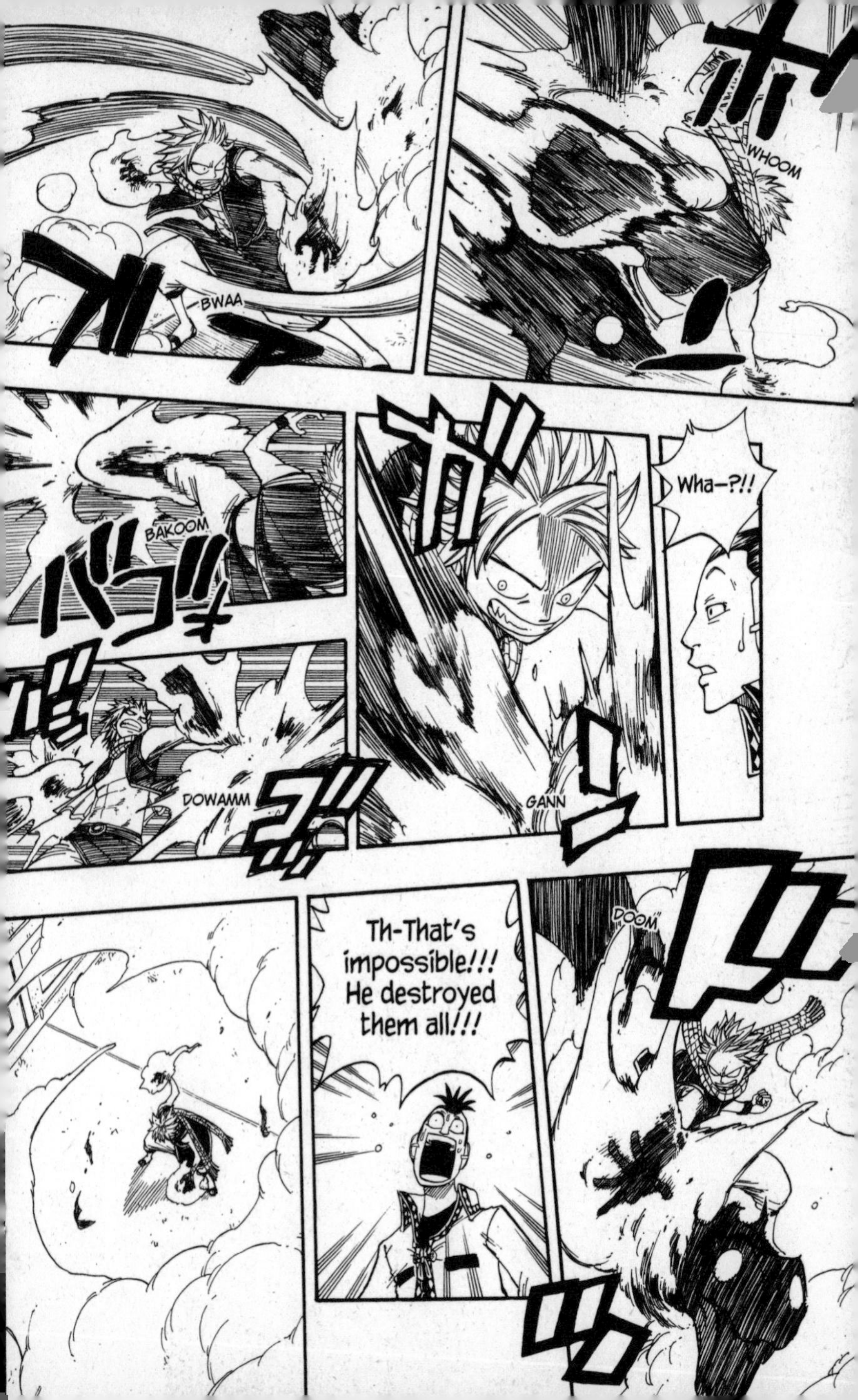
WHOOM
BWAA
Wha–?!!
GANN
BAKOOM
DOWAMM
DOOM
Th-That's impossible!!! He destroyed them all!!!

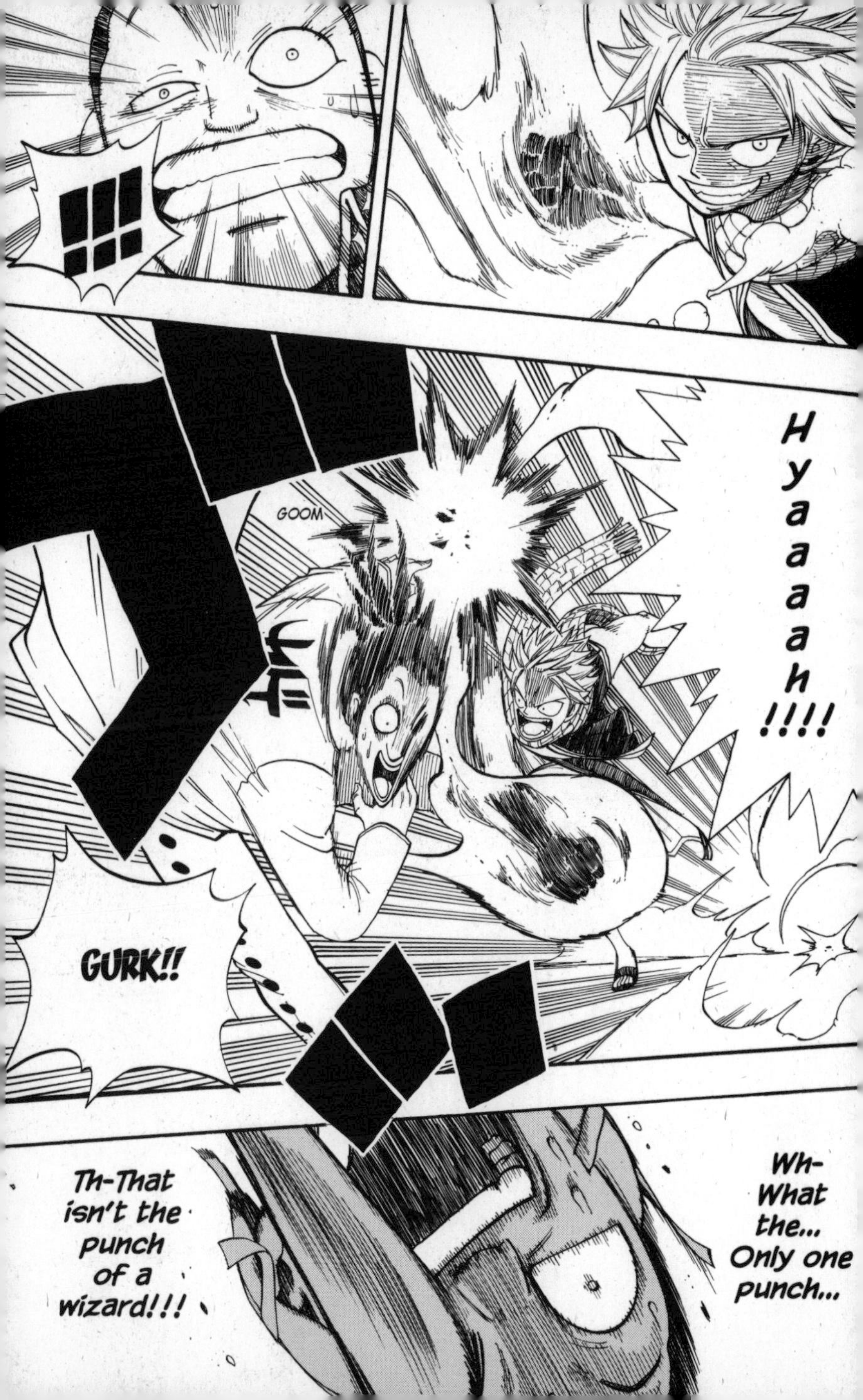
!!!
Hyaaaah!!!!
GOOM
GURK!!
Wh-What the... Only one punch...
Th-That isn't the punch of a wizard!!!

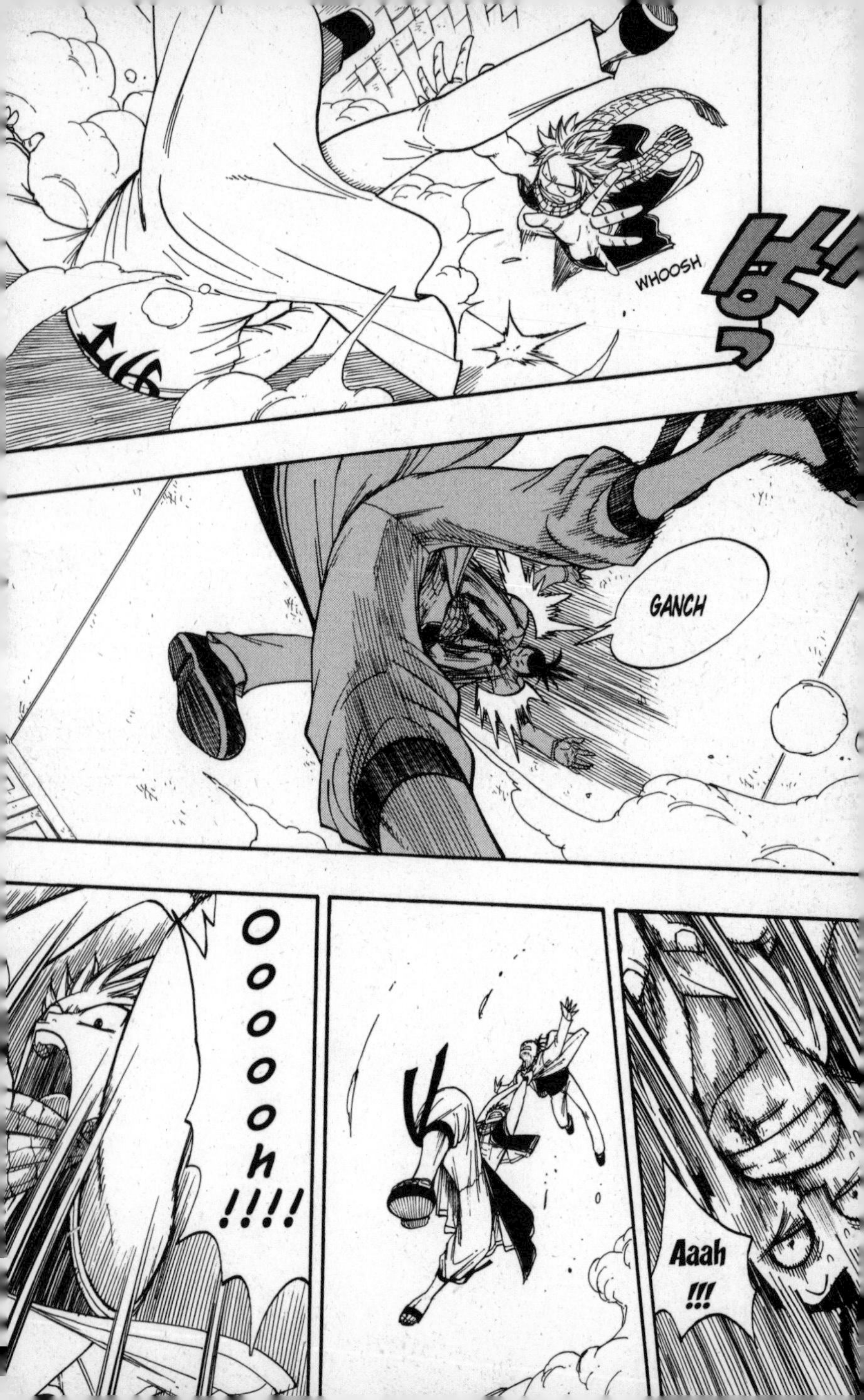
WHOOSH
GANCH
Aaah !!!
Ooooooh !!!!

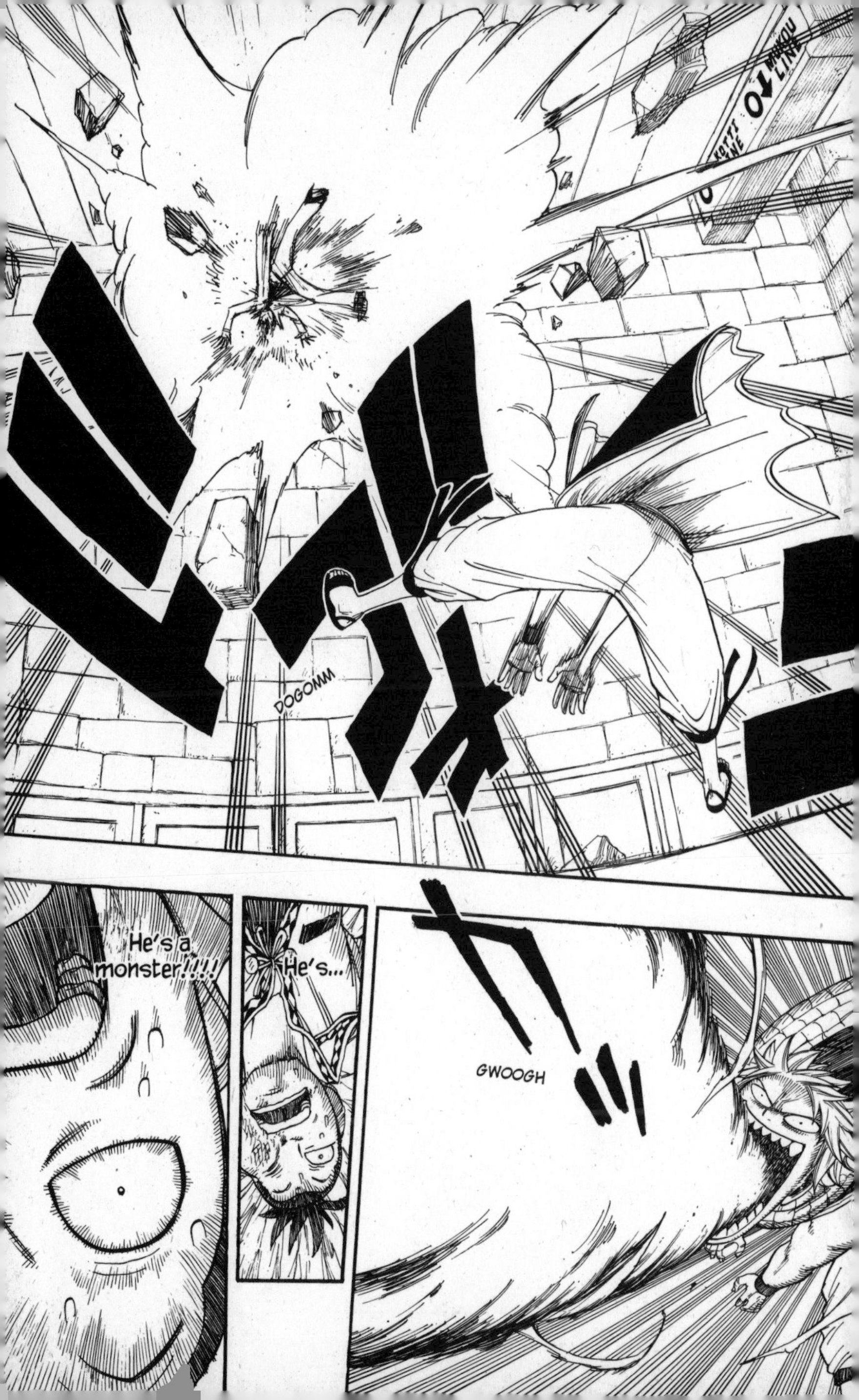
MINKOU LINE
DOGOMM
GWOOGH
He's...
He's a monster!!!!

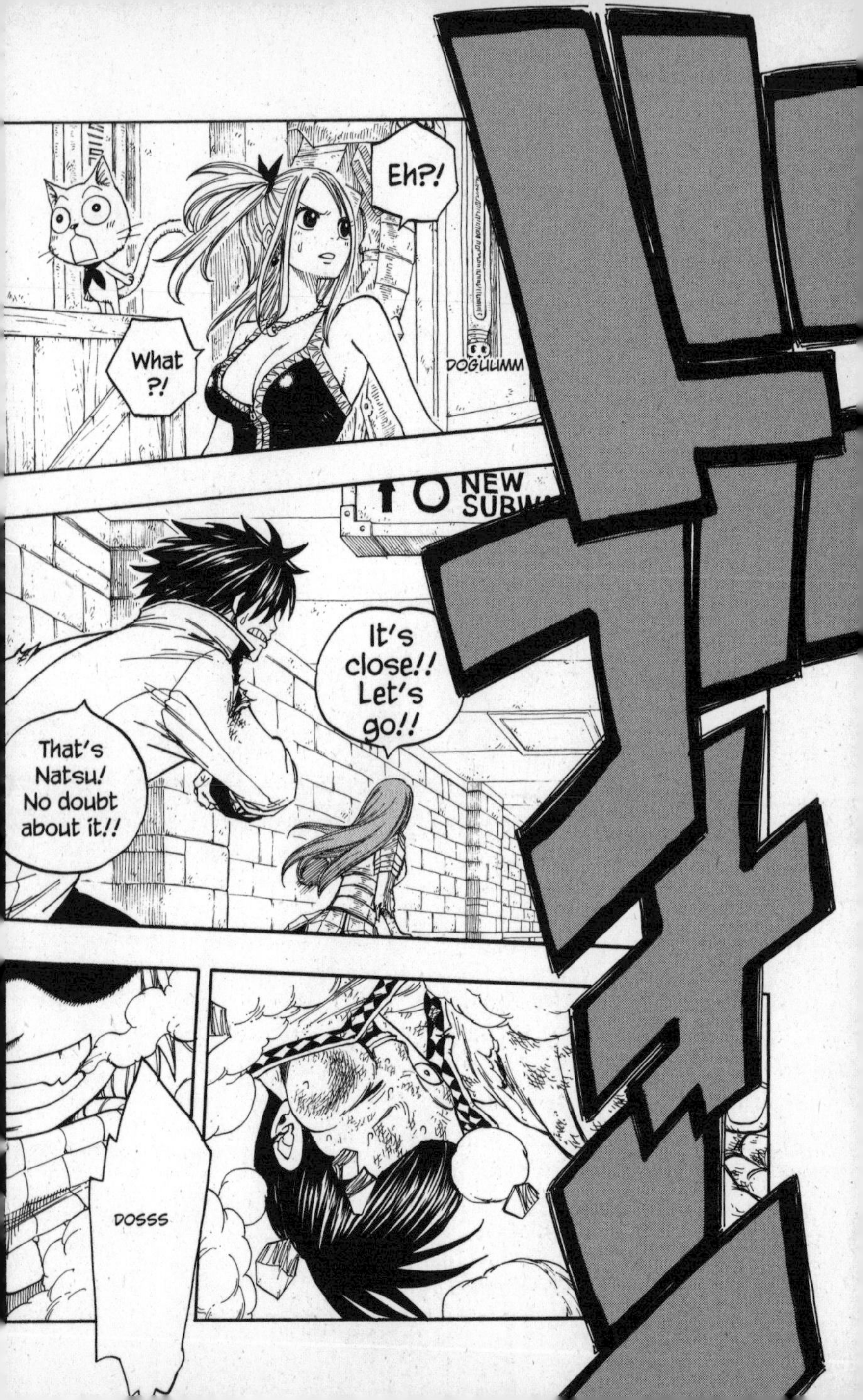
Eh?!
DOGUUMM
What ?!
NEW
It's close!! Let's go!!
That's Natsu! No doubt about it!!
DOSSS

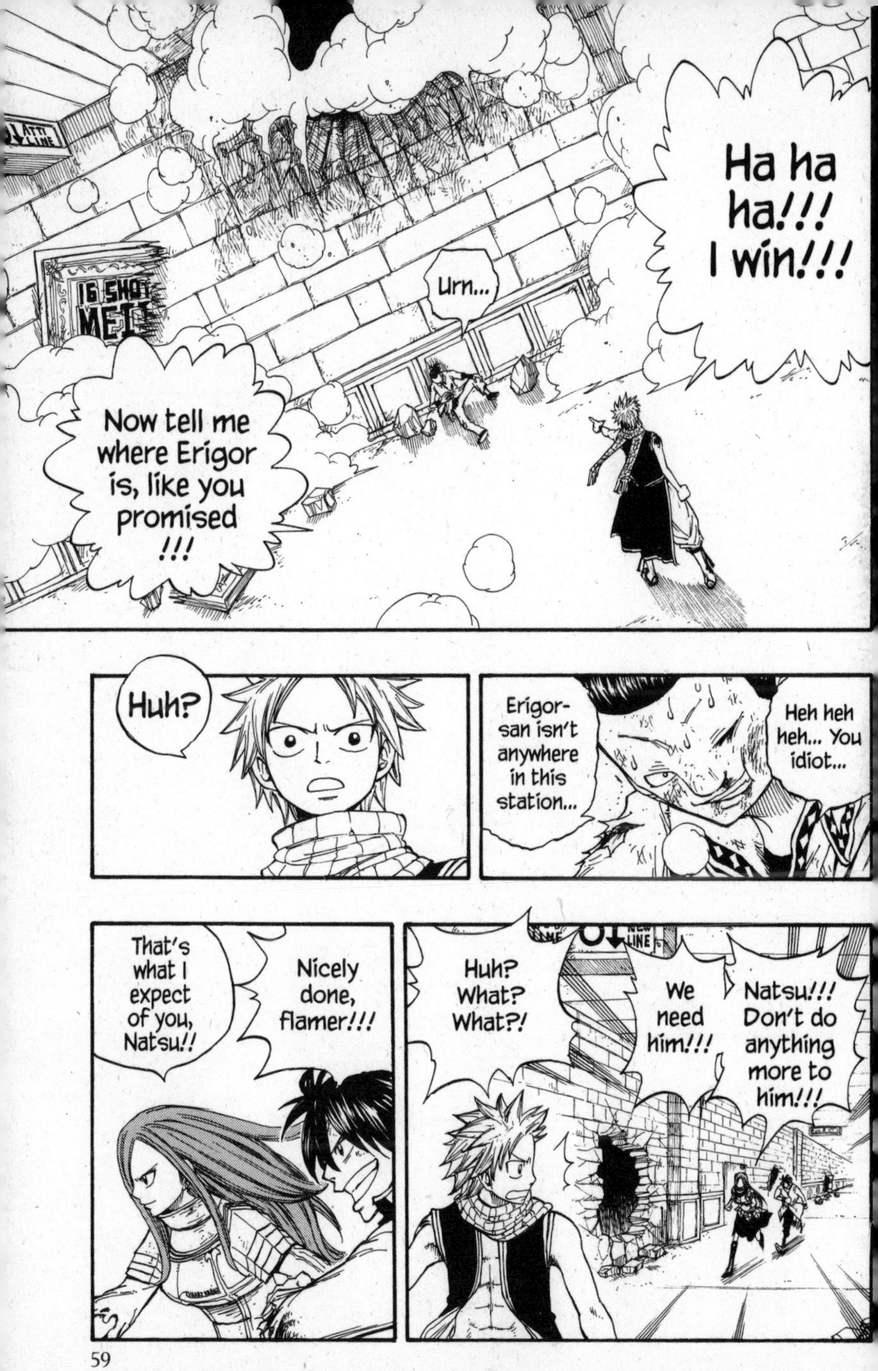
Ha ha ha!!! I win!!!
Urn...
Now tell me where Erigor is, like you promised!!!
Heh heh heh... You idiot...
Erigor-san isn't anywhere in this station...
Huh?
Natsu!!! Don't do anything more to him!!!
We need him!!!
Huh? What? What?!
Nicely done, flamer!!!
That's what I expect of you, Natsu!!

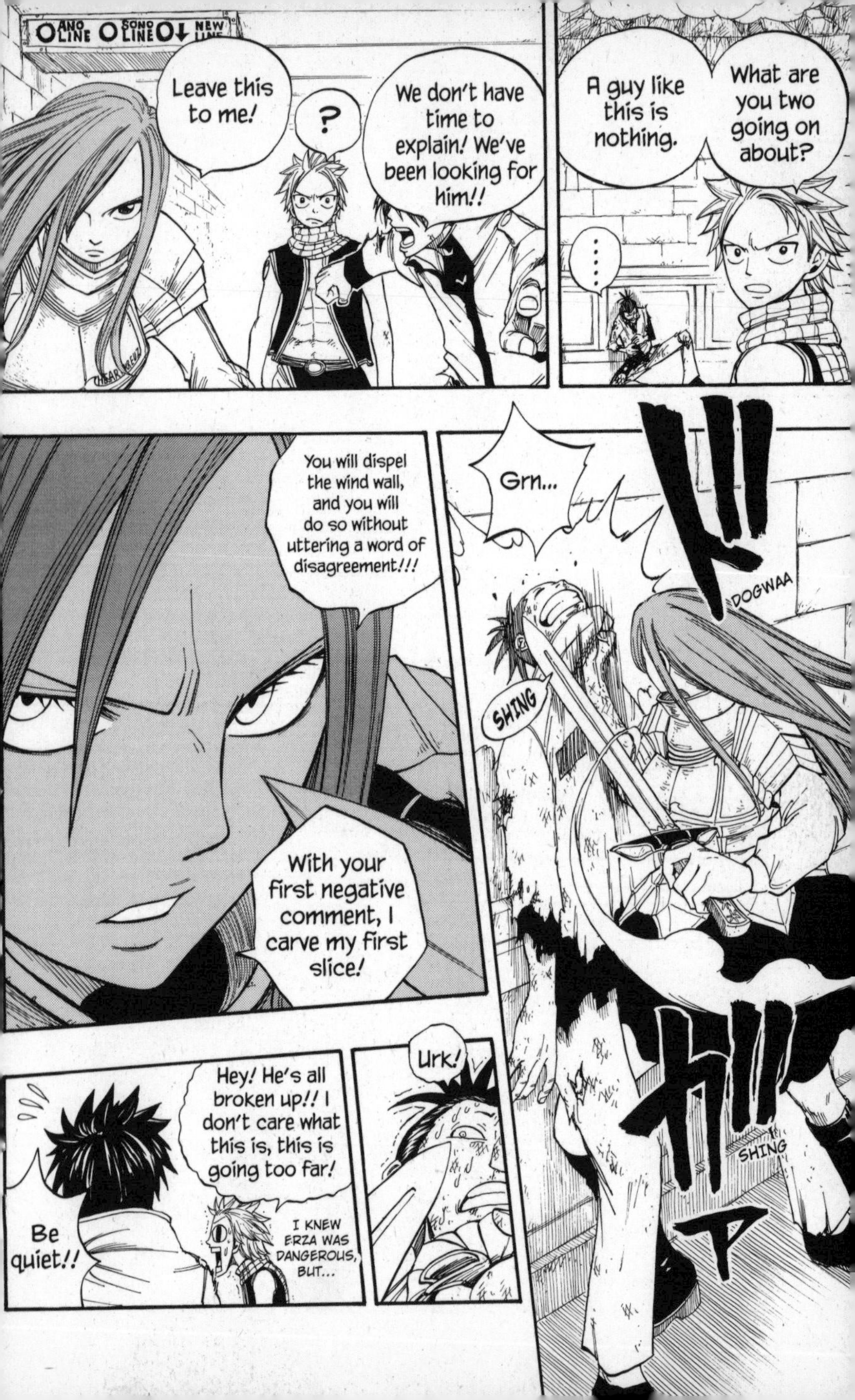
What are you two going on about?
A guy like this is nothing.
……
We don't have time to explain! We've been looking for him!!
?
Leave this to me!
ANO LINE SONO LINE NEW LINE
Grn...
DOGWAA
SHING
SHING
You will dispel the wind wall, and you will do so without uttering a word of disagreement!!!
With your first negative comment, I carve my first slice!
Urk!
Hey! He's all broken up!! I don't care what this is, this is going too far!
Be quiet!!
I KNEW ERZA WAS DANGEROUS, BUT...

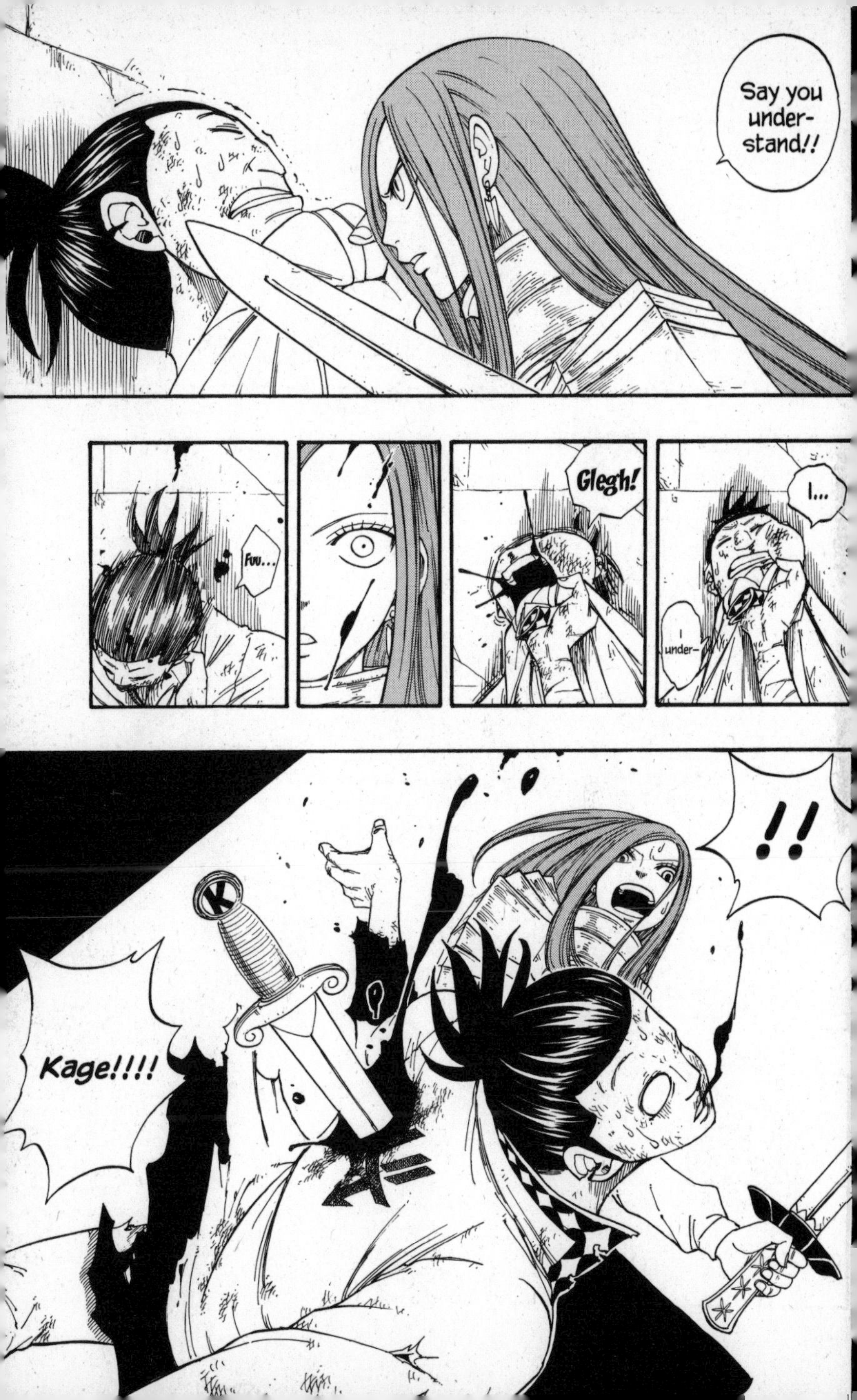

Say you under-stand!!
I...
I under-
Glegh!
Fuu...
!!
Kage!!!!

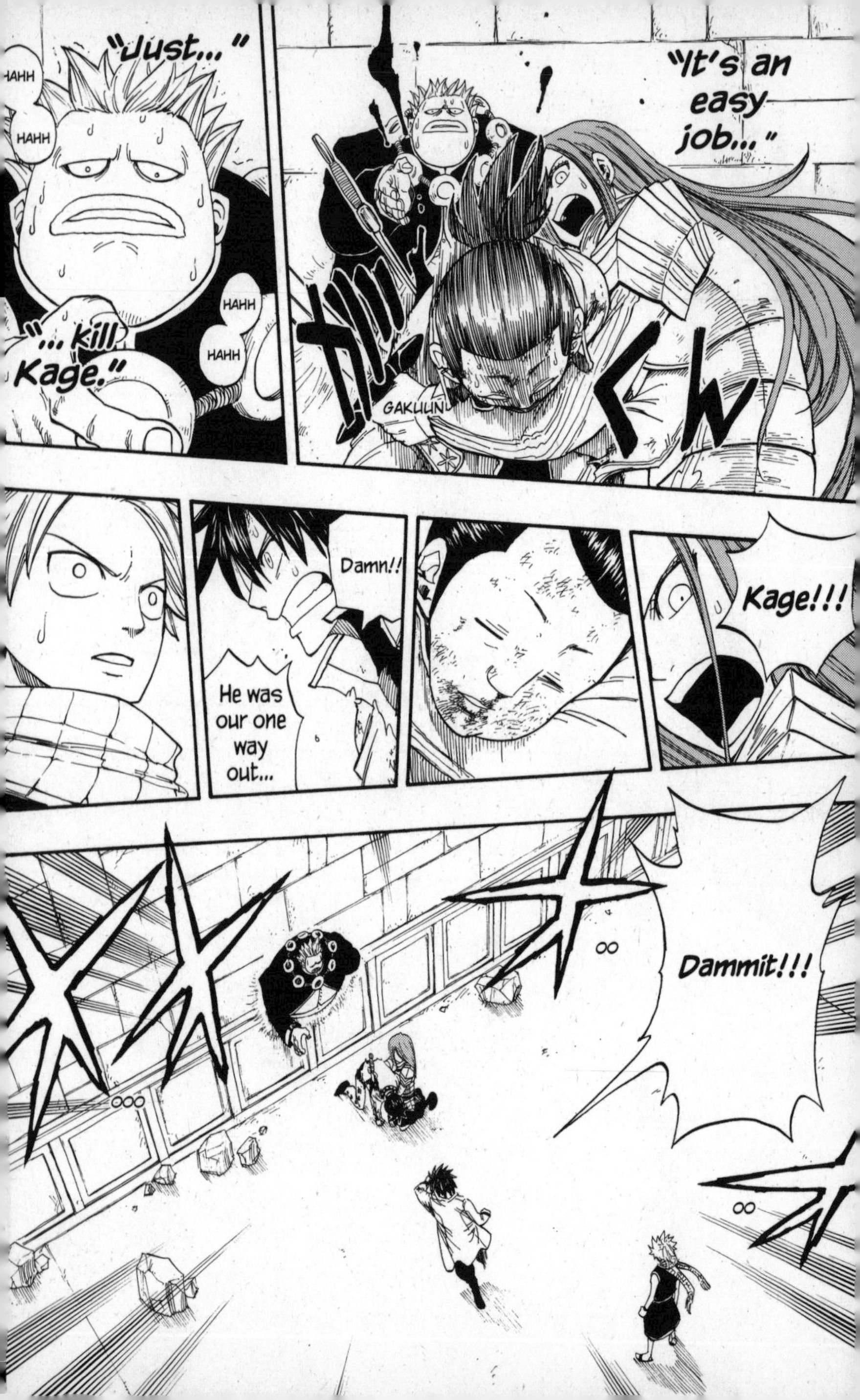
"It's an easy job..."
GAKUUN
"Just..."
HAHH
HAHH
HAHH
HAHH
"...kill Kage."
Kage!!!
Damn!!
He was our one way out...
Dammit!!!

FAIRY TAIL

Chapter 17: The Virgin Magic

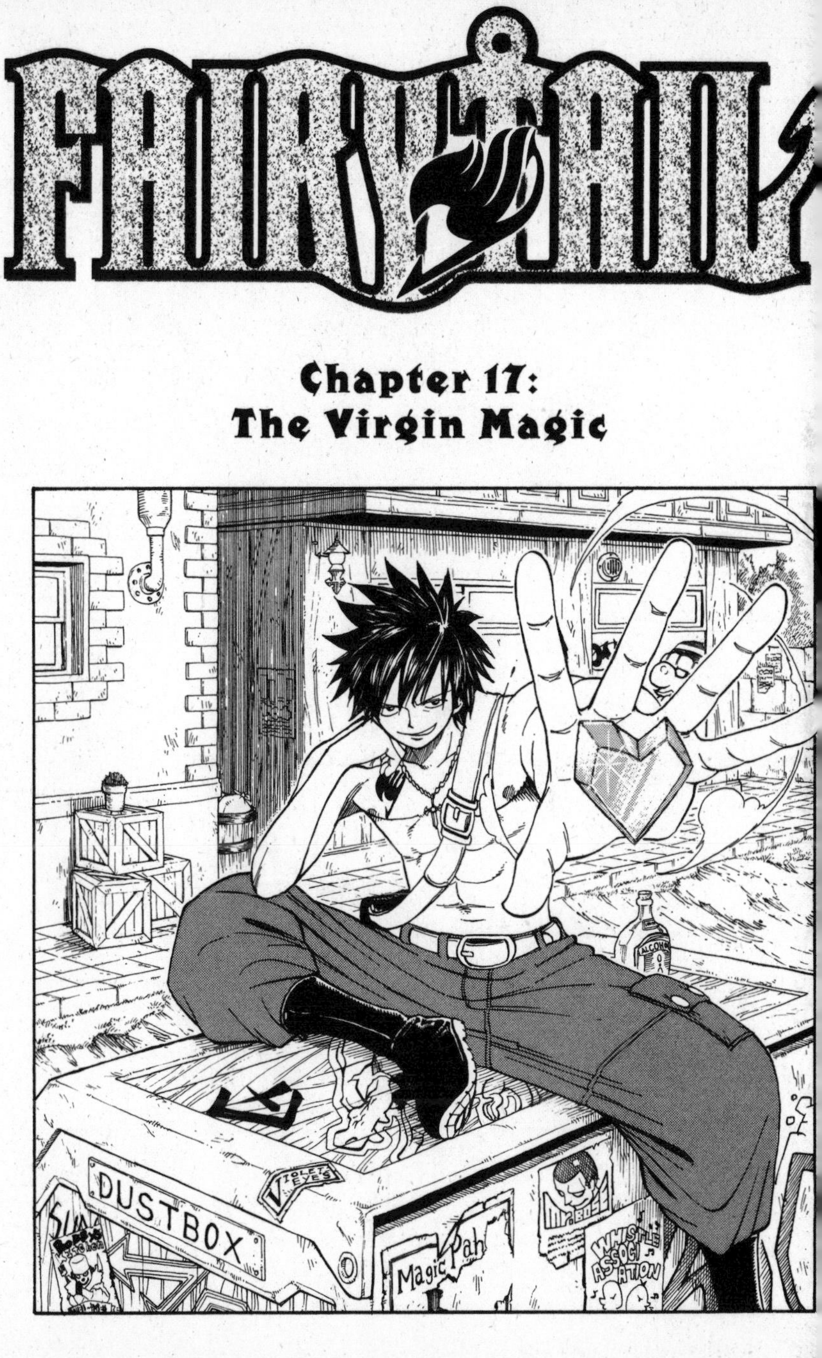
DUSTBOX
VIOLET EYES
Magic Pah
WHISTLE ASSOCI ATION

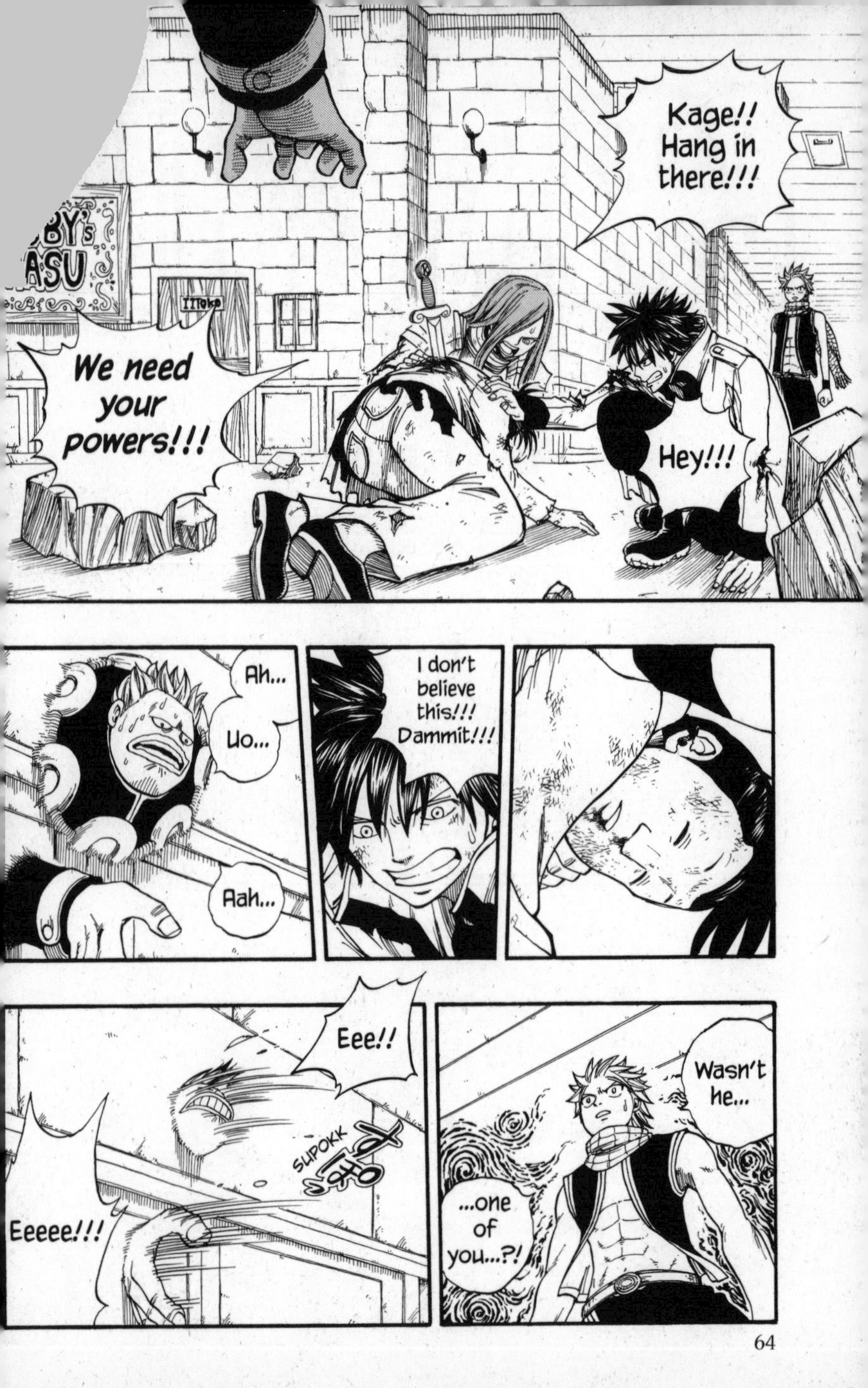
Kage!! Hang in there!!!
Hey!!!
We need your powers!!!
I don't believe this!!! Dammit!!!
Ah...
Uo...
Aah...
Wasn't he...
...one of you...?!
Eee!!
SUPOKK
Eeeee!!!

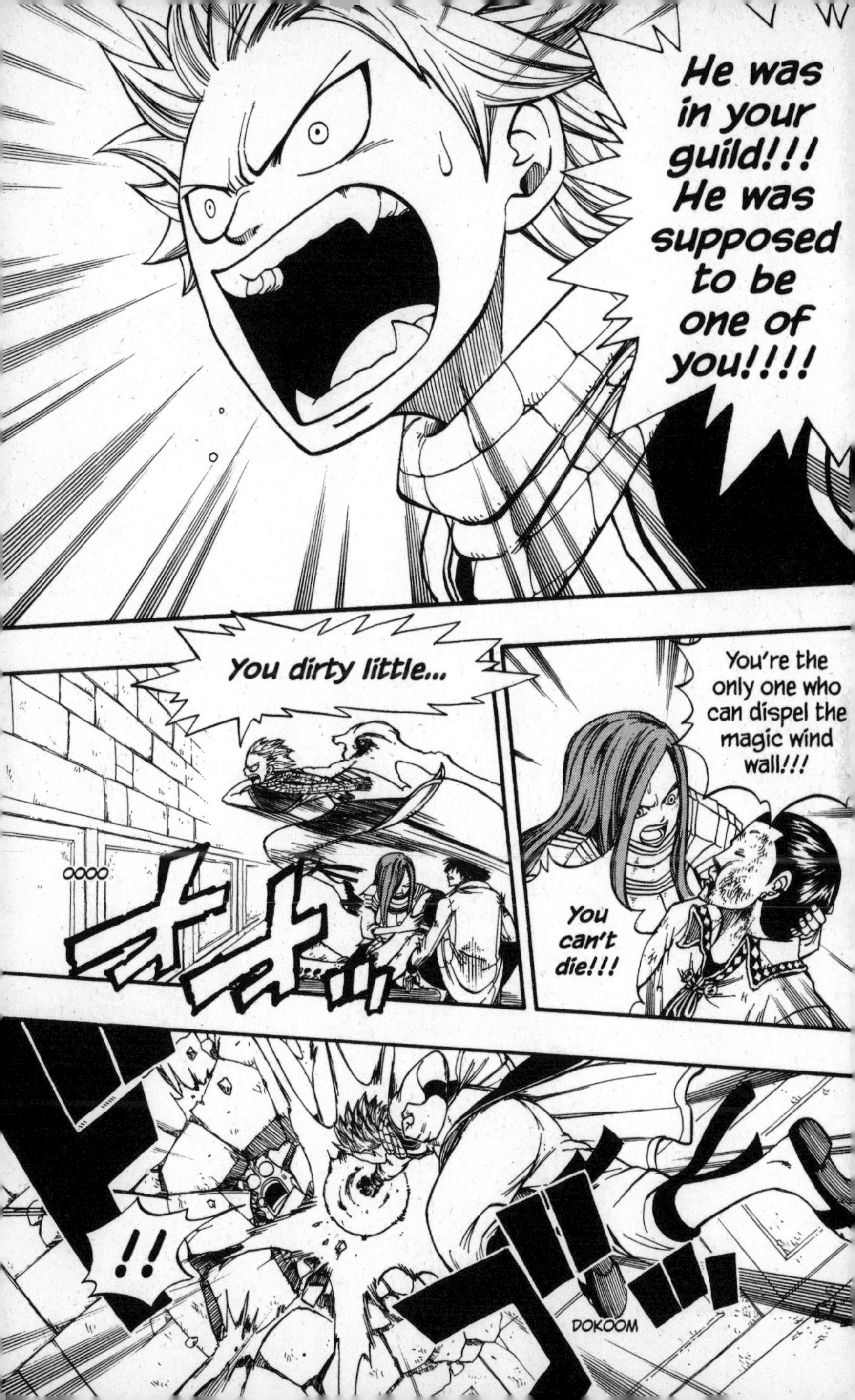
He was in your guild!!! He was supposed to be one of you!!!!
You're the only one who can dispel the magic wind wall!!!
You can't die!!!
You dirty little...
oooo
!!
DOKOOM

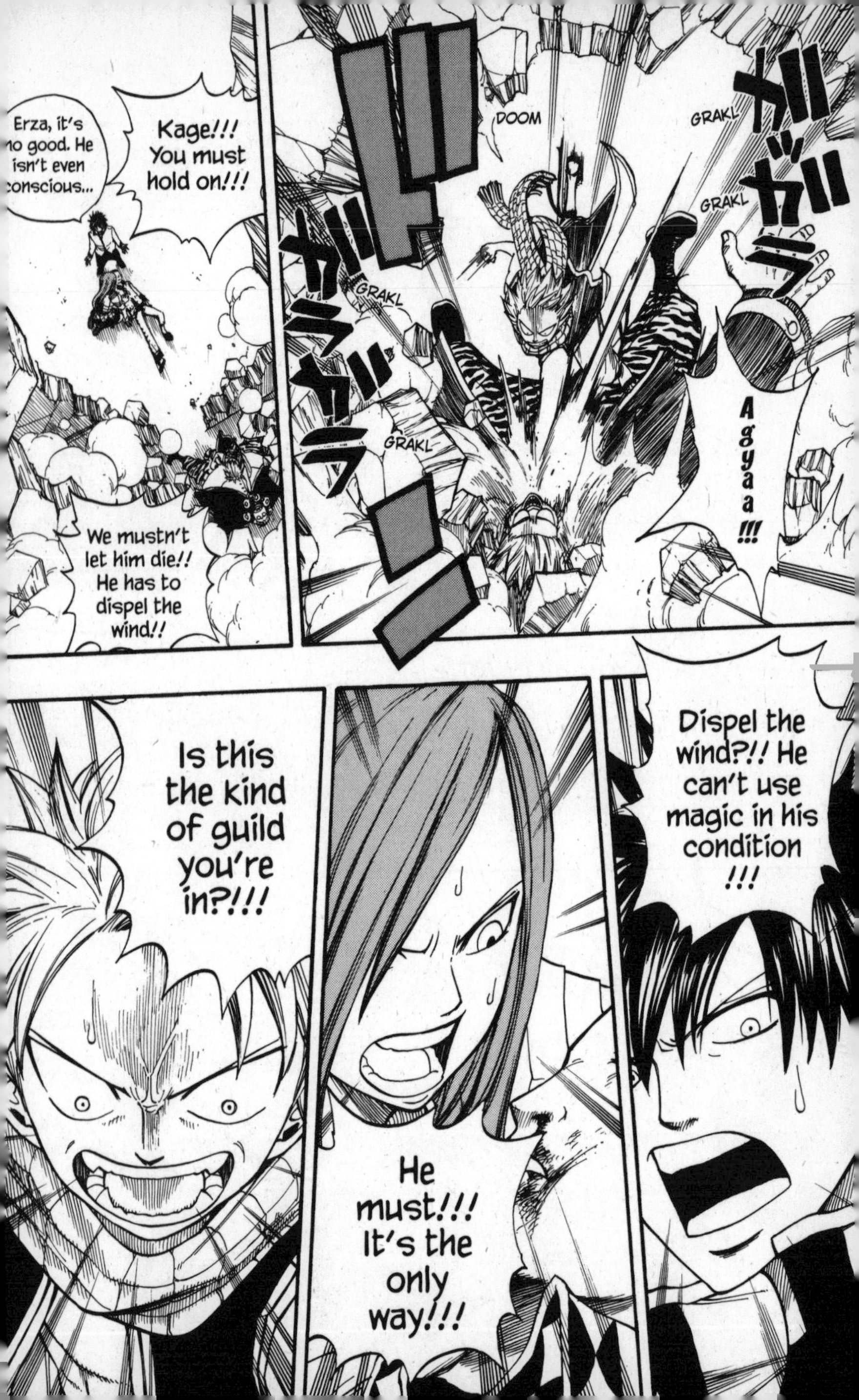
GRAKL
GRAKL
DOOM
GRAKL
GRAKL
Agyaa!!!
Kage!!! You must hold on!!!
Erza, it's no good. He isn't even conscious...
We mustn't let him die!! He has to dispel the wind!!
Dispel the wind?!! He can't use magic in his condition !!!
He must!!! It's the only way!!!
Is this the kind of guild you're in?!!!

Aye.

I-I think we'd only be in the way.

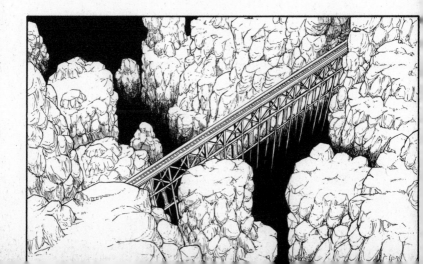

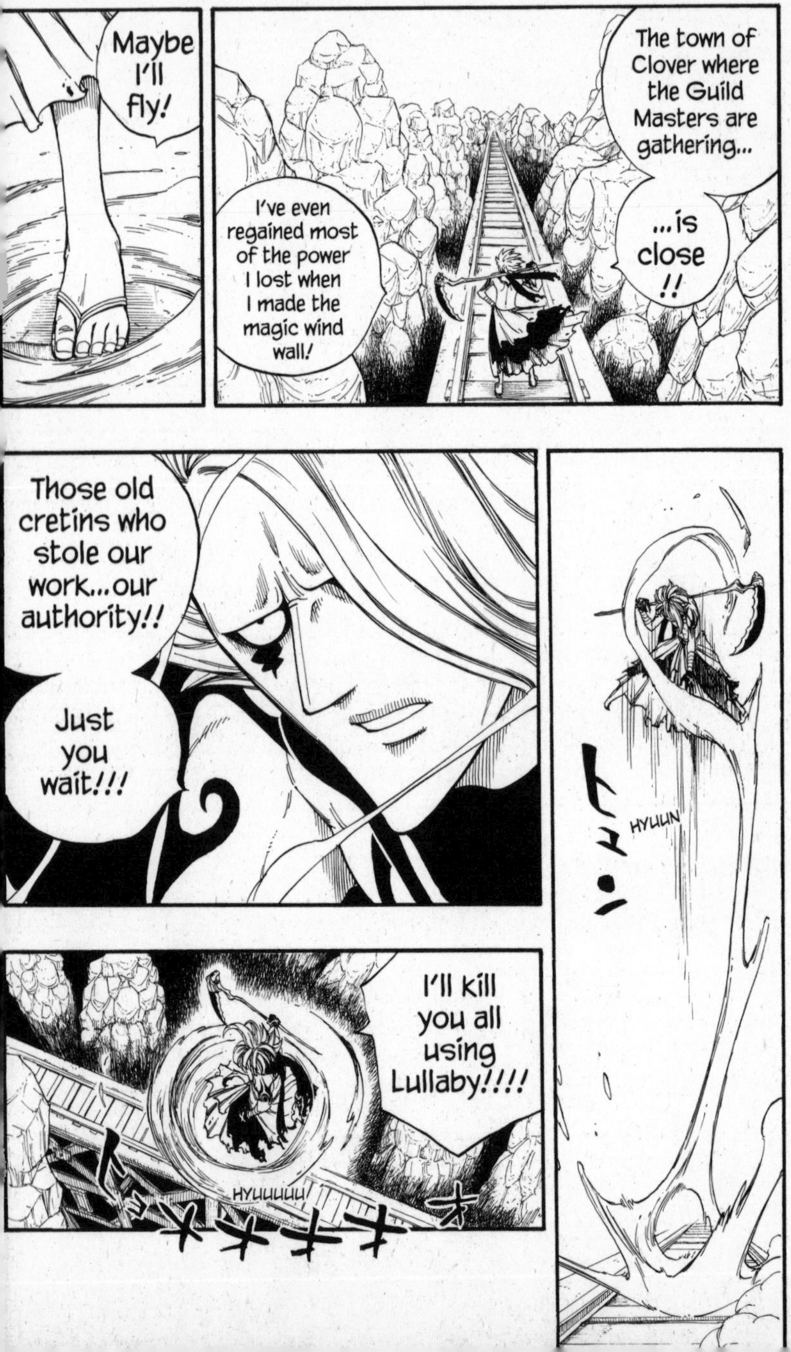
The town of Clover where the Guild Masters are gathering...
...is close!!
I've even regained most of the power I lost when I made the magic wind wall!
Maybe I'll fly!
HYUUN
Those old cretins who stole our work...our authority!!
Just you wait!!!
I'll kill you all using Lullaby!!!!
HYUUUUUU

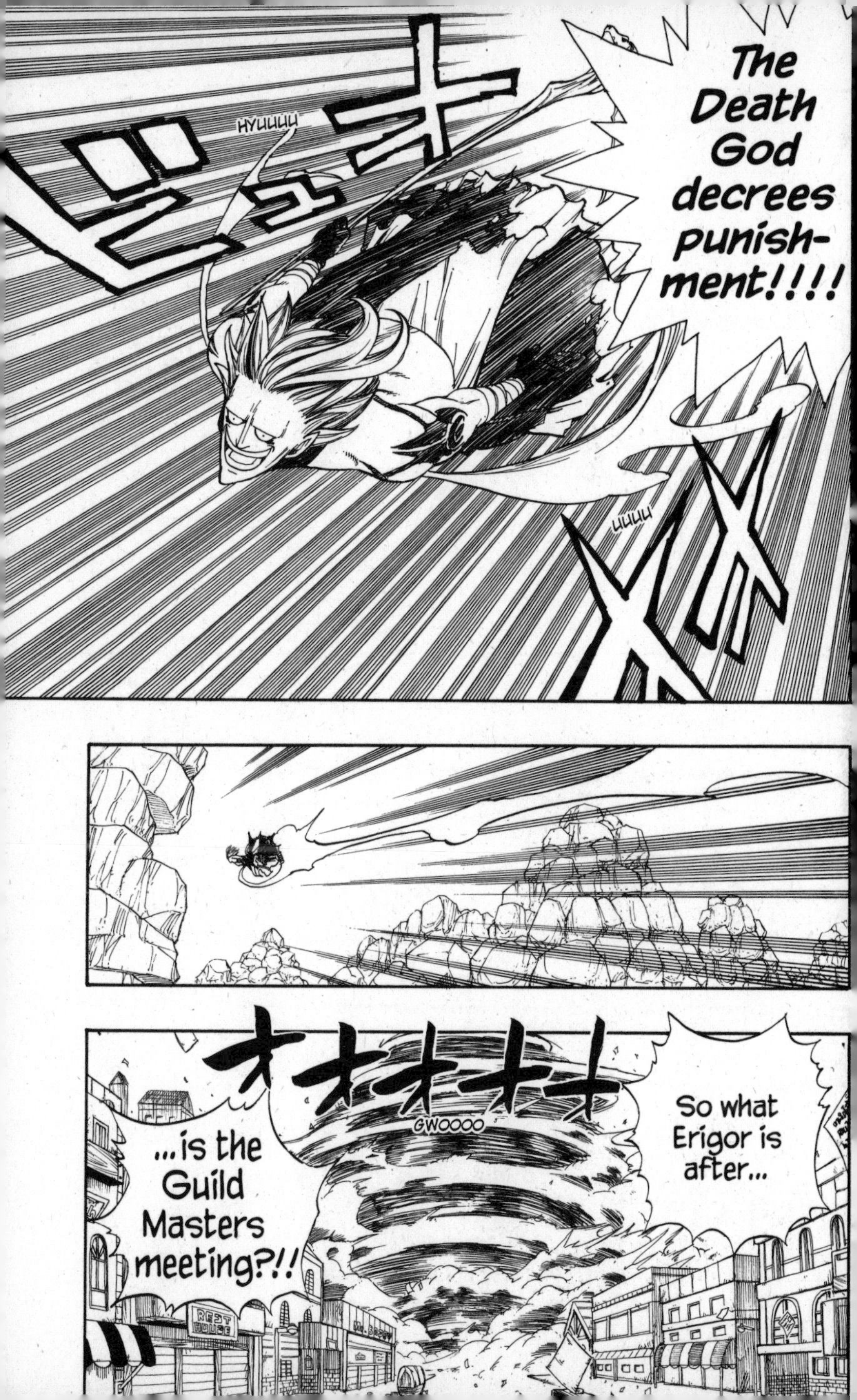
The Death God decrees punish-ment!!!!
HYUUUU
UUUU
So what Erigor is after...
...is the Guild Masters meeting?!!
GWOOOO
REST HOUSE

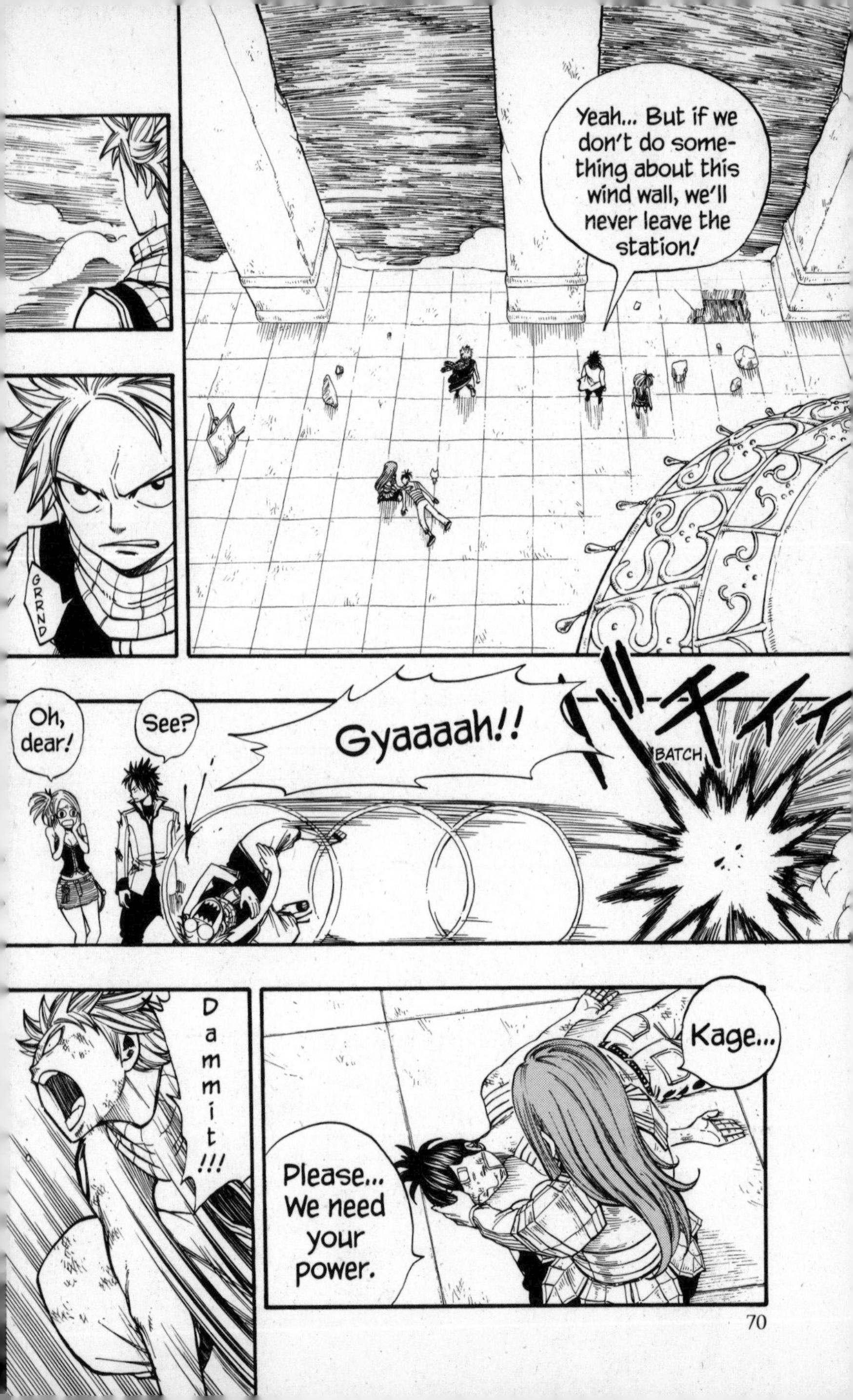
Yeah... But if we don't do something about this wind wall, we'll never leave the station!
GRRND
BATCH
Gyaaaah!!
See?
Oh, dear!
Kage...
Please... We need your power.
Dammit!!!

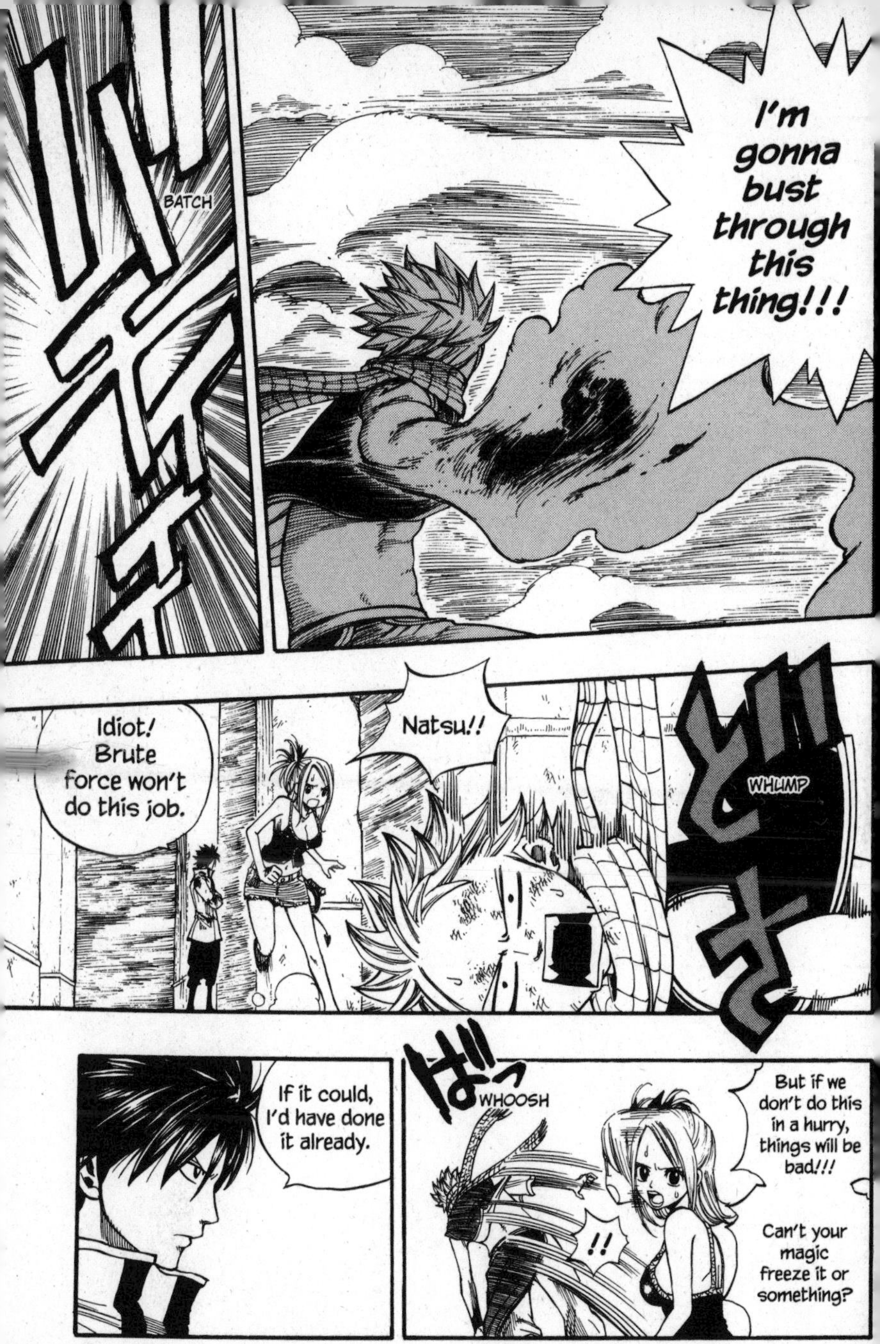
I'm gonna bust through this thing!!!
BATCH
WHUMP
Natsu!!
Idiot! Brute force won't do this job.
But if we don't do this in a hurry, things will be bad!!!
WHOOSH
Can't your magic freeze it or something?
!!
If it could, I'd have done it already.

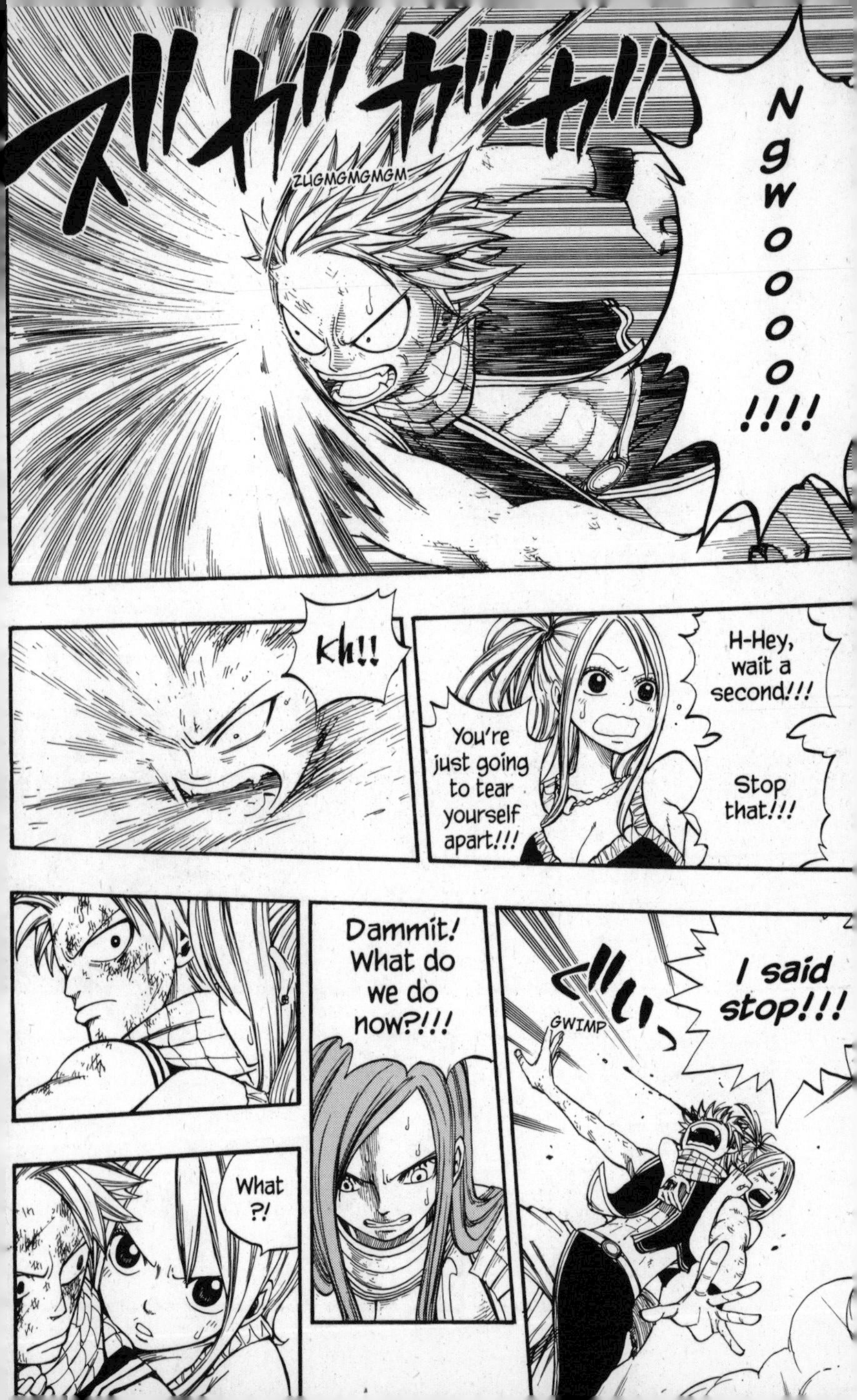
Ngwoooo!!!!
ZUGMGMGMGM
H-Hey, wait a second!!!
Stop that!!!
You're just going to tear yourself apart!!!
Kh!!
I said stop!!!
GWIMP
Dammit! What do we do now?!!!
What ?!

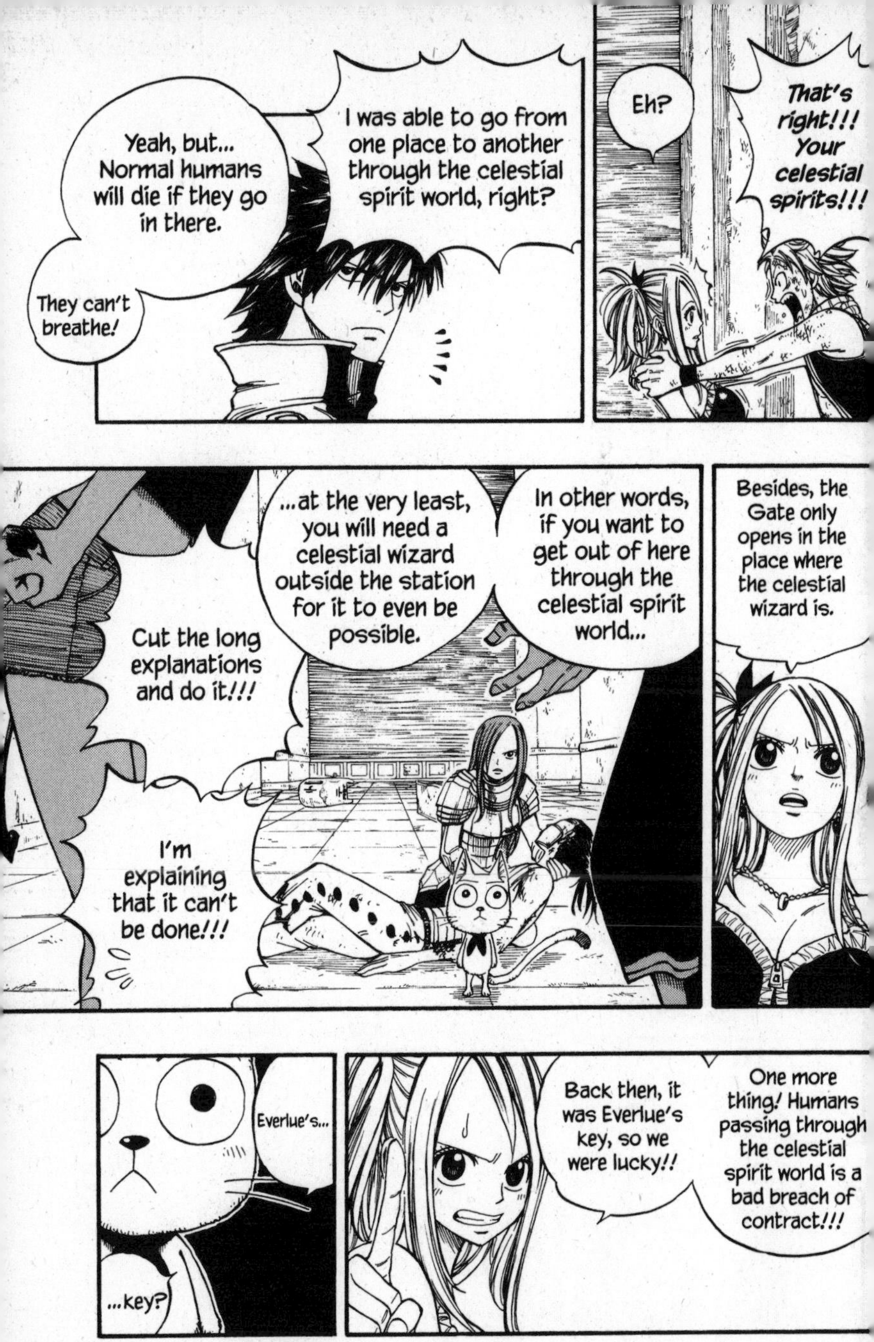

That's right!!! Your celestial spirits!!!
Eh?
I was able to go from one place to another through the celestial spirit world, right?
Yeah, but... Normal humans will die if they go in there.
They can't breathe!
Besides, the Gate only opens in the place where the celestial wizard is.
In other words, if you want to get out of here through the celestial spirit world...
...at the very least, you will need a celestial wizard outside the station for it to even be possible.
Cut the long explanations and do it!!!
I'm explaining that it can't be done!!!
One more thing! Humans passing through the celestial spirit world is a bad breach of contract!!!
Back then, it was Everlue's key, so we were lucky!!
Everlue's...
...key?

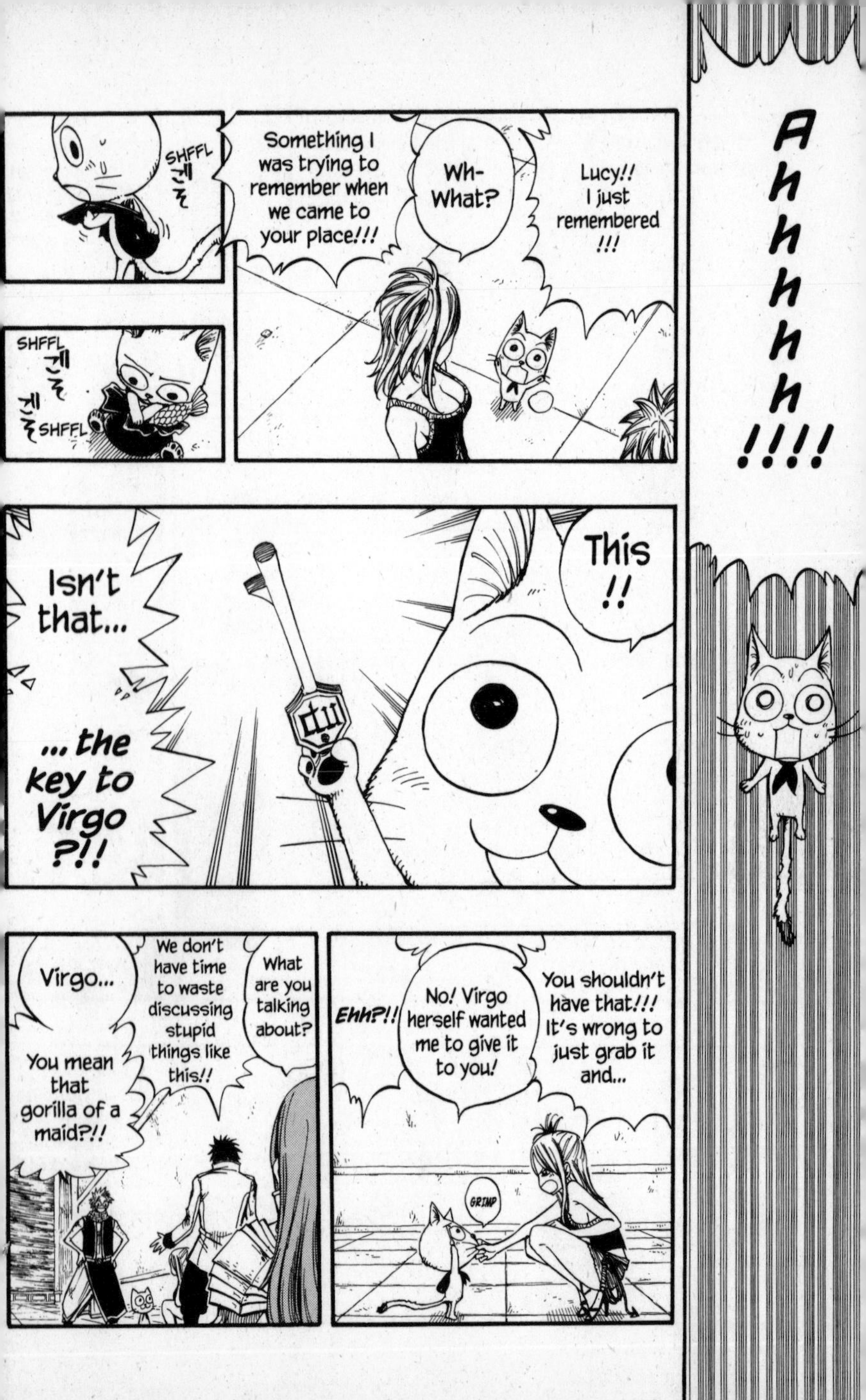

Ahhhhh!!!!
Lucy!! I just remembered!!!
Wh- What?
Something I was trying to remember when we came to your place!!!
SHFFL
SHFFL
SHFFL
This!!
Isn't that...
...the key to Virgo?!!
You shouldn't have that!!! It's wrong to just grab it and...
No! Virgo herself wanted me to give it to you!
Ehh?!!
GRIMP
What are you talking about?
We don't have time to waste discussing stupid things like this!!
Virgo...
You mean that gorilla of a maid?!!

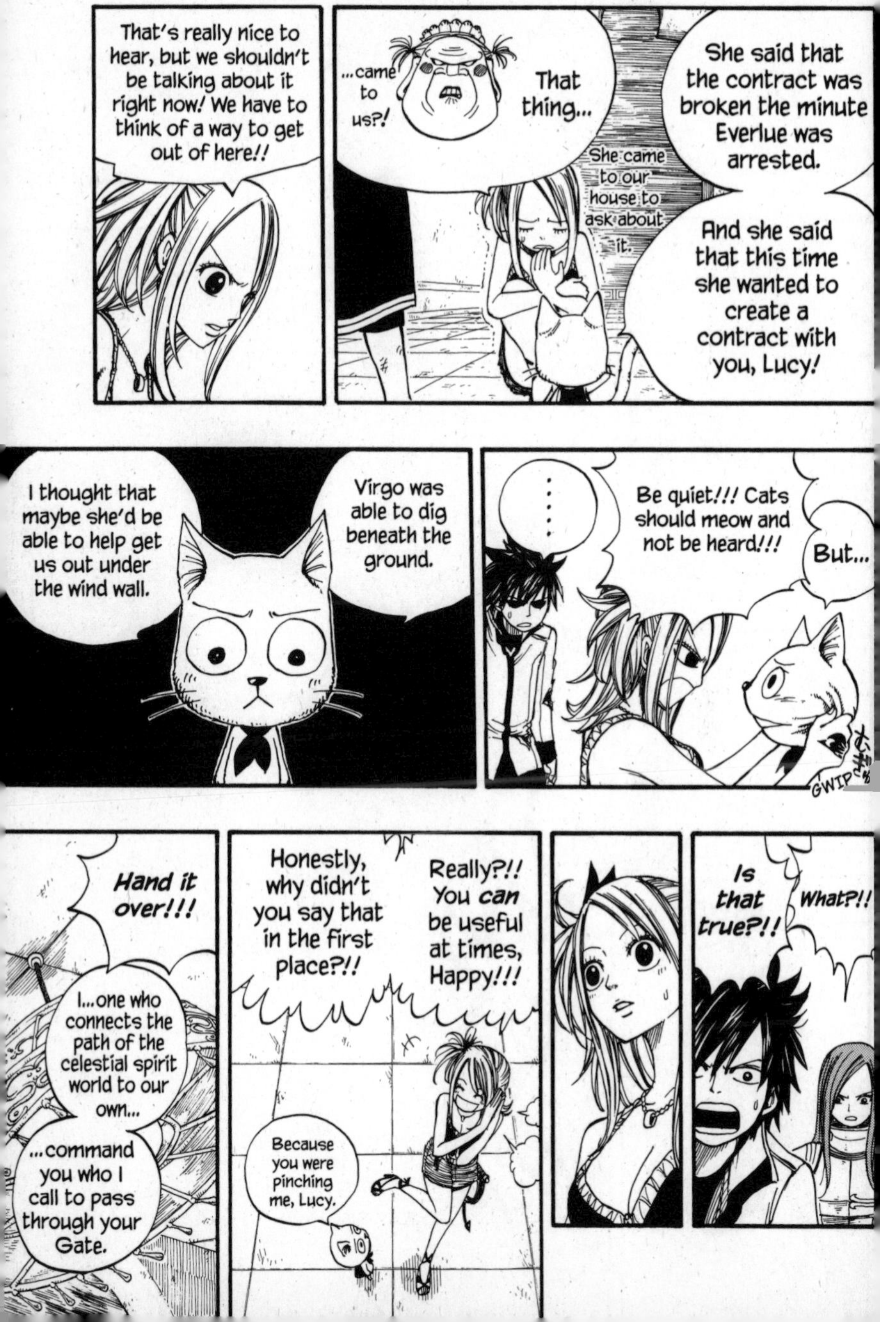
She said that the contract was broken the minute Everlue was arrested.
And she said that this time she wanted to create a contract with you, Lucy!
She came to our house to ask about it.
That thing...
...came to us?!
That's really nice to hear, but we shouldn't be talking about it right now! We have to think of a way to get out of here!!
But...
Be quiet!!! Cats should meow and not be heard!!!
.....
GWIP
Virgo was able to dig beneath the ground.
I thought that maybe she'd be able to help get us out under the wind wall.
What?!!
Is that true?!!
Really?!! You can be useful at times, Happy!!!
Honestly, why didn't you say that in the first place?!!
Because you were pinching me, Lucy.
Hand it over!!!
I...one who connects the path of the celestial spirit world to our own...
...command you who I call to pass through your Gate.

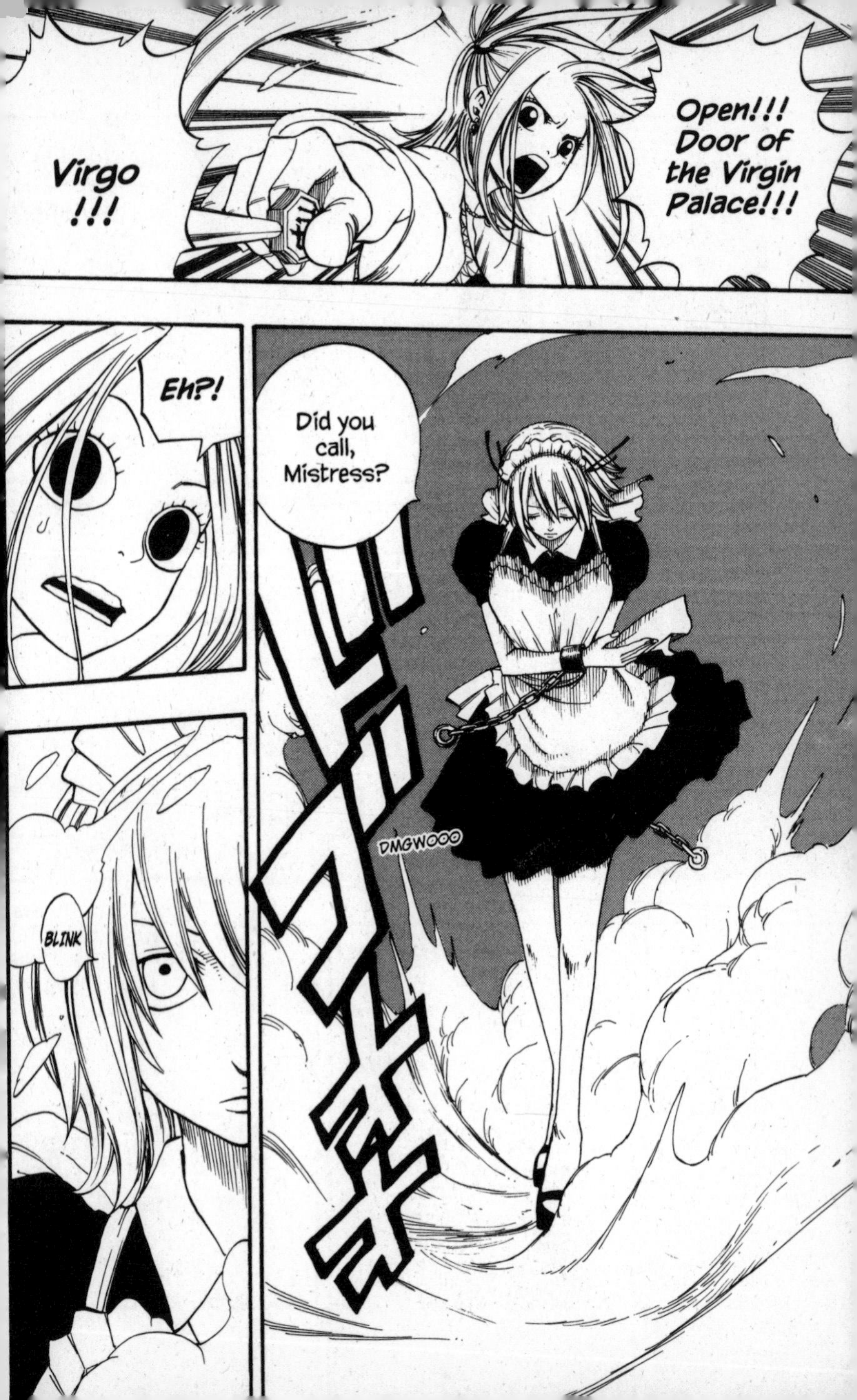
Open!!! Door of the Virgin Palace!!!
Virgo !!!
Did you call, Mistress?
DMGWOOO
Eh?!
BLINK

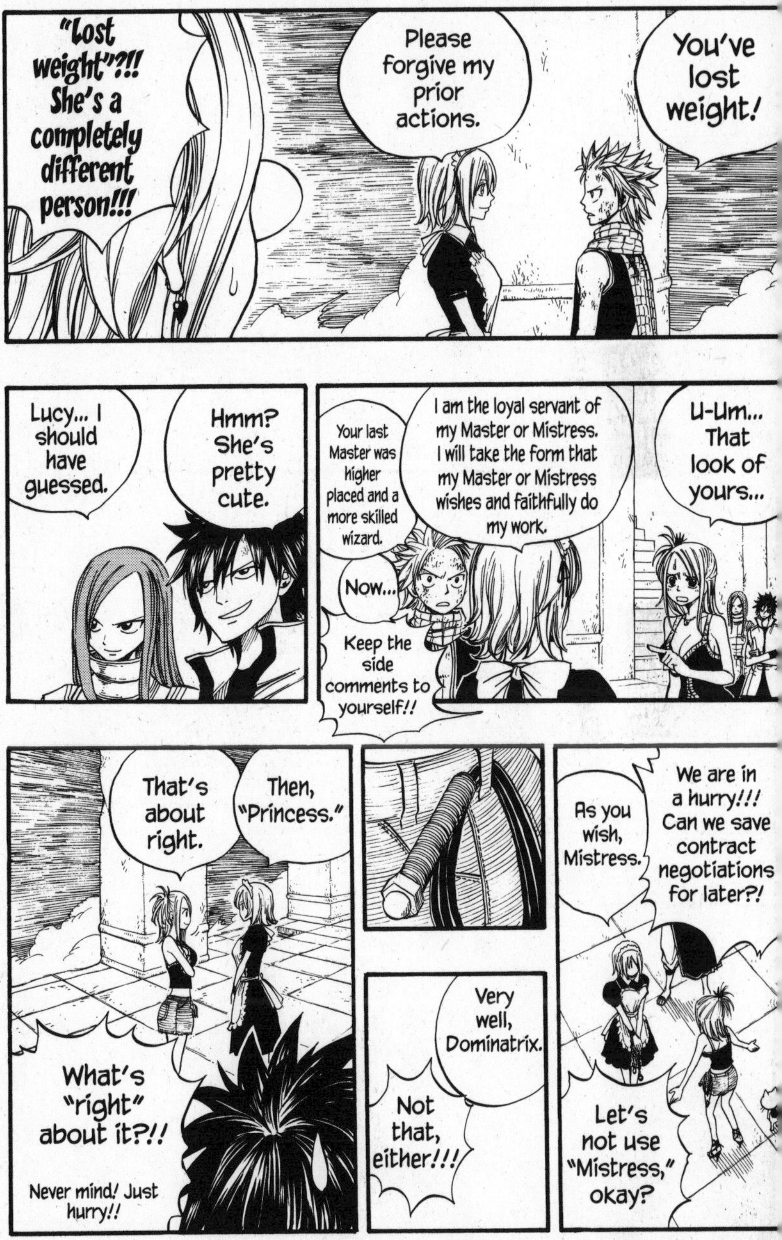
You've lost weight!
Please forgive my prior actions.
"Lost weight"?!! She's a completely different person!!!
U-Um... That look of yours...
I am the loyal servant of my Master or Mistress. I will take the form that my Master or Mistress wishes and faithfully do my work.
Your last Master was higher placed and a more skilled wizard.
Now...
Keep the side comments to yourself!!
Hmm? She's pretty cute.
Lucy... I should have guessed.
We are in a hurry!!! Can we save contract negotiations for later?!
As you wish, Mistress.
Let's not use "Mistress," okay?
Very well, Dominatrix.
Not that, either!!!
Then, "Princess."
That's about right.
What's "right" about it?!!
Never mind! Just hurry!!

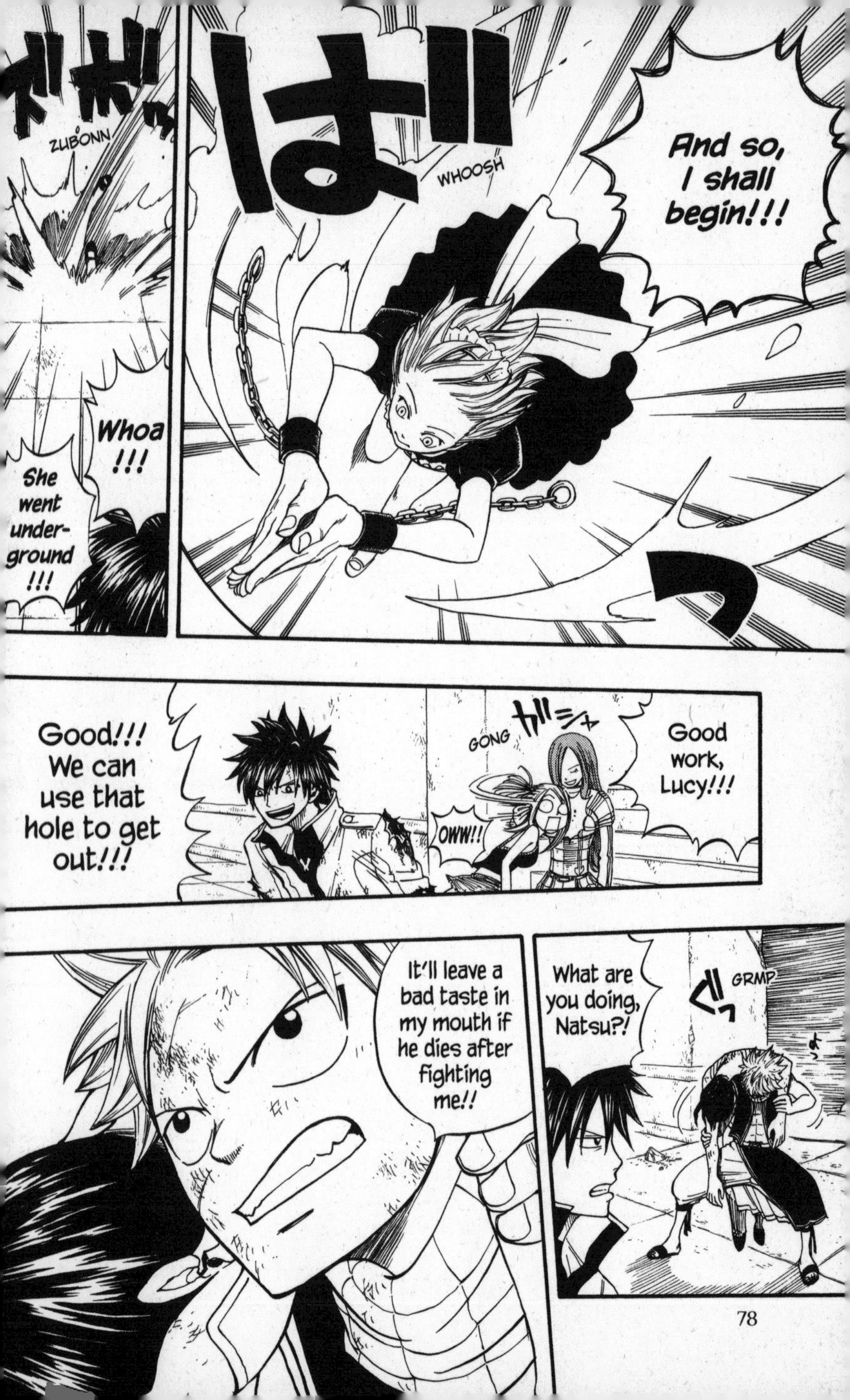
And so, I shall begin!!!
WHOOSH
ZUBONN
Whoa!!!
She went under-ground!!!
Good work, Lucy!!!
GONG
OWW!!
Good!!! We can use that hole to get out!!!
GRMP
What are you doing, Natsu?!
It'll leave a bad taste in my mouth if he dies after fighting me!!

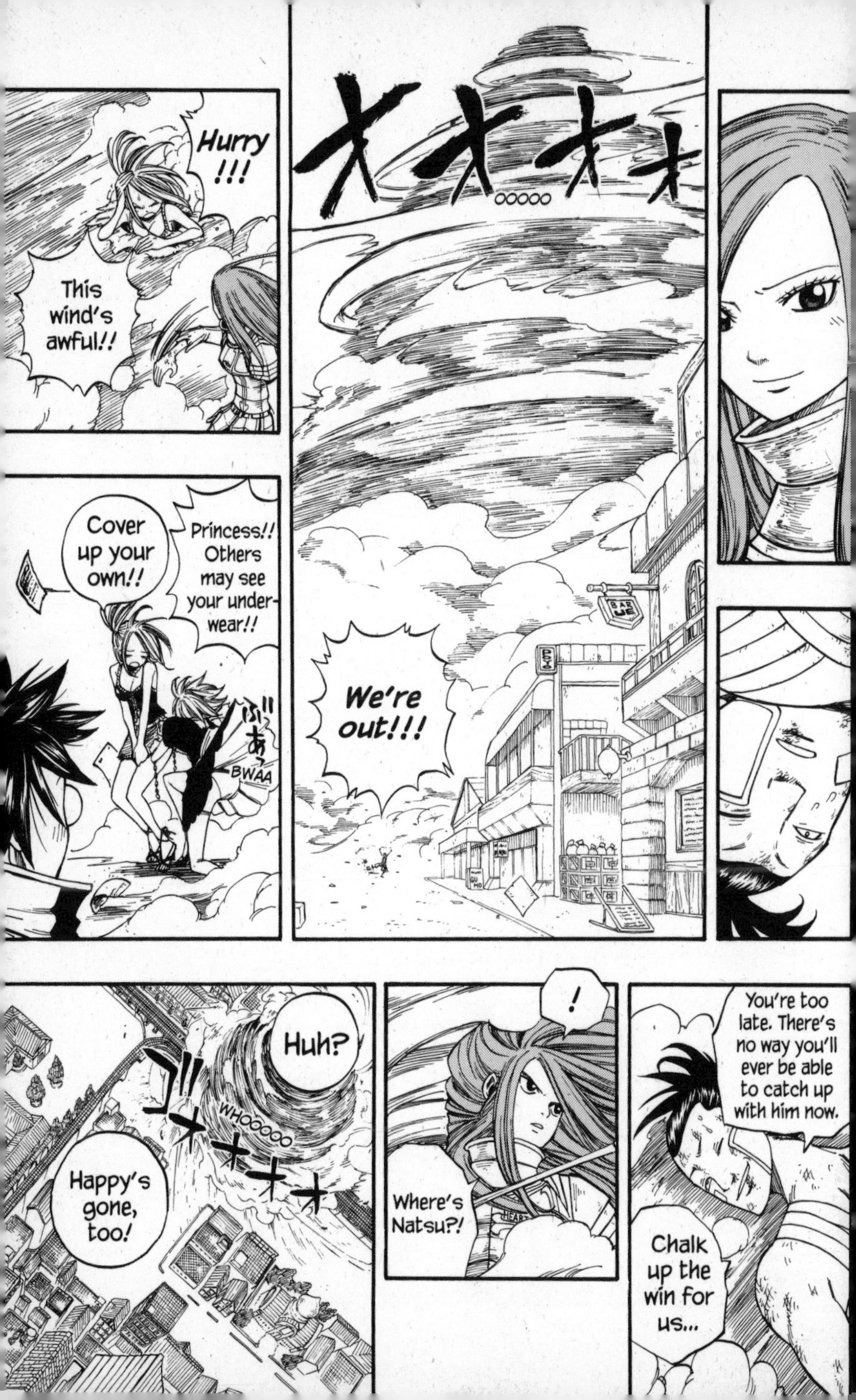
オオオォ
ooooo
We're out!!!
Hurry!!!
This wind's awful!!
Princess!! Others may see your underwear!!
Cover up your own!!
ぶあっ
BWAA
You're too late. There's no way you'll ever be able to catch up with him now.
Chalk up the win for us...
!
Where's Natsu?!
Huh?
WHOOOOO
Happy's gone, too!

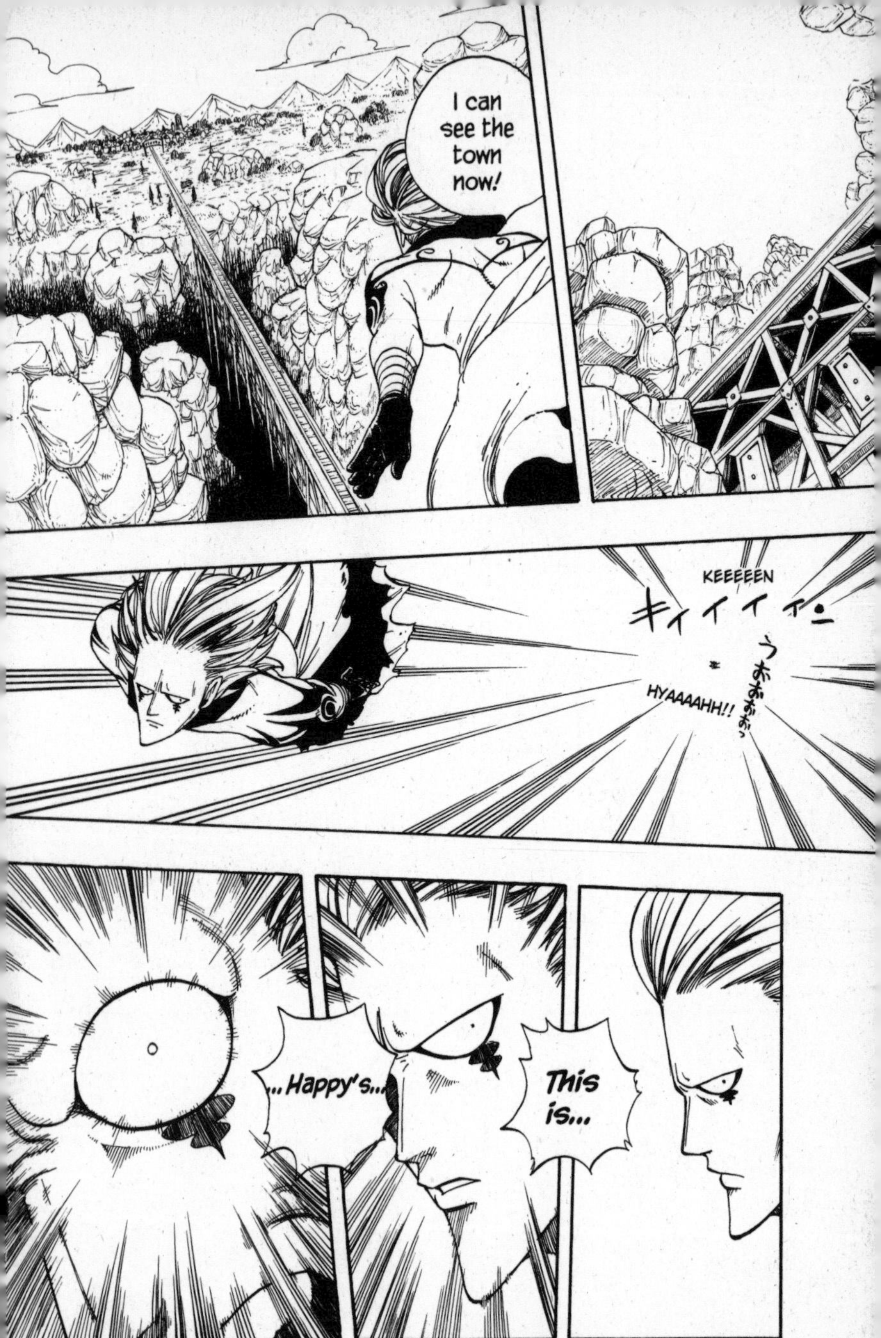
I can see the town now!
KEEEEEN
キィイイイン
HYAAAAHH!!
うおおおおっ
This is...
...Happy's...

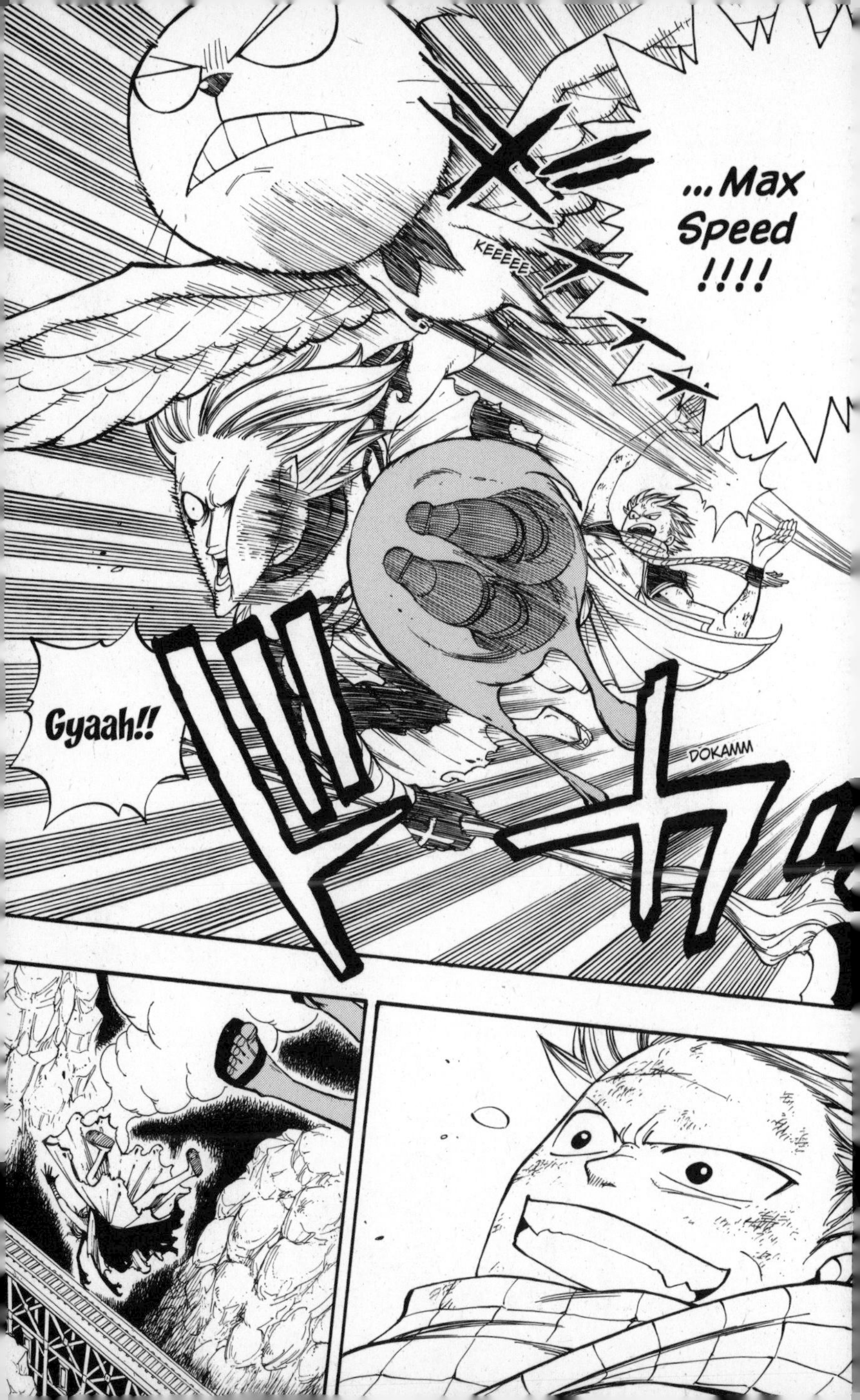
...Max Speed !!!!
KEEEEE
Gyaah!!
DOKAMM

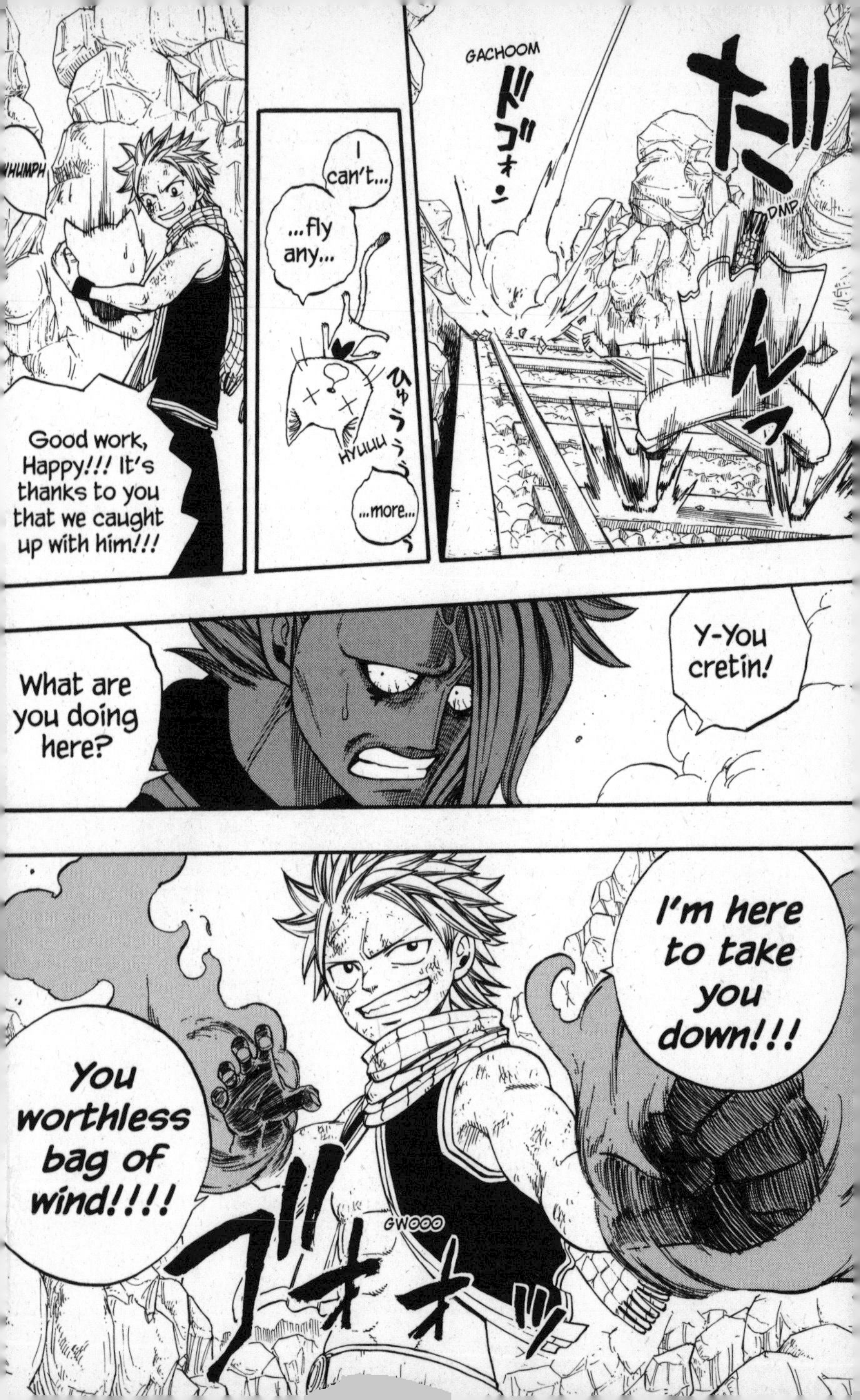

だん
DMP
ドゴォン
GACHOOM
I can't...
...fly any...
...more...
ひゅううう
HYUUU
WHUMPH
Good work, Happy!!! It's thanks to you that we caught up with him!!!
Y-You cretin!
What are you doing here?
I'm here to take you down!!!
You worthless bag of wind!!!!
ブォオオッ
GWOOO

FAIRY TAIL

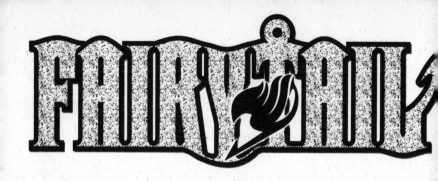

Chapter 18: Fire and Wind

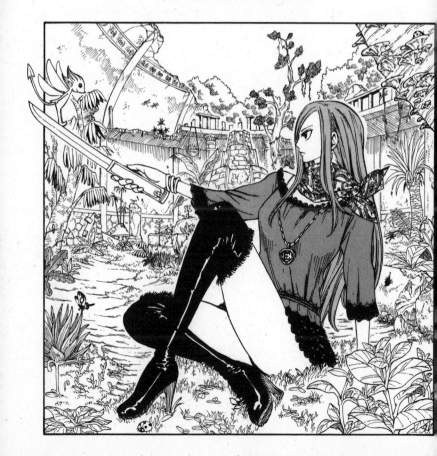

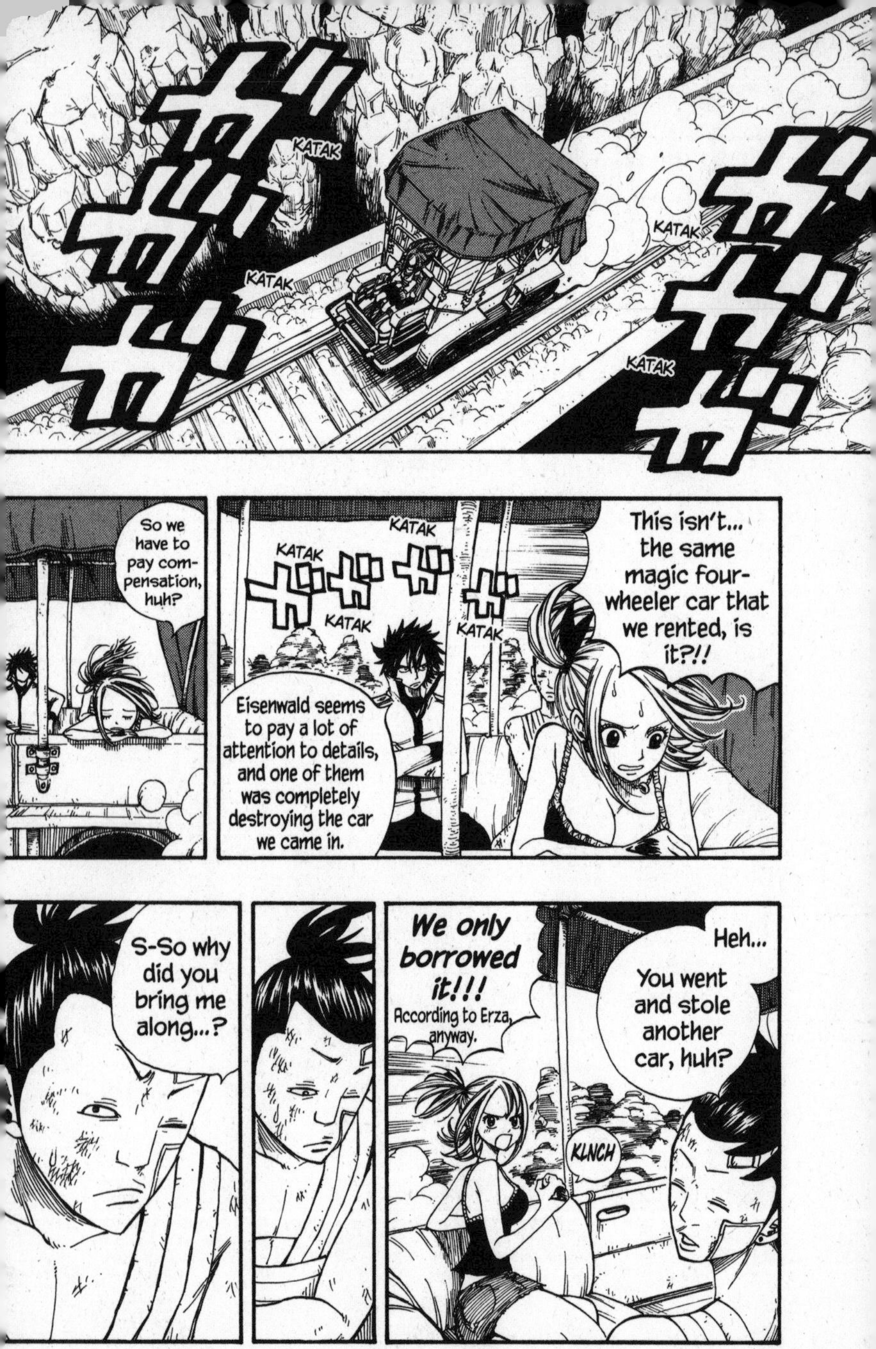
KATAK
KATAK
KATAK
KATAK
KATAK
KATAK
KATAK
KATAK
This isn't... the same magic four-wheeler car that we rented, is it?!!
Eisenwald seems to pay a lot of attention to details, and one of them was completely destroying the car we came in.
So we have to pay compensation, huh?
Heh... You went and stole another car, huh?
We only borrowed it!!!
According to Erza, anyway.
KLNCH
S-So why did you bring me along...?

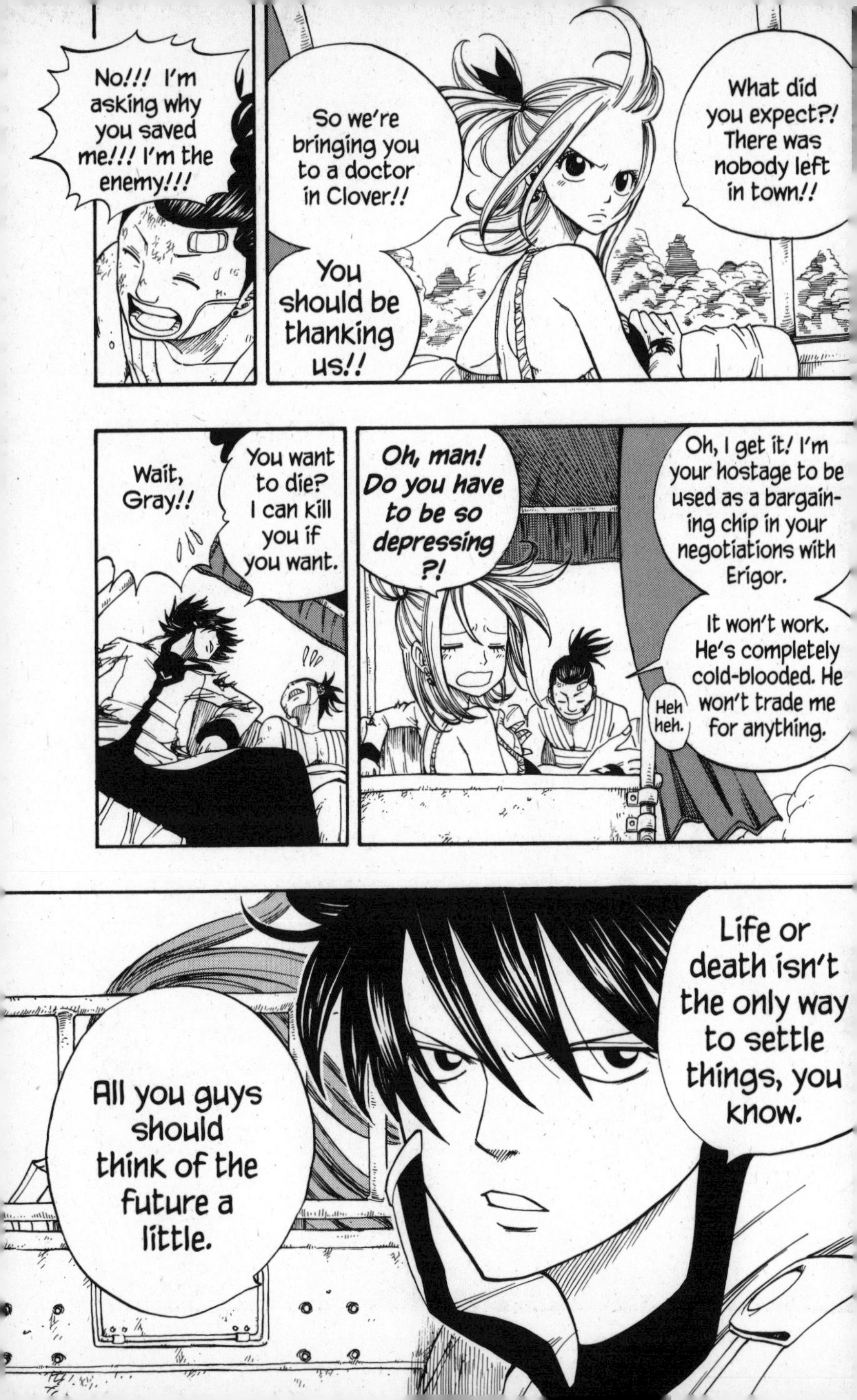
What did you expect?! There was nobody left in town!!
So we're bringing you to a doctor in Clover!!
You should be thanking us!!
No!!! I'm asking why you saved me!!! I'm the enemy!!!
Oh, I get it! I'm your hostage to be used as a bargain-ing chip in your negotiations with Erigor.
It won't work. He's completely cold-blooded. He won't trade me for anything.
Heh heh.
Oh, man! Do you have to be so depressing?!
You want to die? I can kill you if you want.
Wait, Gray!!
Life or death isn't the only way to settle things, you know.
All you guys should think of the future a little.

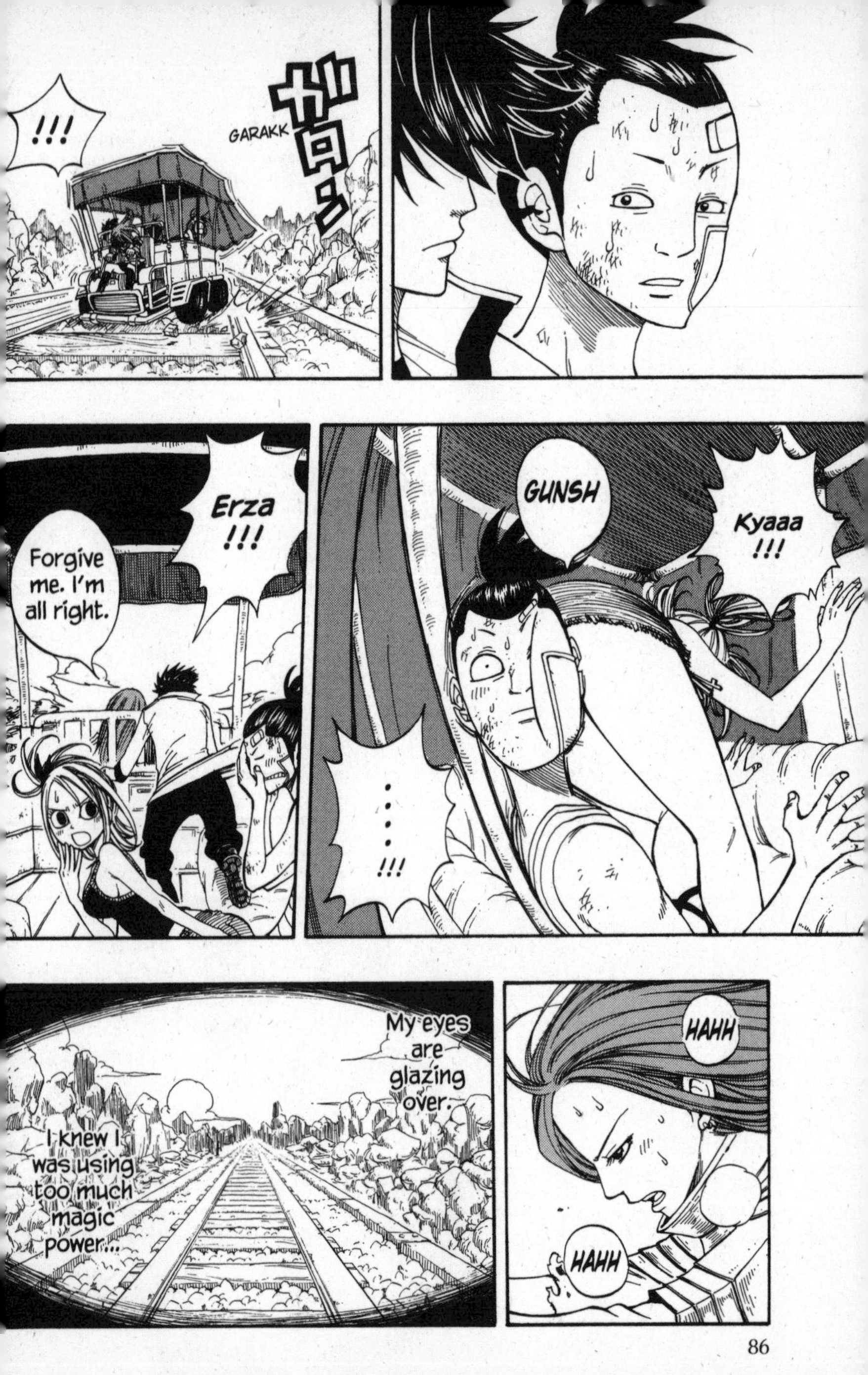
GARAKK
!!!
Kyaaa!!!
GUNSH
......!!!
Erza!!!
Forgive me. I'm all right.
HAHH
HAHH
My eyes are glazing over.
I knew I was using too much magic power...

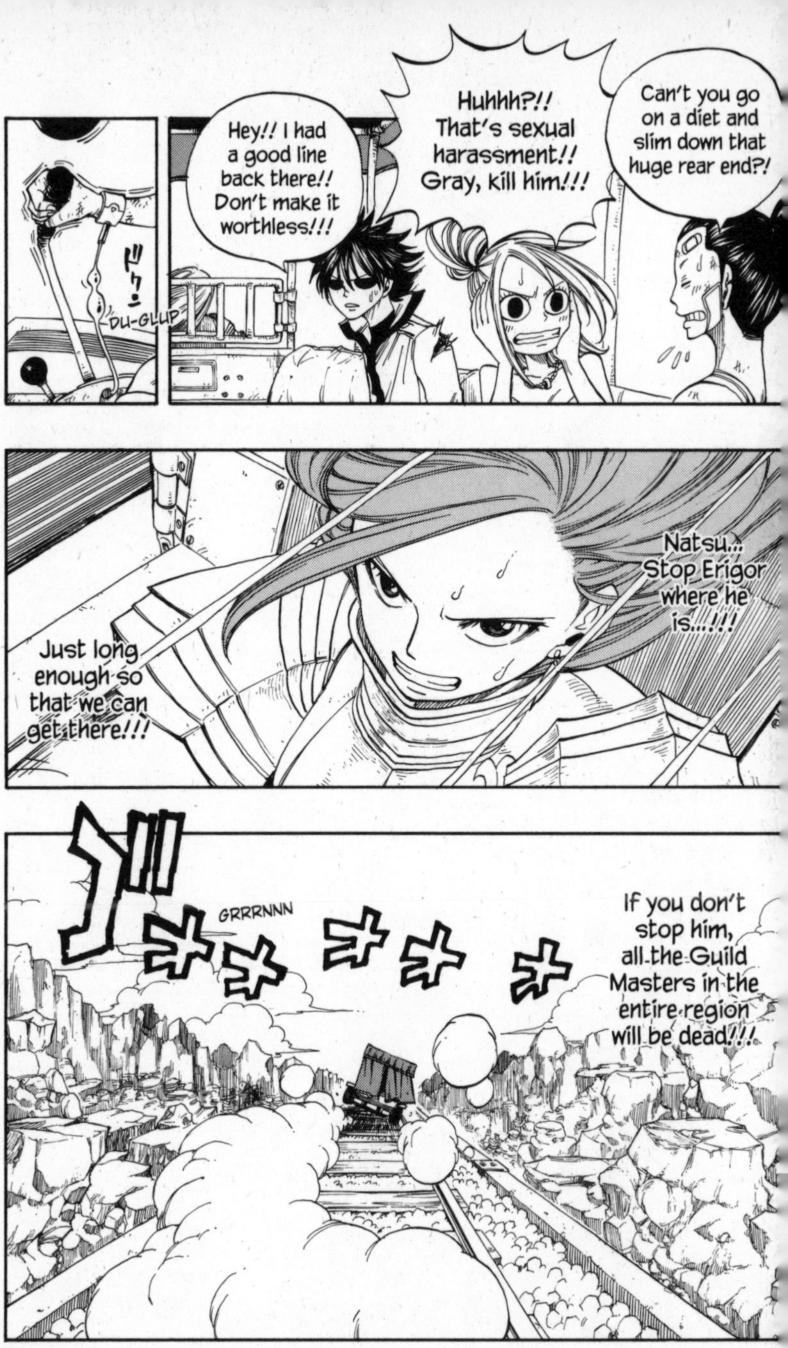
Can't you go on a diet and slim down that huge rear end?!
Huhhh?!! That's sexual harassment!! Gray, kill him!!!
Hey!! I had a good line back there!! Don't make it worthless!!!
DU-GLUP
Natsu... Stop Erigor where he is...!!!
Just long enough so that we can get there!!!
If you don't stop him, all the Guild Masters in the entire region will be dead!!!
GRRRNNN

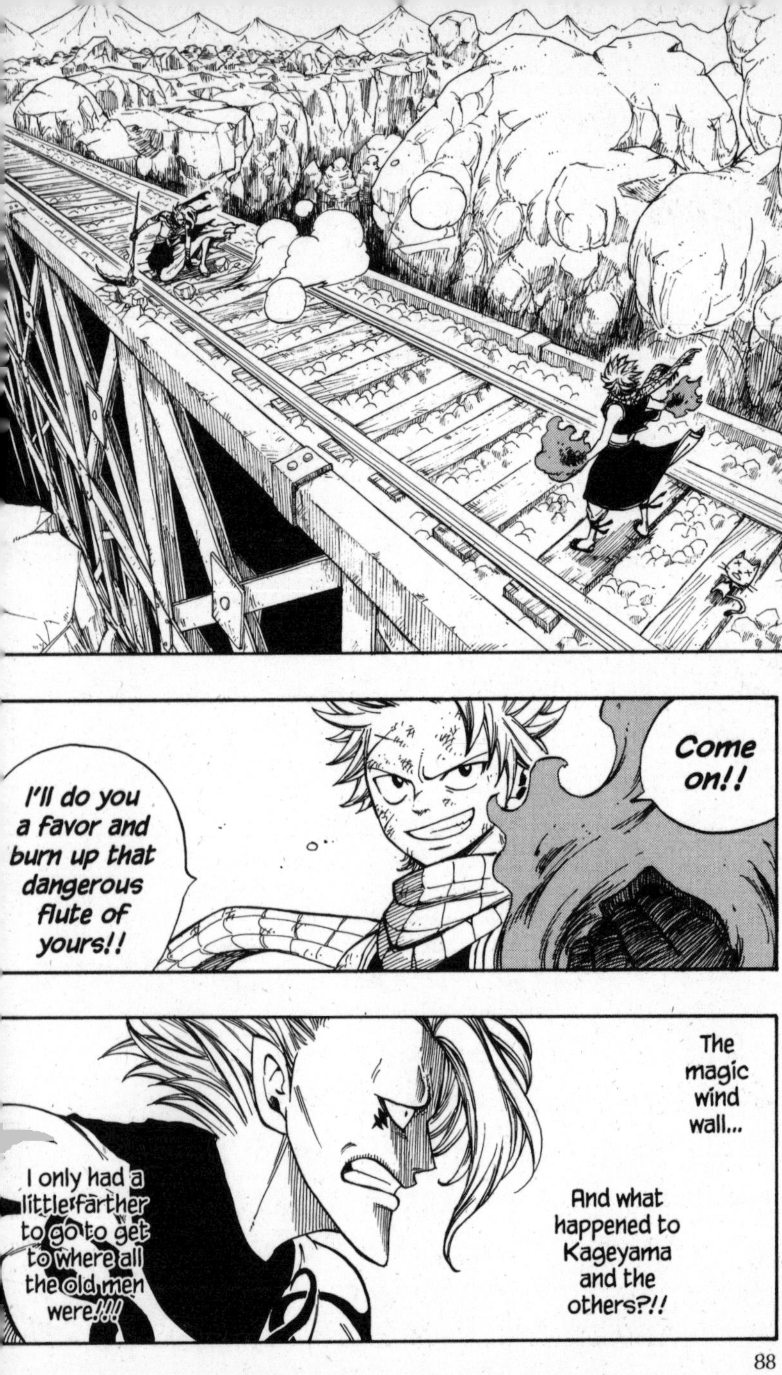
Come on!!
I'll do you a favor and burn up that dangerous flute of yours!!
The magic wind wall...
And what happened to Kageyama and the others?!!
I only had a little farther to go to get to where all the old men were!!!

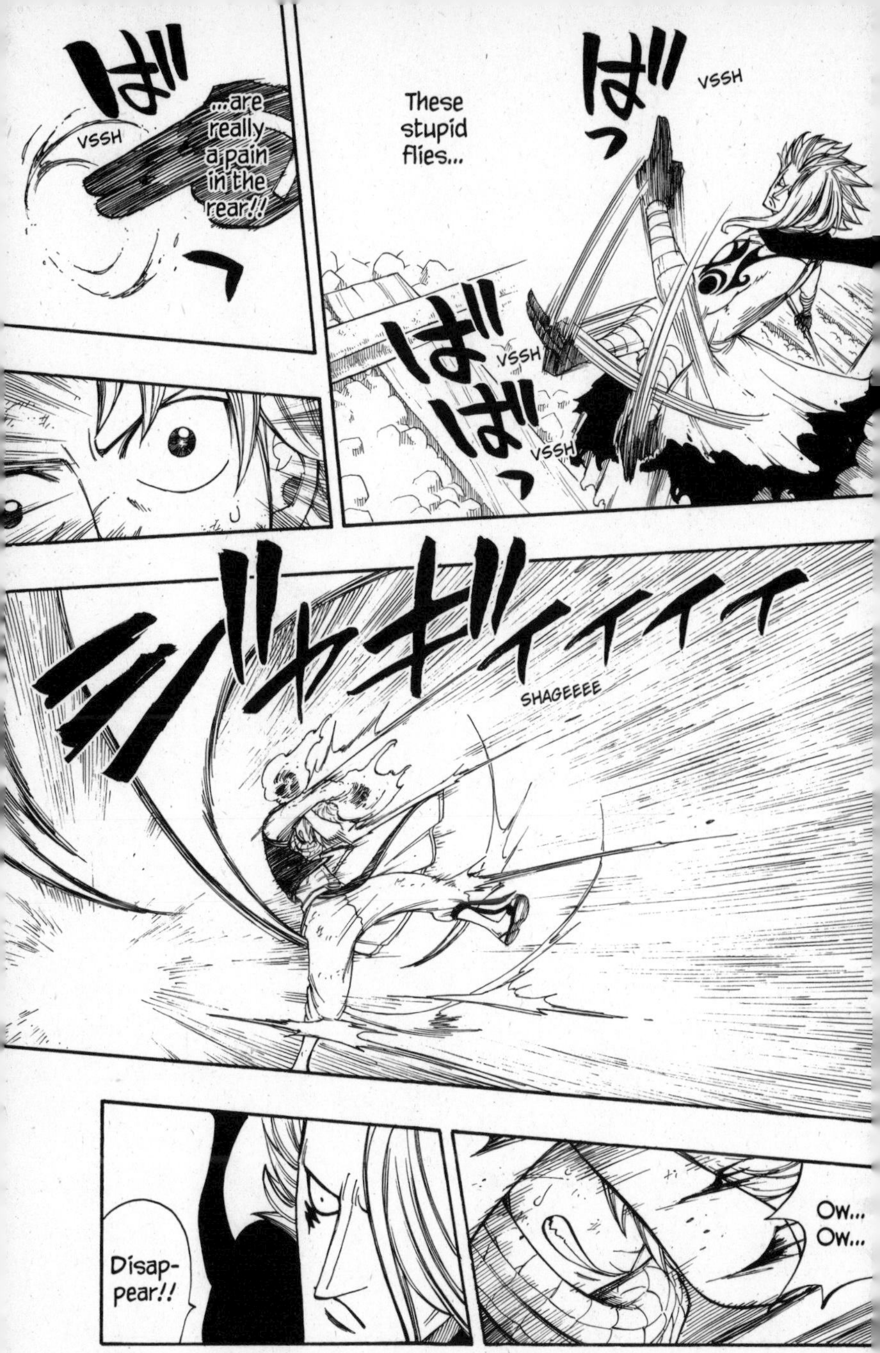
ばっ
VSSH
These stupid flies...
ばばっ
VSSH
VSSH
ばっ
VSSH
...are really a pain in the rear!!
シャギィィィ
SHAGEEEE
Ow... Ow...
Disap-pear!!

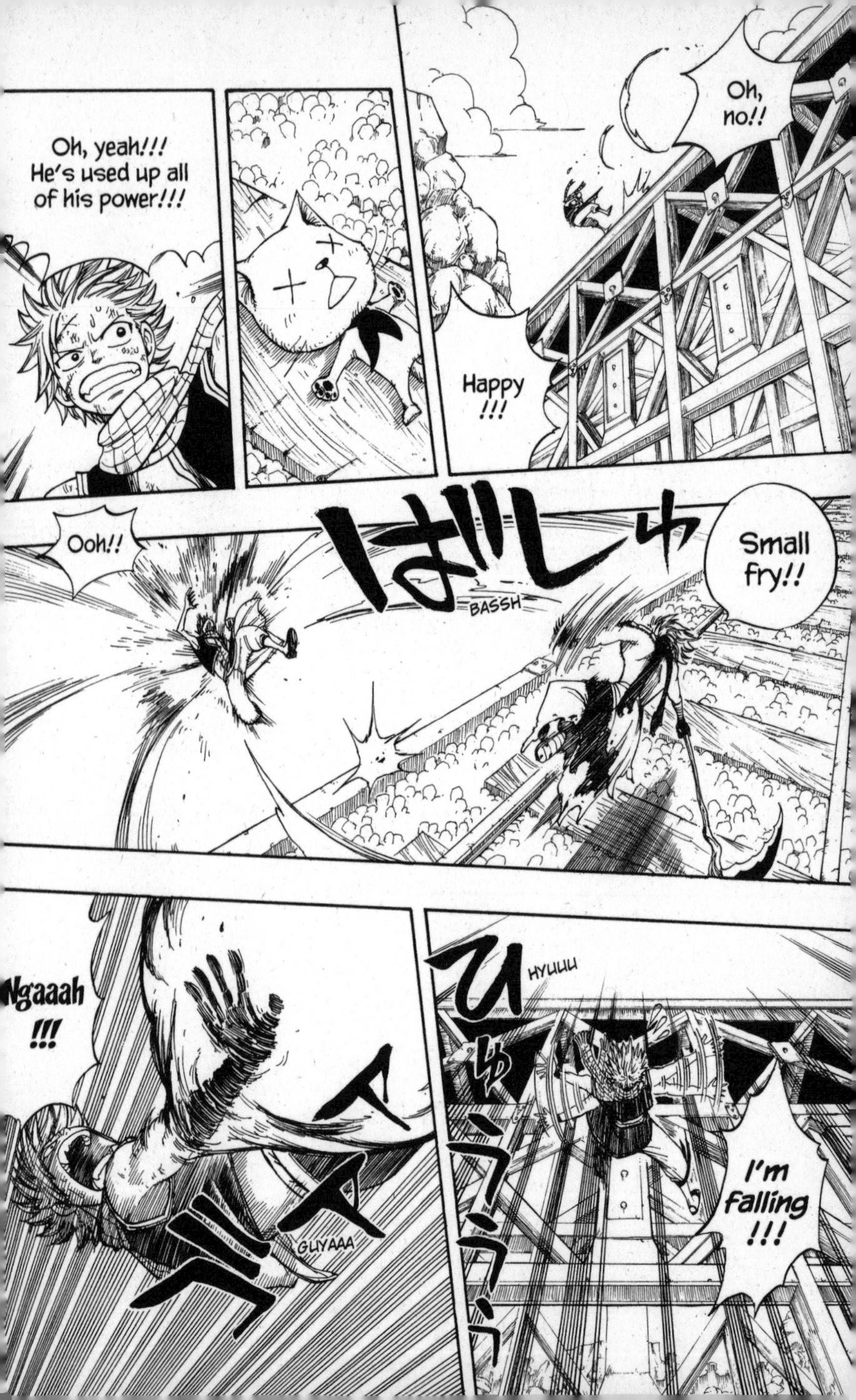
Oh, no!!
Happy !!!
Oh, yeah!!! He's used up all of his power!!!
Small fry!!
ばしゅ
BASSH
Ooh!!
ひゅううう
HYUUU
I'm falling !!!
Ngaaah !!!
ギャア
GUYAAA

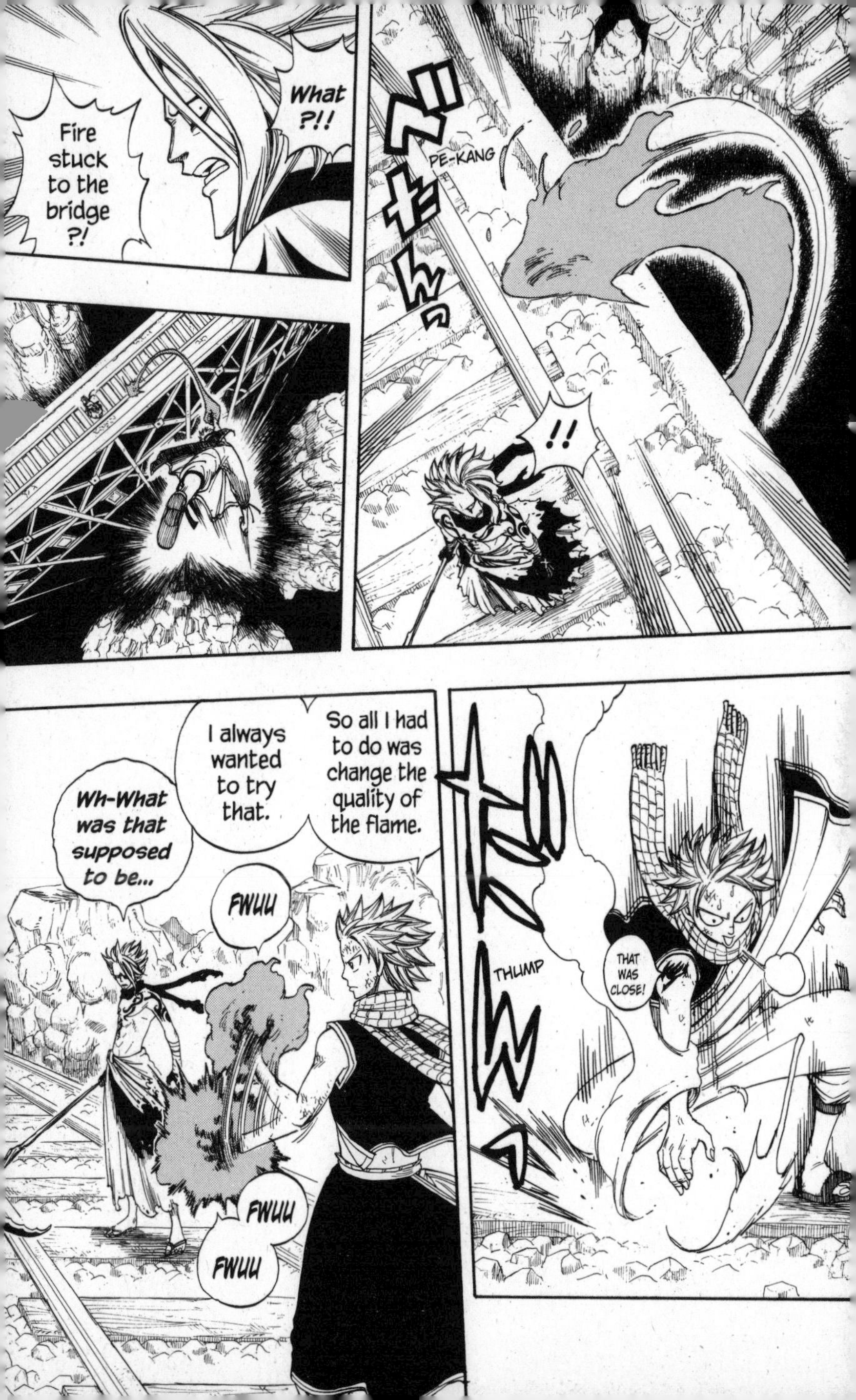
PE-KANG
!!
What ?!!
Fire stuck to the bridge ?!
THUMP
THAT WAS CLOSE!
So all I had to do was change the quality of the flame.
I always wanted to try that.
Wh-What was that supposed to be...
FWUU
FWUU
FWUU

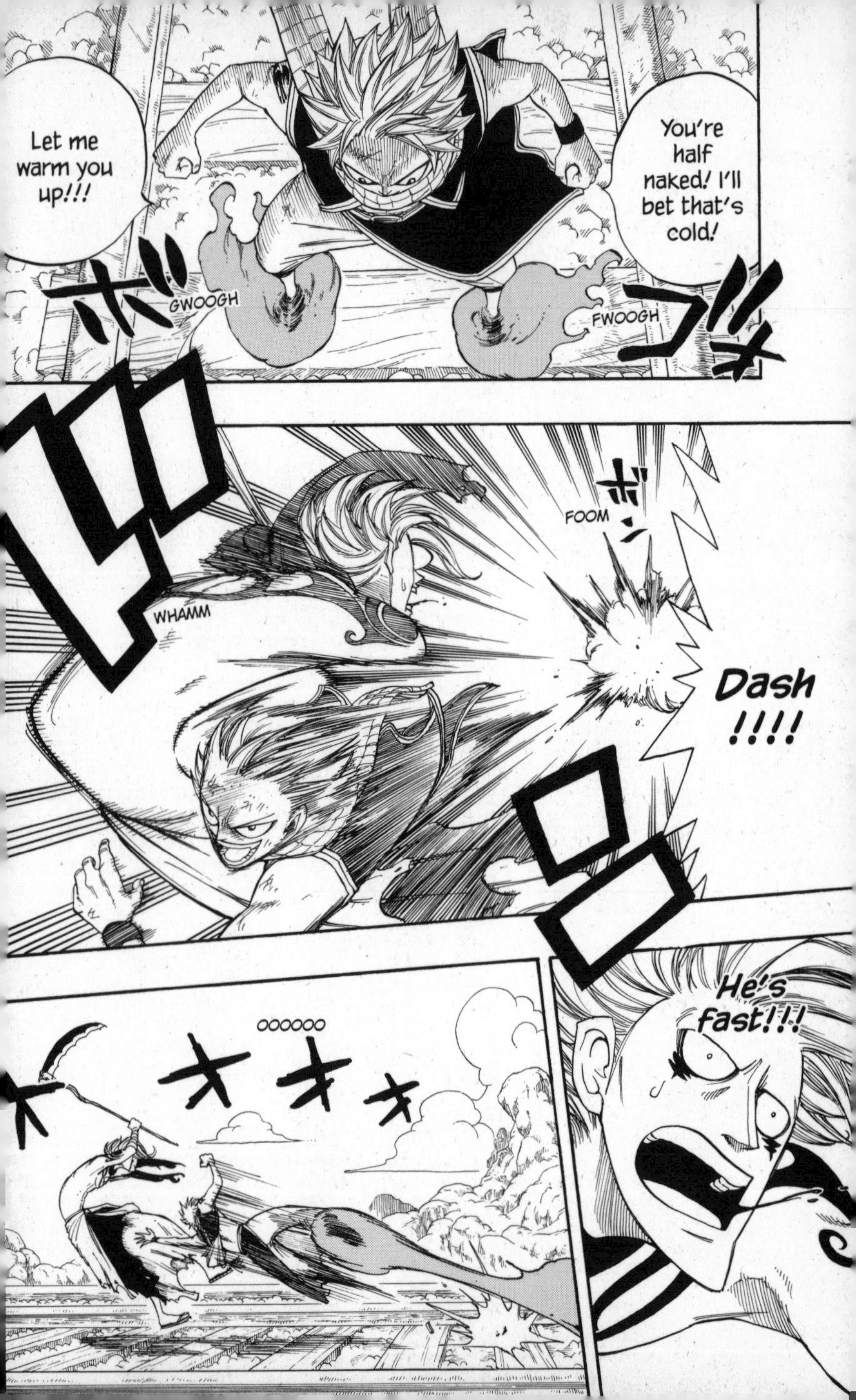
You're half naked! I'll bet that's cold!
Let me warm you up!!!
FWOOGH
GWOOGH
FOOM
Dash!!!!
WHAMM
He's fast!!!
OOOOOO

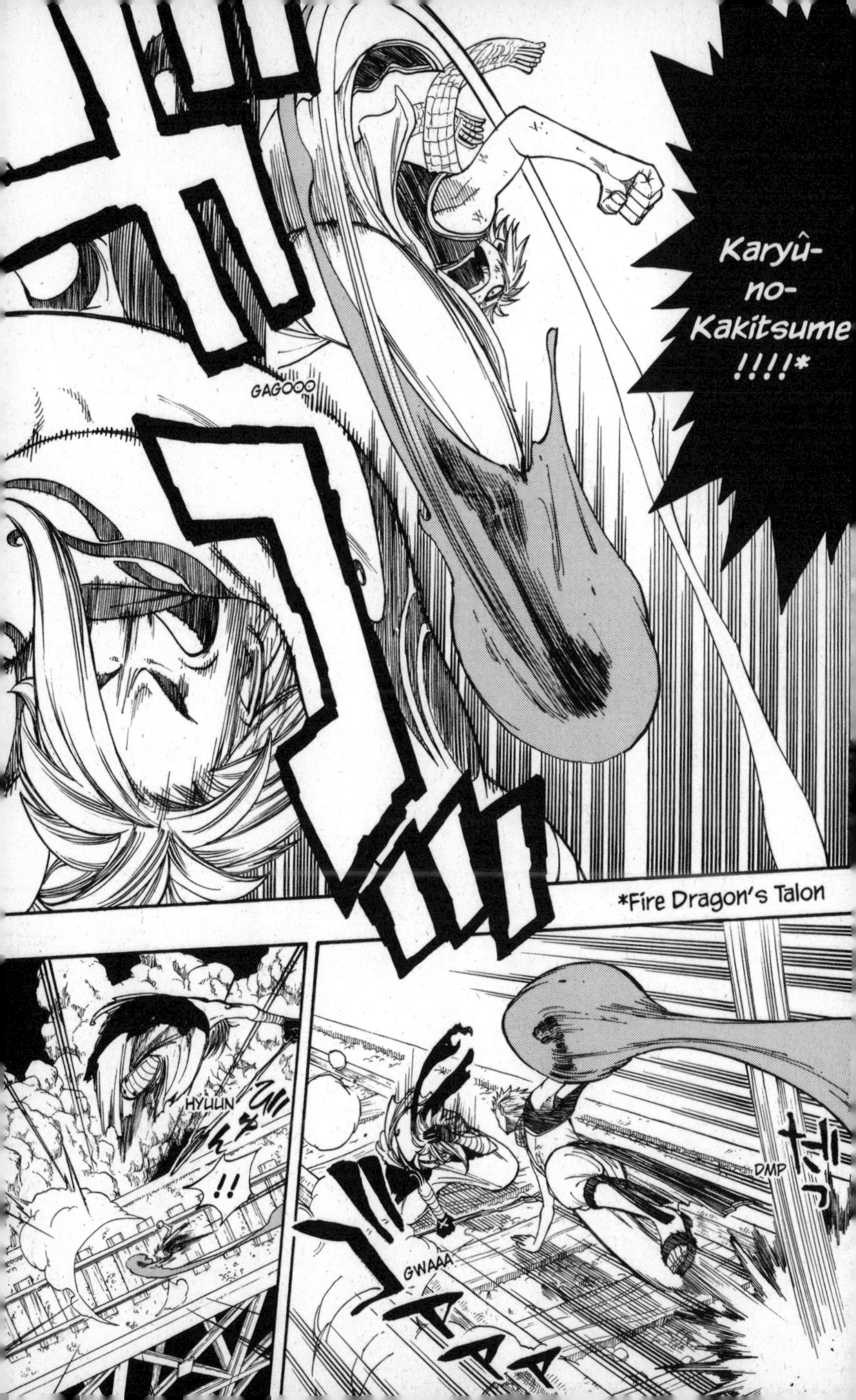
Karyû-
no-
Kakitsume
!!!!*
GAGOOO
*Fire Dragon's Talon
DMP
GWAAA
HYUUN
!!

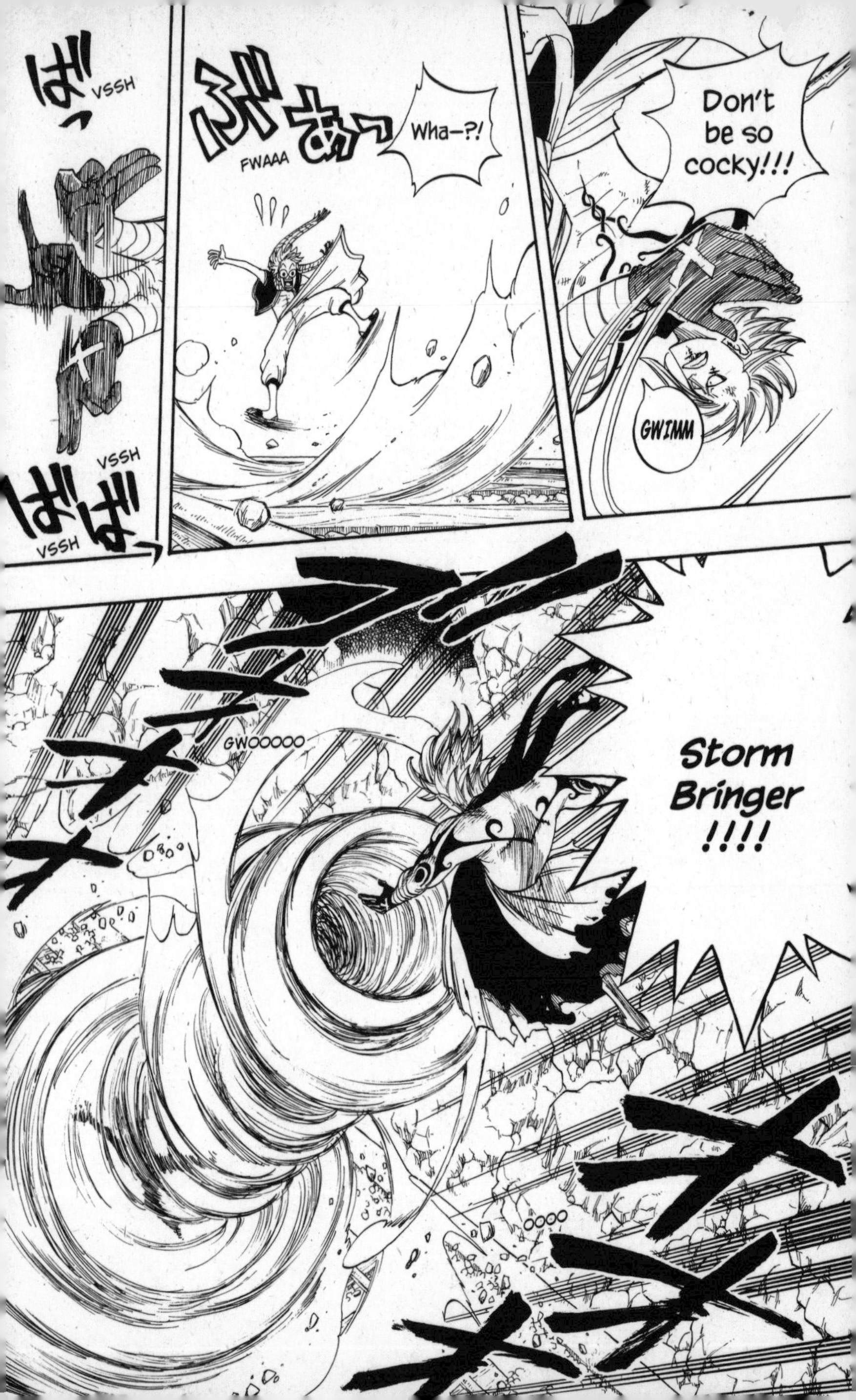
Don't be so cocky!!!
GWIMM
FWAAA
Wha-?!
VSSH
VSSH
VSSH
Storm Bringer !!!!
GWOOOOO
OOOO

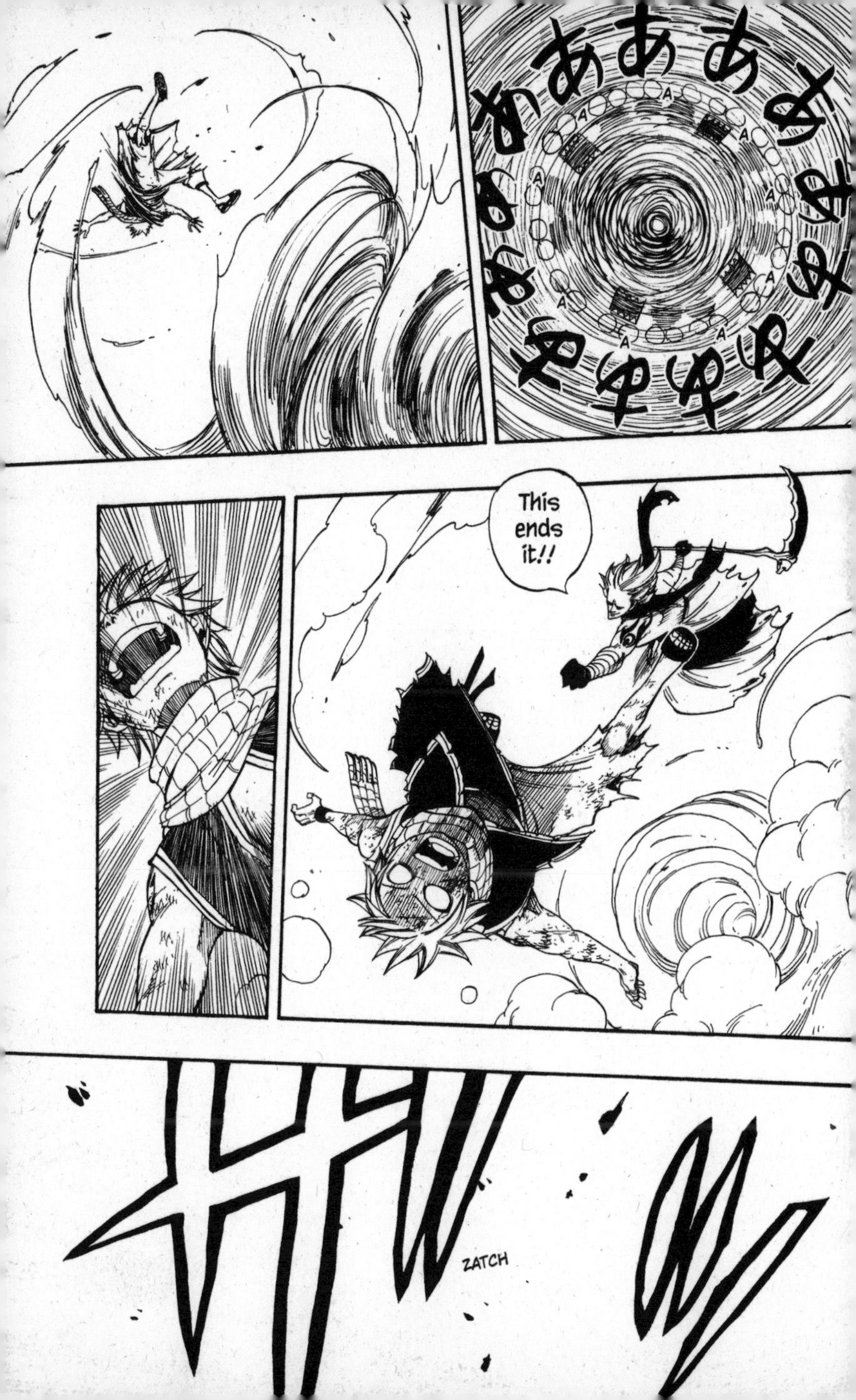
This ends it!!
ZATCH

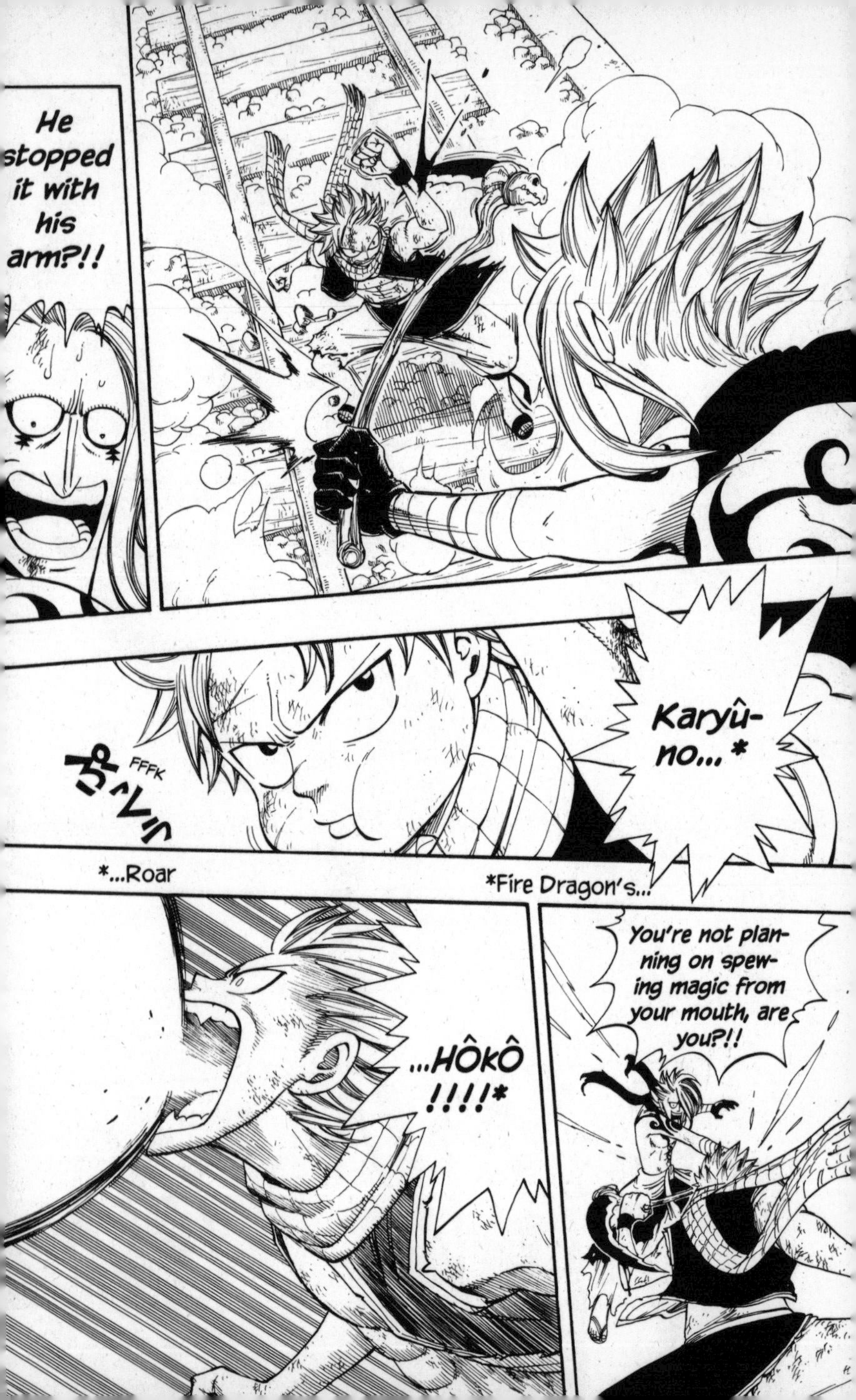
He stopped it with his arm?!!
Karyû-no...*
FFFK
*Fire Dragon's...
You're not planning on spewing magic from your mouth, are you?!!
...HÔKÔ !!!!*
*...Roar

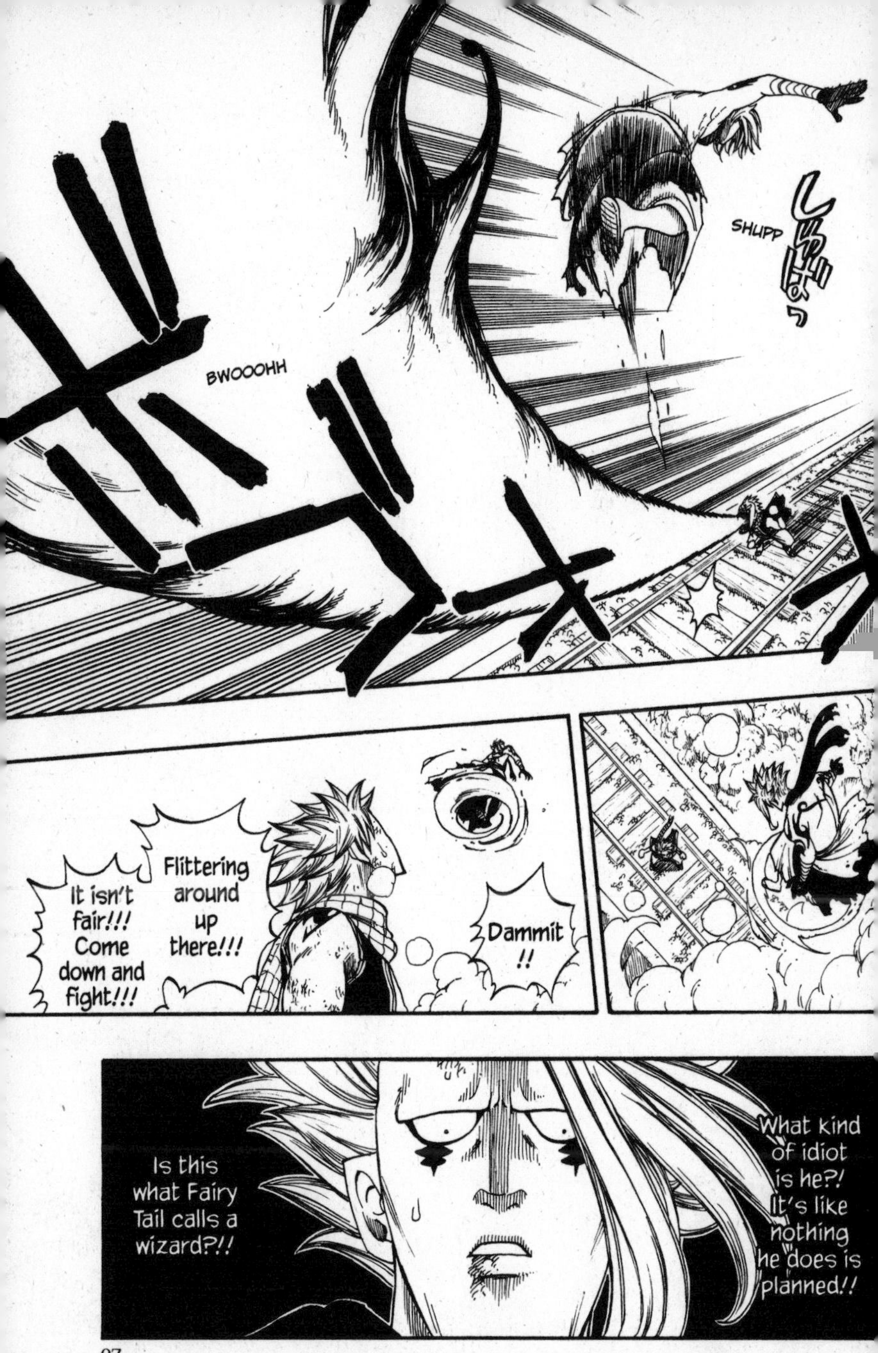
SHUPP
BWOOOHH
Dammit!!
Flittering around up there!!!
It isn't fair!!! Come down and fight!!!
What kind of idiot is he?! It's like nothing he does is planned!!
Is this what Fairy Tail calls a wizard?!!

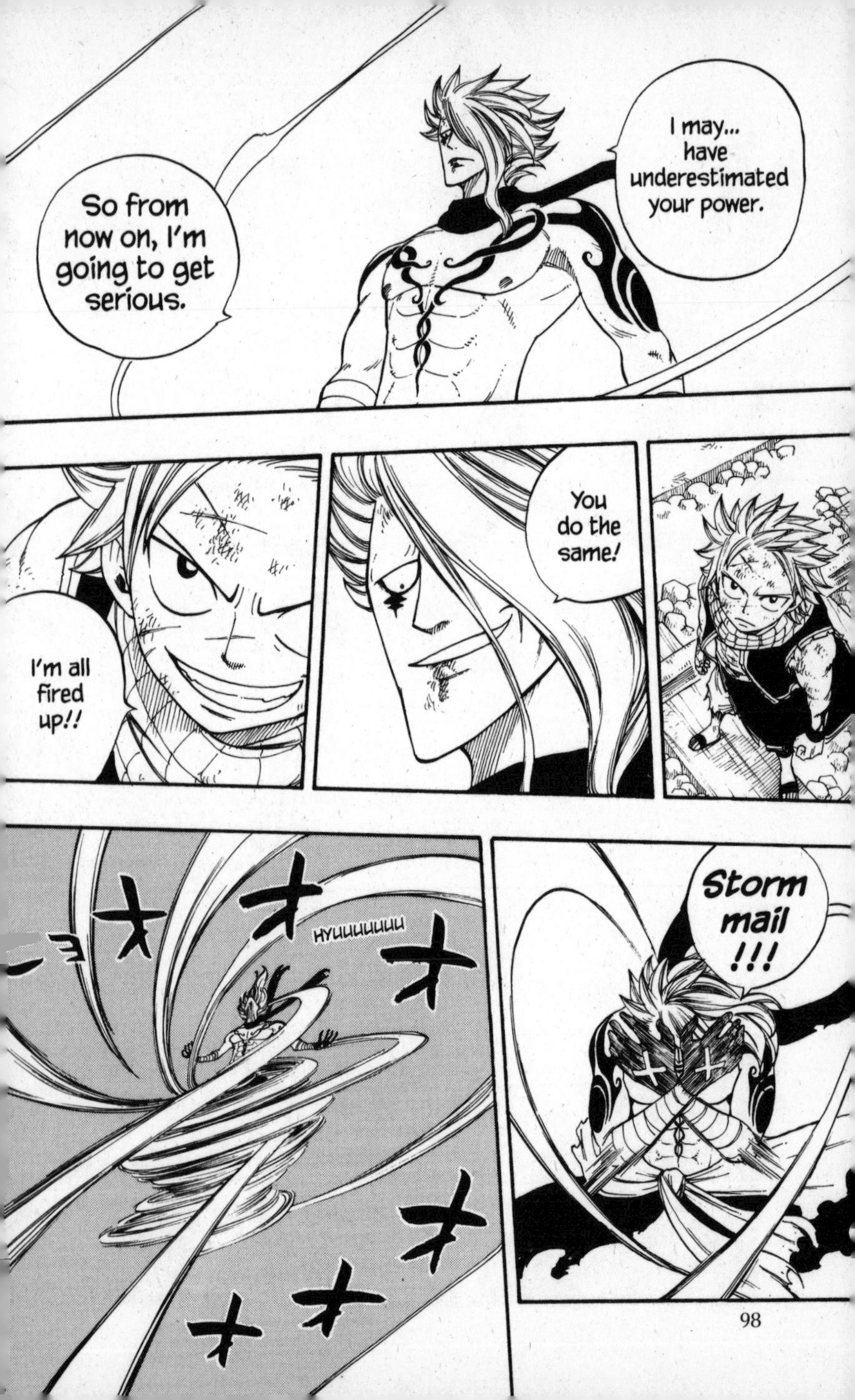
I may... have underestimated your power.
So from now on, I'm going to get serious.
You do the same!
I'm all fired up!!
Storm mail!!!
HYUUUUUUUU

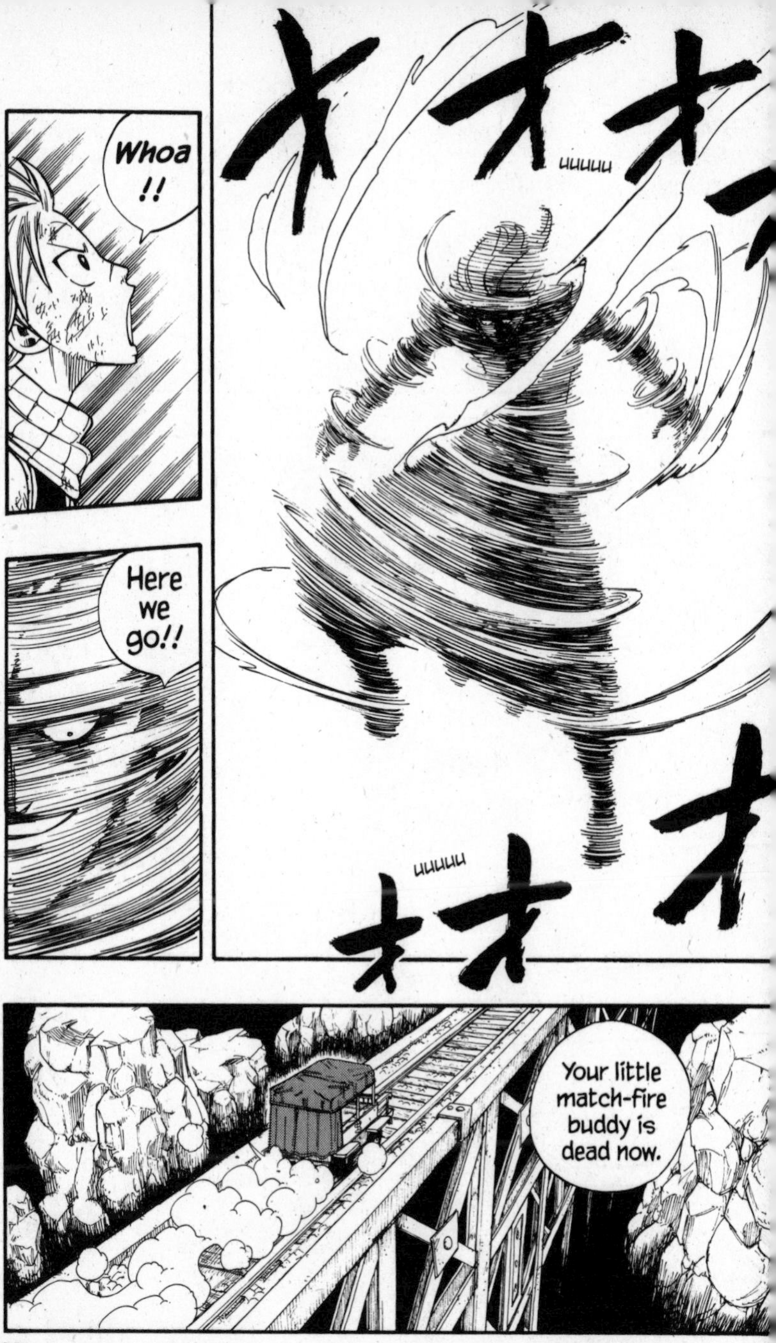
uuuuu
uuuuu
Whoa!!
Here we go!!
Your little match-fire buddy is dead now.

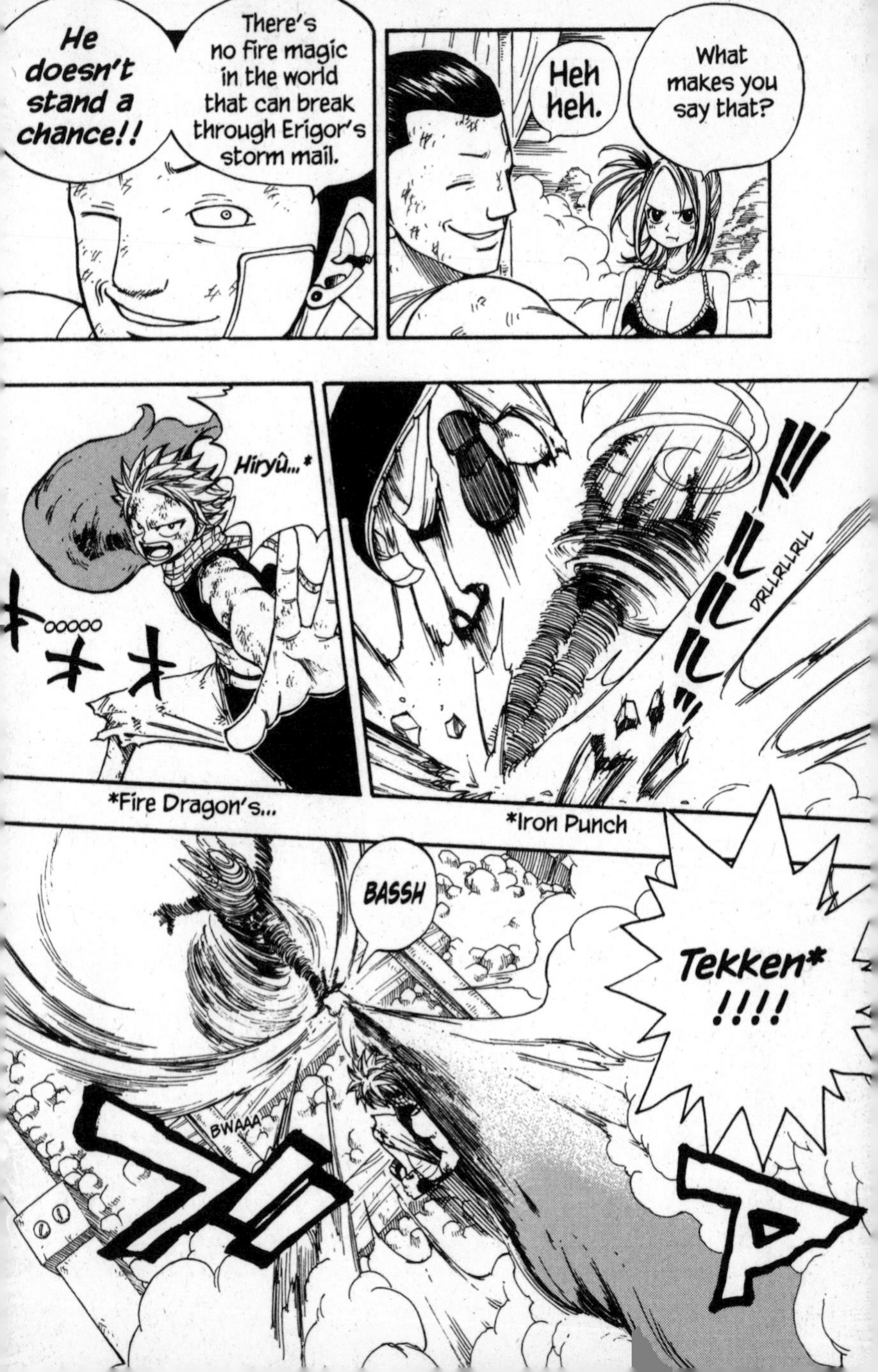

What makes you say that?
Heh heh.
There's no fire magic in the world that can break through Erigor's storm mail.
He doesn't stand a chance!!
DRLLRLLRLL
*Iron Punch
Hiryû...*
ooooo
*Fire Dragon's...
Tekken* !!!!
BASSH
BWAAA

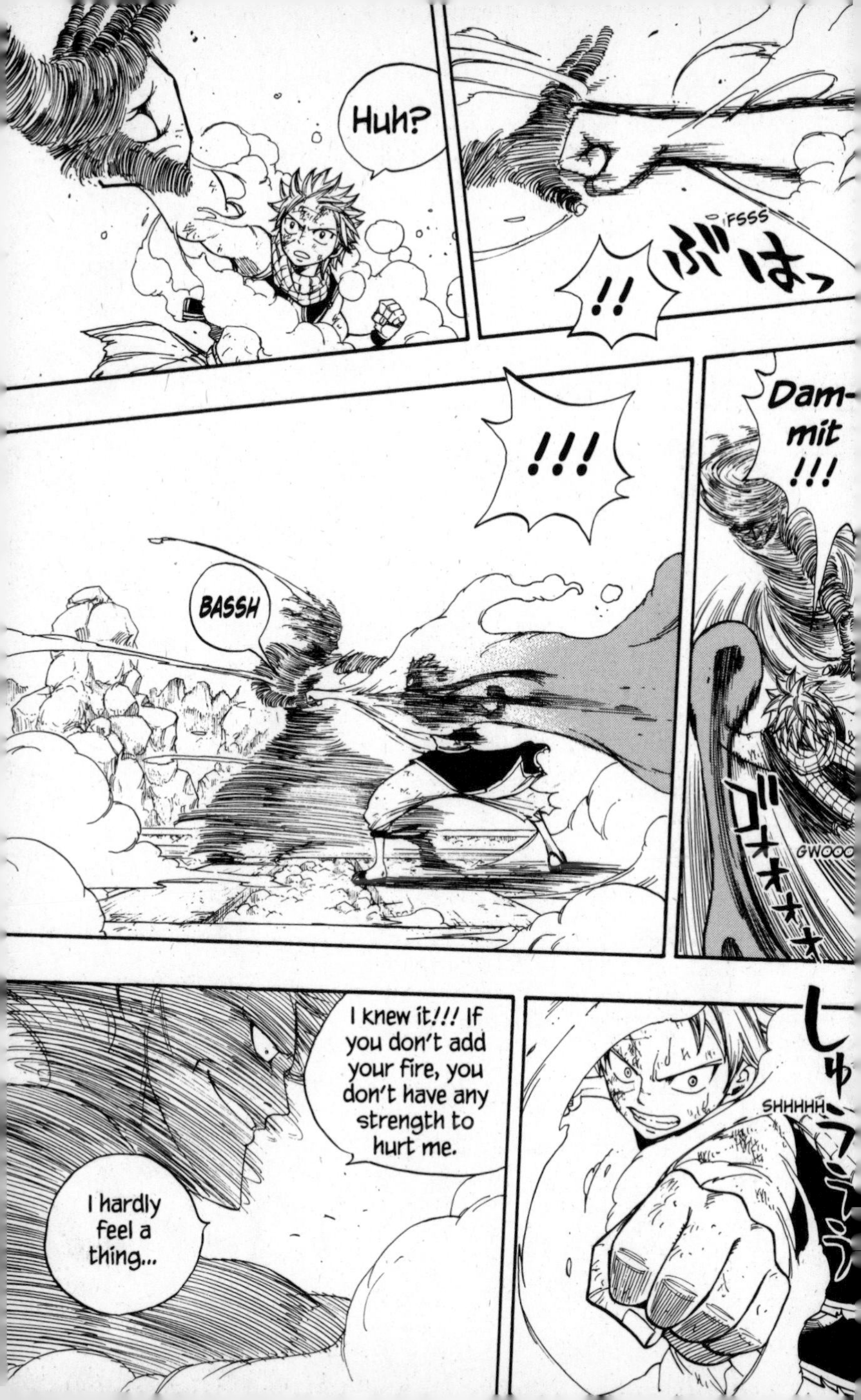
FSSS
ぶはっ
!!
Huh?
Dam-mit!!!
ゴオオオオ
GWOOO
!!!
BASSH
しゅうううう
SHHHHH
I knew it!!! If you don't add your fire, you don't have any strength to hurt me.
I hardly feel a thing...

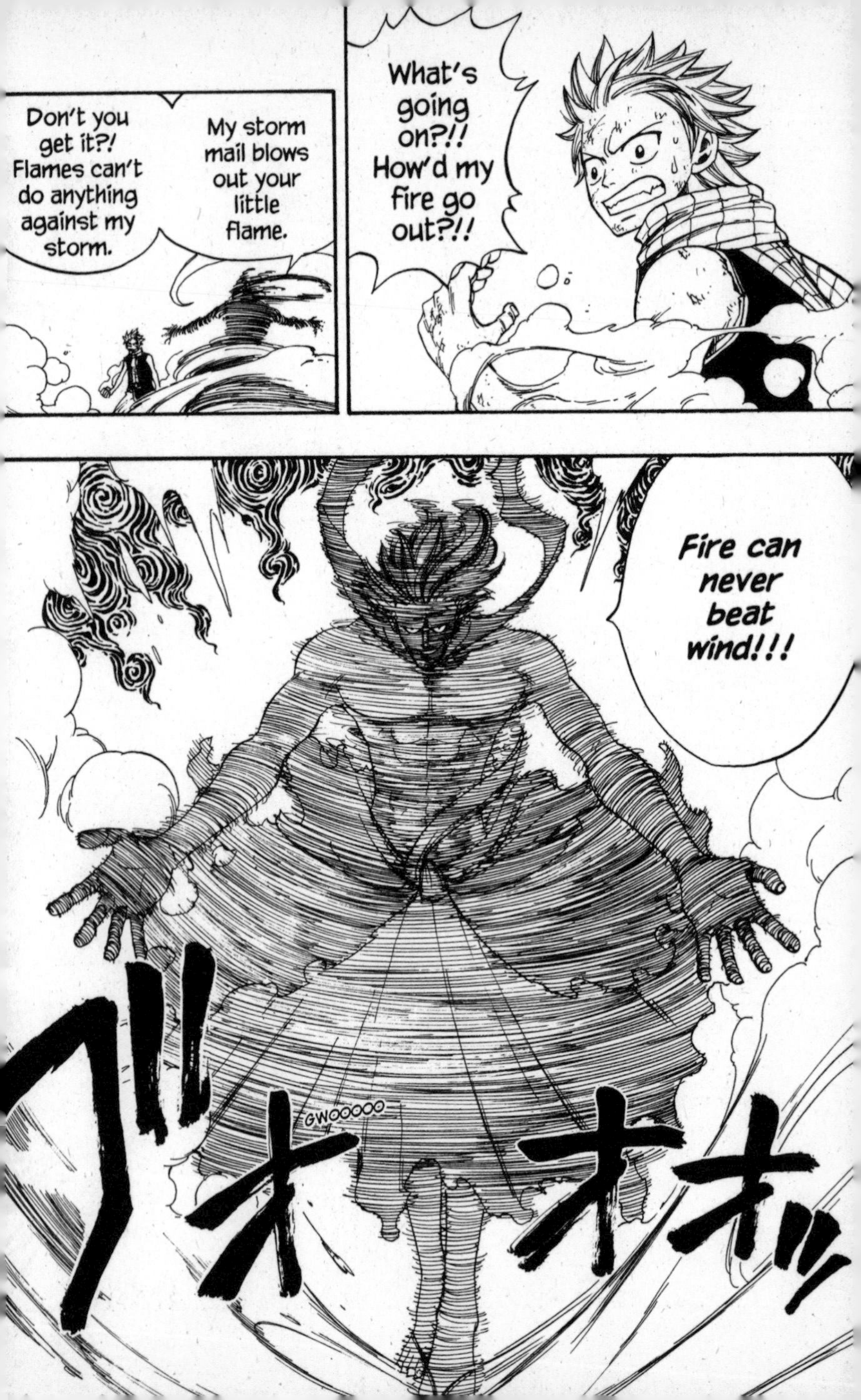

What's going on?!! How'd my fire go out?!!
My storm mail blows out your little flame.
Don't you get it?! Flames can't do anything against my storm.
Fire can never beat wind!!!
ゴオオッ
GWOOOOO

Chapter 19: Impossible! Natsu Can't Win!

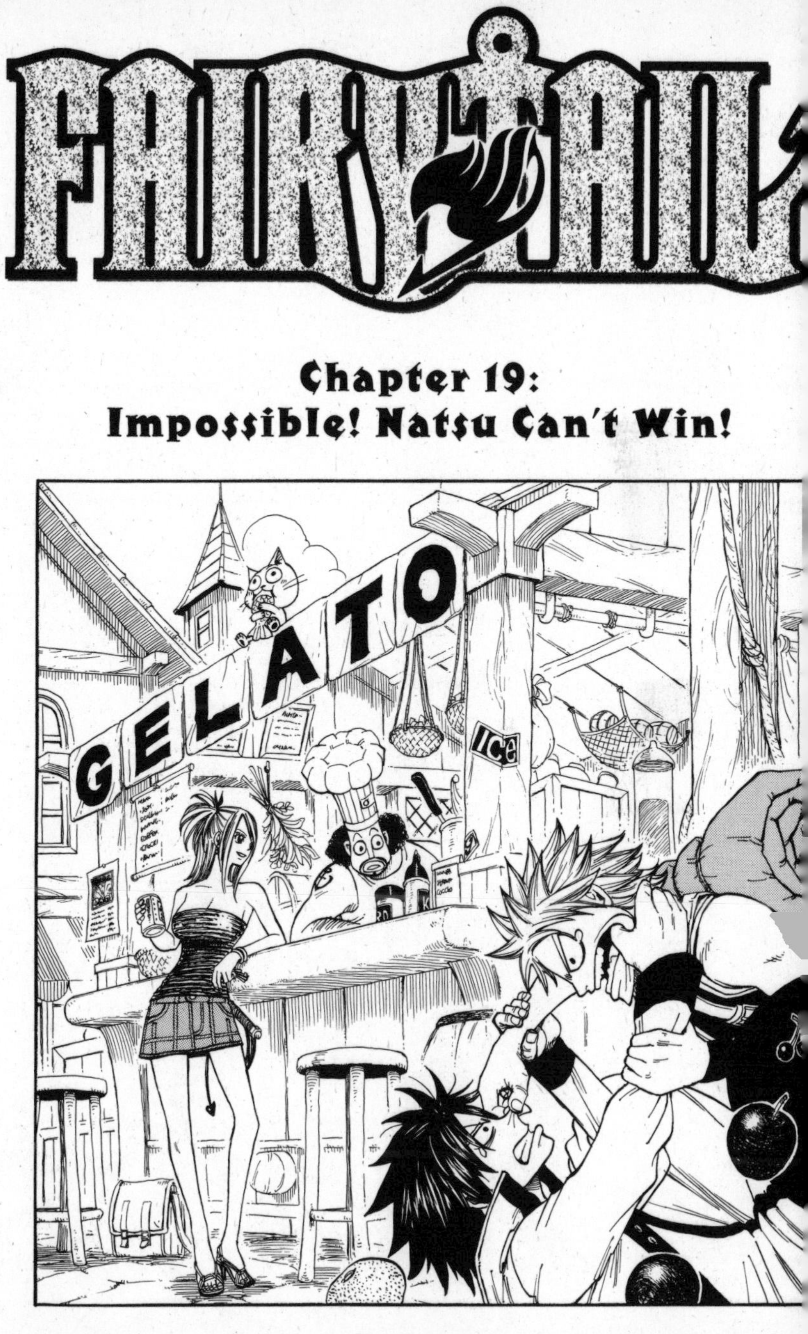
GELATO
ICE

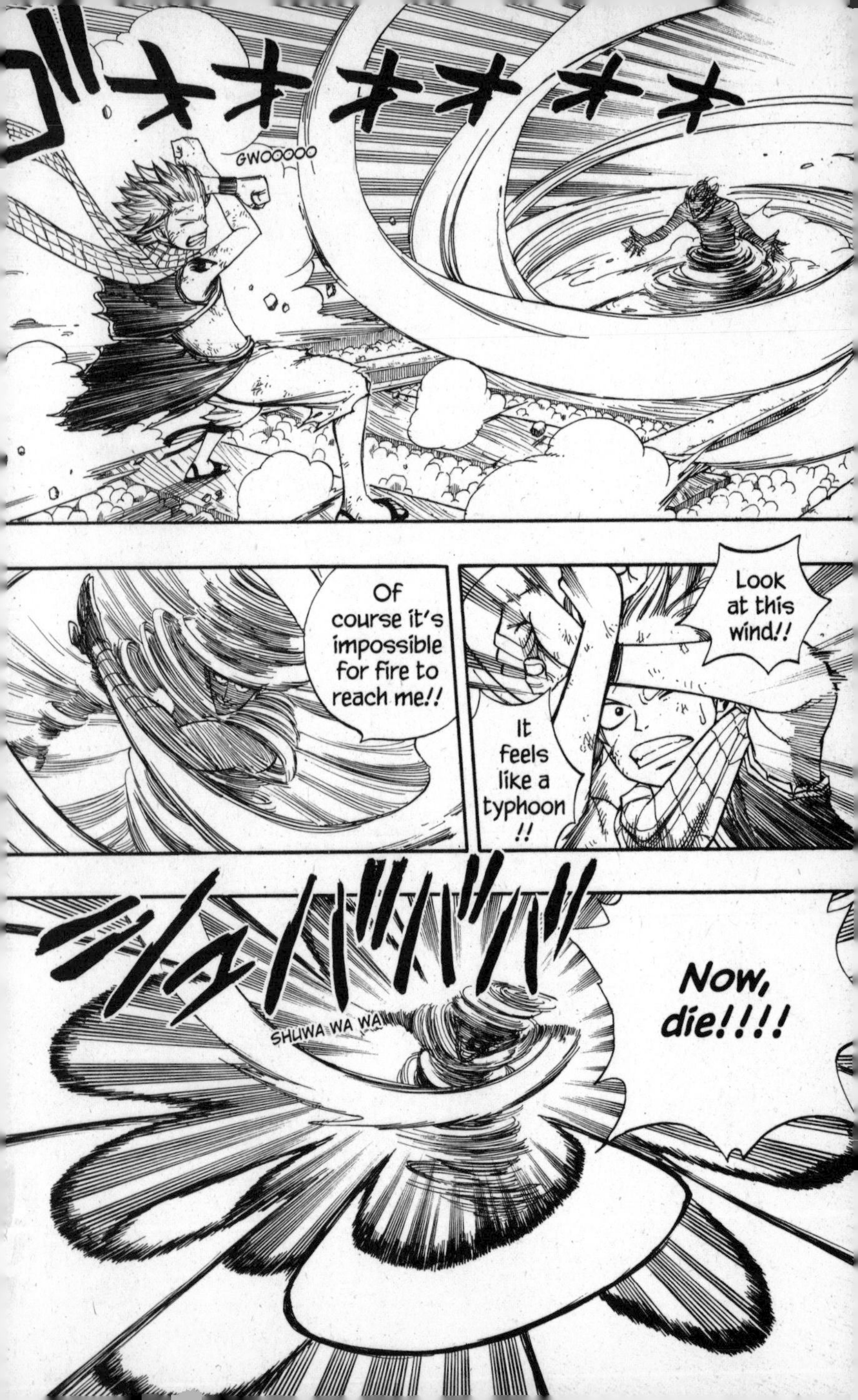
GWOOOOO
Look at this wind!!
It feels like a typhoon!!
Of course it's impossible for fire to reach me!!
Now, die!!!!
SHUWA WA WA

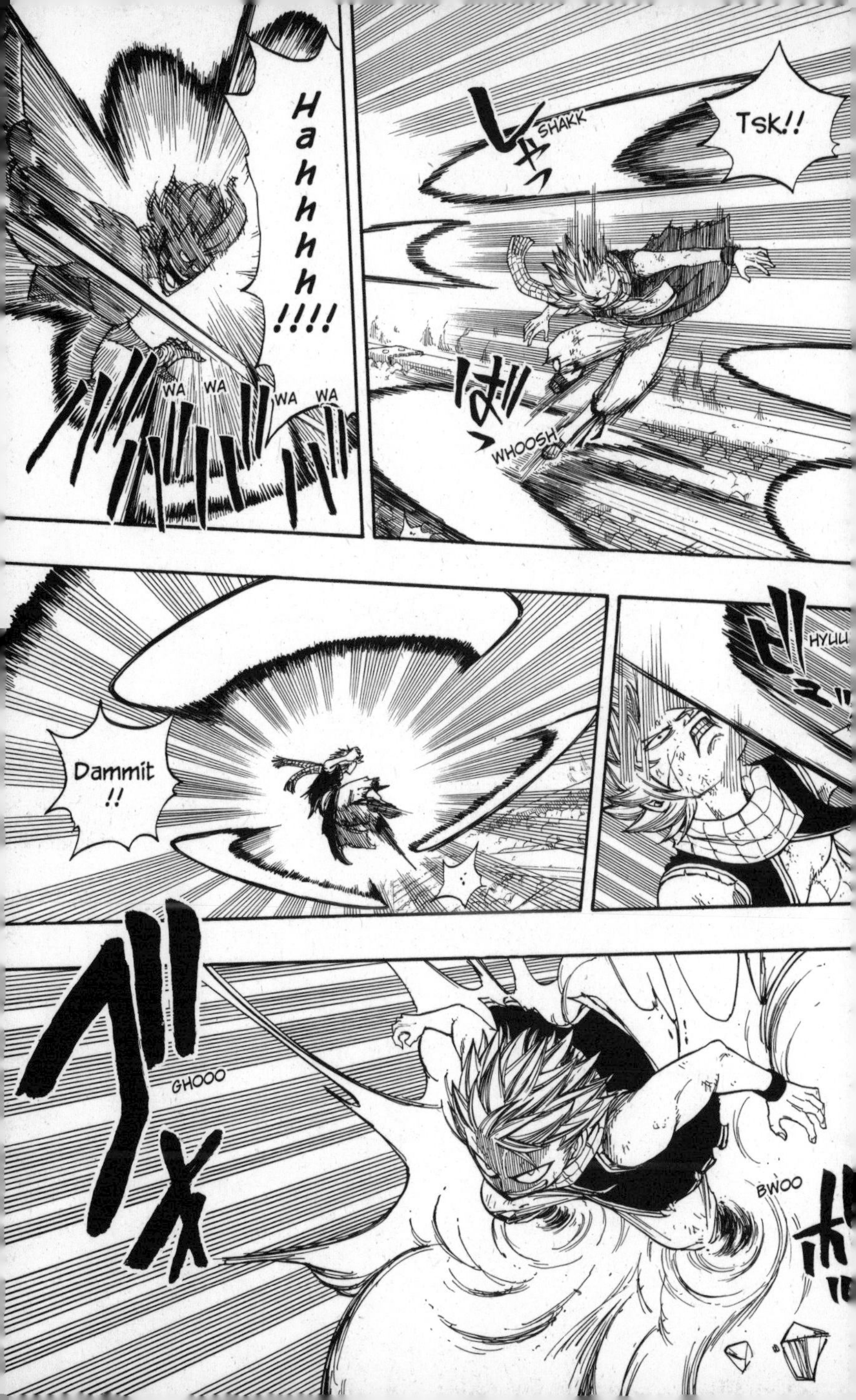
TSK!!
SHAKK
WHOOSH
Hahhhhh!!!!
WA WA WA WA
HYUU
Dammit!!
GHOOO
BWOO

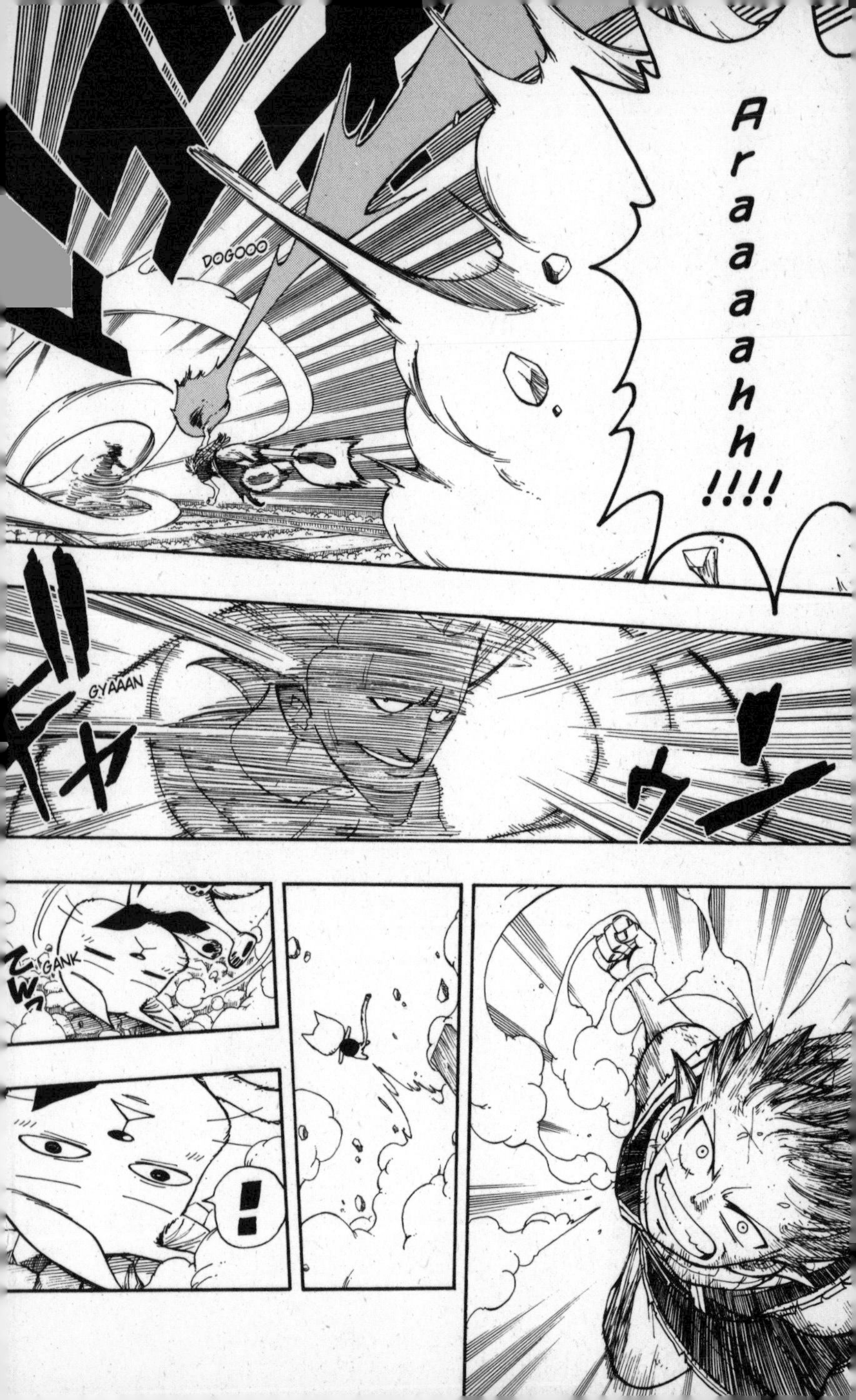
Araaaahh!!!!
DOGOOO
GYAAAN
GANK
!

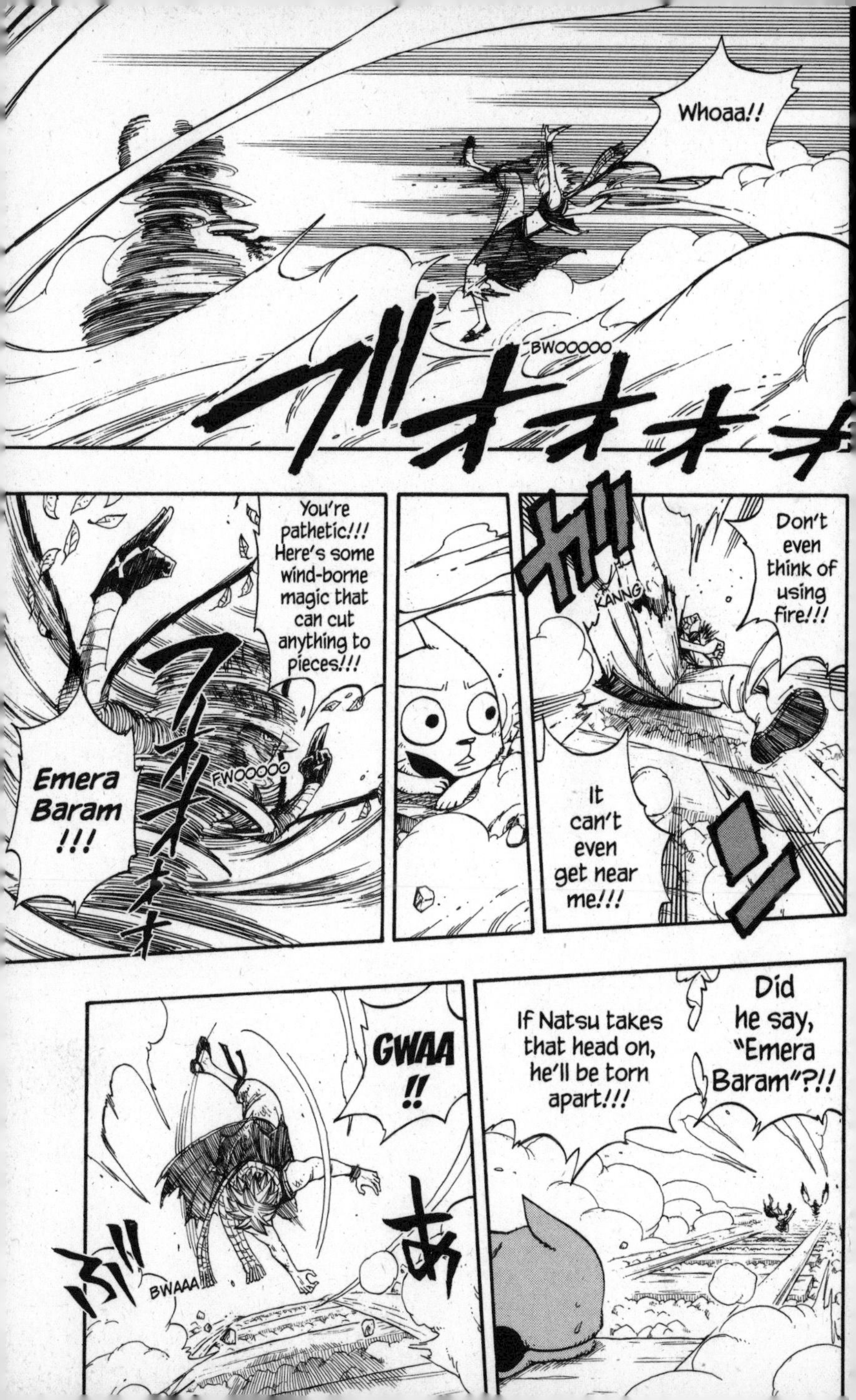
Whoaa!!
BWOOOOO
Don't even think of using fire!!!
KANNG
It can't even get near me!!!
You're pathetic!!! Here's some wind-borne magic that can cut anything to pieces!!!
FWOOOOO
Emera Baram!!!
Did he say, "Emera Baram"?!!
If Natsu takes that head on, he'll be torn apart!!!
GWAA!!
BWAAA

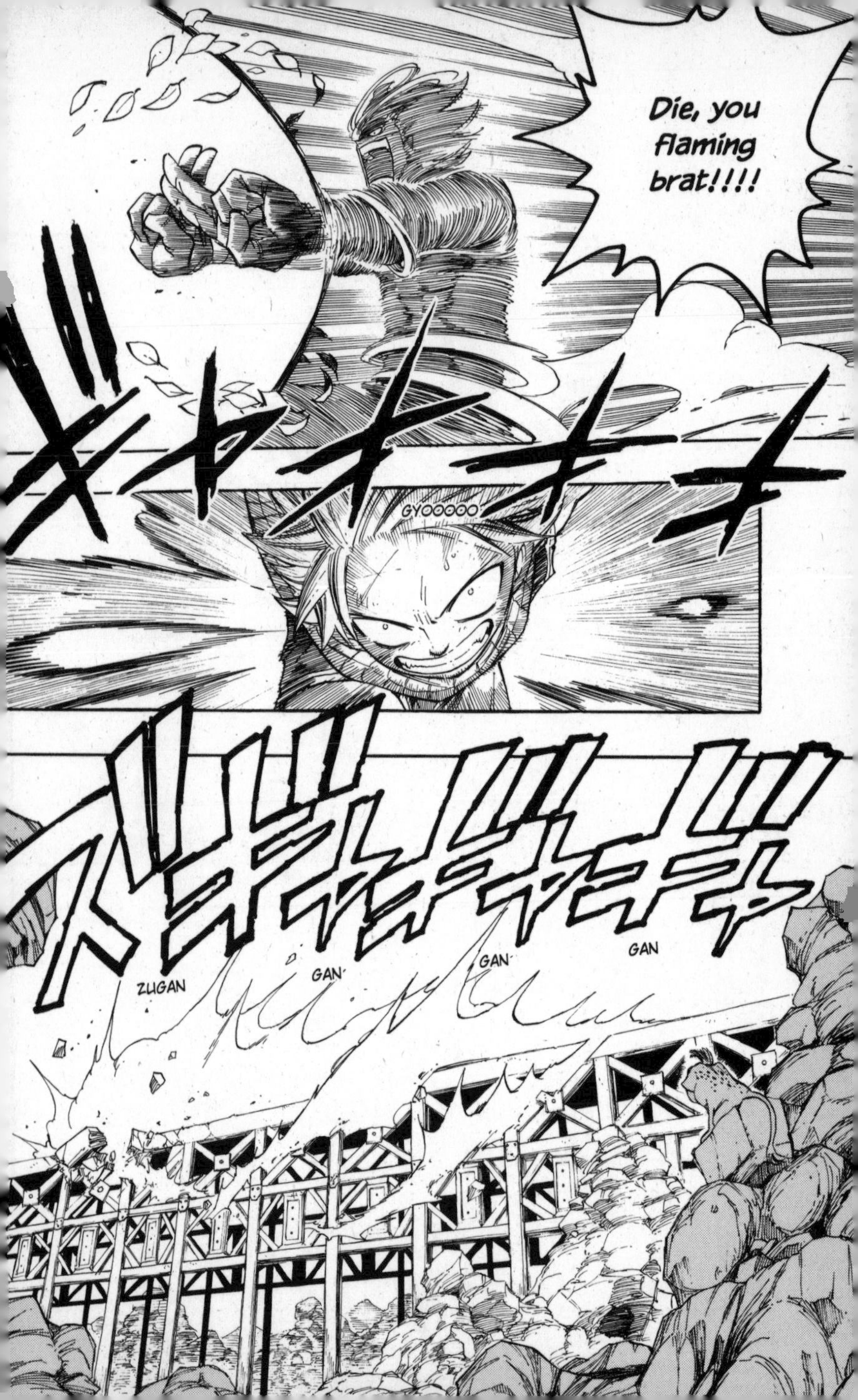
Die, you flaming brat!!!!
GYOOOOO
ZUGAN
GAN
GAN
GAN

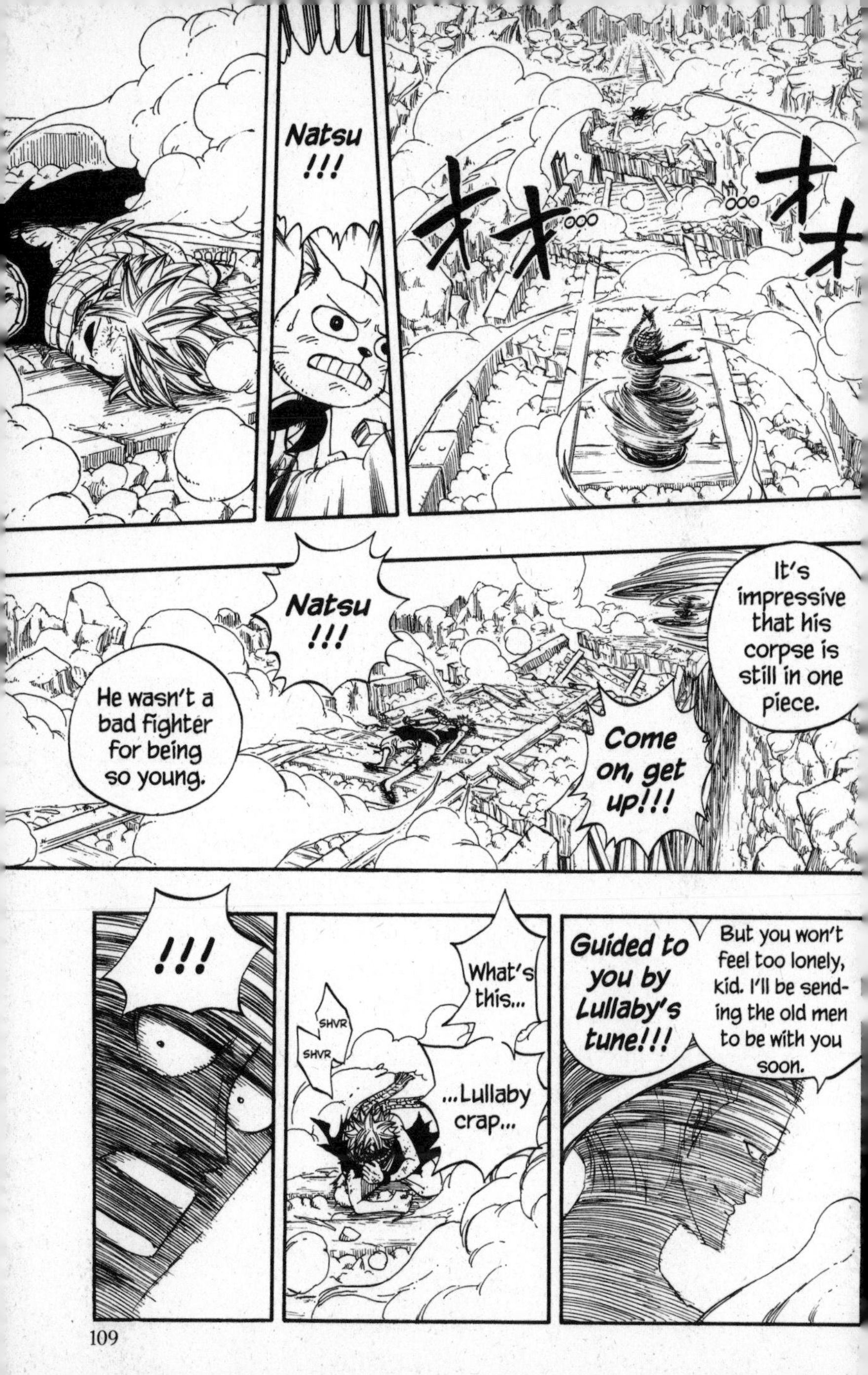
オオ...
オオ...
Natsu!!!
It's impressive that his corpse is still in one piece.
Natsu!!!
Come on, get up!!!
He wasn't a bad fighter for being so young.
But you won't feel too lonely, kid. I'll be sending the old men to be with you soon.
Guided to you by Lullaby's tune!!!
What's this...
SHVR
SHVR
...Lullaby crap...
!!!

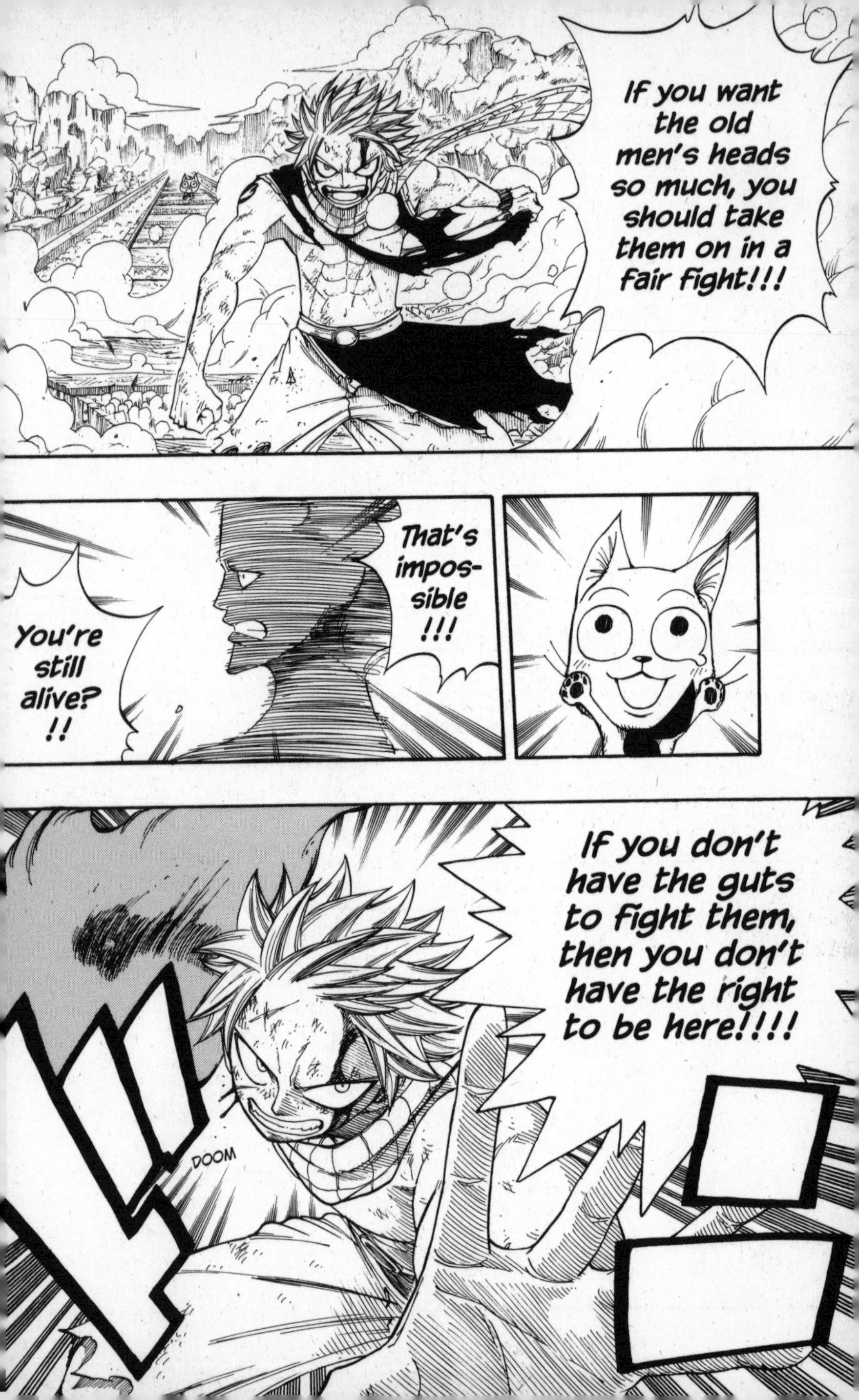
If you want the old men's heads so much, you should take them on in a fair fight!!!
That's impossible!!!
You're still alive?!!
If you don't have the guts to fight them, then you don't have the right to be here!!!!
DOOM

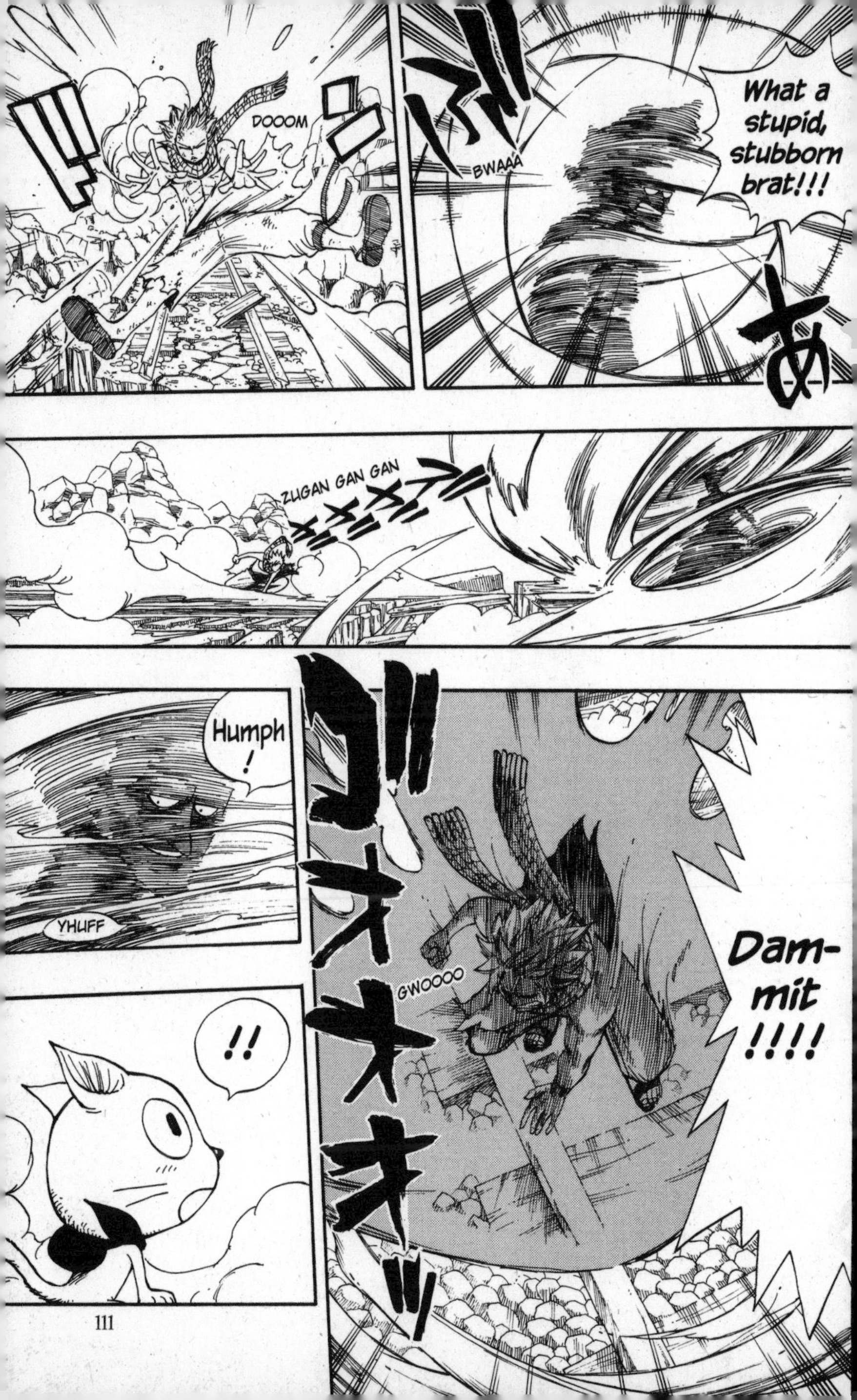
What a stupid, stubborn brat!!!
BWAAA
DOOOM
ZUGAN GAN GAN
Dam-mit!!!!
GWOOOO
Humph!
YHUFF
!!

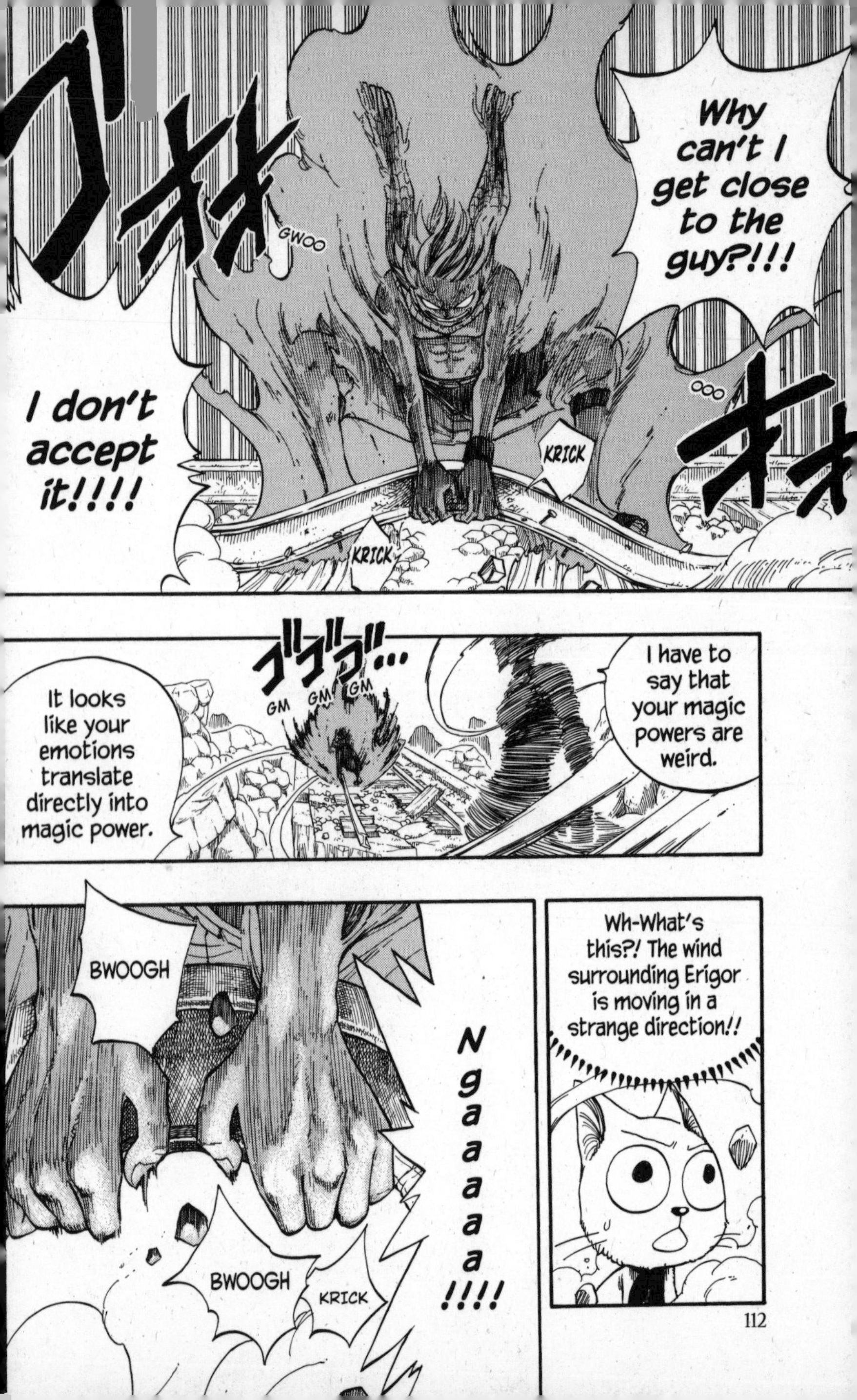
Why can't I get close to the guy?!!!
OOO
KRICK
GWOO
KRICK
I don't accept it!!!!
I have to say that your magic powers are weird.
GM GM GM
It looks like your emotions translate directly into magic power.
Wh-What's this?! The wind surrounding Erigor is moving in a strange direction!!
BWOOGH
Ngaaaaaa!!!!
BWOOGH
KRICK

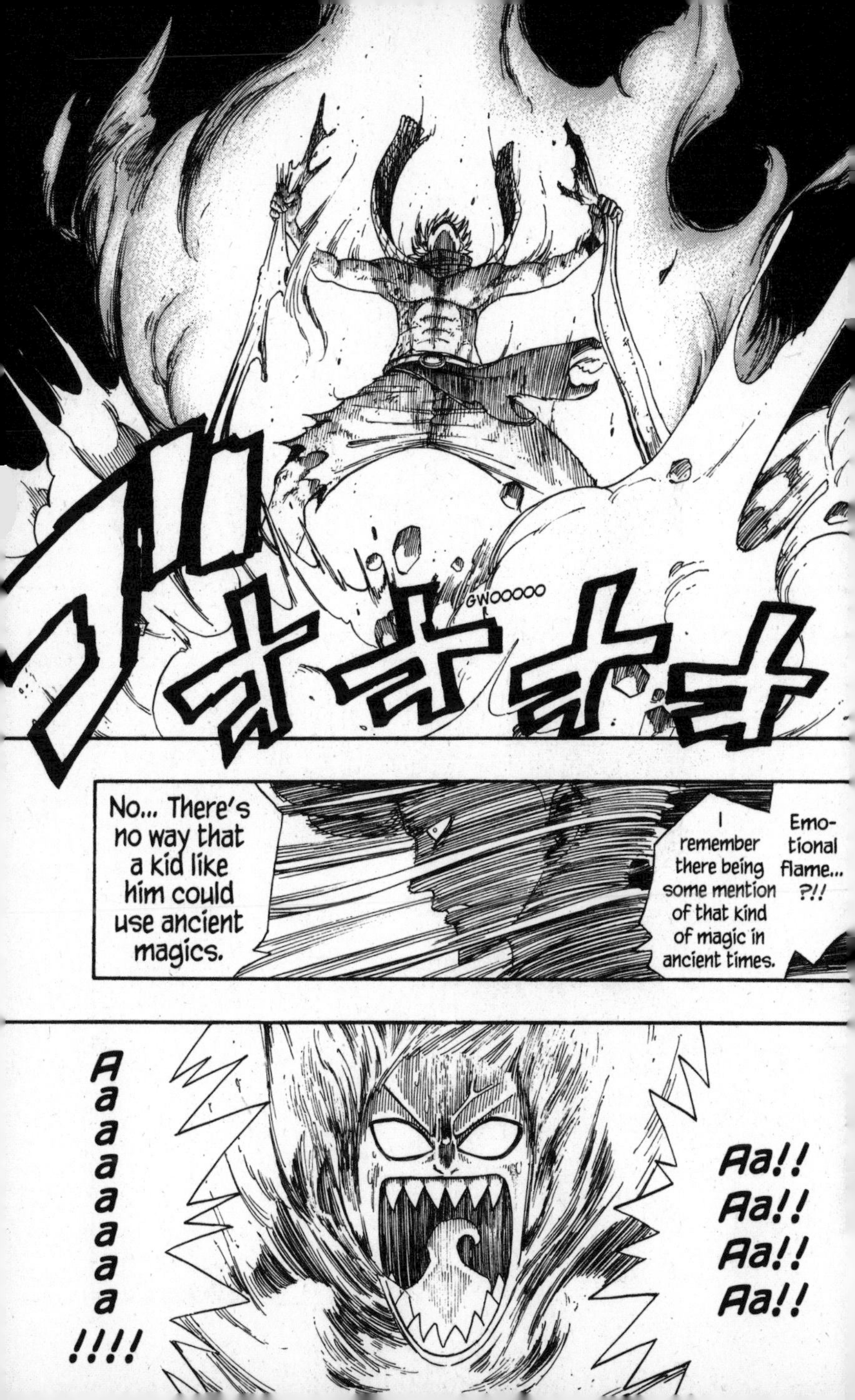
ゴォォォォ
GWOOOOO
Emo-tional flame...?!!
I remember there being some mention of that kind of magic in ancient times.
No... There's no way that a kid like him could use ancient magics.
Aa!! Aa!! Aa!! Aa!!
Aaaaaaaa!!!!

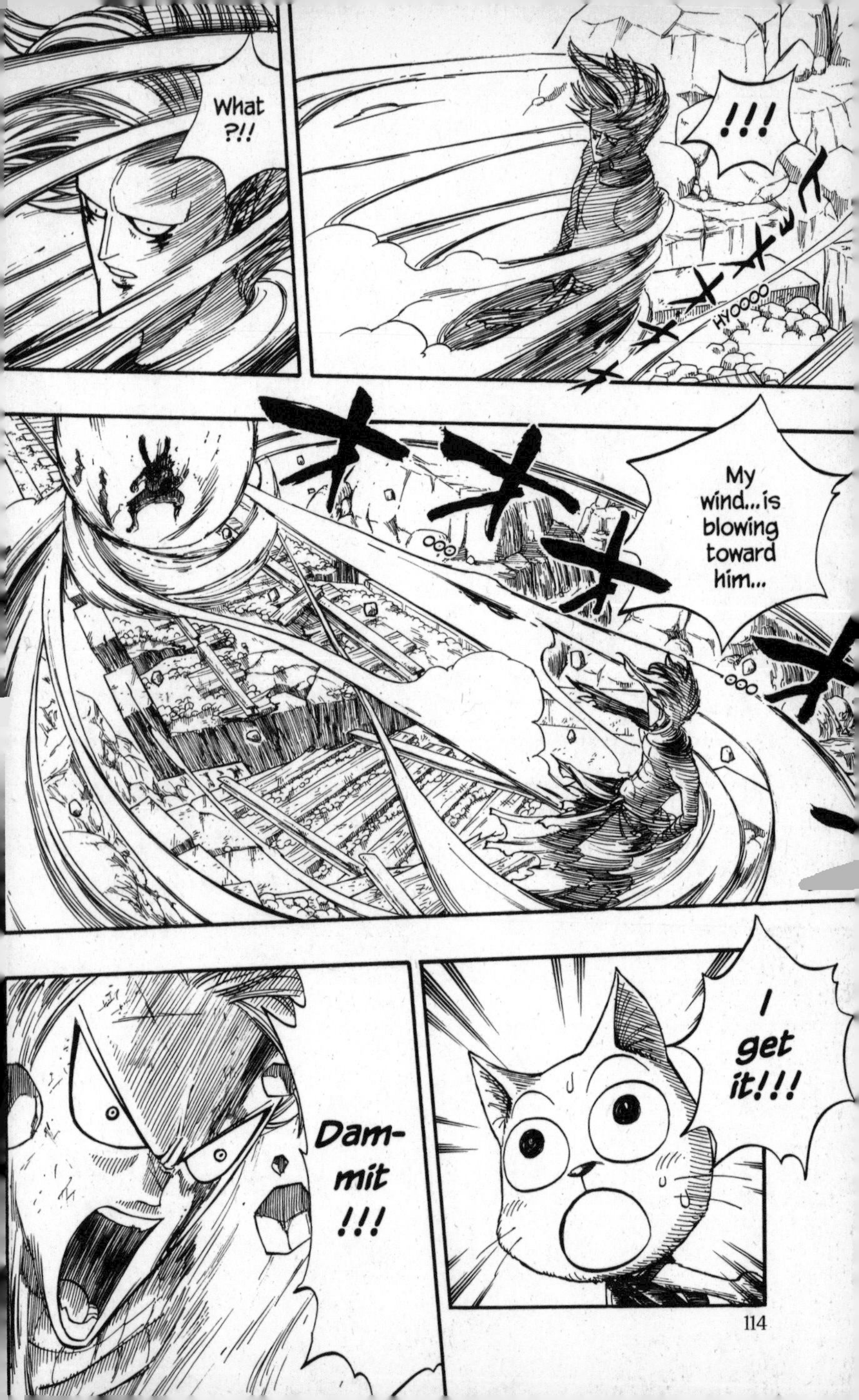
!!!
HYOOOO
What ?!!
My wind...is blowing toward him...
I get it!!!
Dam-mit !!!

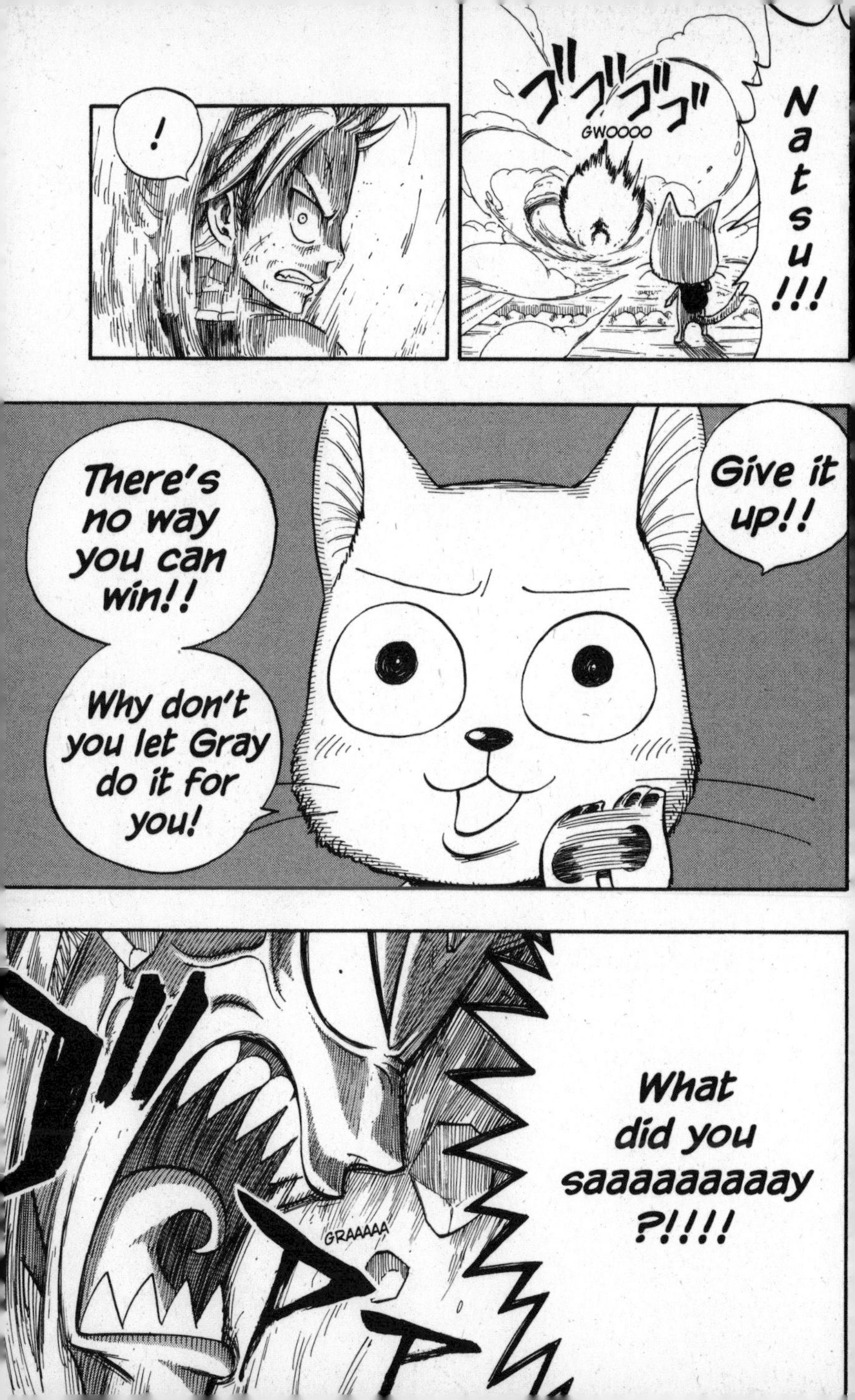
GWOOOO
Natsu!!!
!
Give it up!!
There's no way you can win!!
Why don't you let Gray do it for you!
What did you saaaaaaaaay?!!!!
GRAAAAA

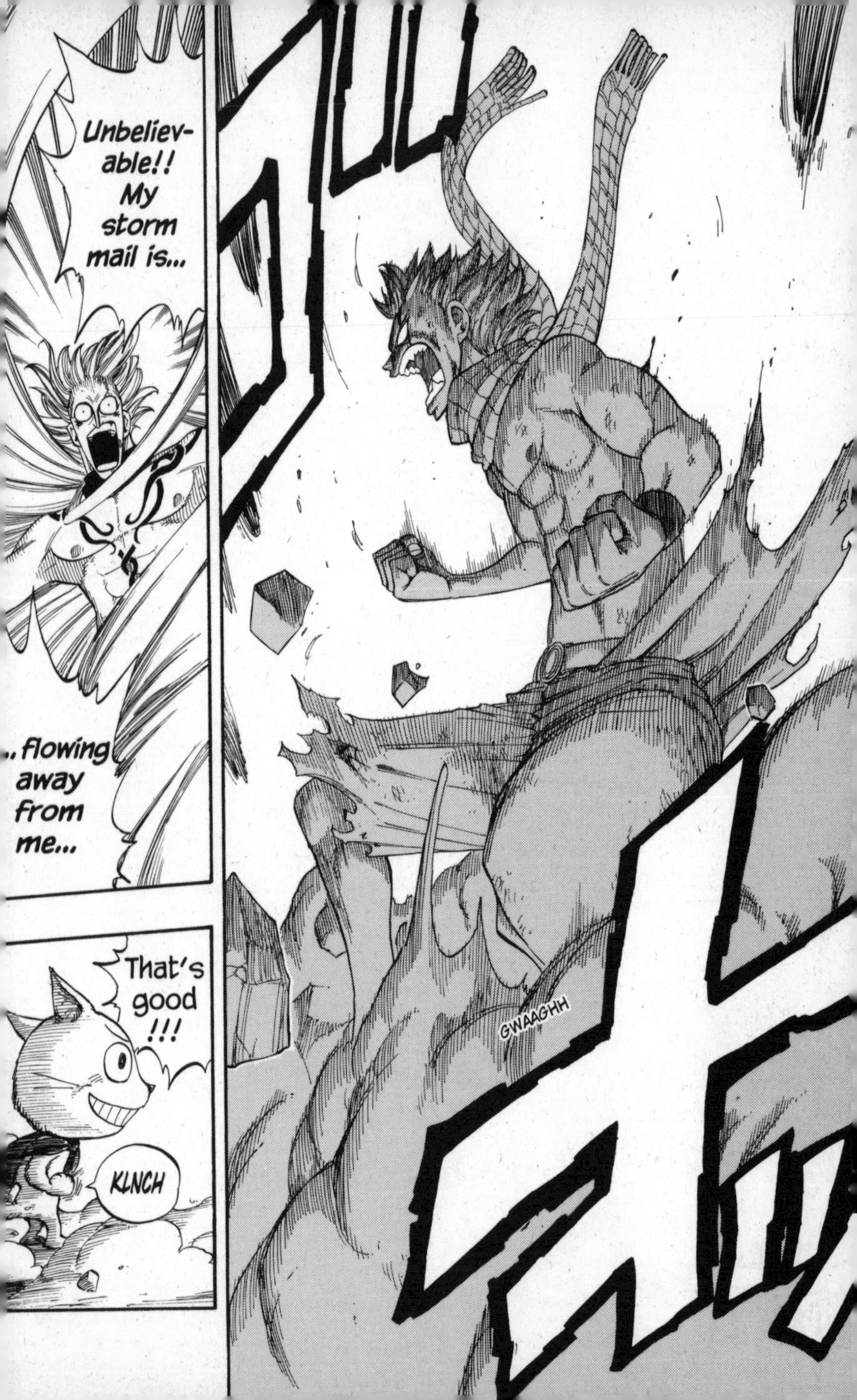
GWAAGHH
Unbelievable!! My storm mail is...
..flowing away from me...
That's good!!!
KLNCH

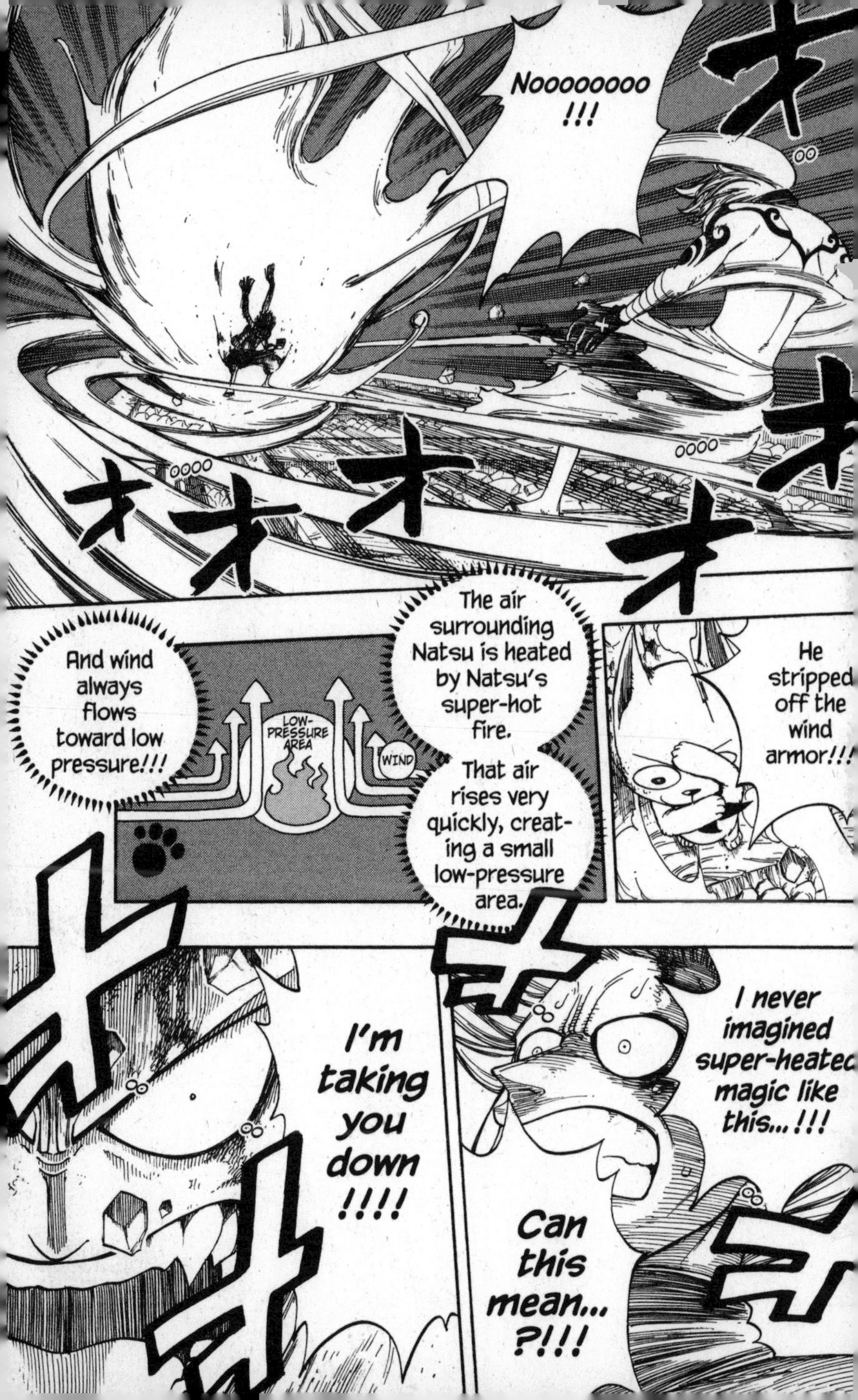
Noooooooo !!!
oo
oooo
oooo
He stripped off the wind armor!!!
The air surrounding Natsu is heated by Natsu's super-hot fire.
That air rises very quickly, creat-ing a small low-pressure area.
And wind always flows toward low pressure!!!
LOW-PRESSURE AREA
WIND
I never imagined super-heated magic like this...!!!
Can this mean...?!!!
I'm taking you down!!!!

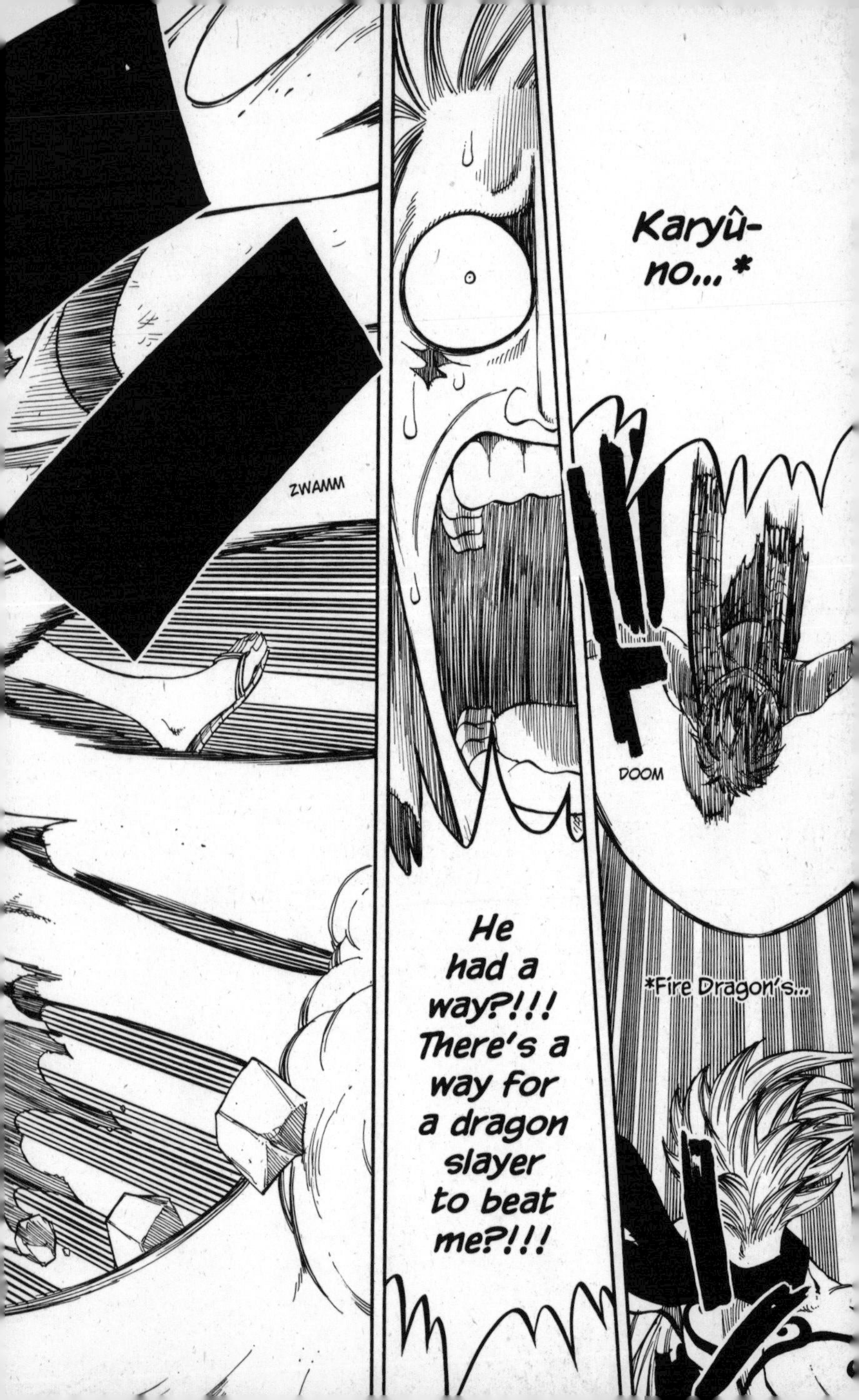
Karyû-no...*
DOOM
*Fire Dragon's...
He had a way?!!! There's a way for a dragon slayer to beat me?!!!
ZWAMM

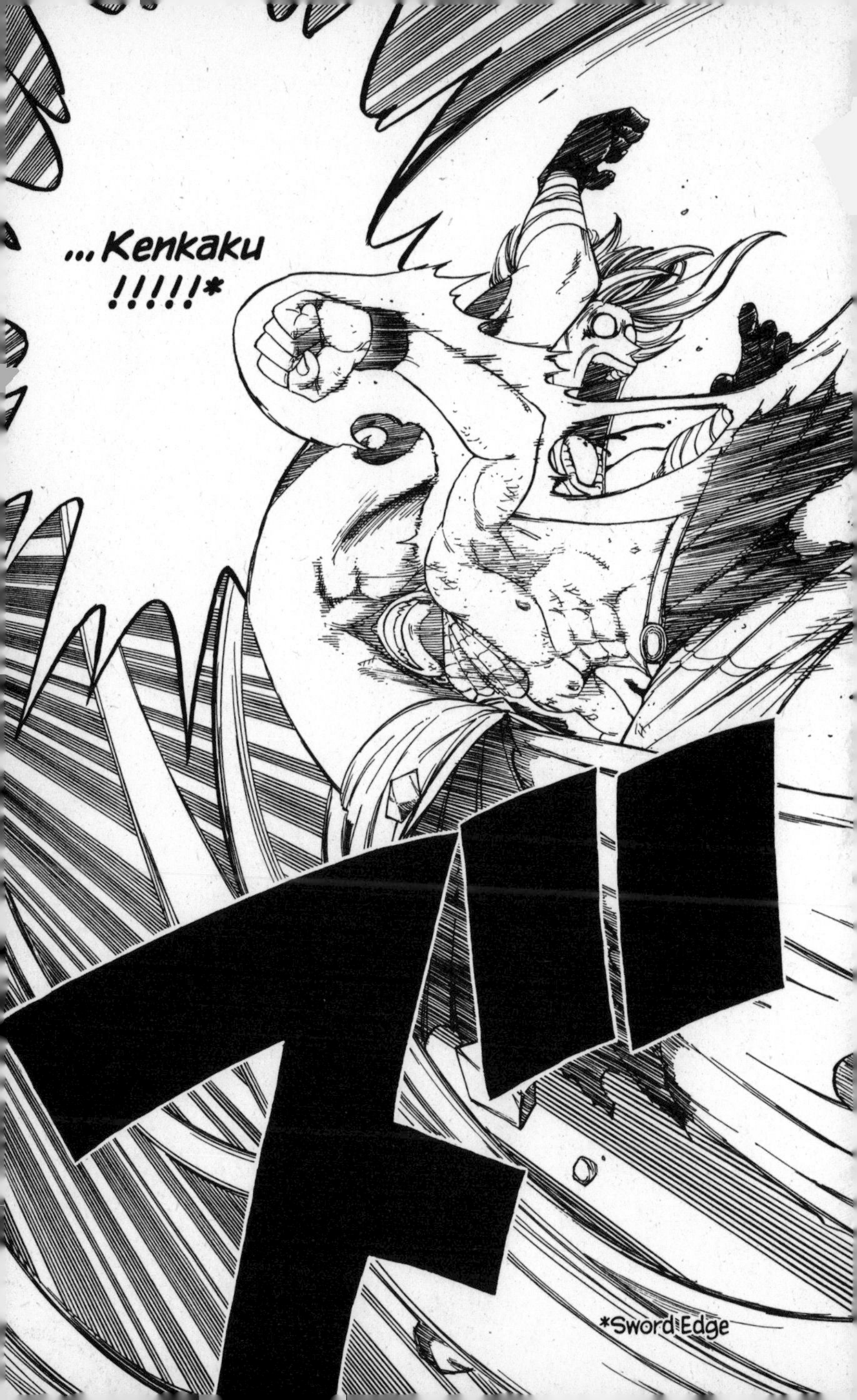
...Kenkaku !!!!!*
*Sword Edge

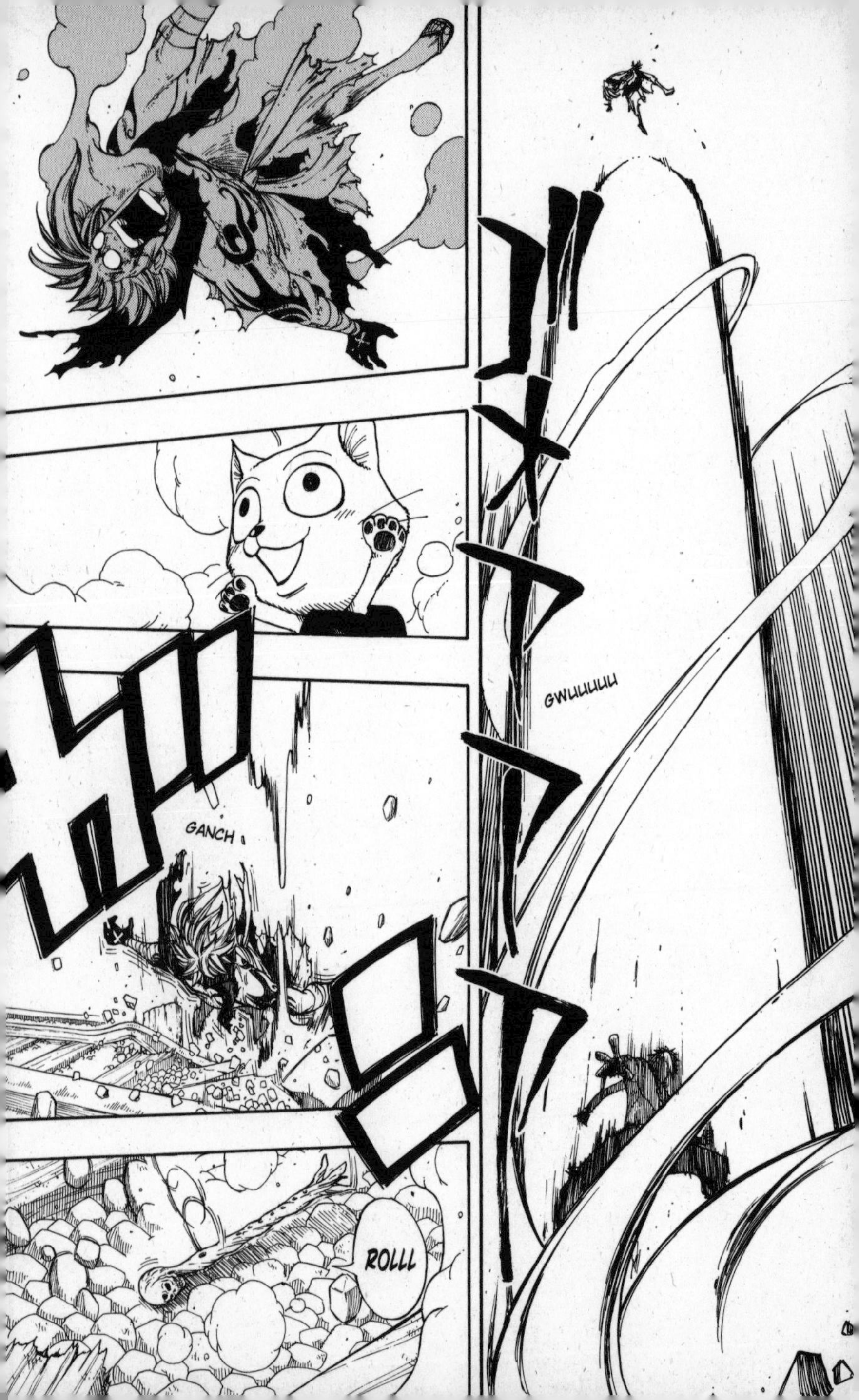
GWUUUUU
GANCH
ROLLL

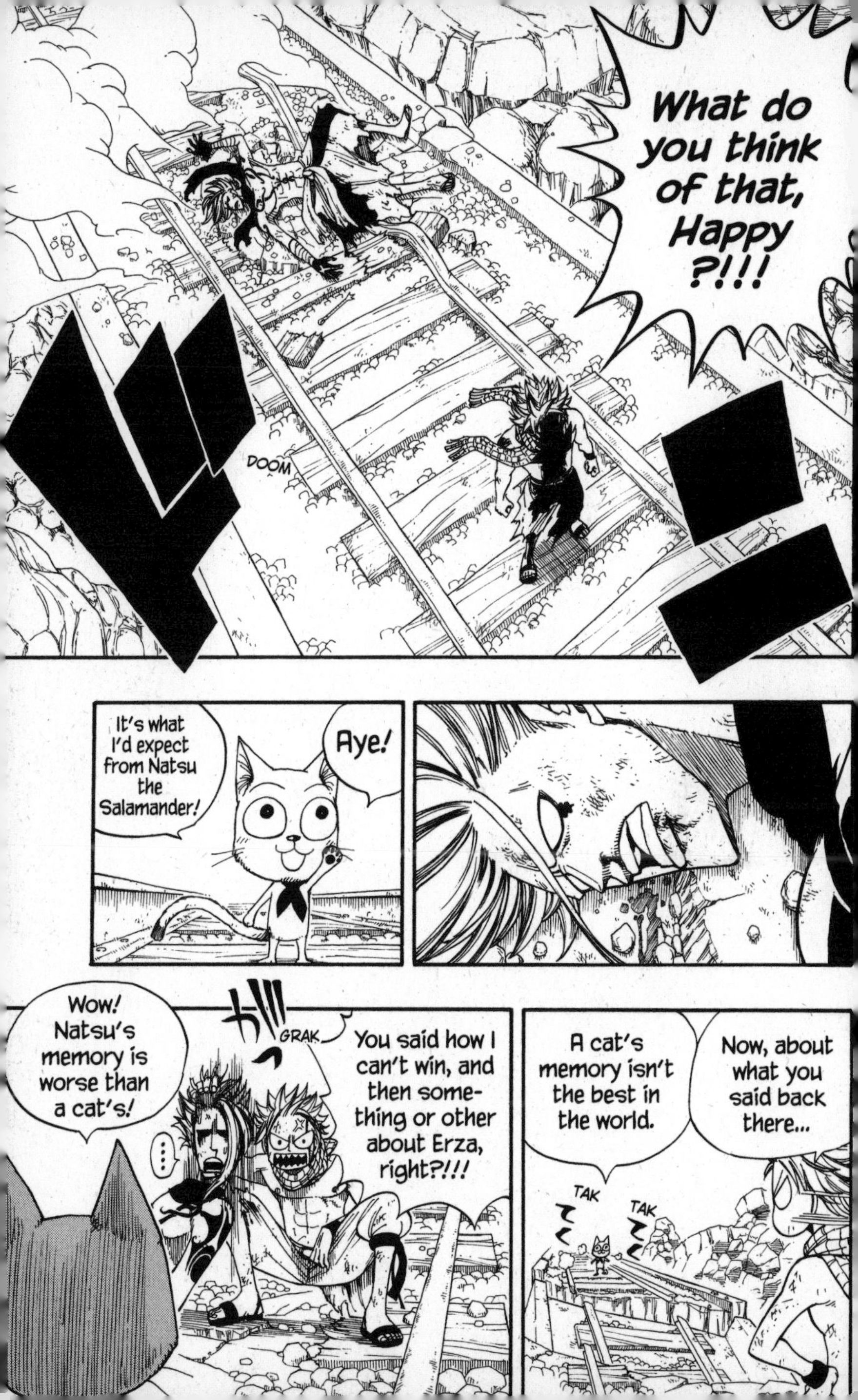
What do you think of that, Happy?!!!
DOOM
Aye!
It's what I'd expect from Natsu the Salamander!
Now, about what you said back there...
A cat's memory isn't the best in the world.
TAK
TAK
You said how I can't win, and then some-thing or other about Erza, right?!!!
GRAK
....
Wow! Natsu's memory is worse than a cat's!

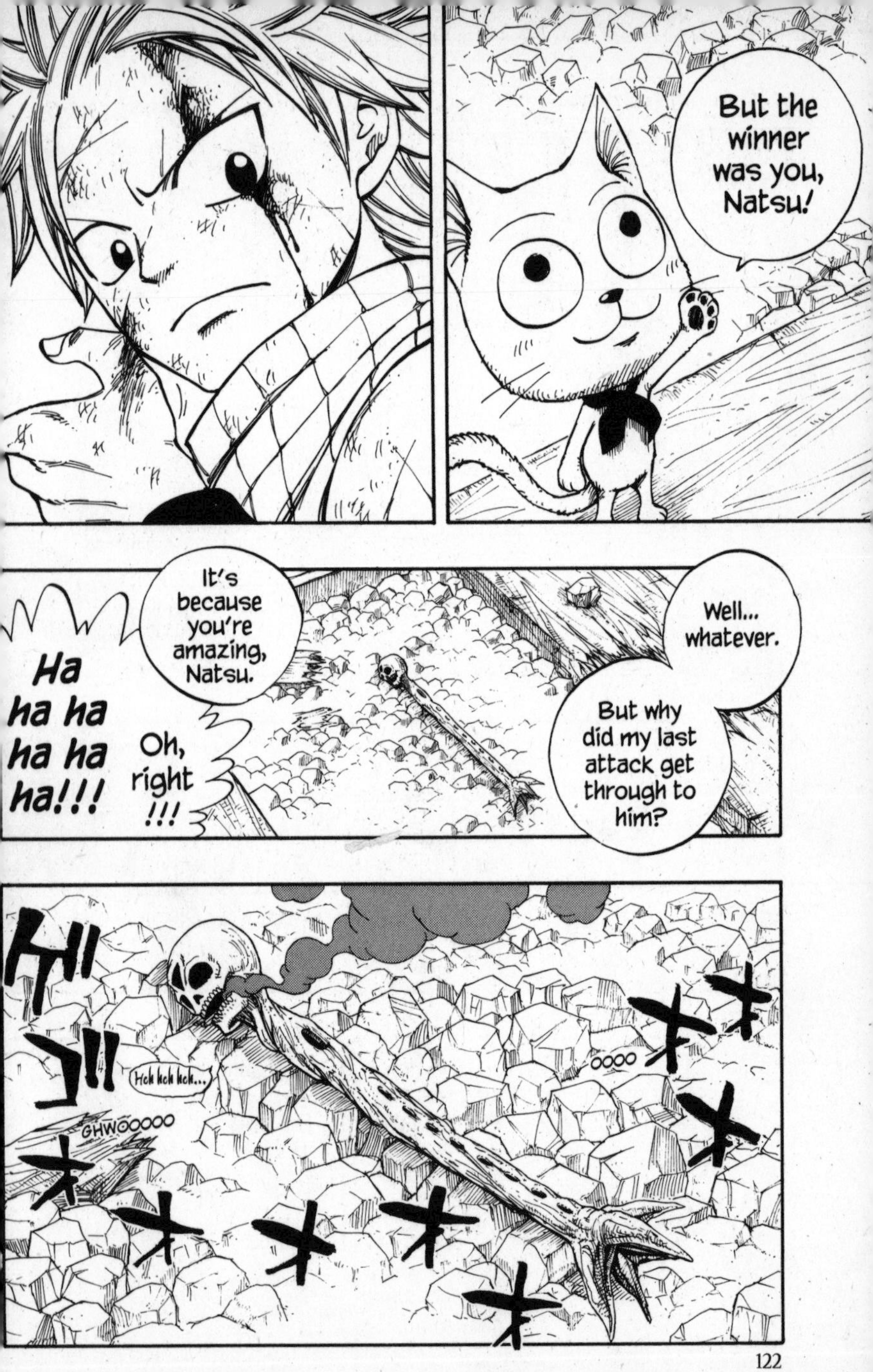

But the winner was you, Natsu!
Well... whatever.
But why did my last attack get through to him?
It's because you're amazing, Natsu.
Oh, right!!!
Ha ha ha ha ha ha!!!
oooo
Heh heh heh...
GHWOOOOO

FAIRY TAIL

Chapter 20: To Live Strong

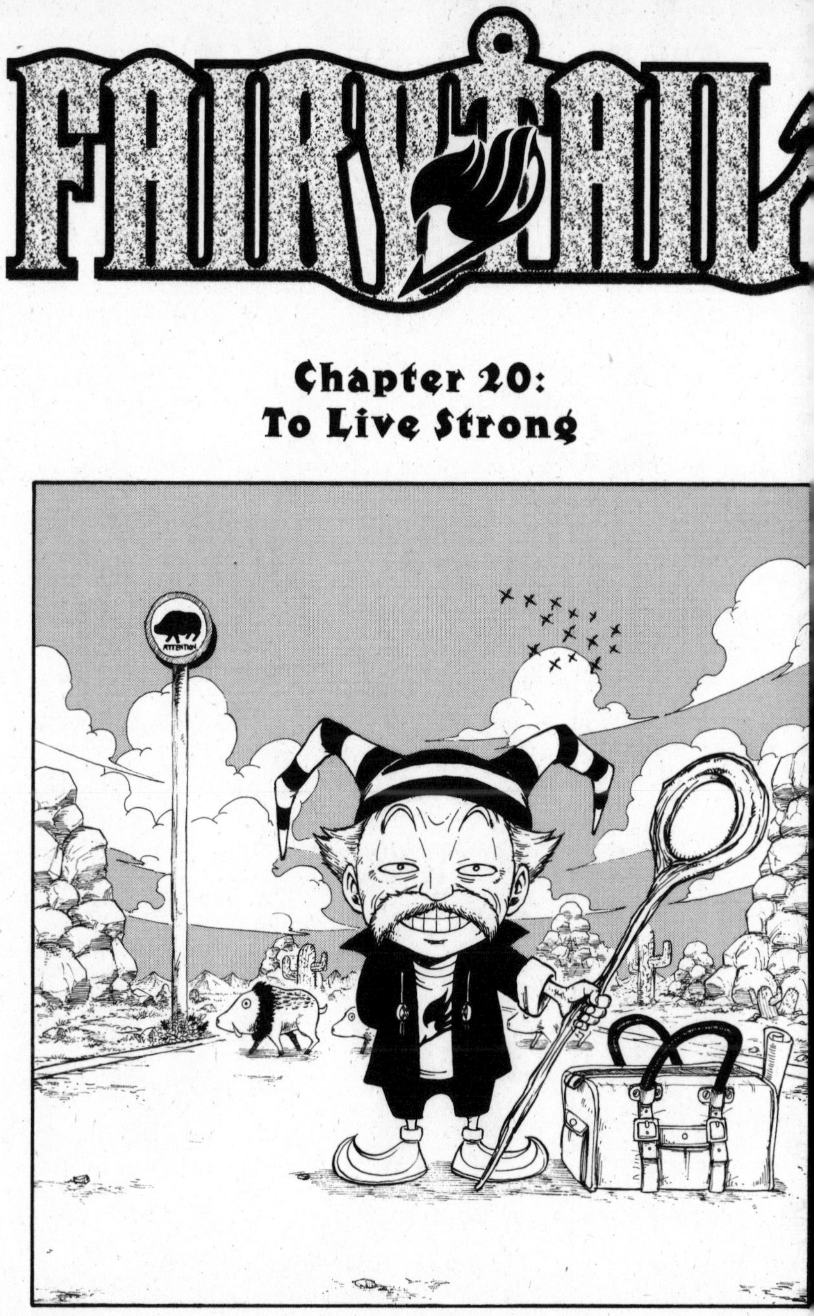
ATTENTION

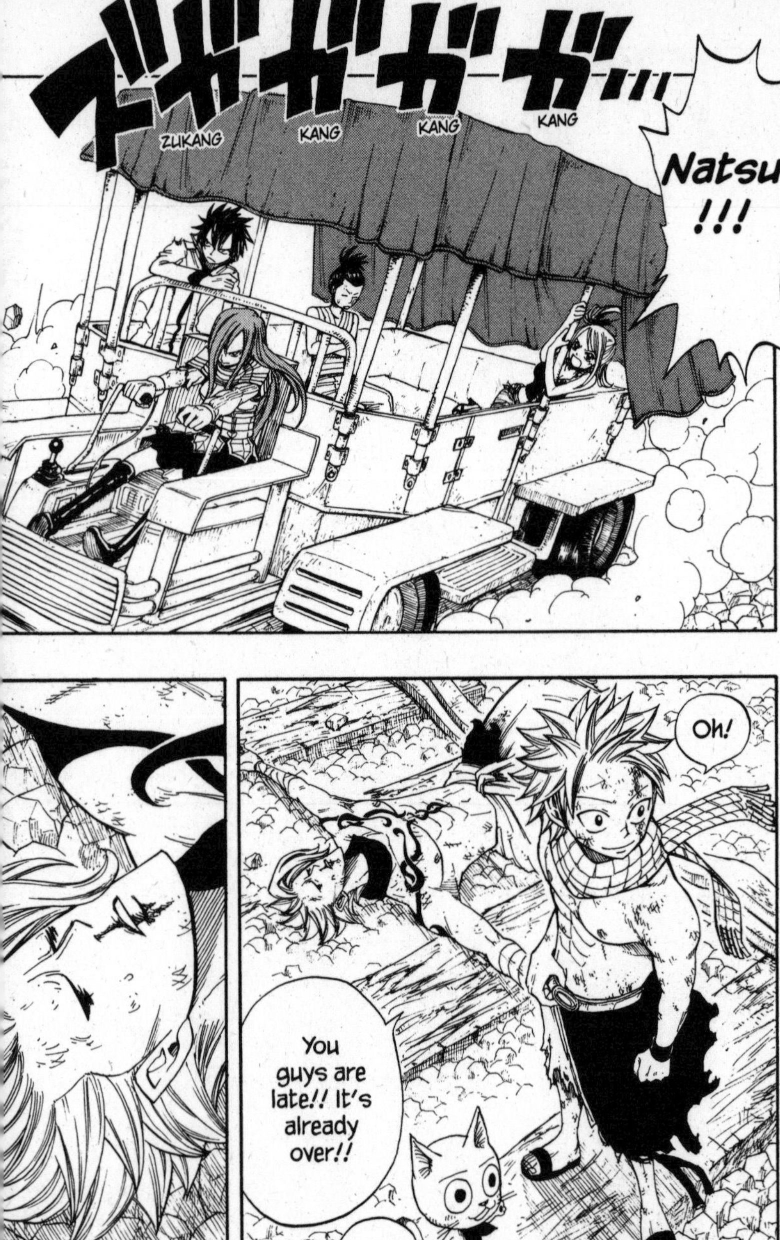
Natsu!!!
ズガガガガ…
ZUKANG KANG KANG KANG
Oh!
You guys are late!! It's already over!!
Aye!

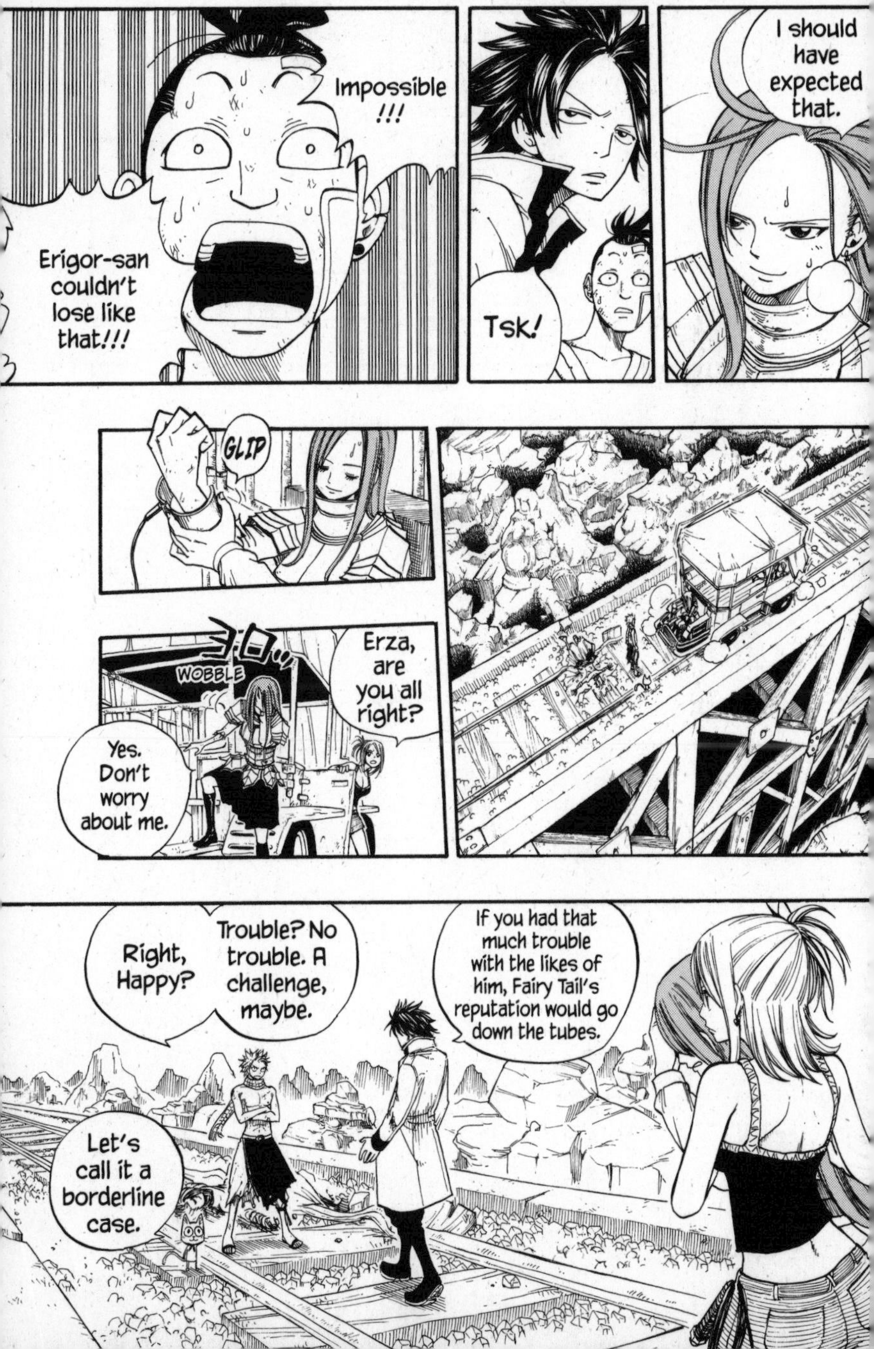
I should have expected that.
Tsk!
Impossible!!!
Erigor-san couldn't lose like that!!!
GLIP
Erza, are you all right?
WOBBLE
Yes. Don't worry about me.
If you had that much trouble with the likes of him, Fairy Tail's reputation would go down the tubes.
Trouble? No trouble. A challenge, maybe.
Right, Happy?
Let's call it a borderline case.

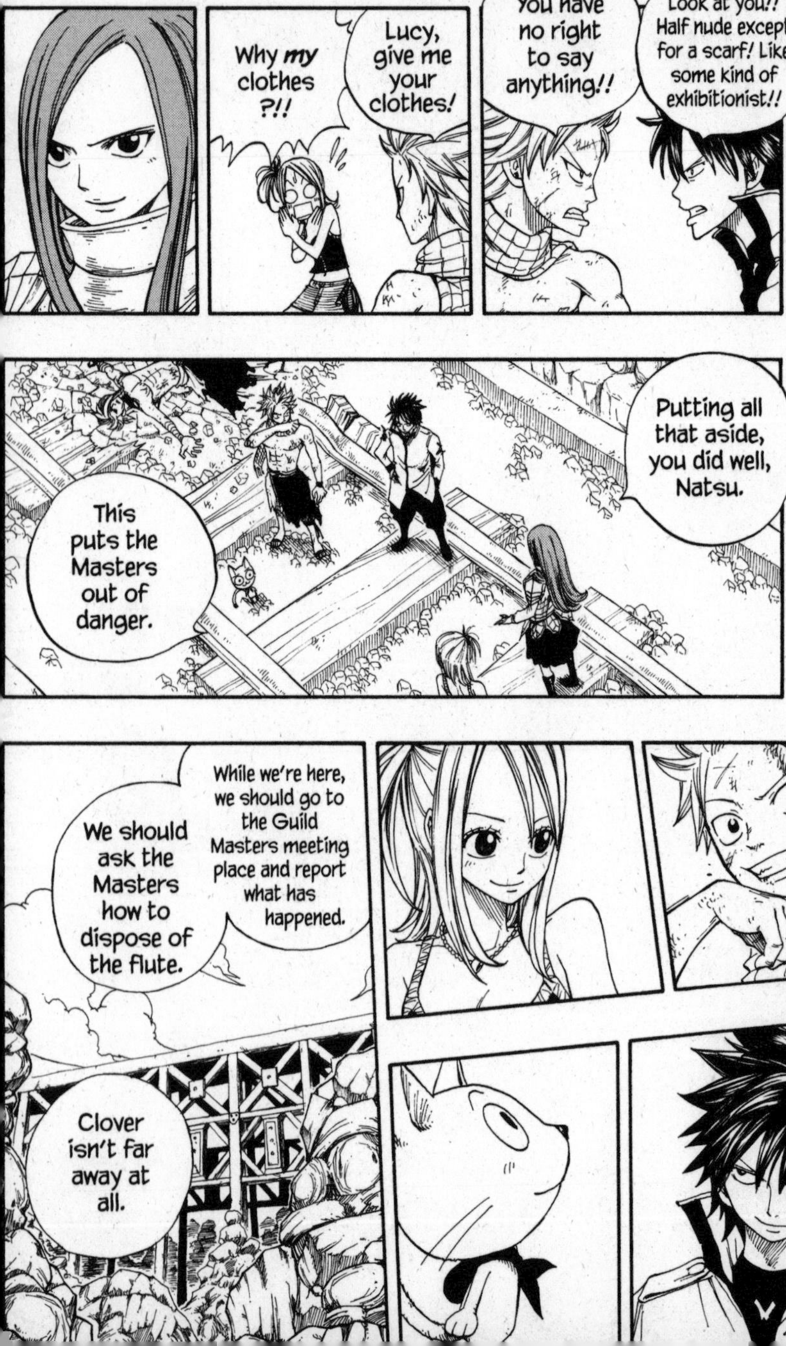

Look at you!! Half nude except for a scarf! Like some kind of exhibitionist!!
You have no right to say anything!!
Lucy, give me your clothes!
Why *my* clothes?!!
Putting all that aside, you did well, Natsu.
This puts the Masters out of danger.
While we're here, we should go to the Guild Masters meeting place and report what has happened.
We should ask the Masters how to dispose of the flute.
Clover isn't far away at all.

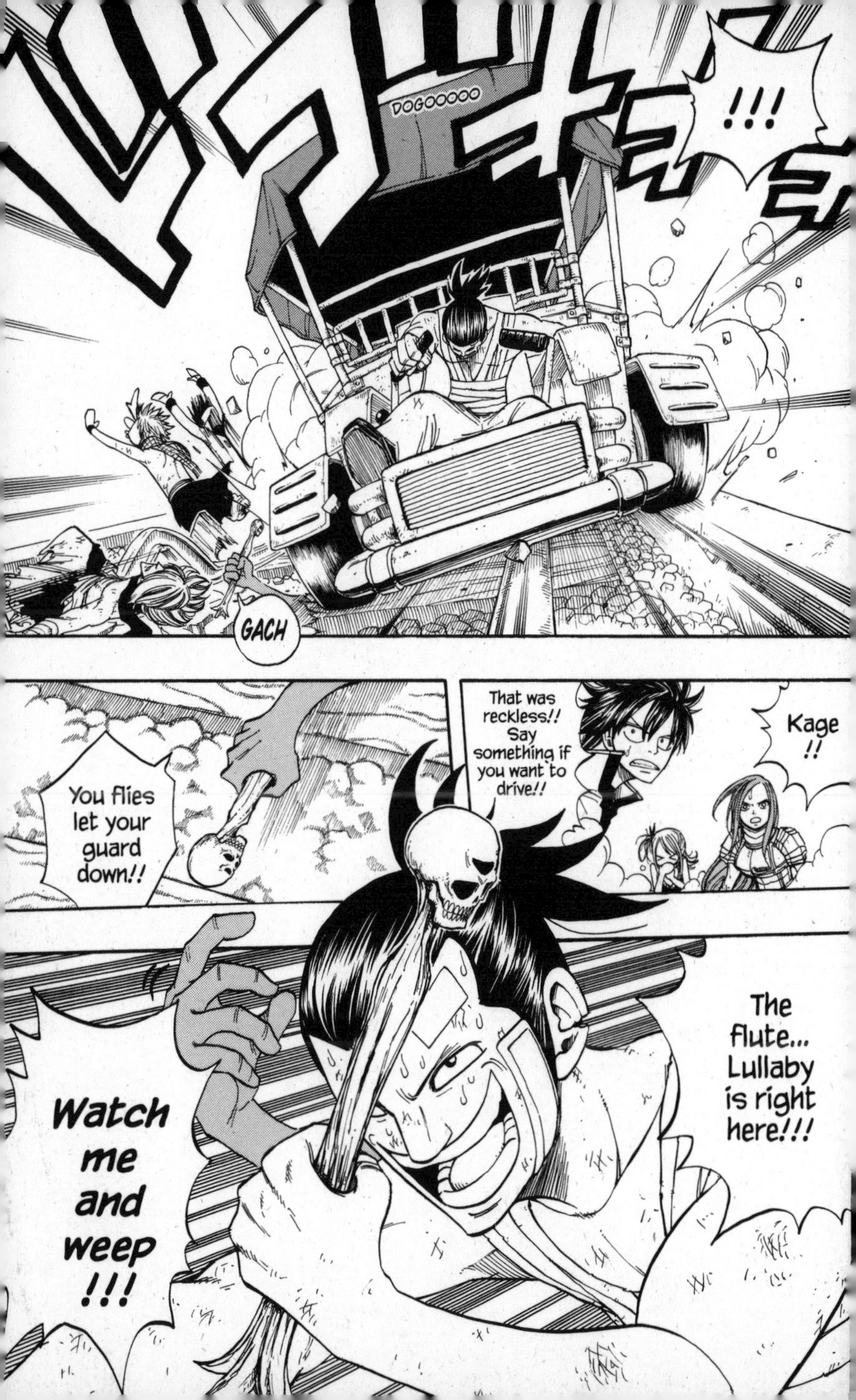
!!!
DOGOOOOO
GACH
Kage !!
That was reckless!! Say something if you want to drive!!
You flies let your guard down!!
The flute... Lullaby is right here!!!
Watch me and weep!!!

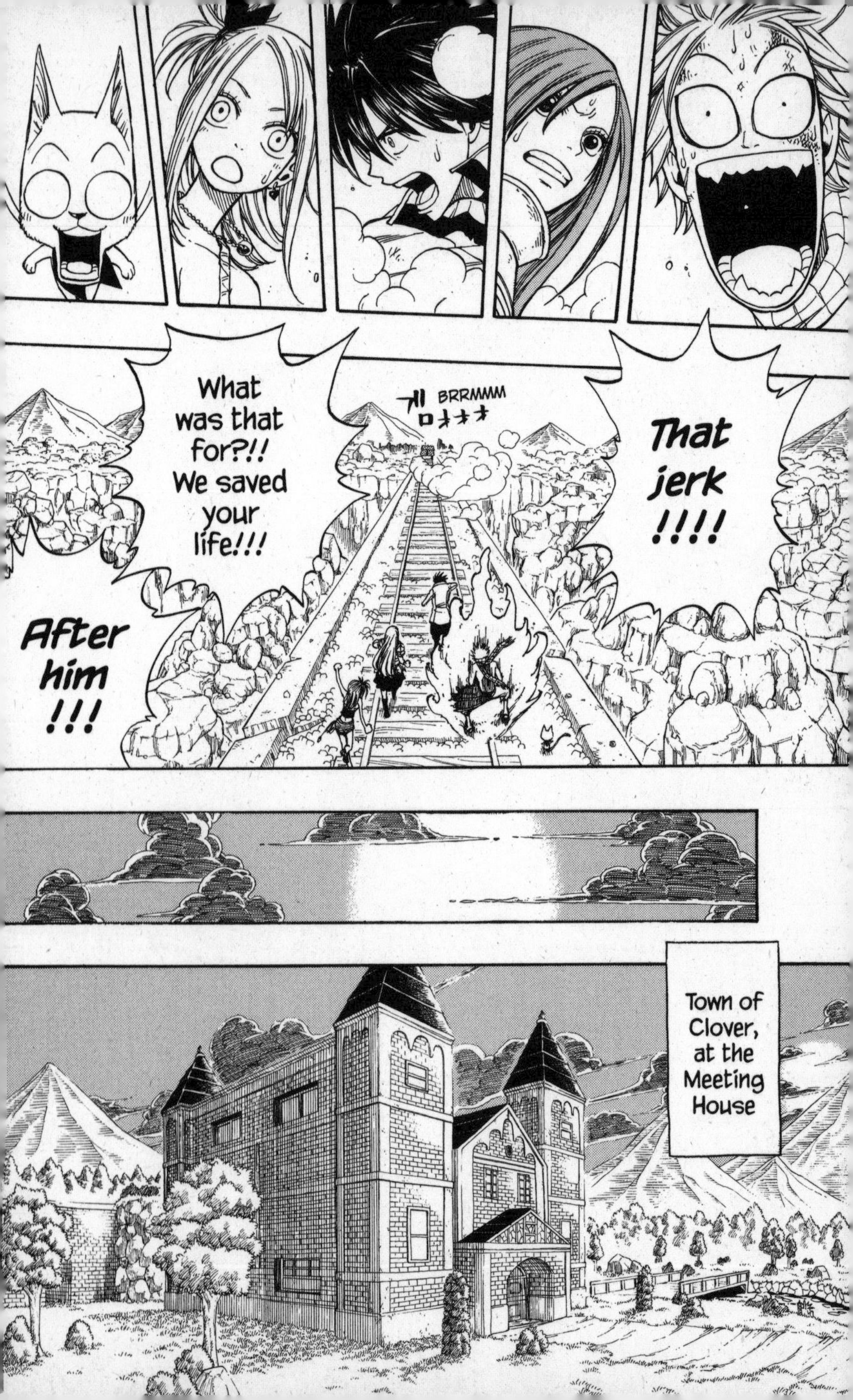
That jerk !!!!
BRRMMM
What was that for?!! We saved your life!!!
After him !!!
Town of Clover, at the Meeting House

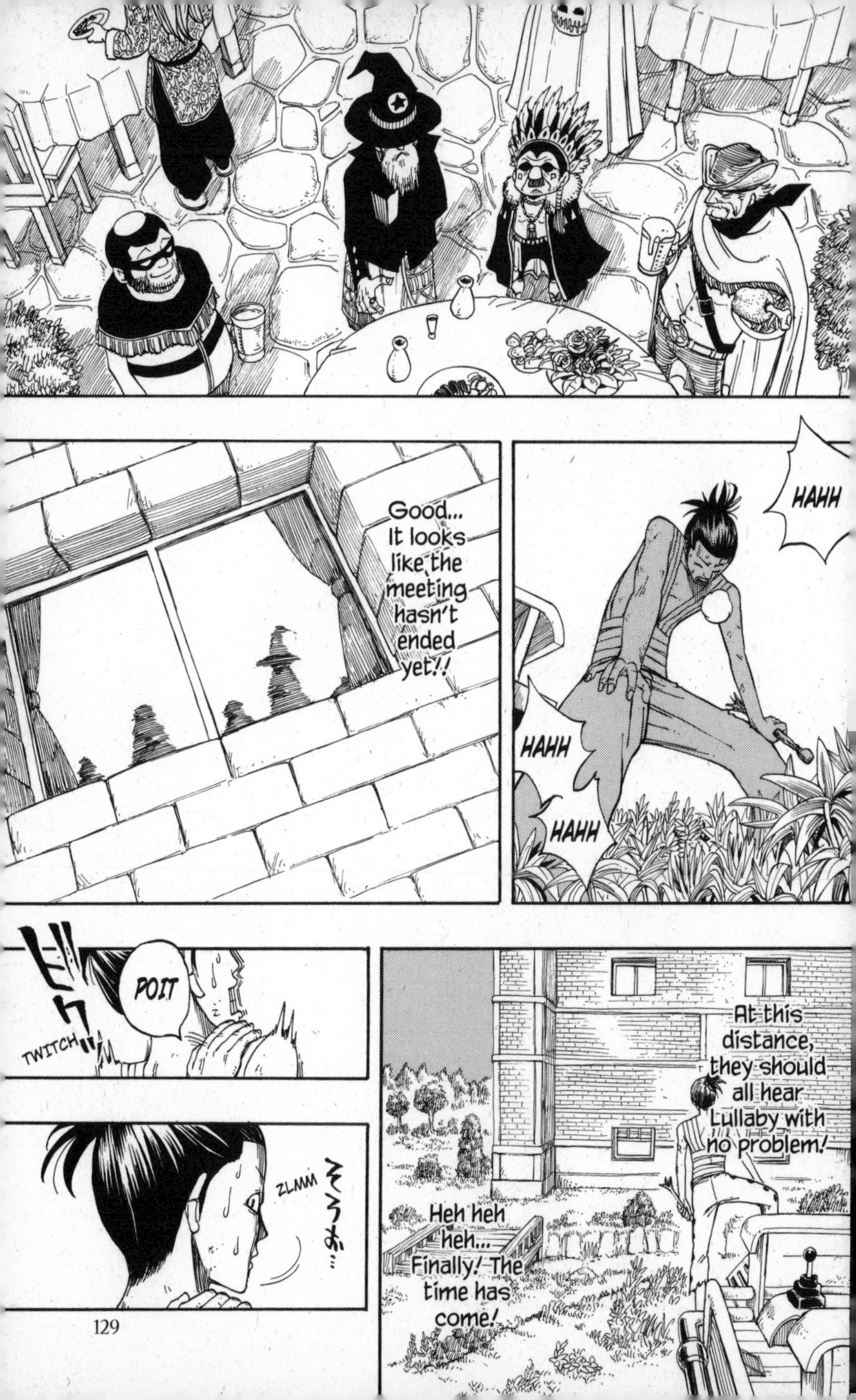
HAHH
HAHH
HAHH
Good... It looks like the meeting hasn't ended yet!!
At this distance, they should all hear Lullaby with no problem!
Heh heh heh... Finally! The time has come!
POIT
TWITCH
ZLMM

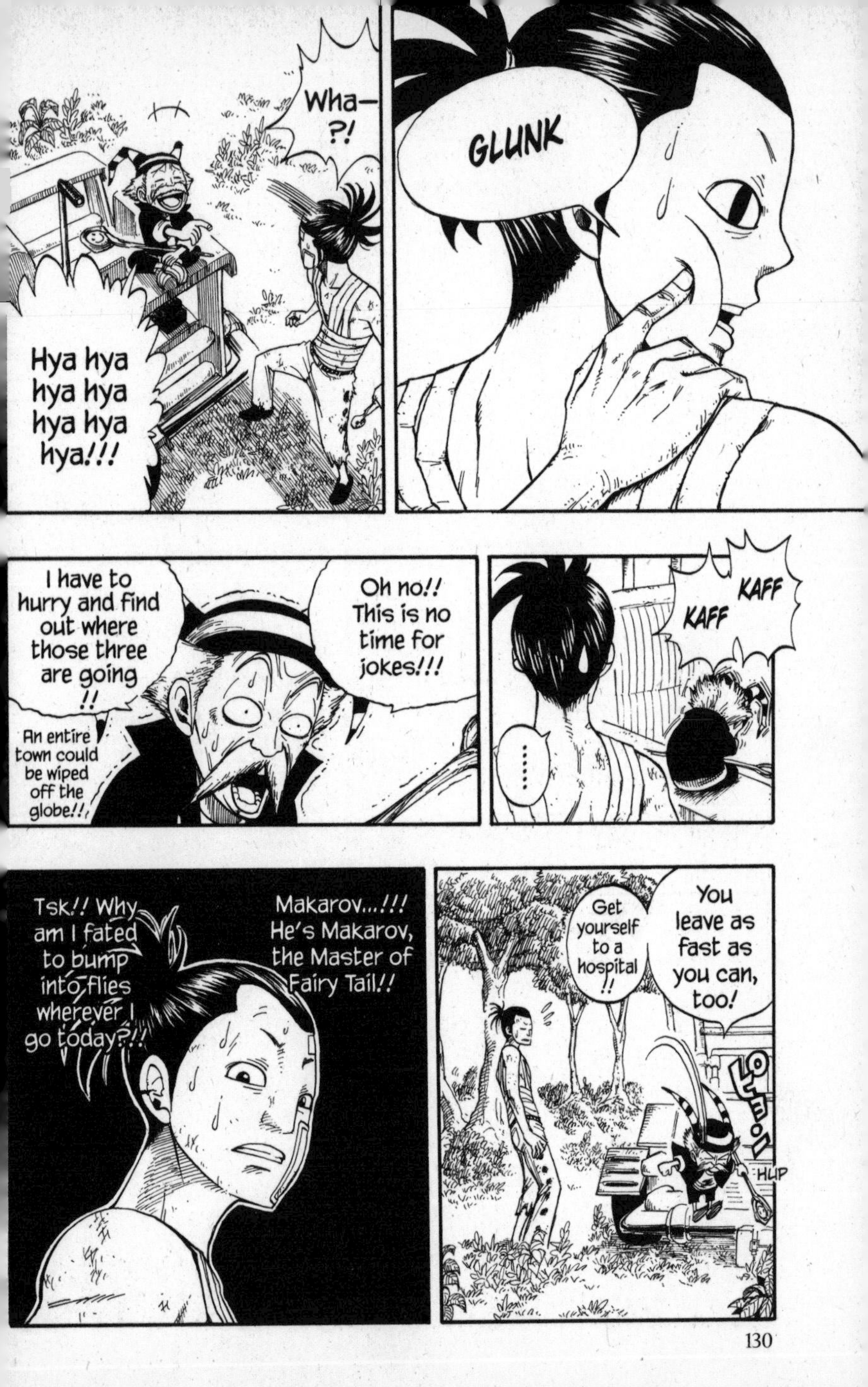
GLUNK
Wha—?!
Hya hya hya hya hya hya hya!!!
KAFF
KAFF
......
Oh no!! This is no time for jokes!!!
I have to hurry and find out where those three are going!!
An entire town could be wiped off the globe!!
You leave as fast as you can, too!
Get yourself to a hospital!!
HUP
Makarov...!!! He's Makarov, the Master of Fairy Tail!!
Tsk!! Why am I fated to bump into flies wherever I go today?!!

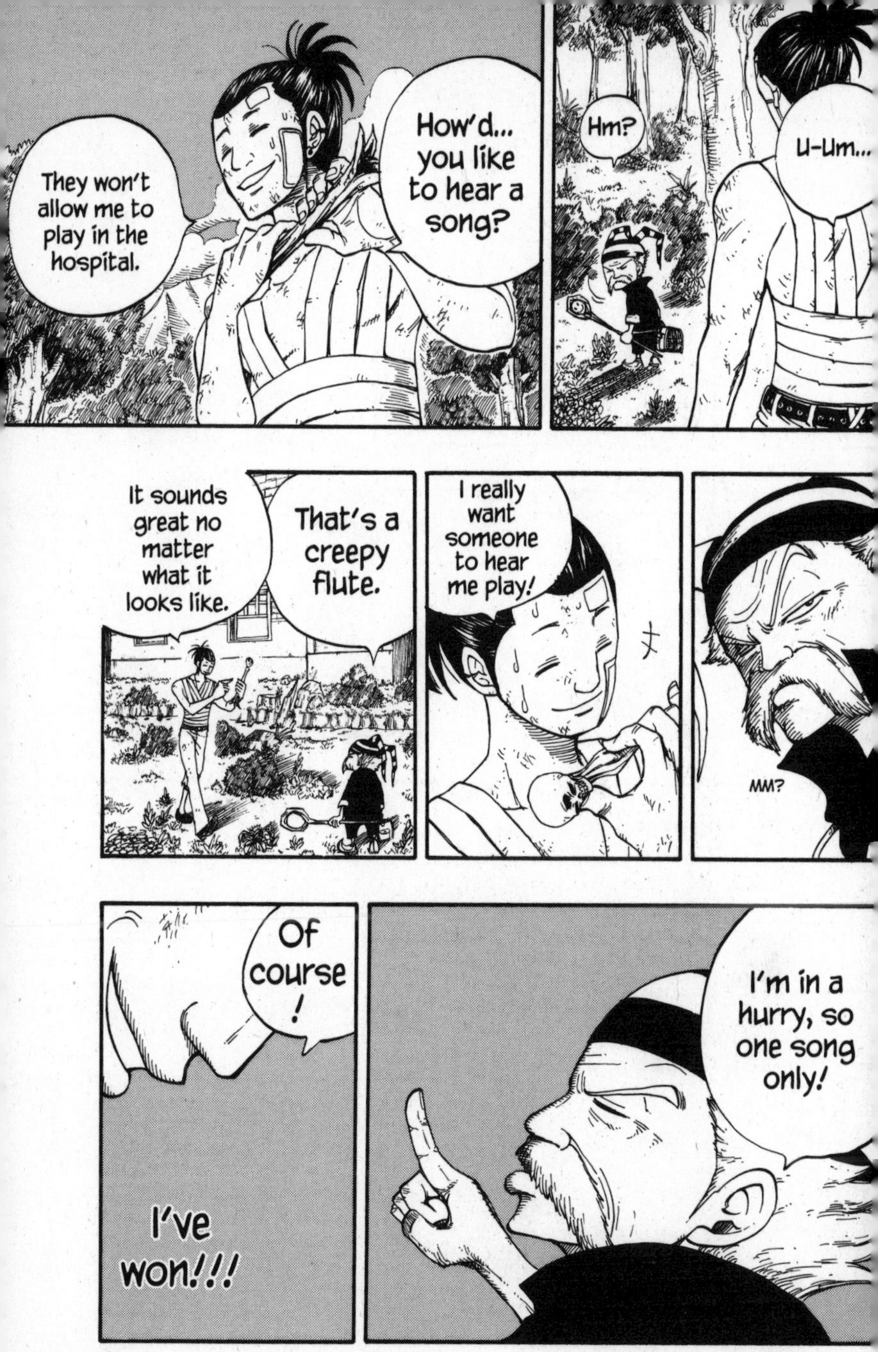
U-um...
Hm?
How'd... you like to hear a song?
They won't allow me to play in the hospital.
MM?
I really want someone to hear me play!
That's a creepy flute.
It sounds great no matter what it looks like.
I'm in a hurry, so one song only!
Of course!
I've won!!!

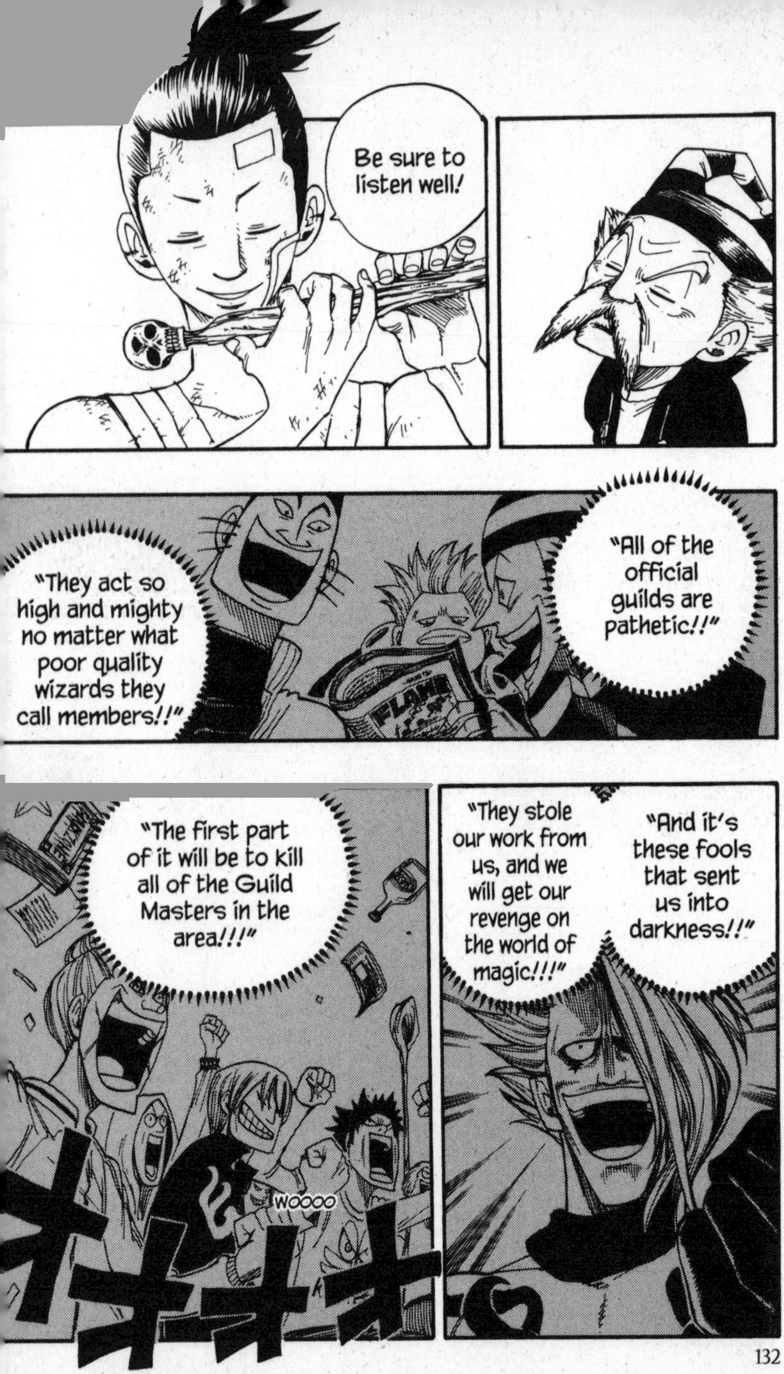
Be sure to listen well!
"All of the official guilds are pathetic!!"
"They act so high and mighty no matter what poor quality wizards they call members!!"
"And it's these fools that sent us into darkness!!"
"They stole our work from us, and we will get our revenge on the world of magic!!!"
"The first part of it will be to kill all of the Guild Masters in the area!!!"
WOOOO

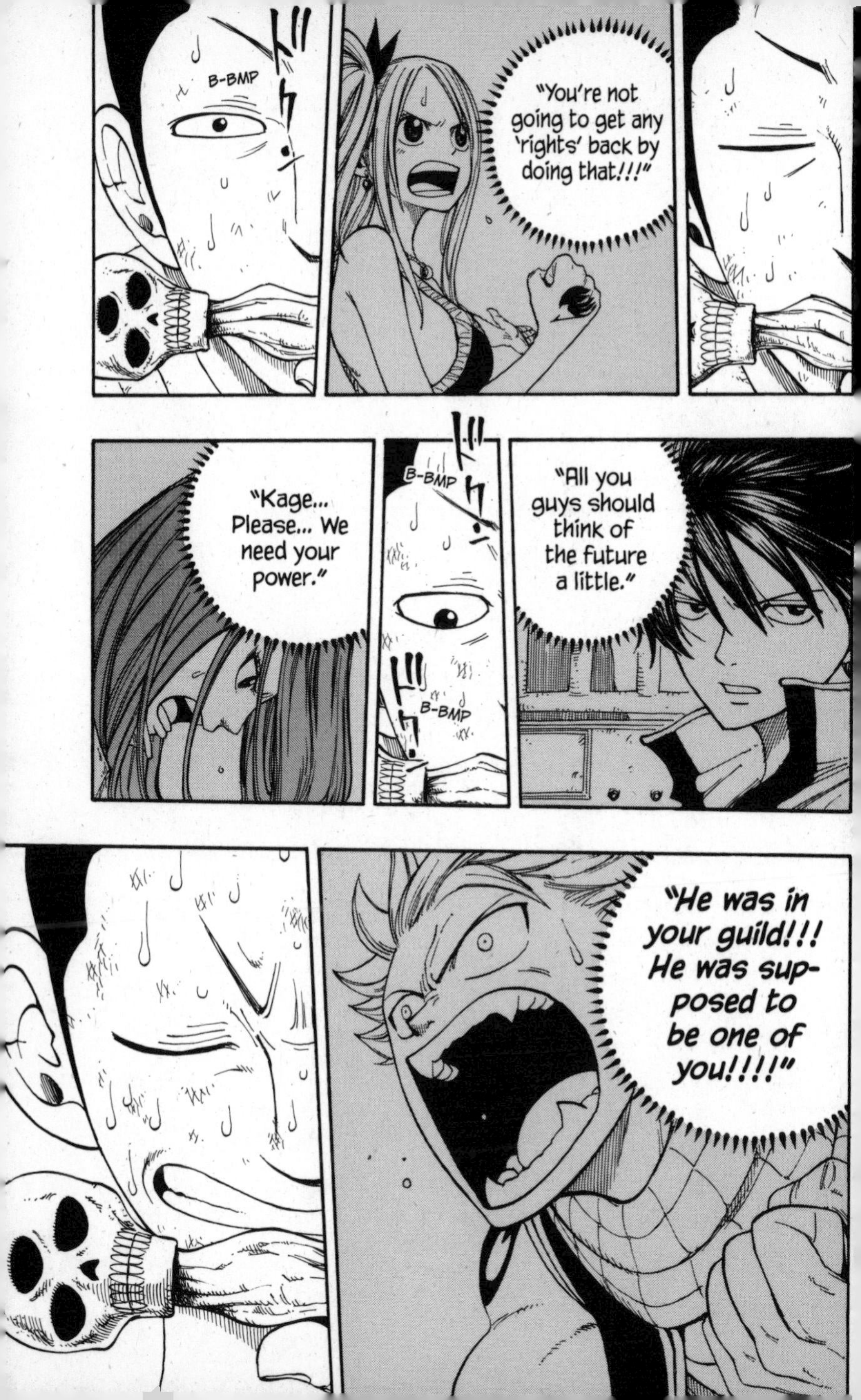
"You're not going to get any 'rights' back by doing that!!!"
B-BMP
"All you guys should think of the future a little."
B-BMP
B-BMP
"Kage... Please... We need your power."
"He was in your guild!!! He was supposed to be one of you!!!!"

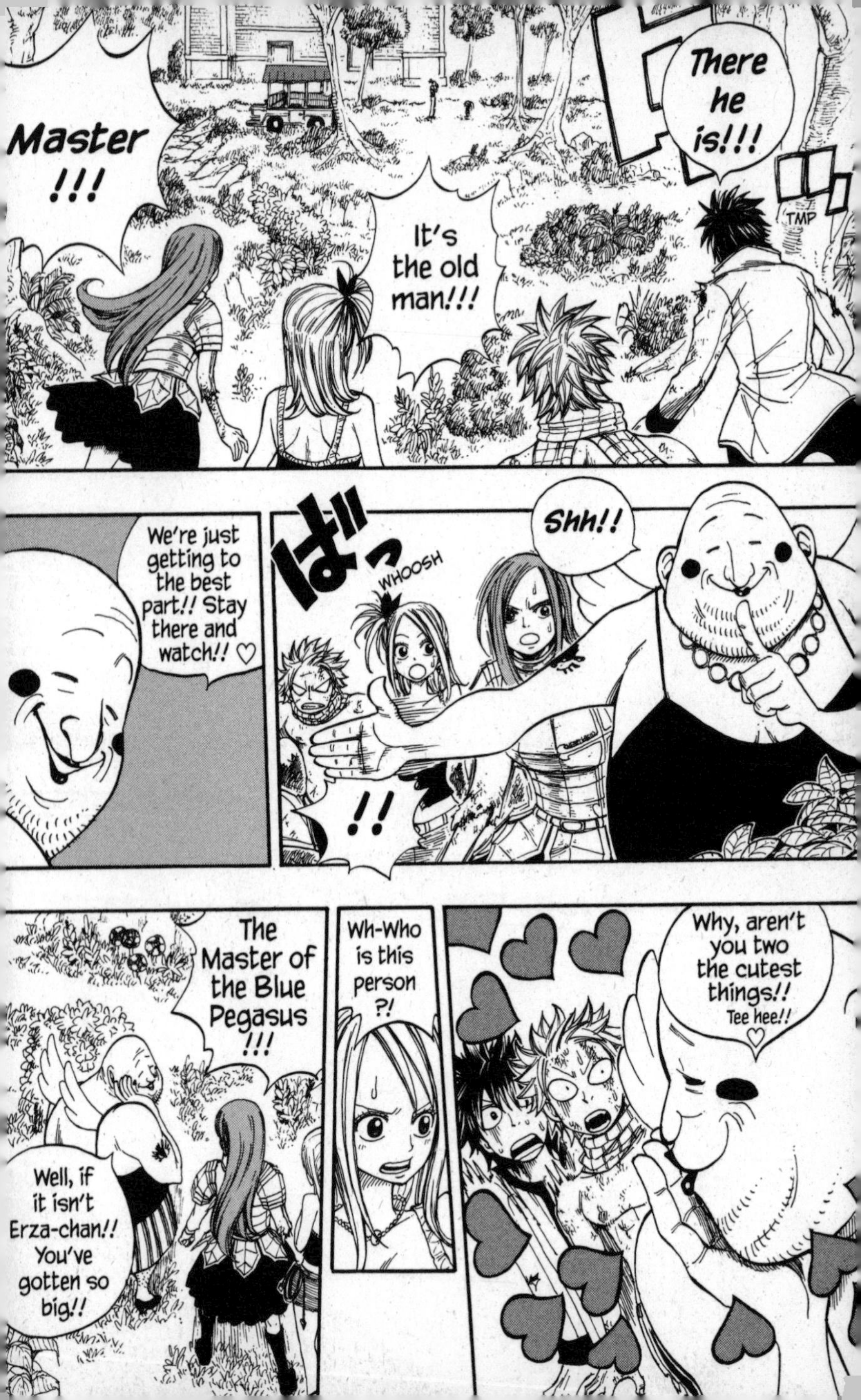
There he is!!!
TMP
It's the old man!!!
Master!!!
Shh!!
ばっ
WHOOSH
!!
We're just getting to the best part!! Stay there and watch!! ♡
Why, aren't you two the cutest things!! Tee hee!! ♡
Wh-Who is this person?!
The Master of the Blue Pegasus!!!
Well, if it isn't Erza-chan!! You've gotten so big!!

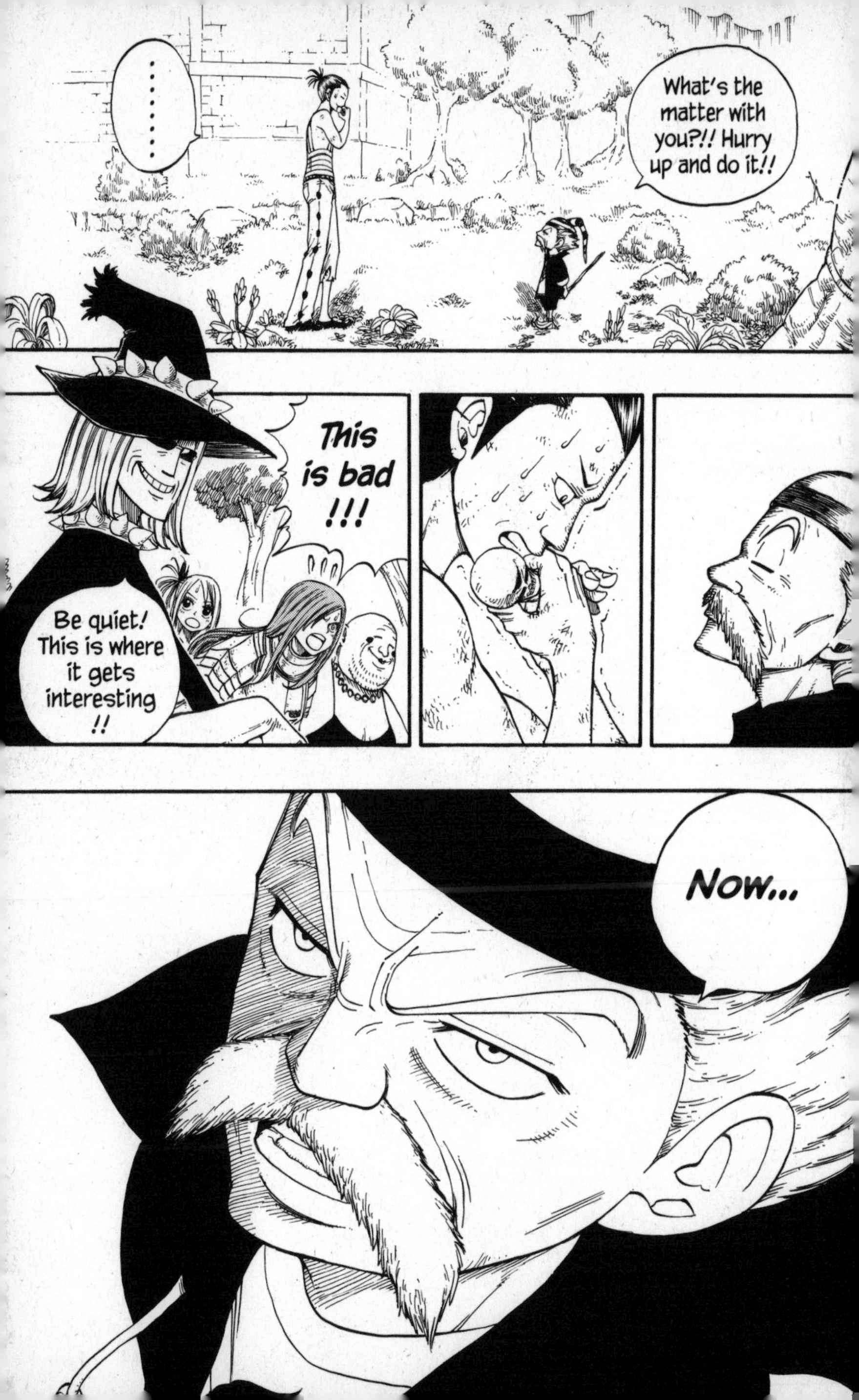
What's the matter with you?!! Hurry up and do it!!
......
This is bad!!!
Be quiet! This is where it gets interesting!!
Now...

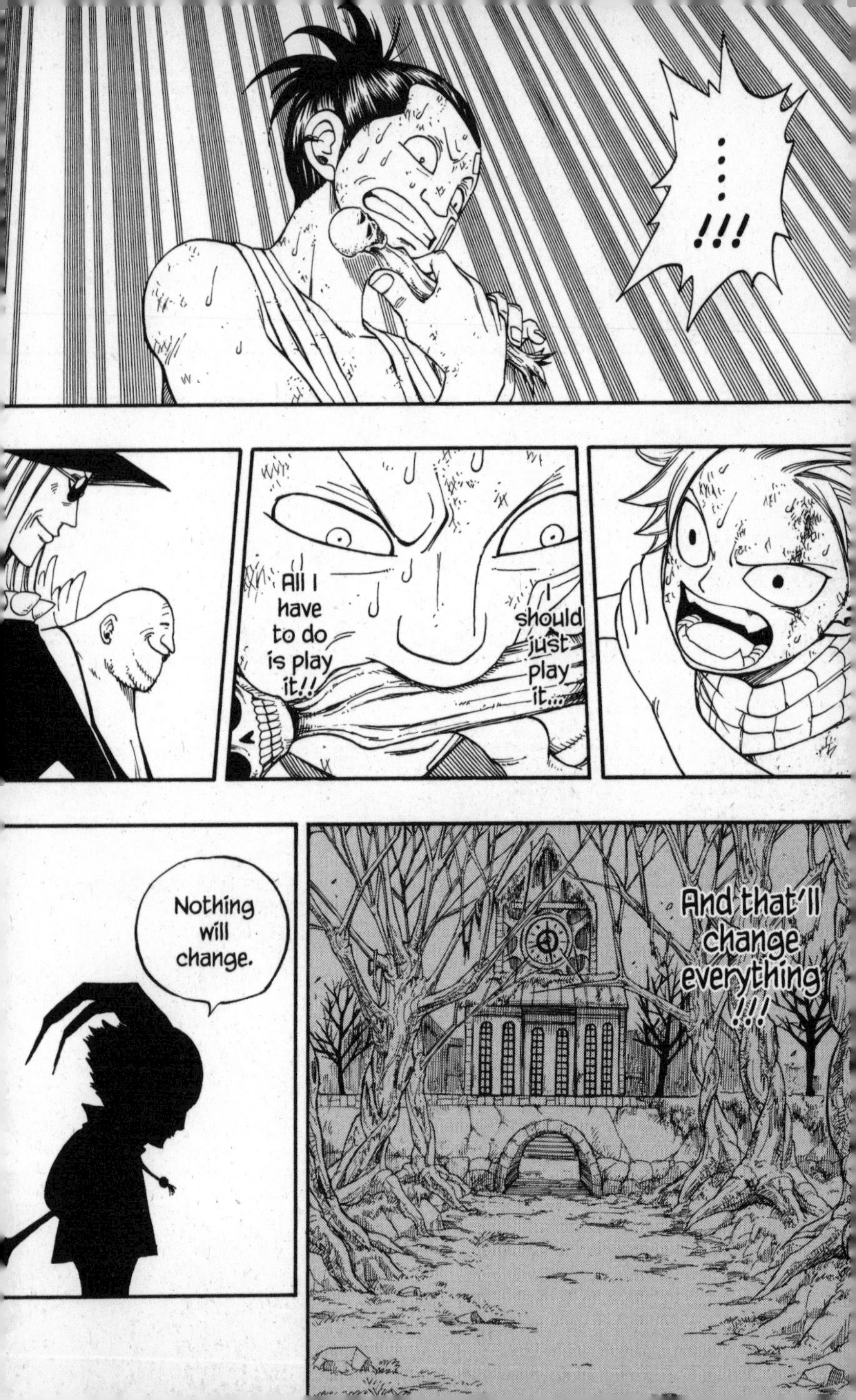
……!!!
I should just play it...
All I have to do is play it!!
And that'll change everything!!!
Nothing will change.

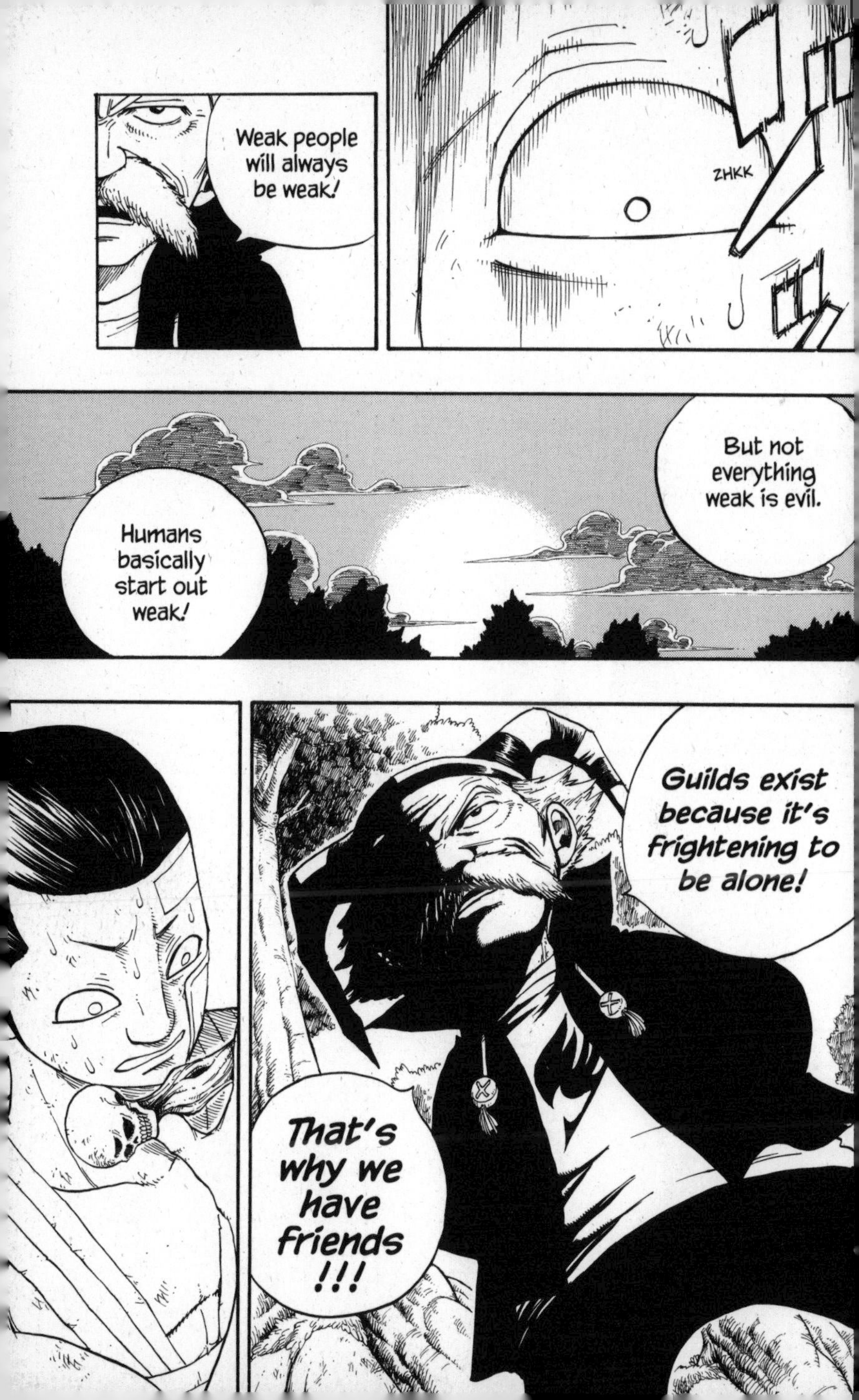
ZHKK
Weak people will always be weak!
But not everything weak is evil.
Humans basically start out weak!
Guilds exist because it's frightening to be alone!
That's why we have friends!!!

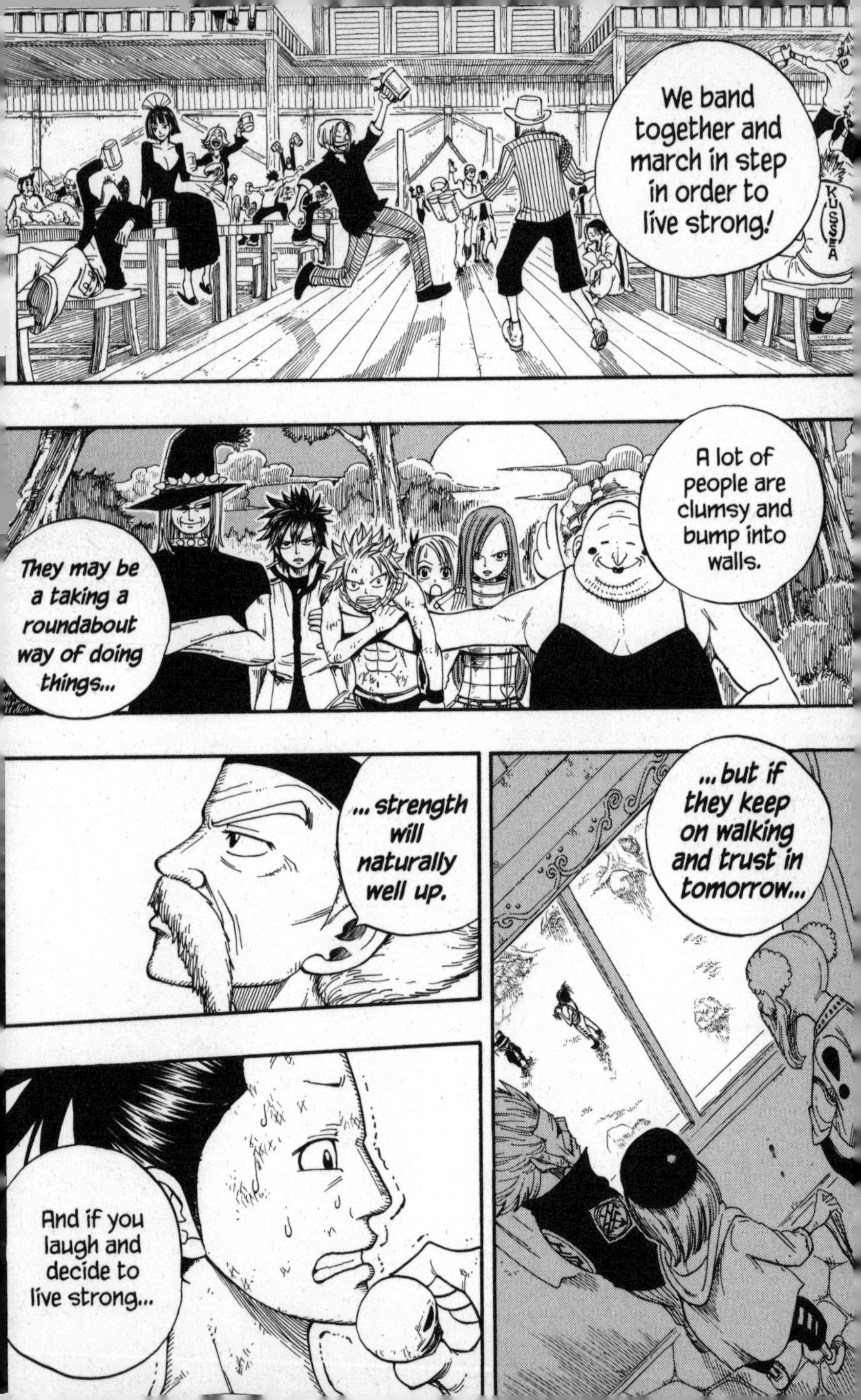

We band together and march in step in order to live strong!
KUSSEA
A lot of people are clumsy and bump into walls.
They may be a taking a roundabout way of doing things...
...but if they keep on walking and trust in tomorrow...
...strength will naturally well up.
And if you laugh and decide to live strong...

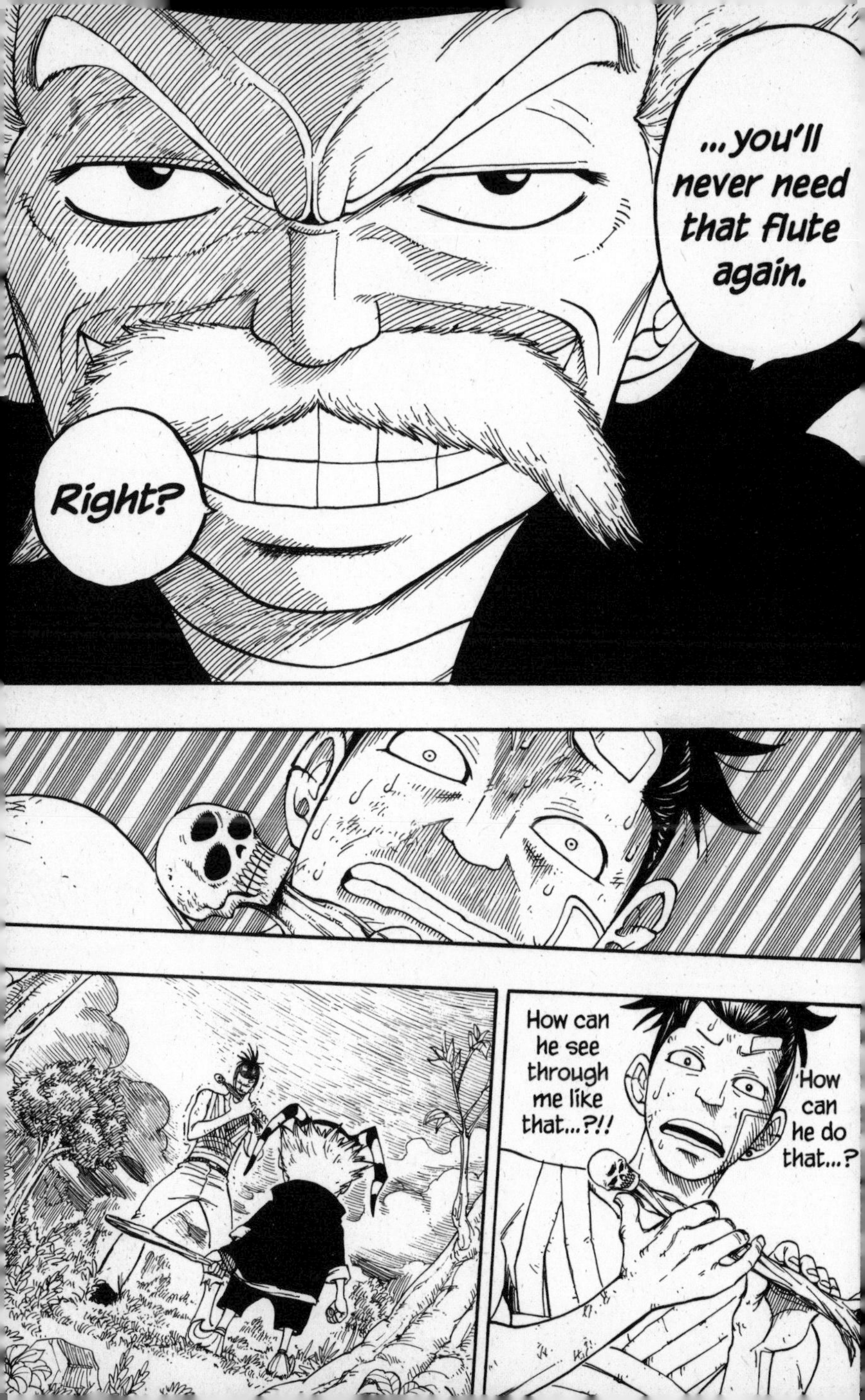
...you'll never need that flute again.
Right?
How can he do that...?
How can he see through me like that...?!!

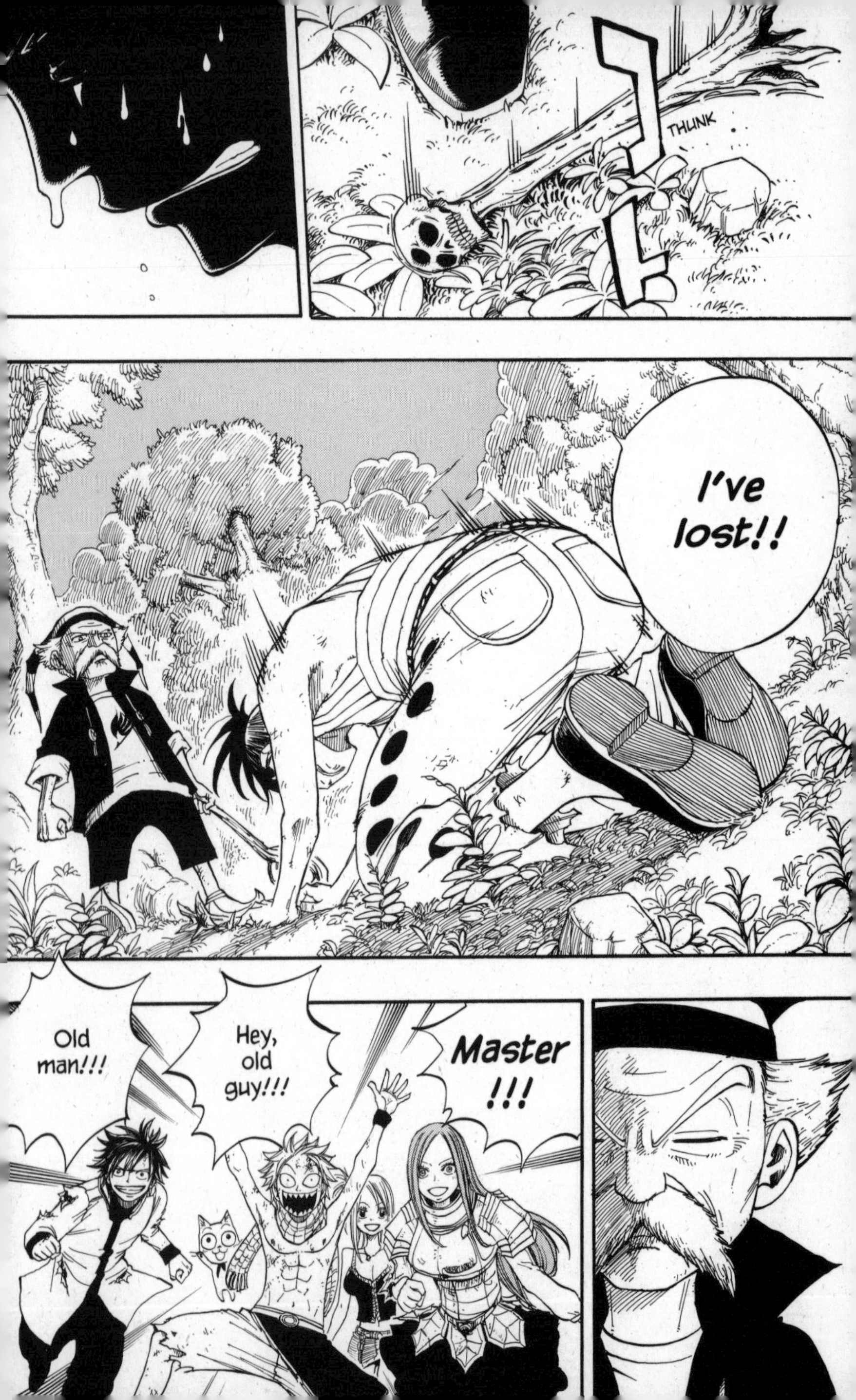
THUNK
I've lost!!
Master !!!
Hey, old guy!!!
Old man!!!

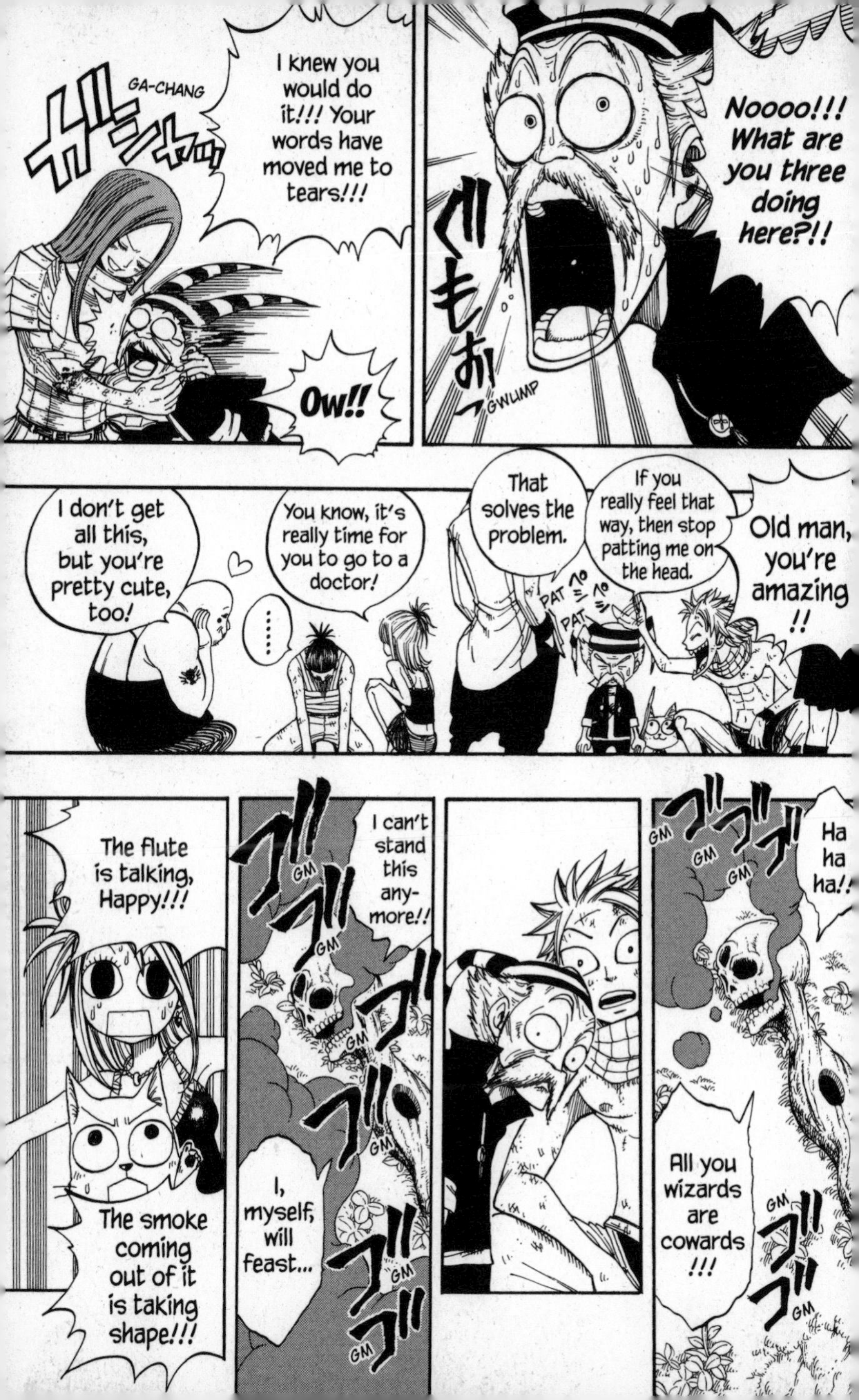
Noooo!!! What are you three doing here?!!
GWUMP
GA-CHANG
I knew you would do it!!! Your words have moved me to tears!!!
Ow!!
Old man, you're amazing!!
If you really feel that way, then stop patting me on the head.
PAT PAT
That solves the problem.
You know, it's really time for you to go to a doctor!
......
I don't get all this, but you're pretty cute, too!
Ha ha ha!!
GM GM GM
All you wizards are cowards!!!
GM GM
I can't stand this any-more!!
GM GM GM
I, myself, will feast...
GM GM
The flute is talking, Happy!!!
The smoke coming out of it is taking shape!!!

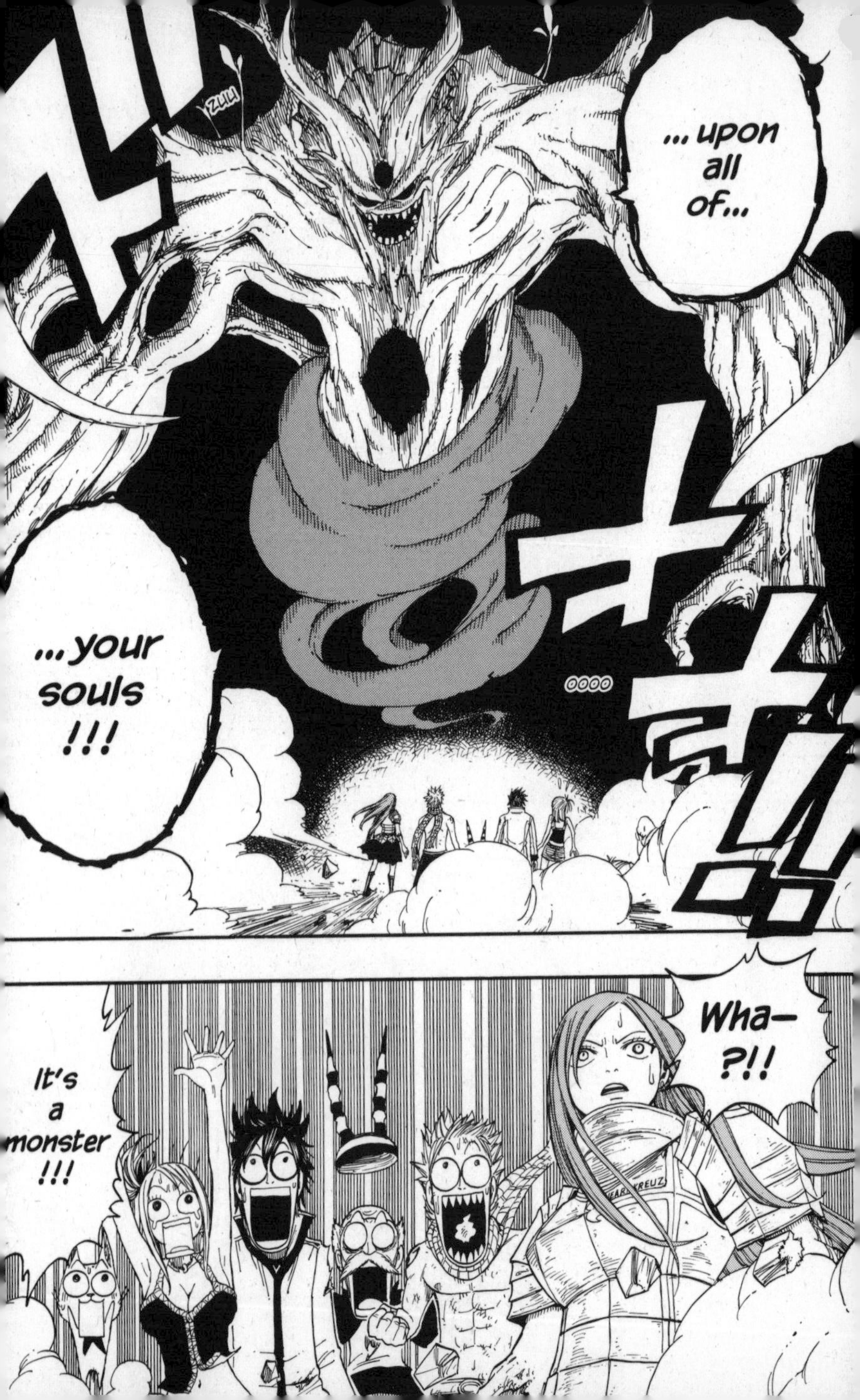

...upon all of...
zuu
...your souls!!!
oooo
Wha-?!!
It's a monster!!!

FAIRY TAIL

Chapter 21: The Most Powerful Team!!!

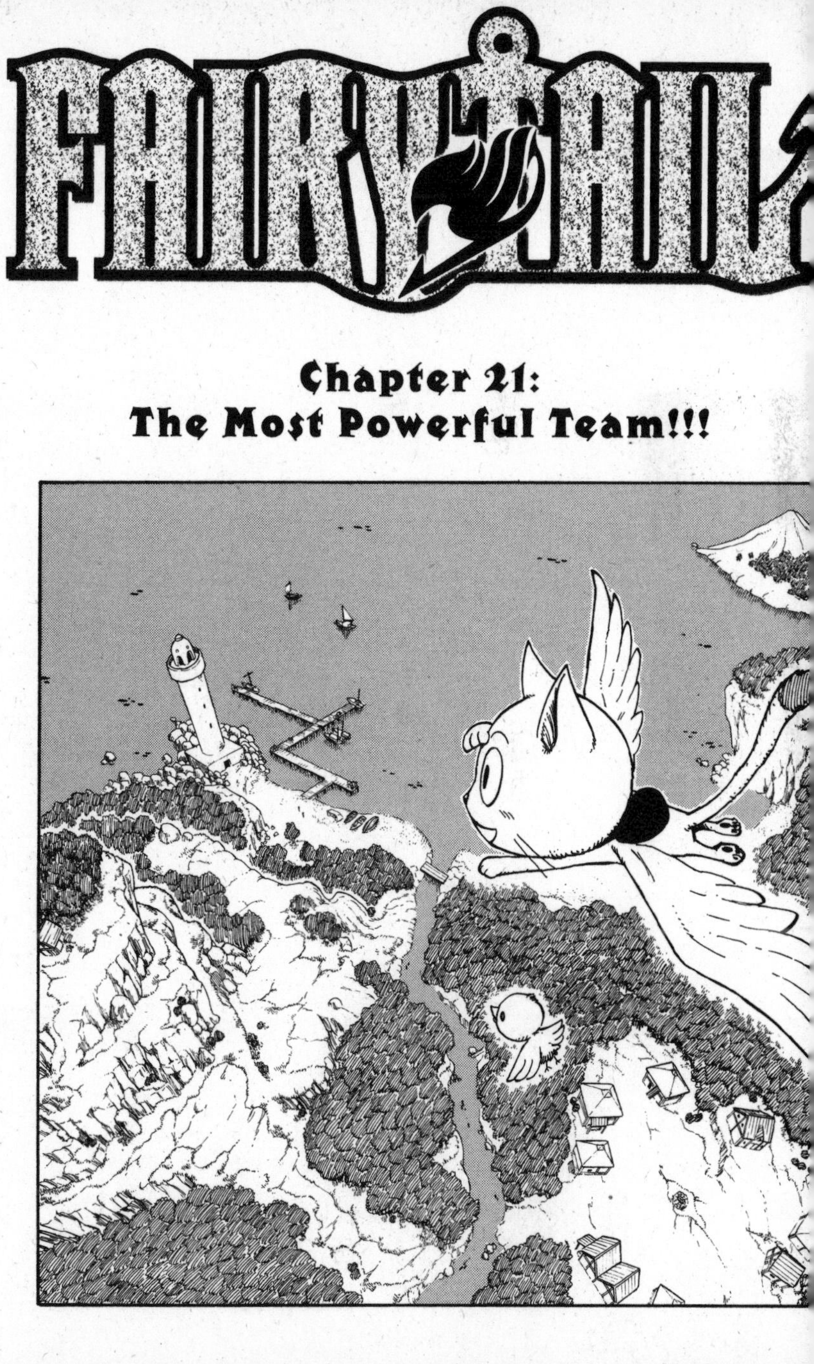

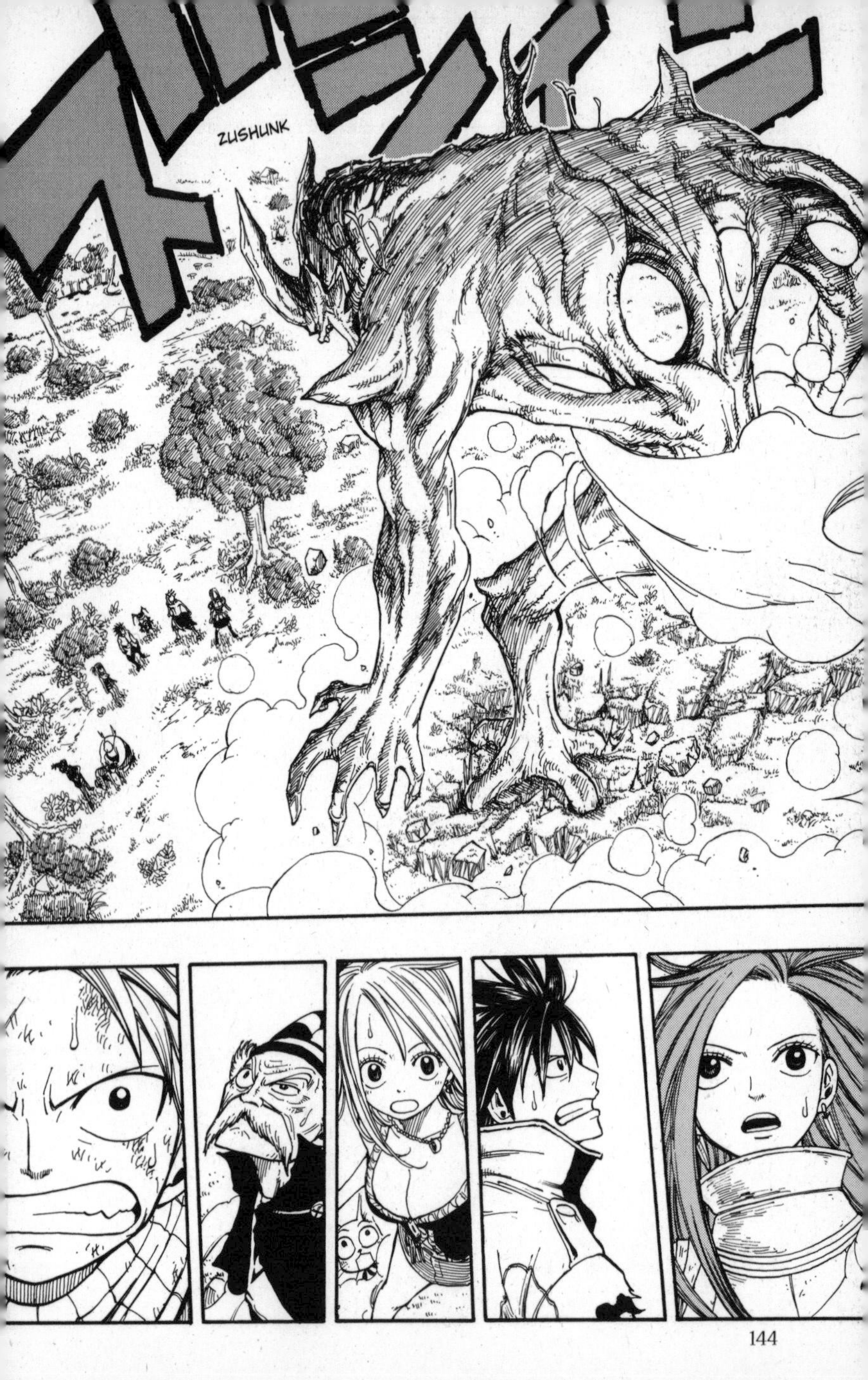
ZUSHUNK

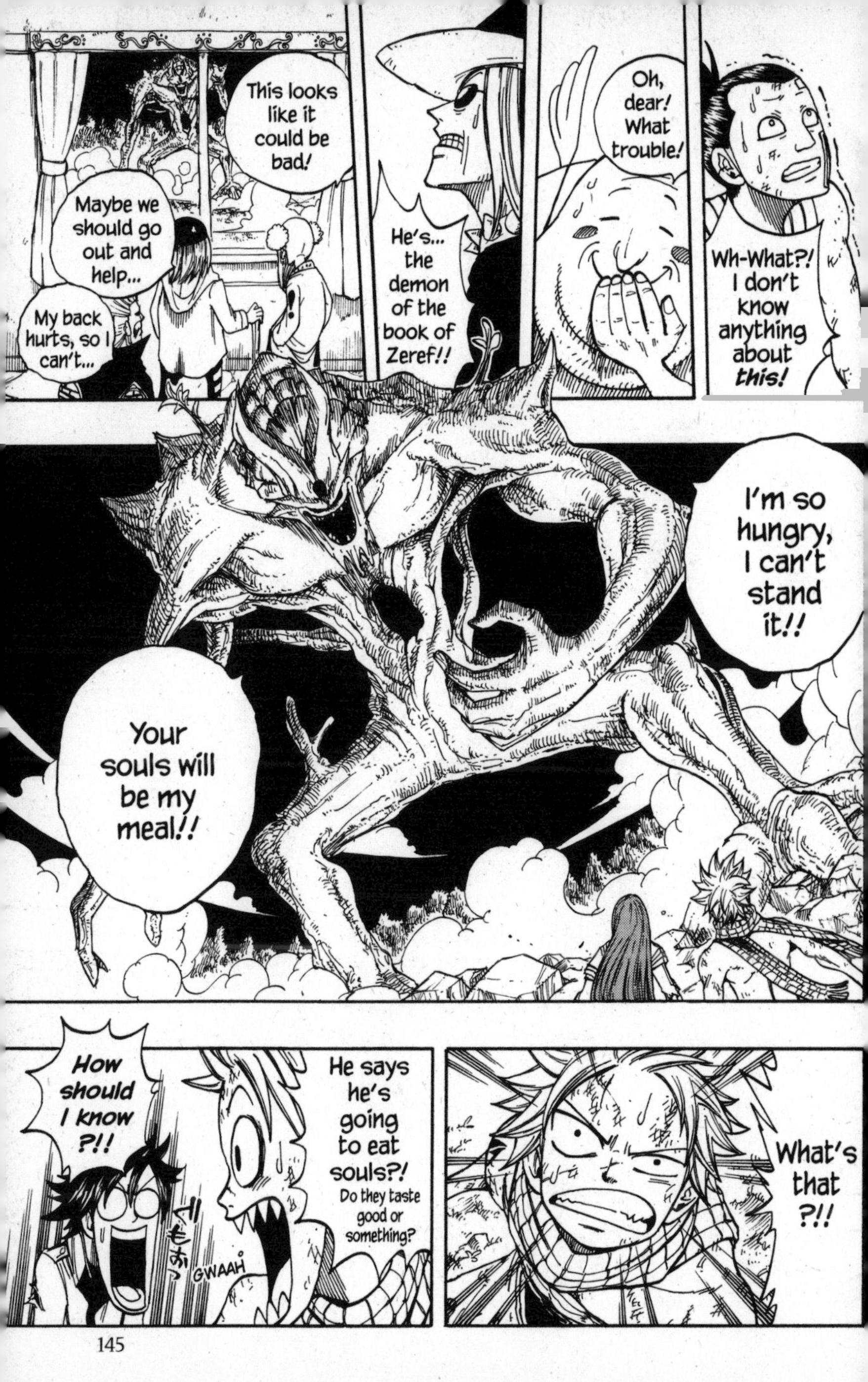
Wh-What?! I don't know anything about this!
Oh, dear! What trouble!
He's... the demon of the book of Zeref!!
This looks like it could be bad!
Maybe we should go out and help...
My back hurts, so I can't...
I'm so hungry, I can't stand it!!
Your souls will be my meal!!
What's that ?!!
He says he's going to eat souls?!
Do they taste good or something?
How should I know ?!!
GWAAH

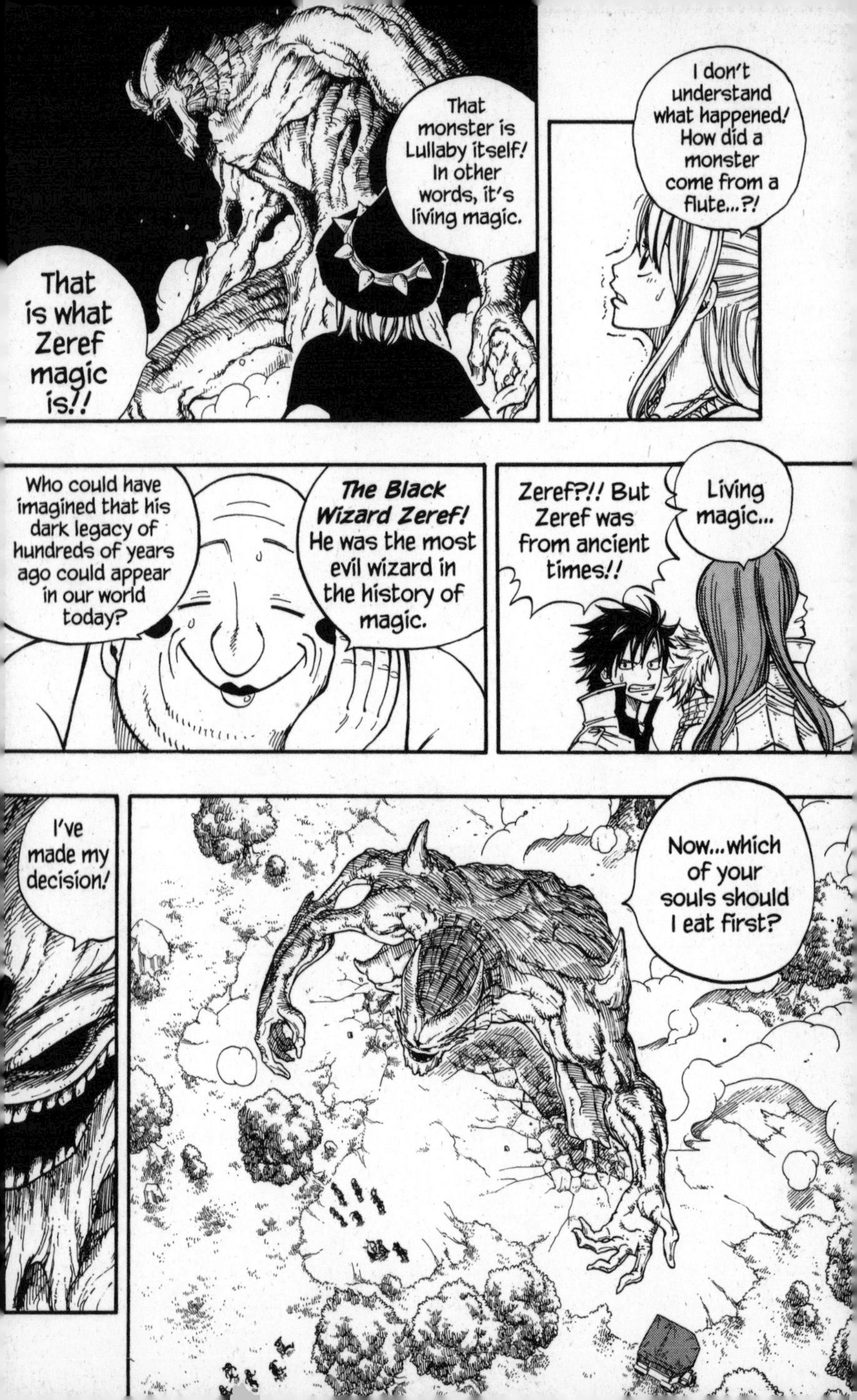
I don't understand what happened! How did a monster come from a flute...?!
That monster is Lullaby itself! In other words, it's living magic.
That is what Zeref magic is!!
Living magic...
Zeref?!! But Zeref was from ancient times!!
The Black Wizard Zeref! He was the most evil wizard in the history of magic.
Who could have imagined that his dark legacy of hundreds of years ago could appear in our world today?
Now...which of your souls should I eat first?
I've made my decision!

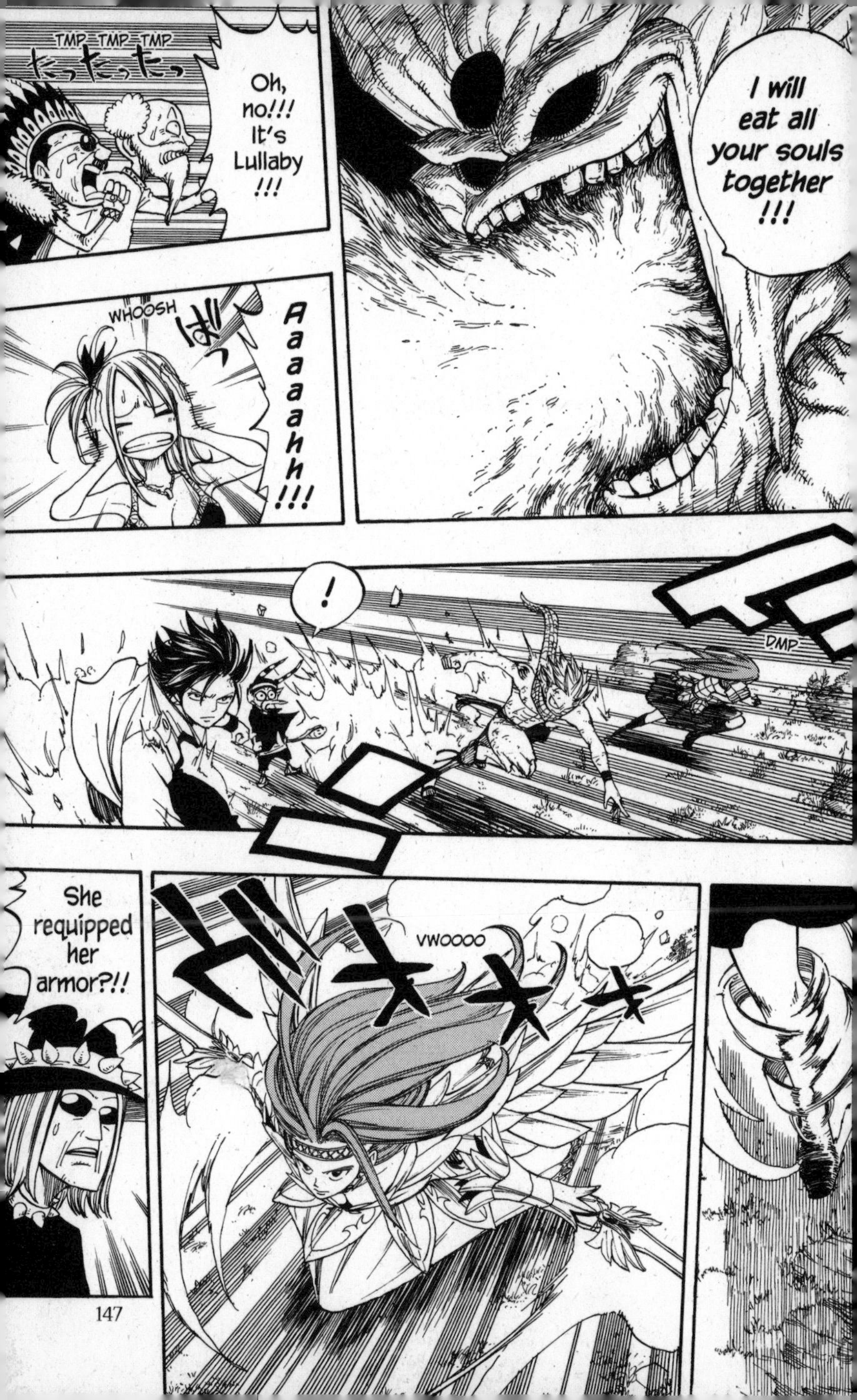
I will eat all your souls together!!!
TMP TMP TMP
たっ たっ たっ
Oh, no!!! It's Lullaby!!!
WHOOSH
ばっ
Aaaaaahh!!!
!
DMP
VWOOOO
She requipped her armor?!!

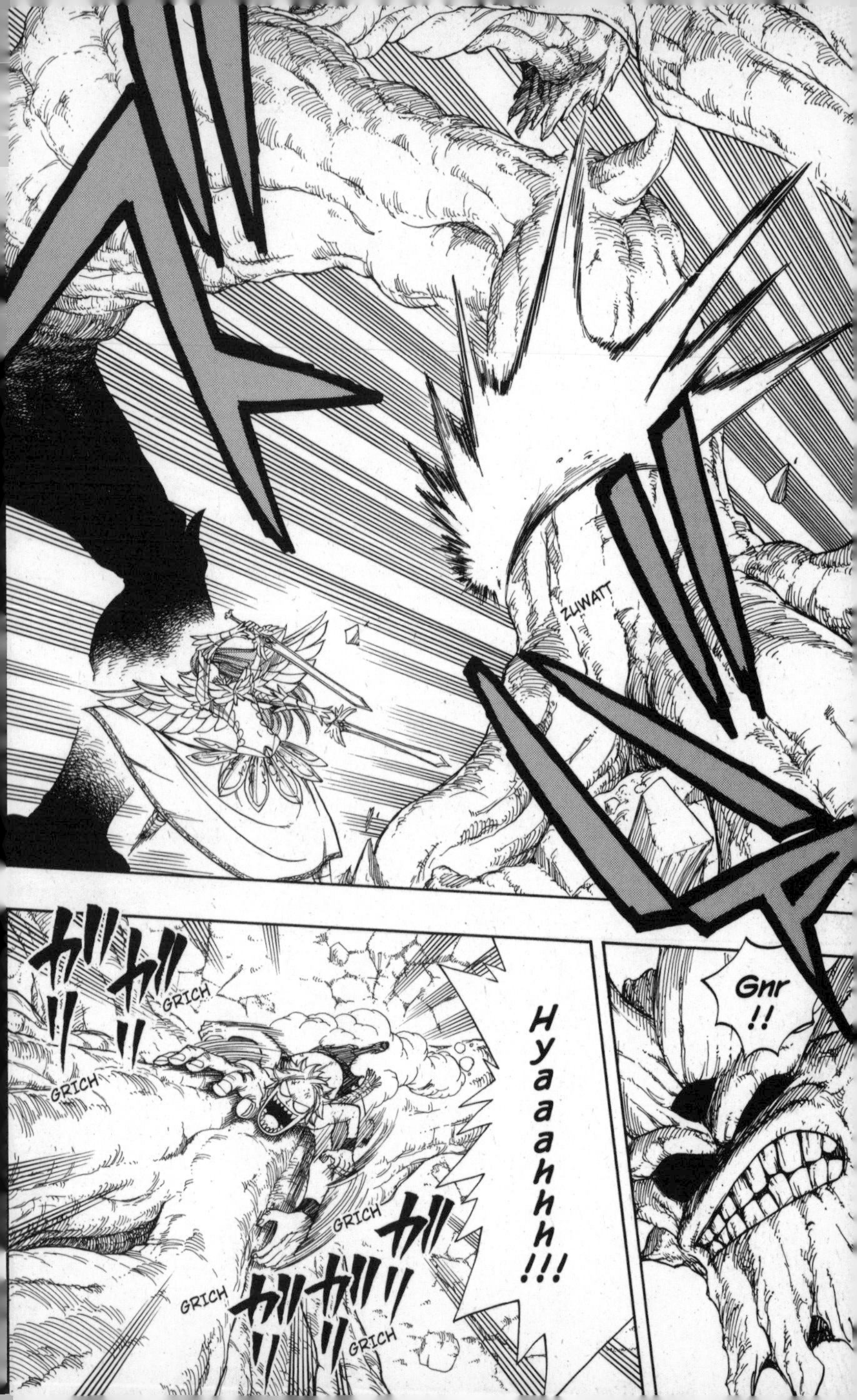
ZUWATT
Gnr !!
Hyaaaahhhh!!!
GRICH
GRICH
GRICH
GRICH
GRICH

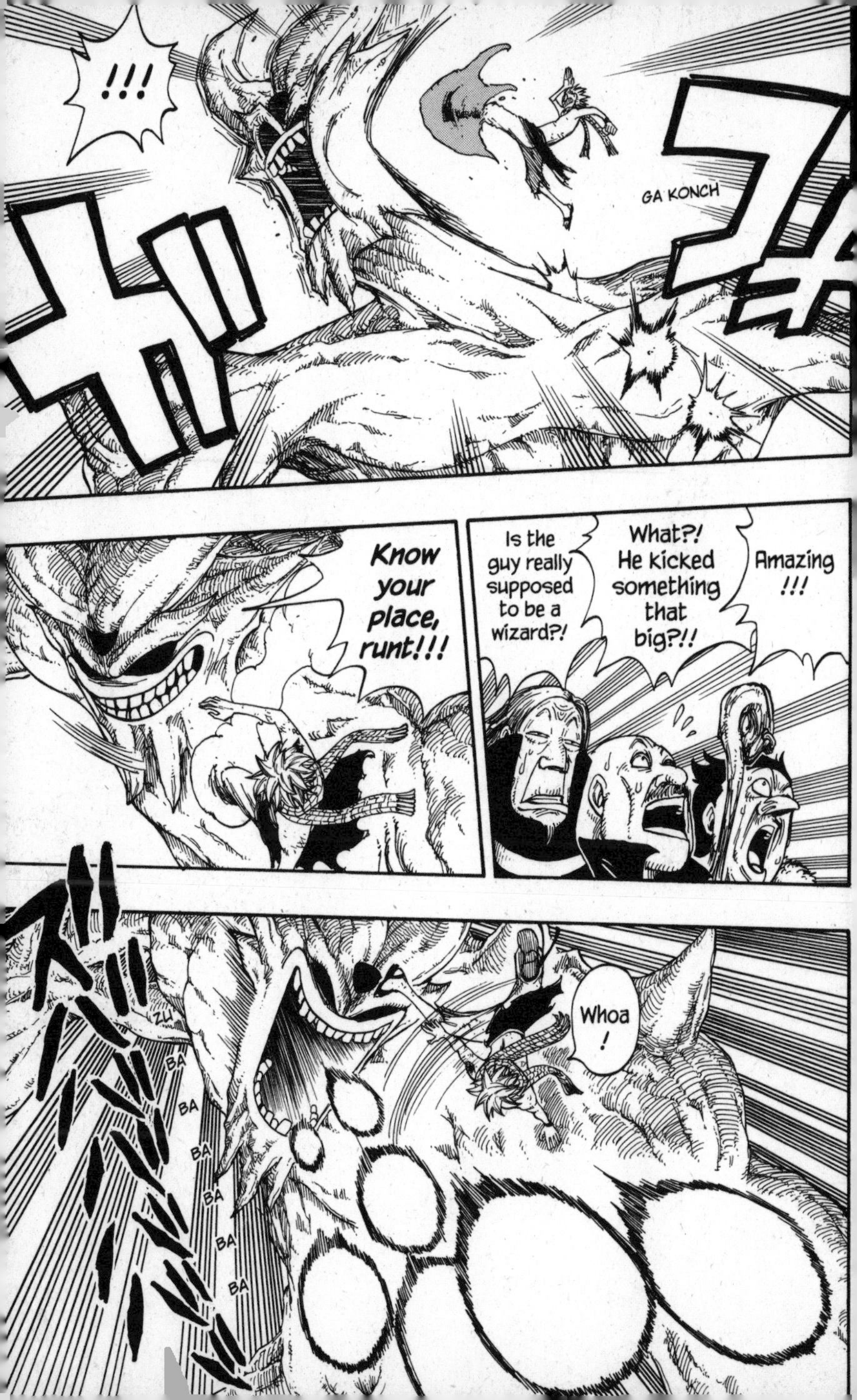
GA KONCH
!!!
Amazing!!!
What?! He kicked something that big?!!
Is the guy really supposed to be a wizard?!
Know your place, runt!!!
Whoa!
ZU
BA BA BA BA BA BA

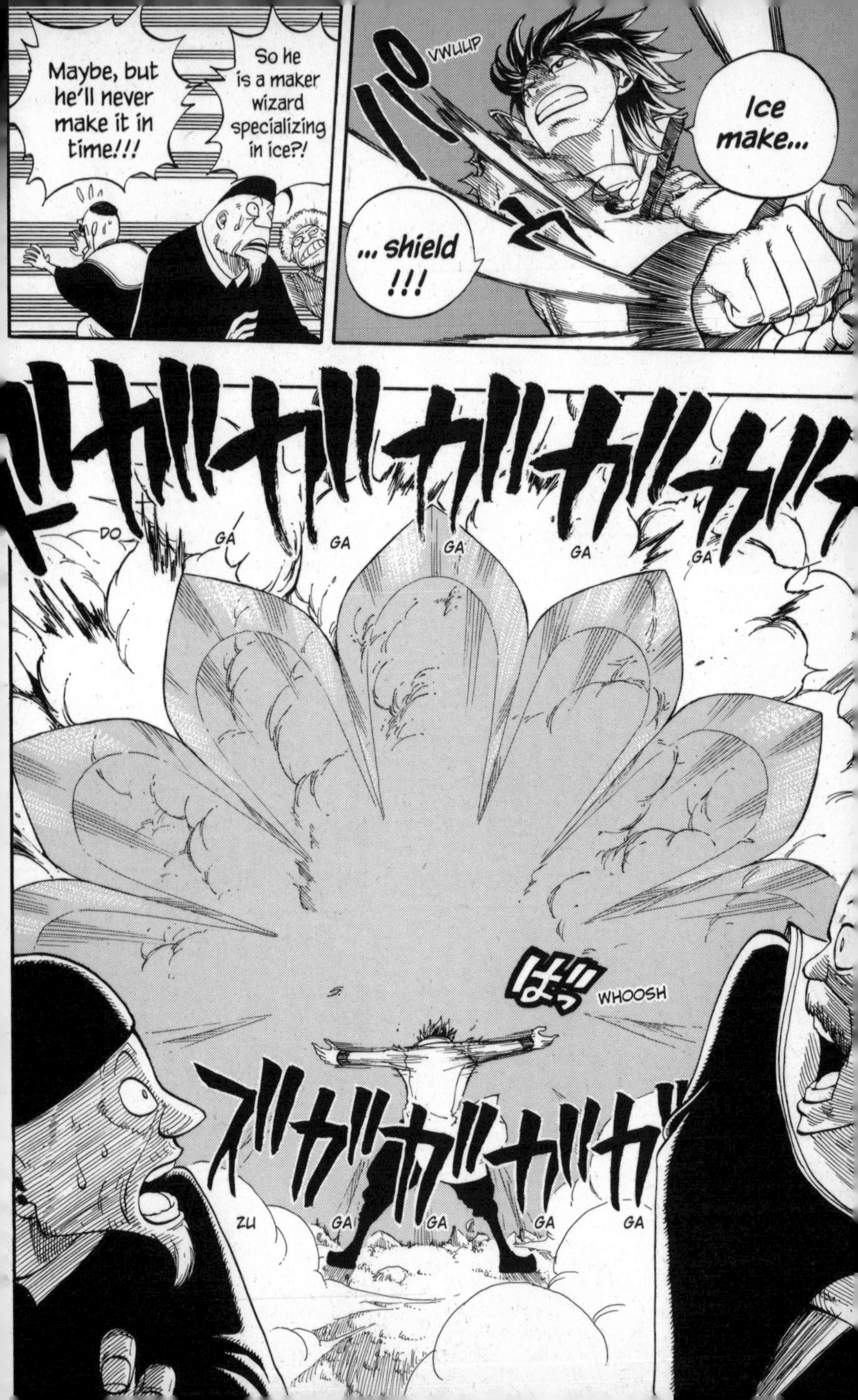
VWULP
Ice make...
... shield !!!
So he is a maker wizard specializing in ice?!
Maybe, but he'll never make it in time!!!
DO GA GA GA GA GA
WHOOSH
ZU GA GA GA GA

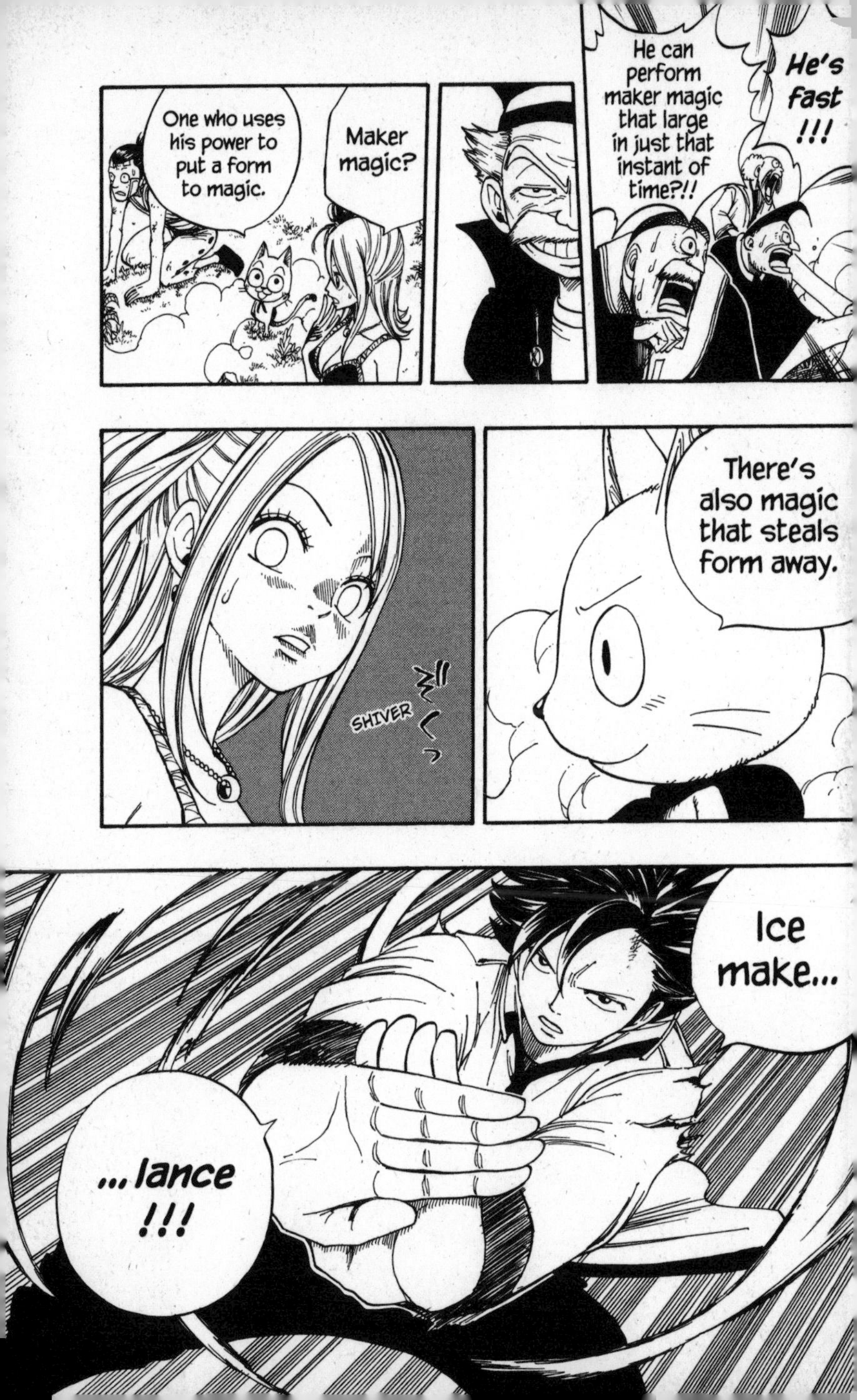
He can perform maker magic that large in just that instant of time?!!
He's fast!!!
Maker magic?
One who uses his power to put a form to magic.
There's also magic that steals form away.
SHIVER
Ice make...
...lance!!!

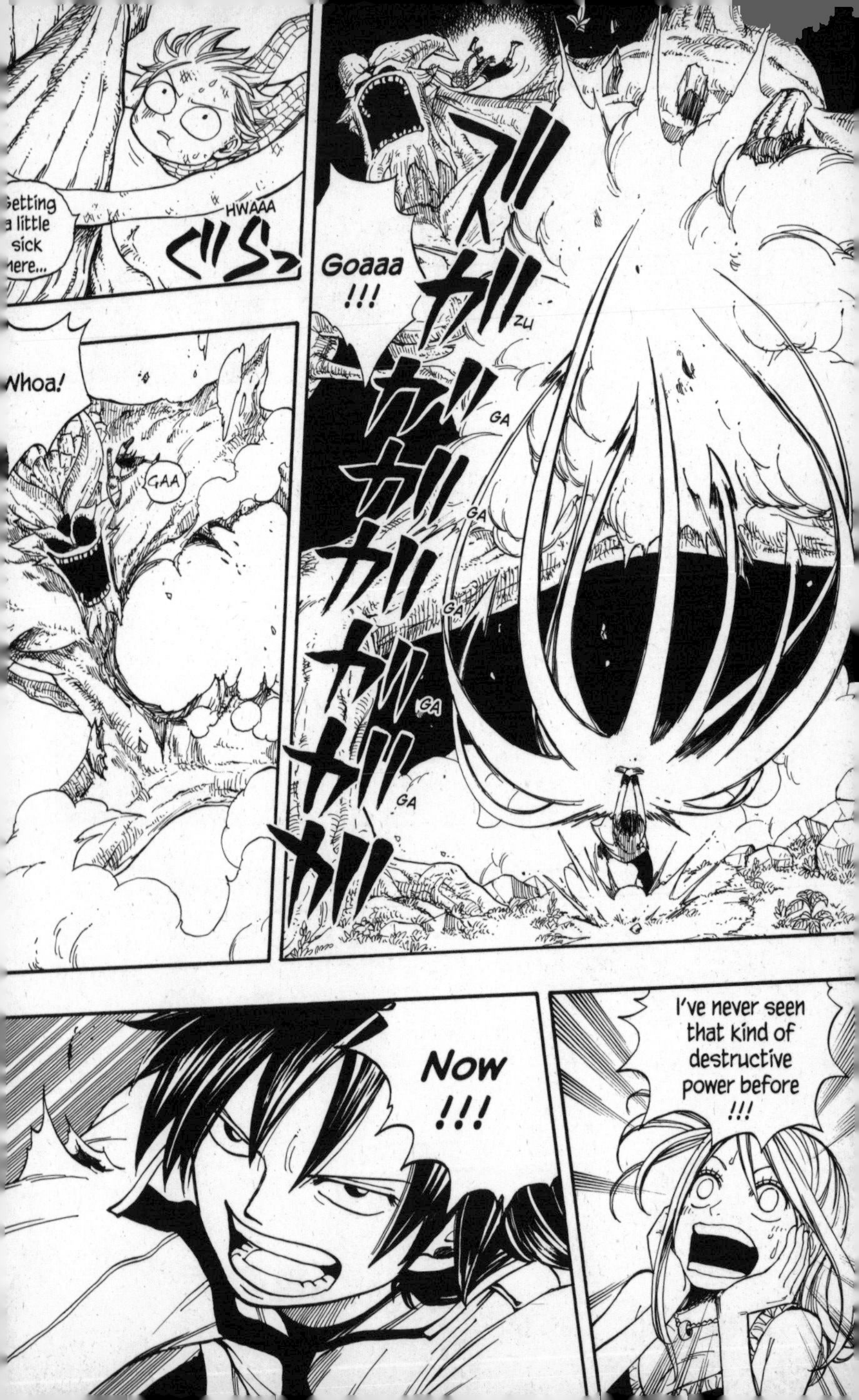
Goaaa !!!
ZU
GA
GA
GA
GA
GA
Getting a little sick here...
HWAAA
Whoa!
GAA
I've never seen that kind of destructive power before !!!
Now !!!

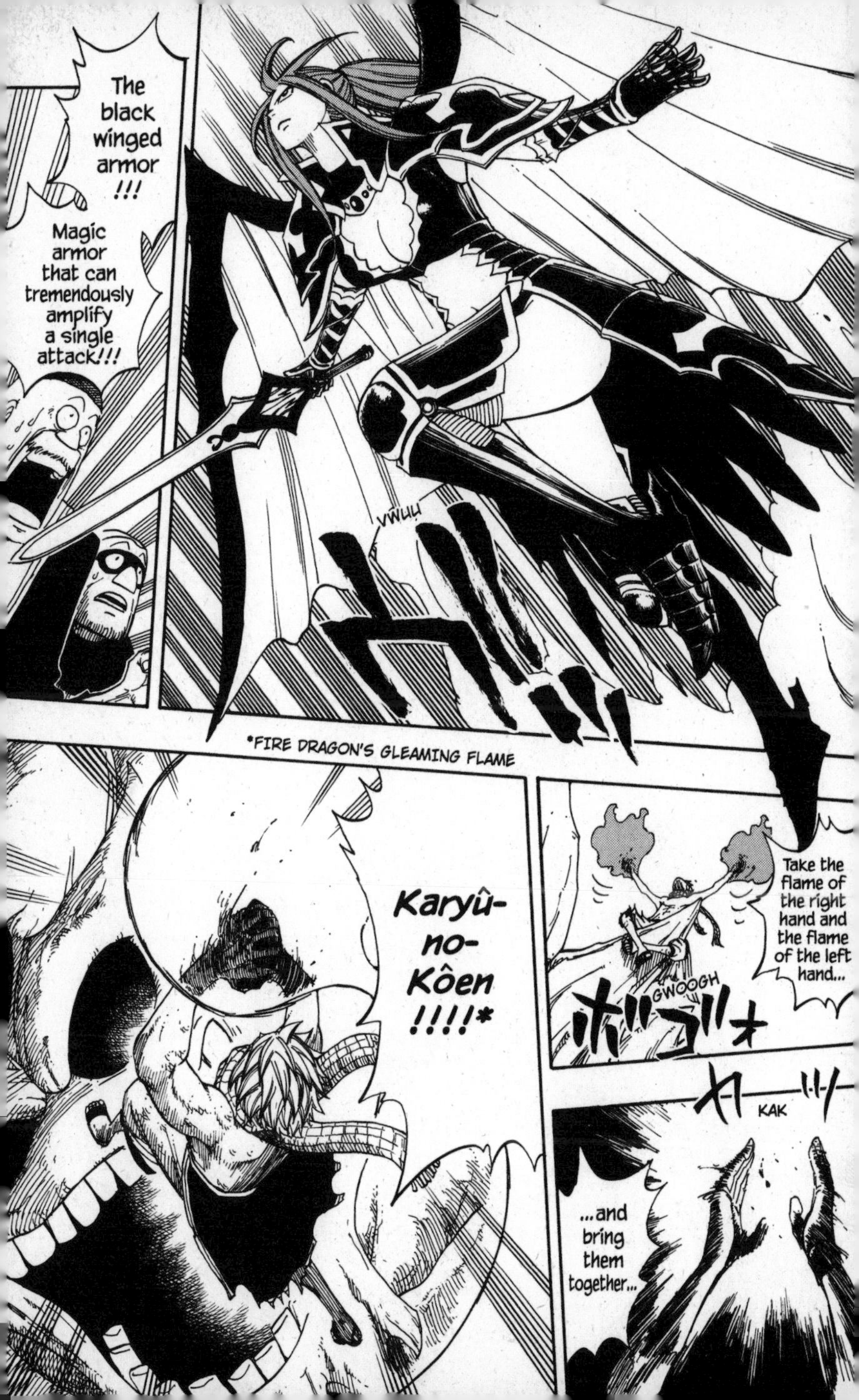
VWUU
The black winged armor!!!
Magic armor that can tremendously amplify a single attack!!!
Take the flame of the right hand and the flame of the left hand...
GWOOGH
KAK
...and bring them together...
Karyû-no-Kôen!!!!*
*FIRE DRAGON'S GLEAMING FLAME

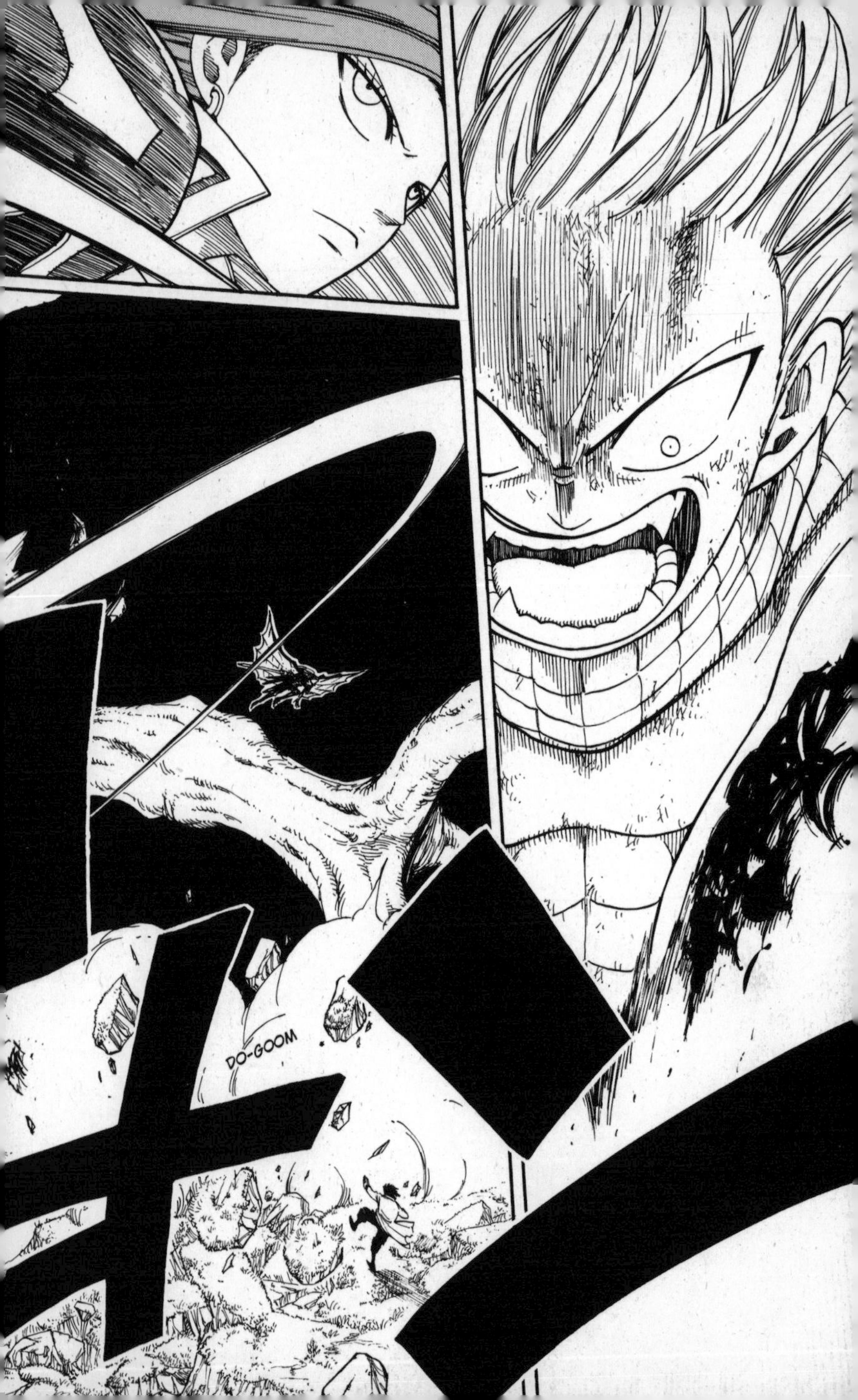
DO-GOOM

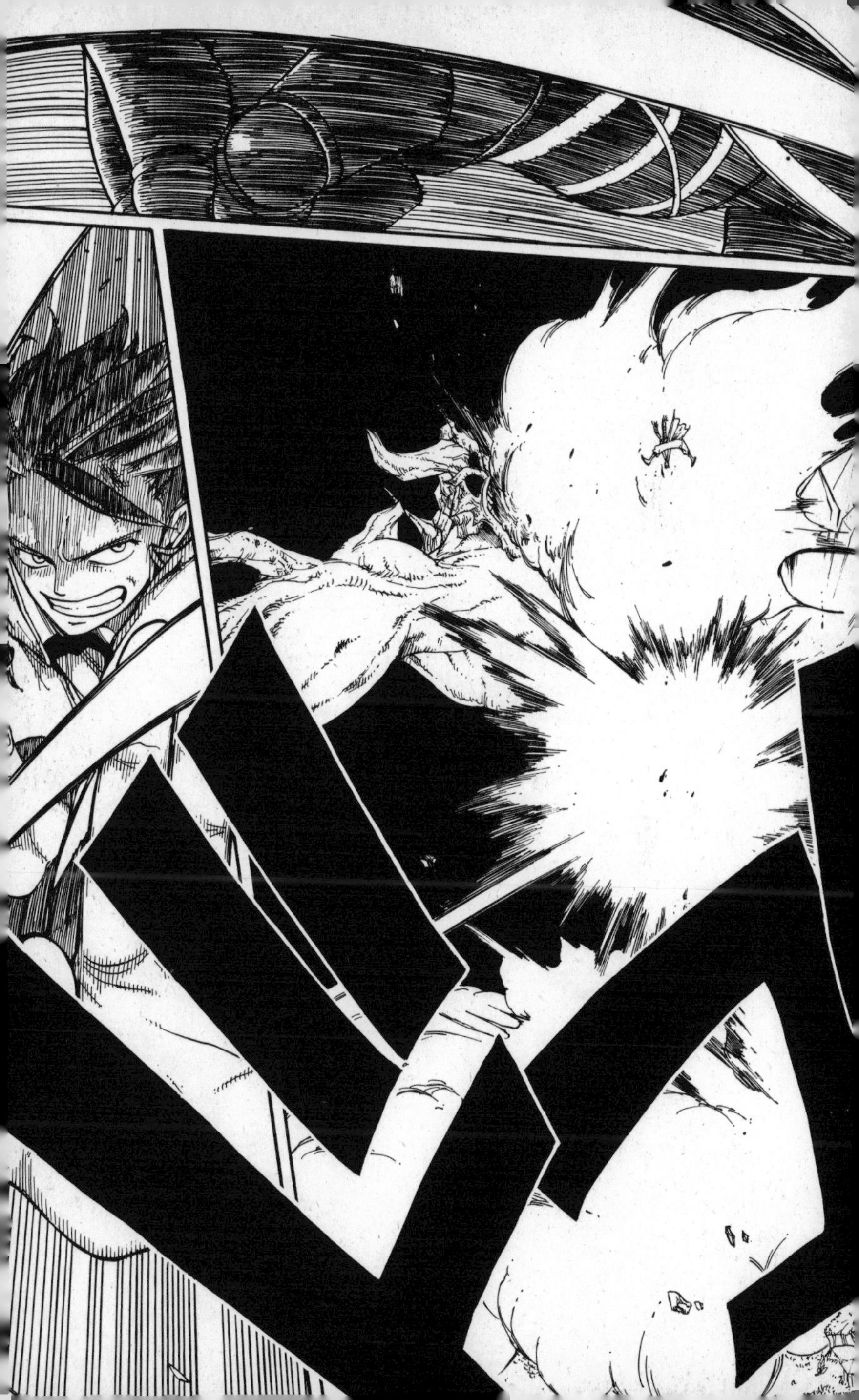

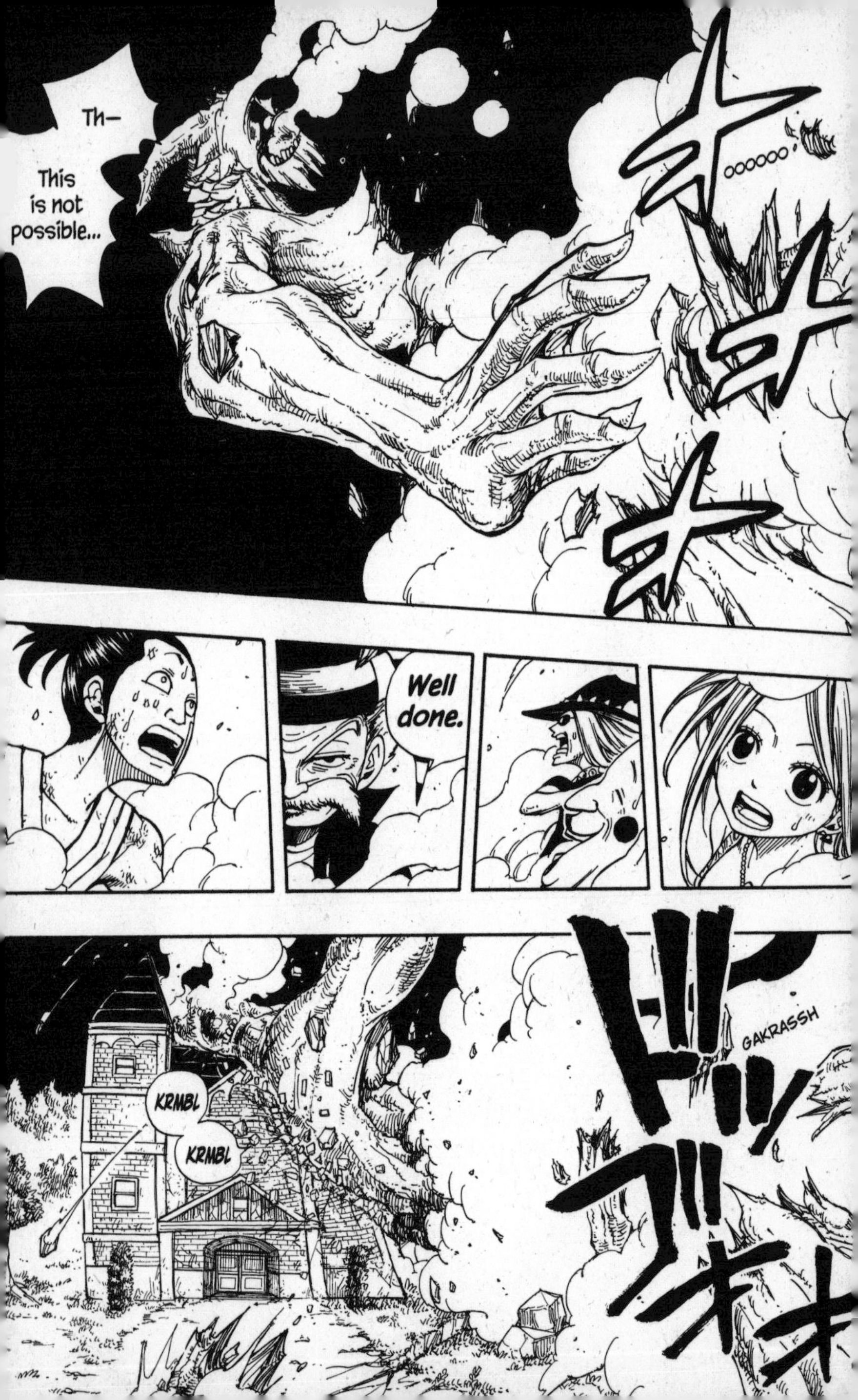

oooooo
Th—
This is not possible...
Well done.
GAKRASSH
KRMBL
KRMBL

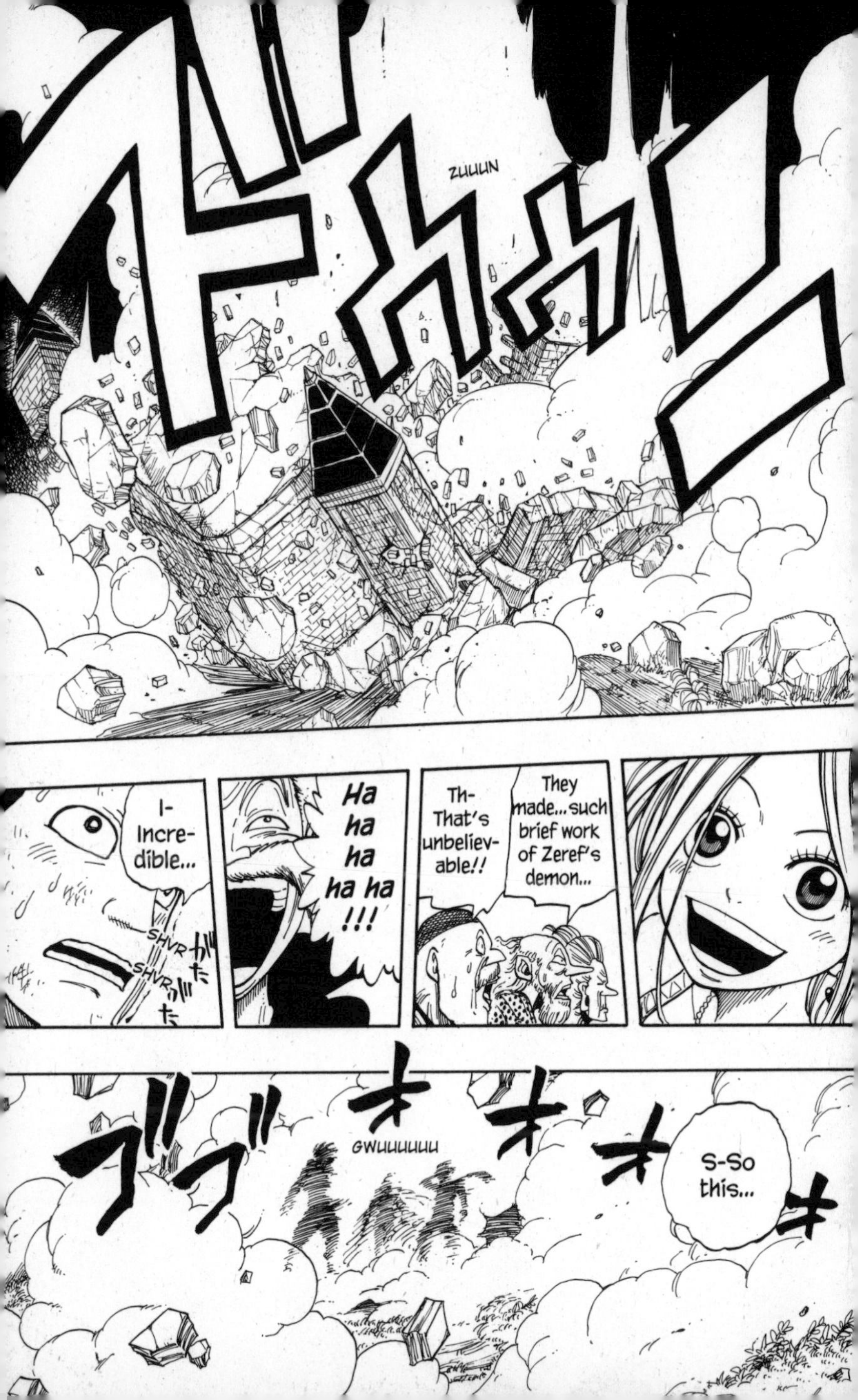
ZUUUN
They made... such brief work of Zeref's demon...
Th- That's unbelievable!!
Ha ha ha ha ha!!!
I- Incredible...
SHVR SHVR
S-So this...
GWUUUUUU

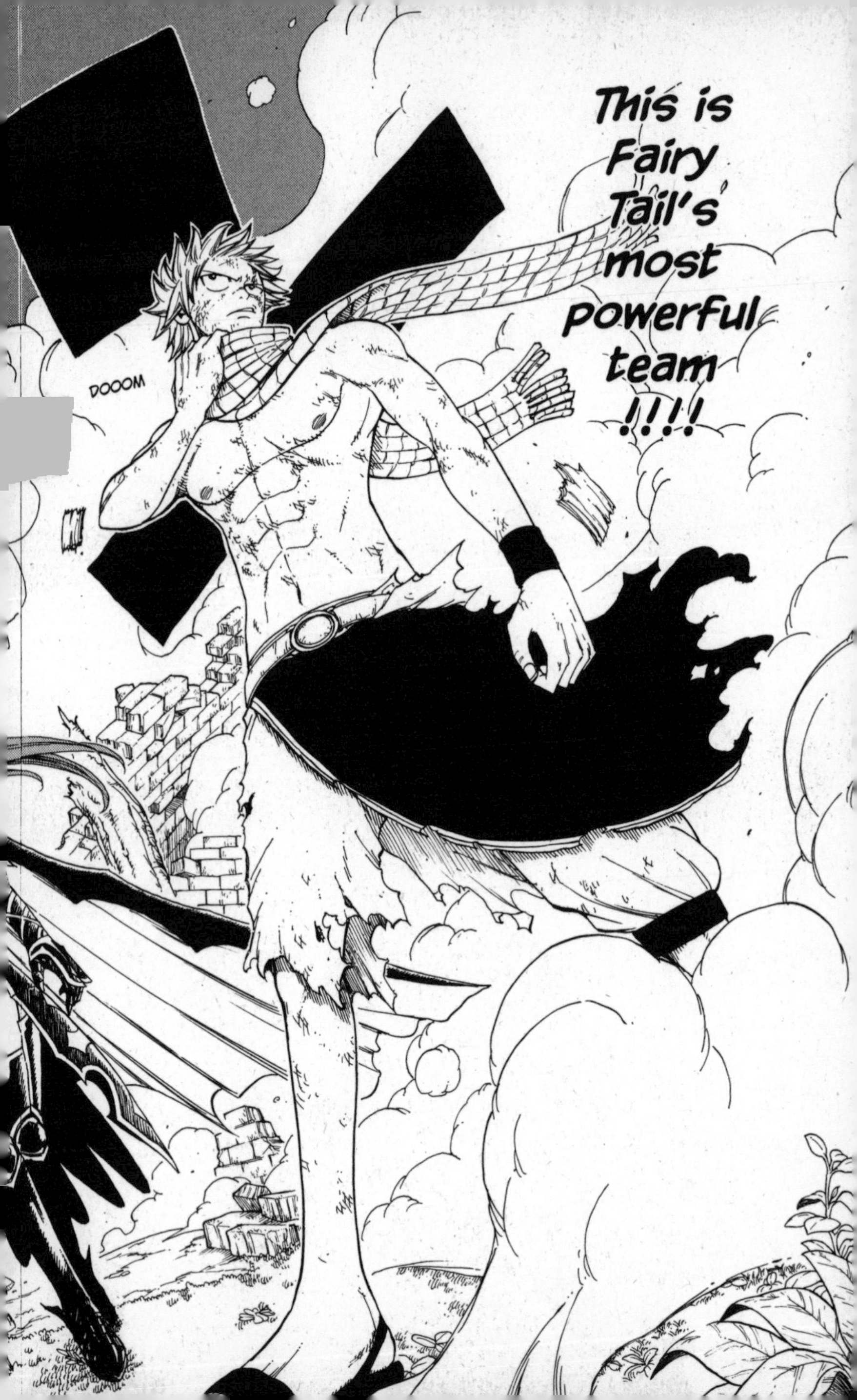
This is Fairy Tail's most powerful team !!!!
DOOOM

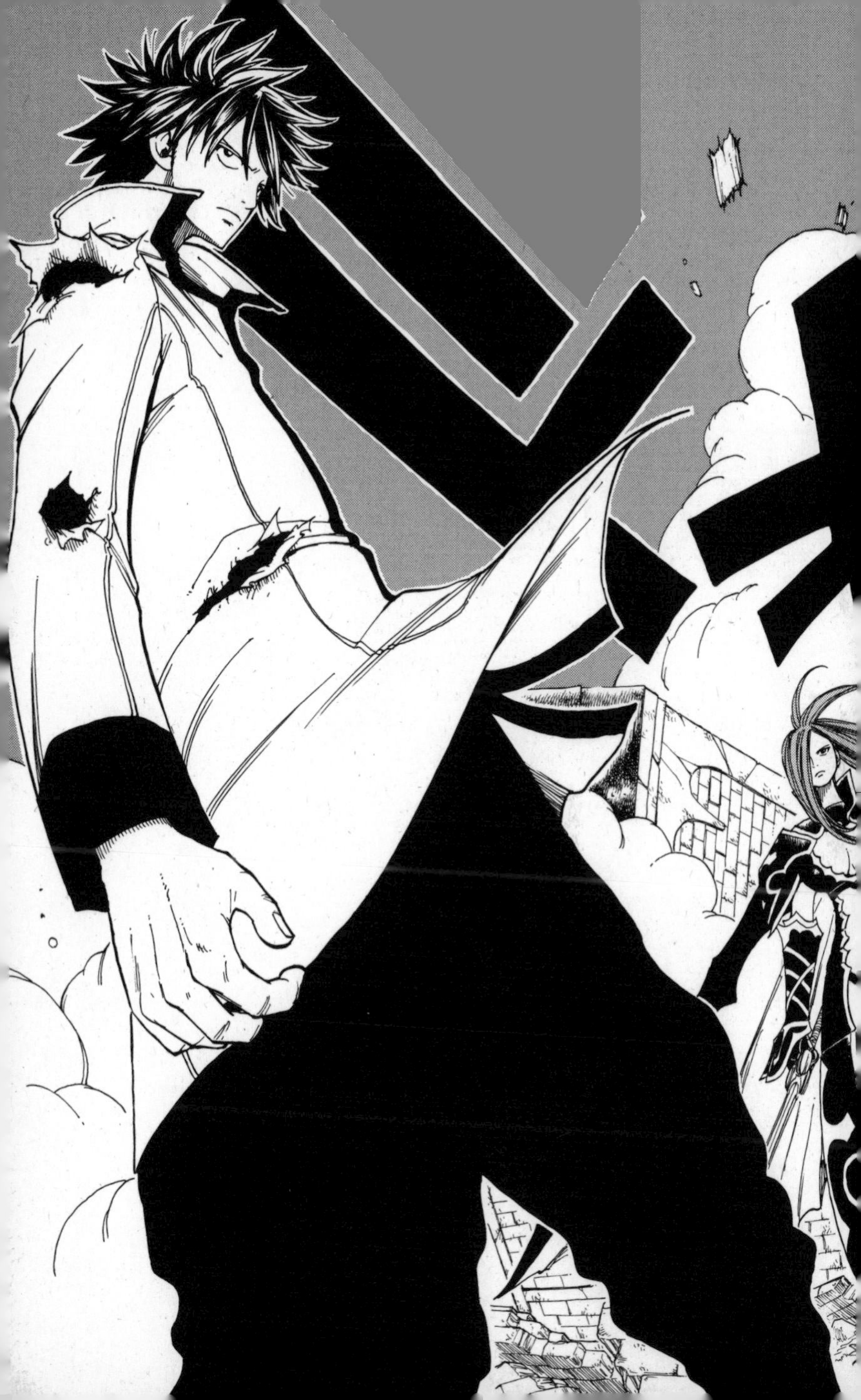

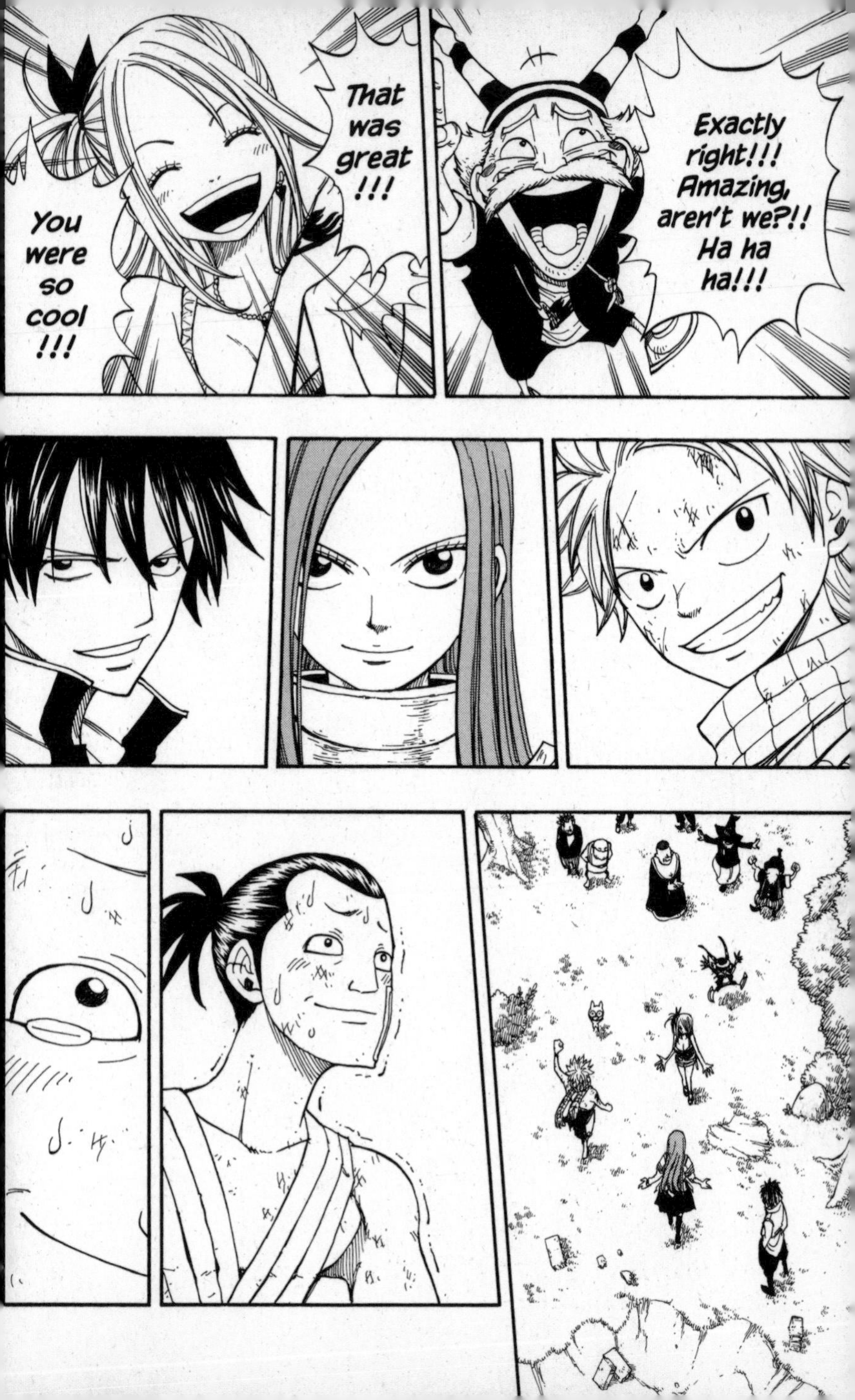
Exactly right!!! Amazing, aren't we?!! Ha ha ha!!!
That was great!!!
You were so cool!!!

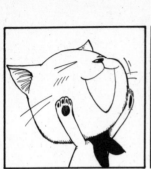

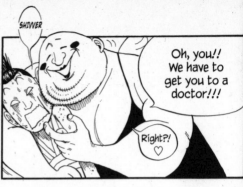

SHIVVER
Oh, you!! We have to get you to a doctor!!!
Right?! ♡
Well, I don't understand the whole story yet, but it looks like we owe a debt to Fairy Tail.
Yes.
I don't know what to say!!! Hya hya hya hya hya!!!
Hya... aa...
!!
Hm?
SNEAK
そろ〜
!!!

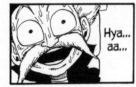

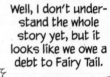

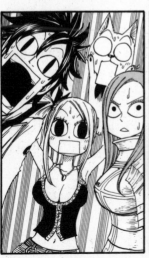

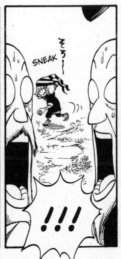

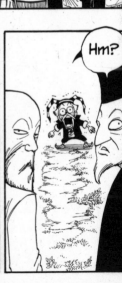

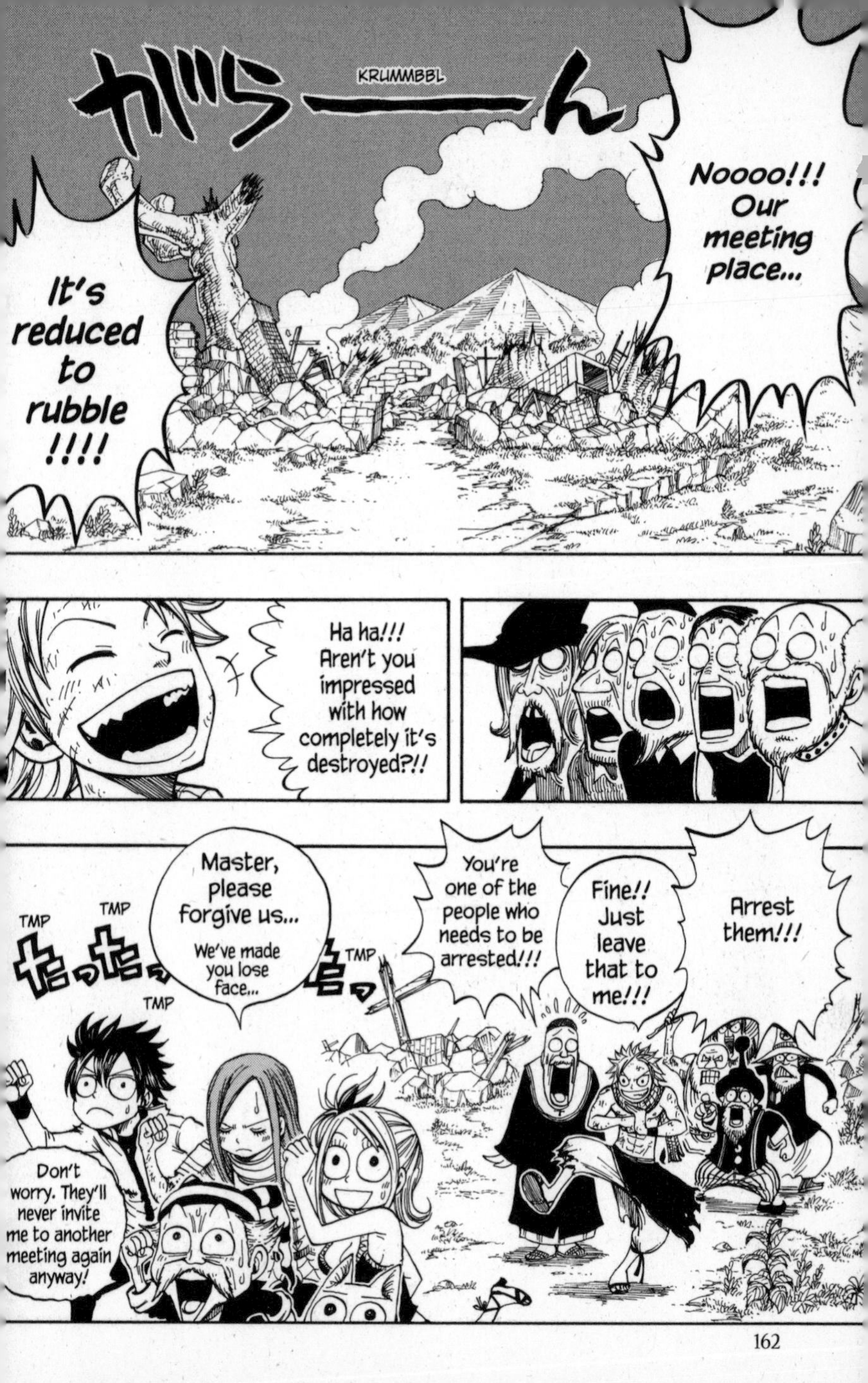
がらーーーん
KRUMMBBL
Noooo!!! Our meeting place...
It's reduced to rubble !!!!
Ha ha!!! Aren't you impressed with how completely it's destroyed?!!
Arrest them!!!
Fine!! Just leave that to me!!!
You're one of the people who needs to be arrested!!!
TMP
Master, please forgive us...
We've made you lose face...
TMP
TMP
TMP
Don't worry. They'll never invite me to another meeting again anyway!

FAIRY TAIL

Chapter 22: Natsu vs. Erza

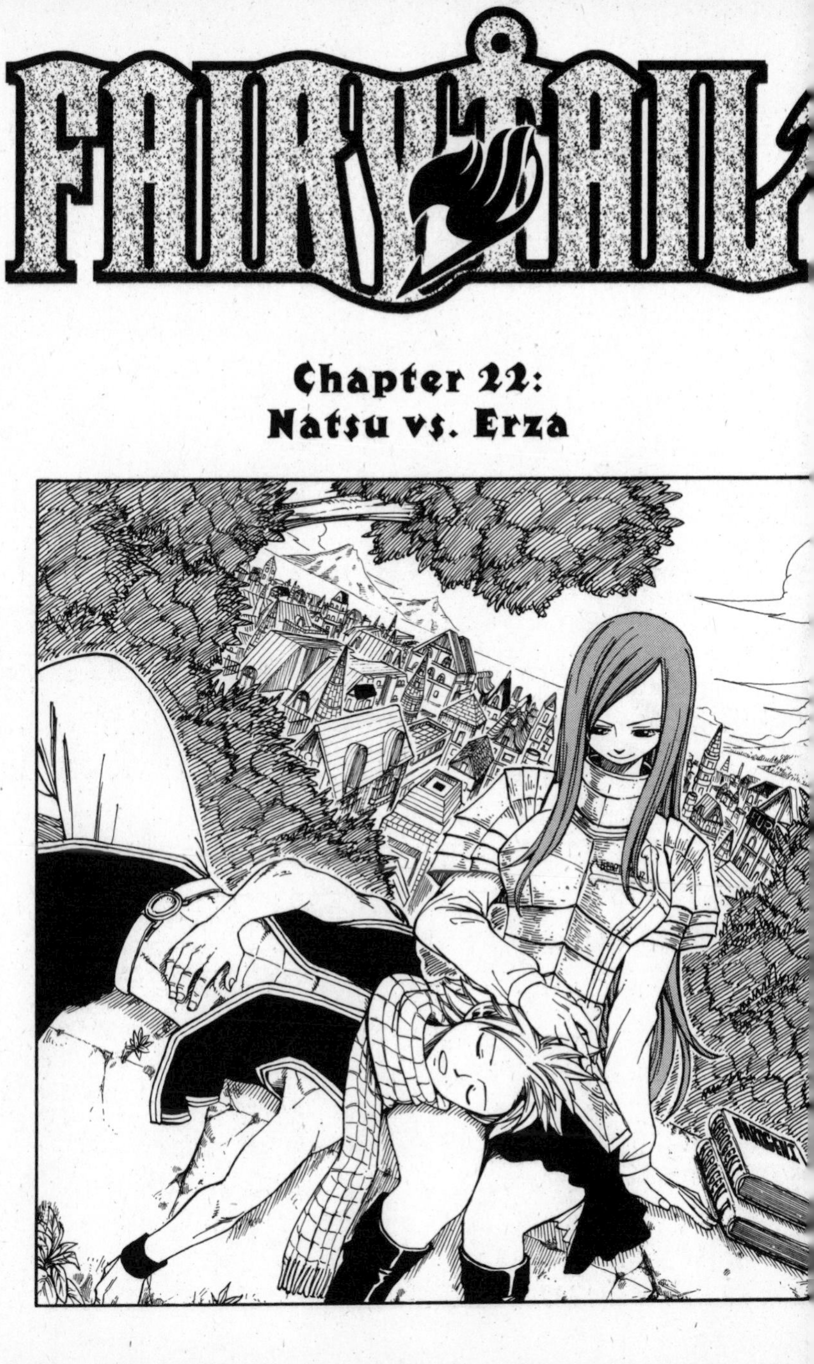

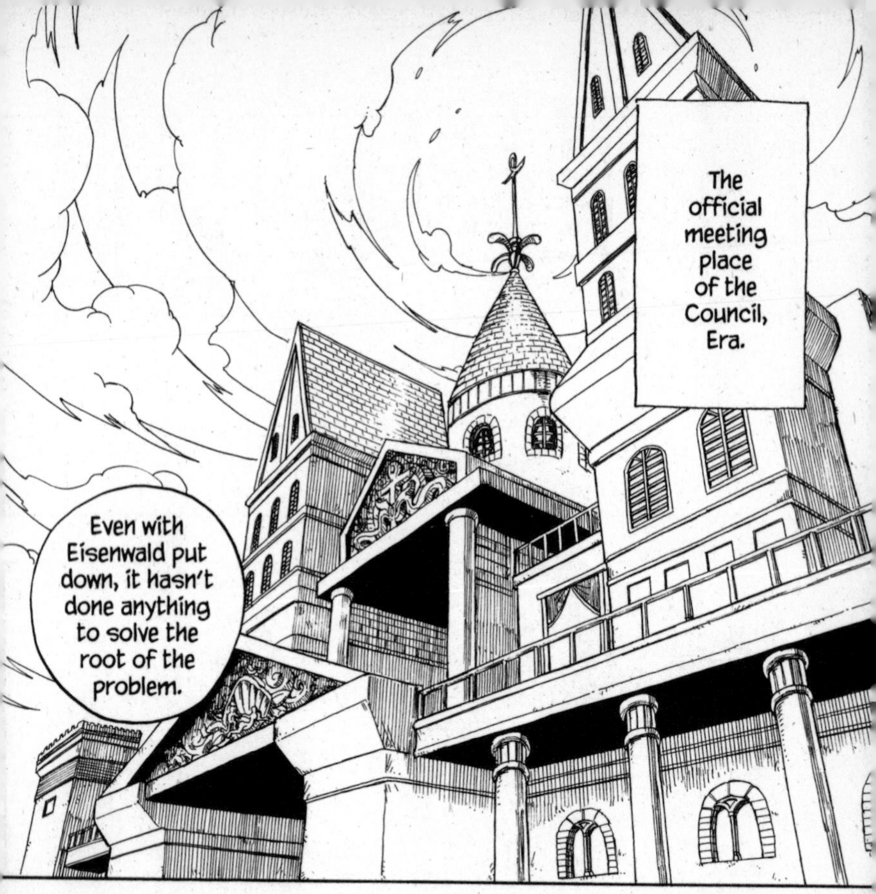
The official meeting place of the Council, Era.
Even with Eisenwald put down, it hasn't done anything to solve the root of the problem.

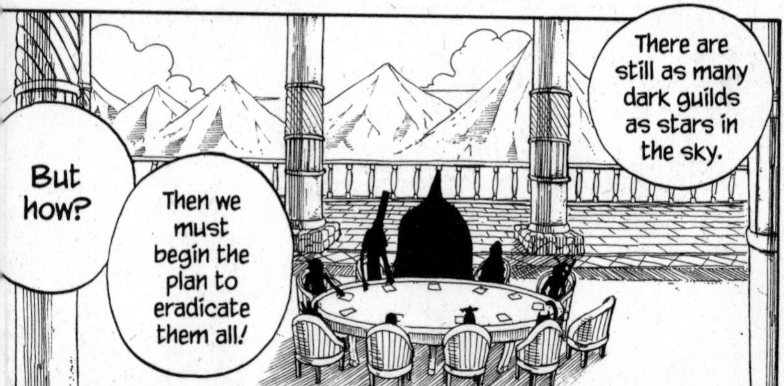
There are still as many dark guilds as stars in the sky.
Then we must begin the plan to eradicate them all!
But how?

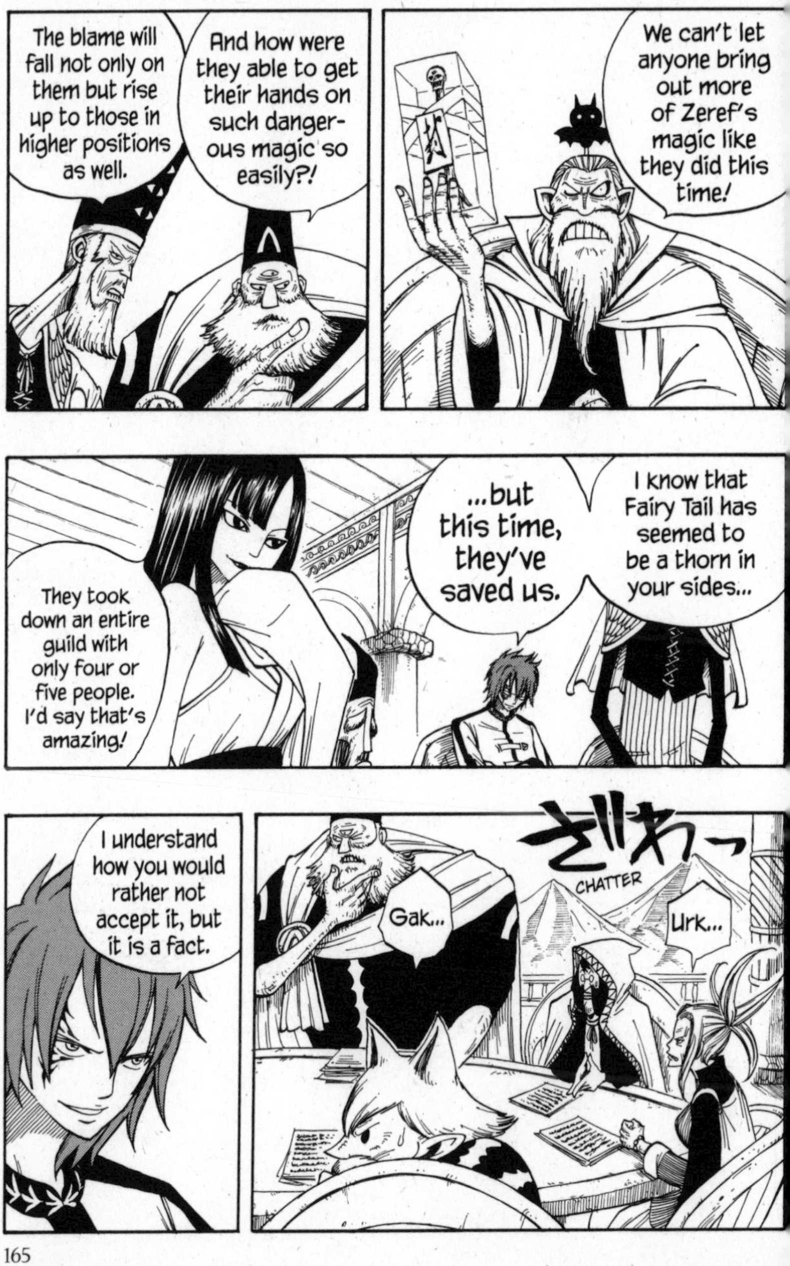
We can't let anyone bring out more of Zeref's magic like they did this time!
And how were they able to get their hands on such danger-ous magic so easily?!
The blame will fall not only on them but rise up to those in higher positions as well.
I know that Fairy Tail has seemed to be a thorn in your sides...
...but this time, they've saved us.
They took down an entire guild with only four or five people. I'd say that's amazing!
ざわっ
CHATTER
Urk...
Gak...
I understand how you would rather not accept it, but it is a fact.

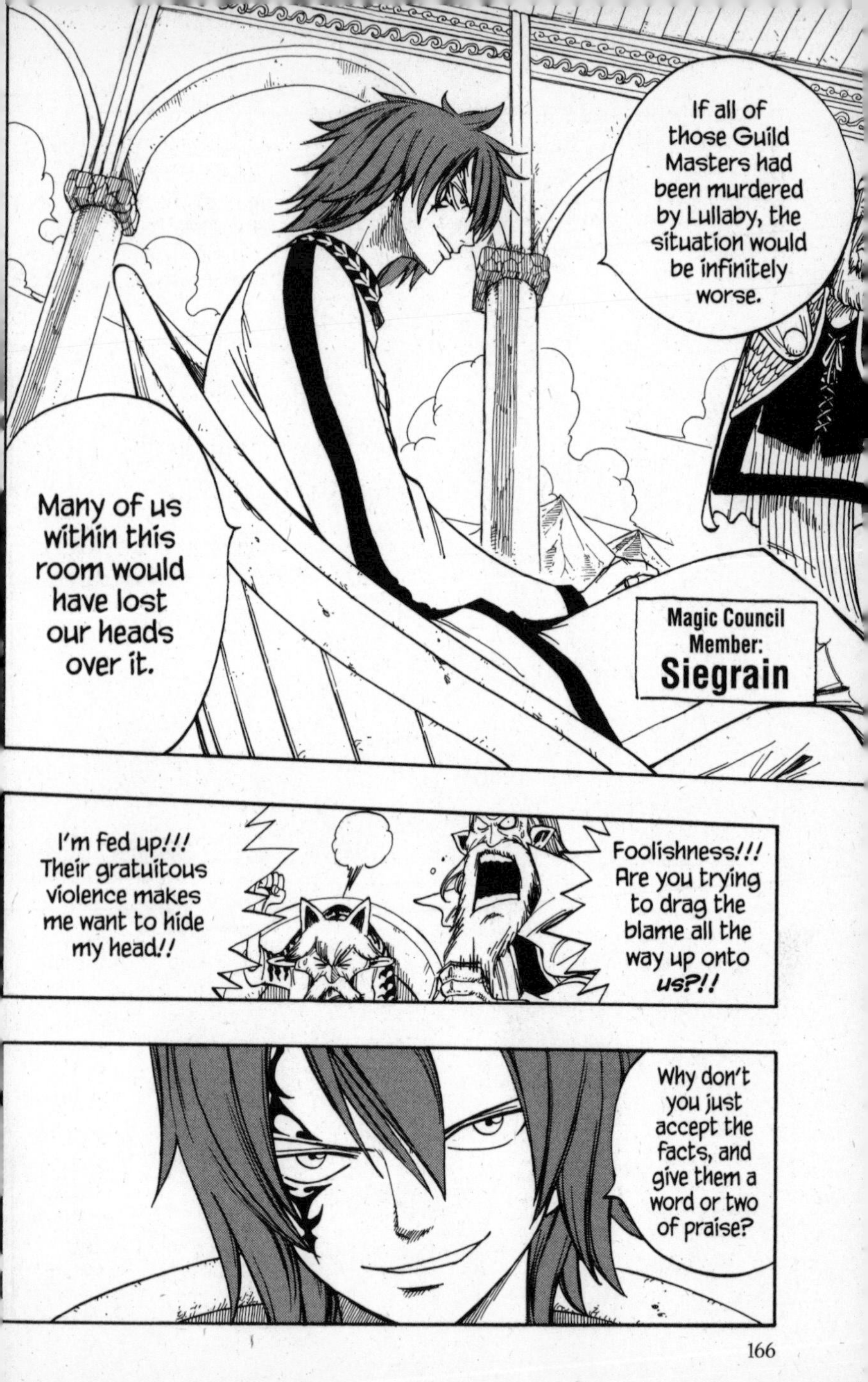
If all of those Guild Masters had been murdered by Lullaby, the situation would be infinitely worse.
Many of us within this room would have lost our heads over it.
Magic Council Member: Siegrain
Foolishness!!! Are you trying to drag the blame all the way up onto *us?!!*
I'm fed up!!! Their gratuitous violence makes me want to hide my head!!
Why don't you just accept the facts, and give them a word or two of praise?

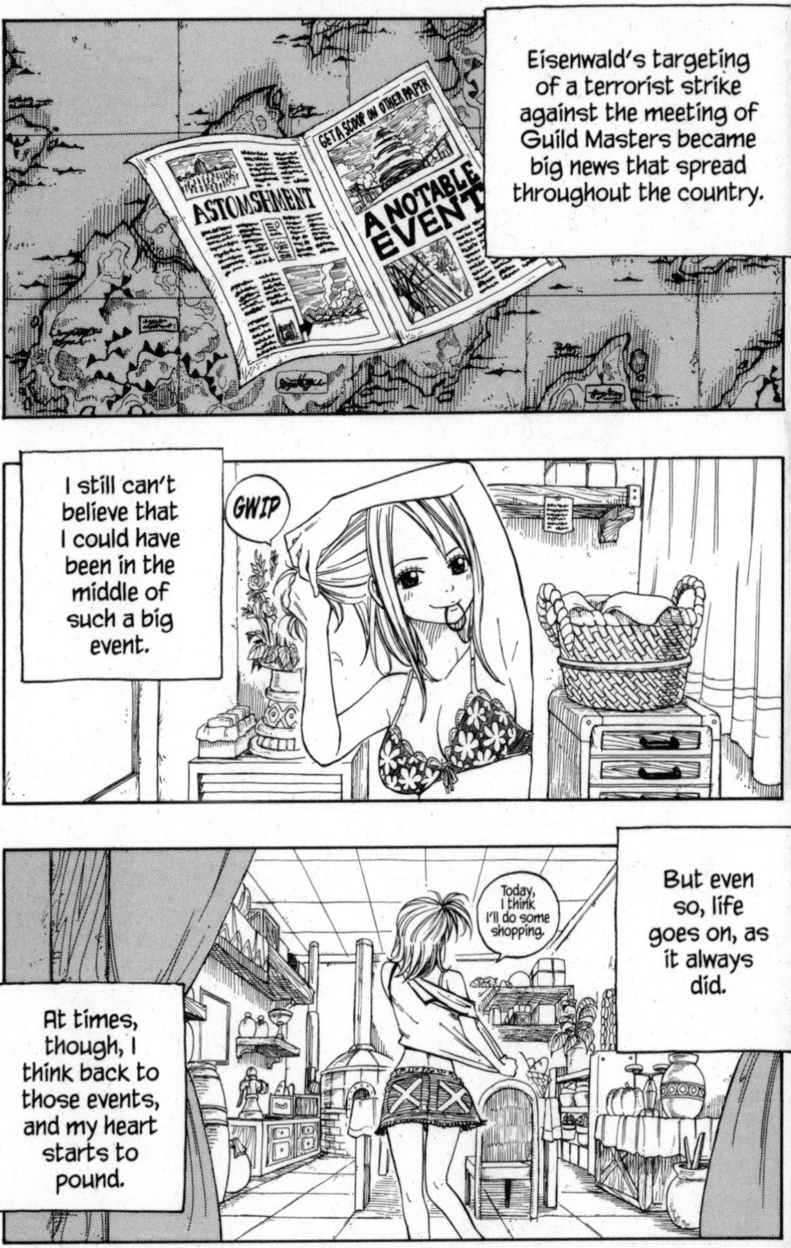
Eisenwald's targeting of a terrorist strike against the meeting of Guild Masters became big news that spread throughout the country.
GET A SCOOP ON OTHER PAPER
A NOTABLE EVENT
ASTOMSHMENT
GWIP
I still can't believe that I could have been in the middle of such a big event.
But even so, life goes on, as it always did.
Today, I think I'll do some shopping.
At times, though, I think back to those events, and my heart starts to pound.

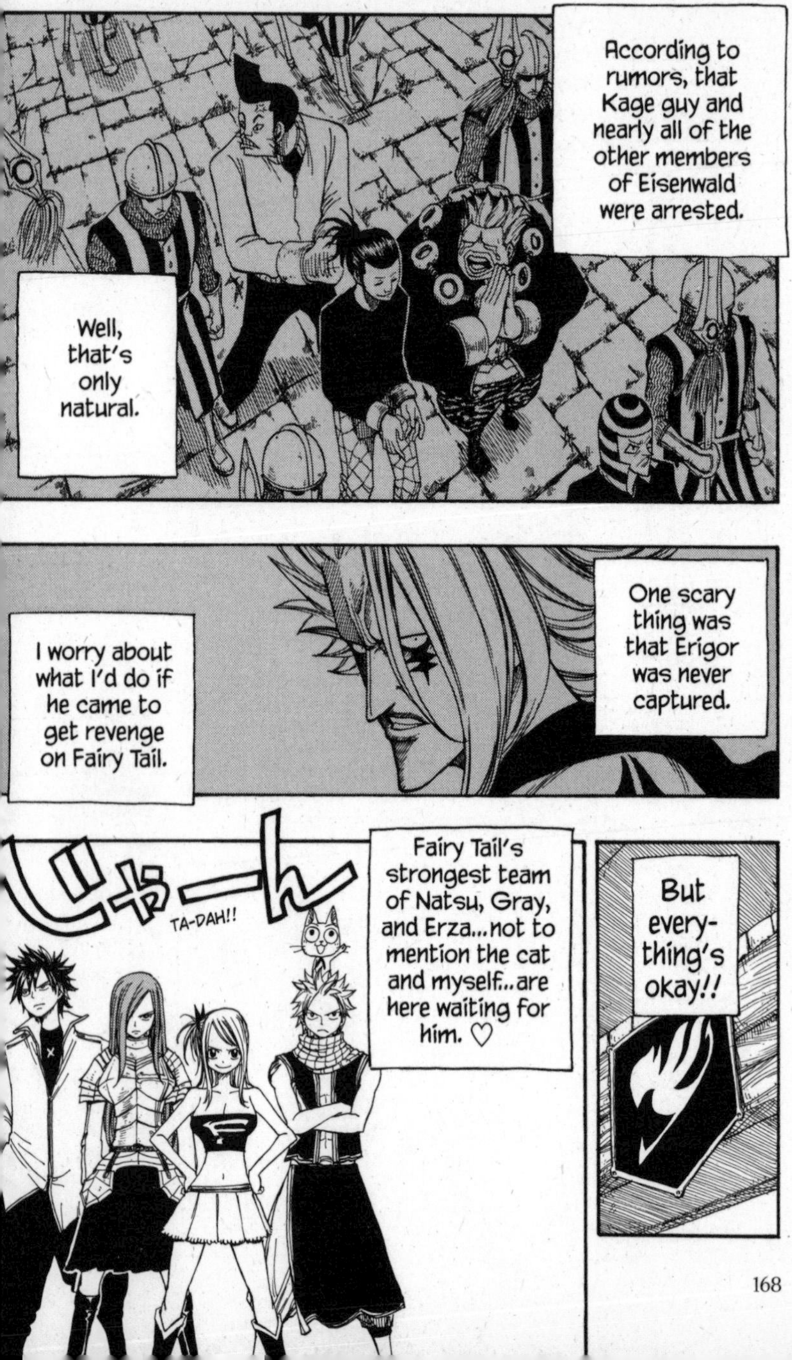
According to rumors, that Kage guy and nearly all of the other members of Eisenwald were arrested.
Well, that's only natural.
One scary thing was that Erigor was never captured.
I worry about what I'd do if he came to get revenge on Fairy Tail.
But everything's okay!!
Fairy Tail's strongest team of Natsu, Gray, and Erza...not to mention the cat and myself...are here waiting for him. ♡
じゃーん
TA-DAH!!

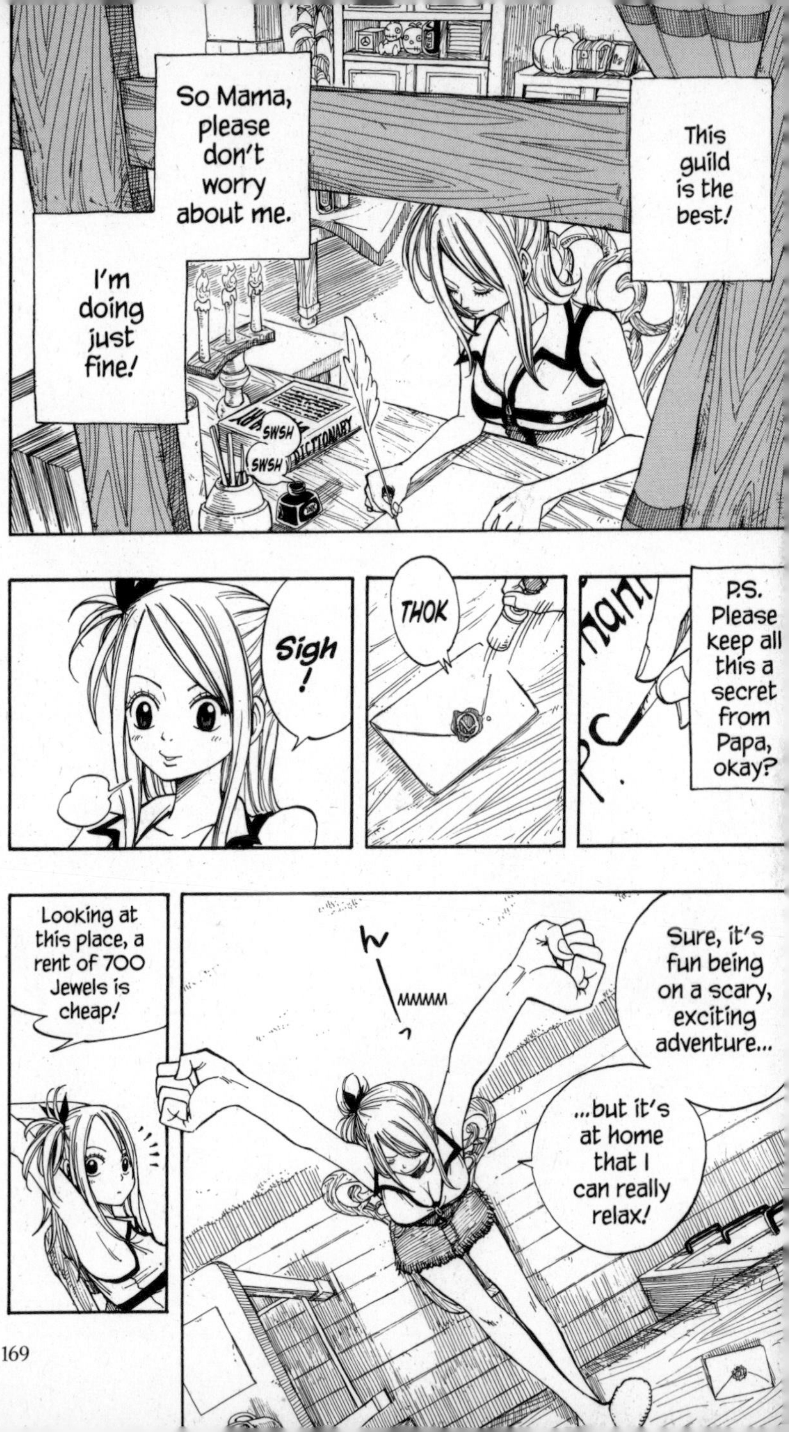
This guild is the best!
So Mama, please don't worry about me.
I'm doing just fine!
SWSH
SWSH
DICTIONARY
P.S. Please keep all this a secret from Papa, okay?
THOK
Sigh!
Sure, it's fun being on a scary, exciting adventure...
...but it's at home that I can really relax!
Looking at this place, a rent of 700 Jewels is cheap!

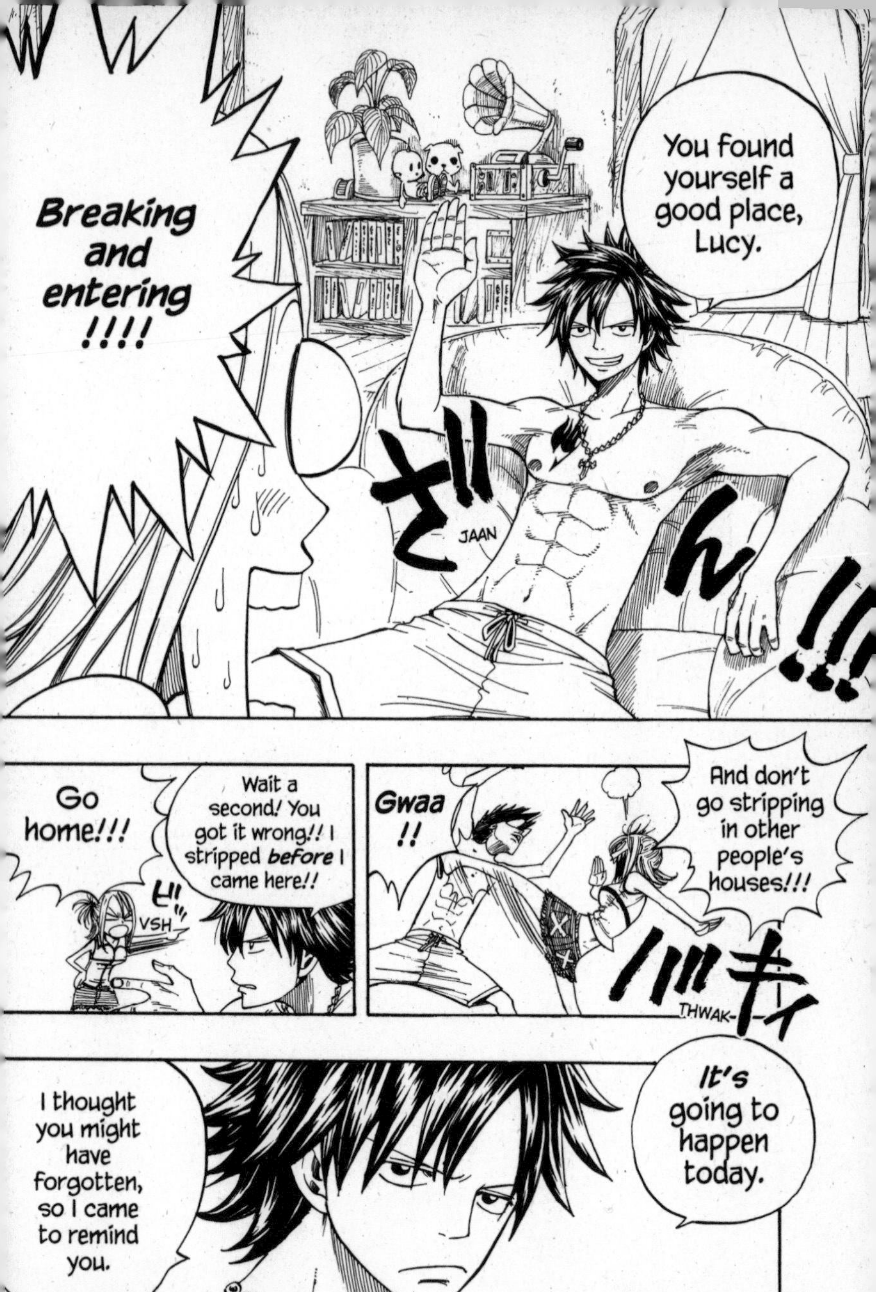
You found yourself a good place, Lucy.
JAAN
Breaking and entering!!!!
And don't go stripping in other people's houses!!!
Gwaa!!
THWAK-
Wait a second! You got it wrong!! I stripped *before* I came here!!
Go home!!!
VSH
It's going to happen today.
I thought you might have forgotten, so I came to remind you.

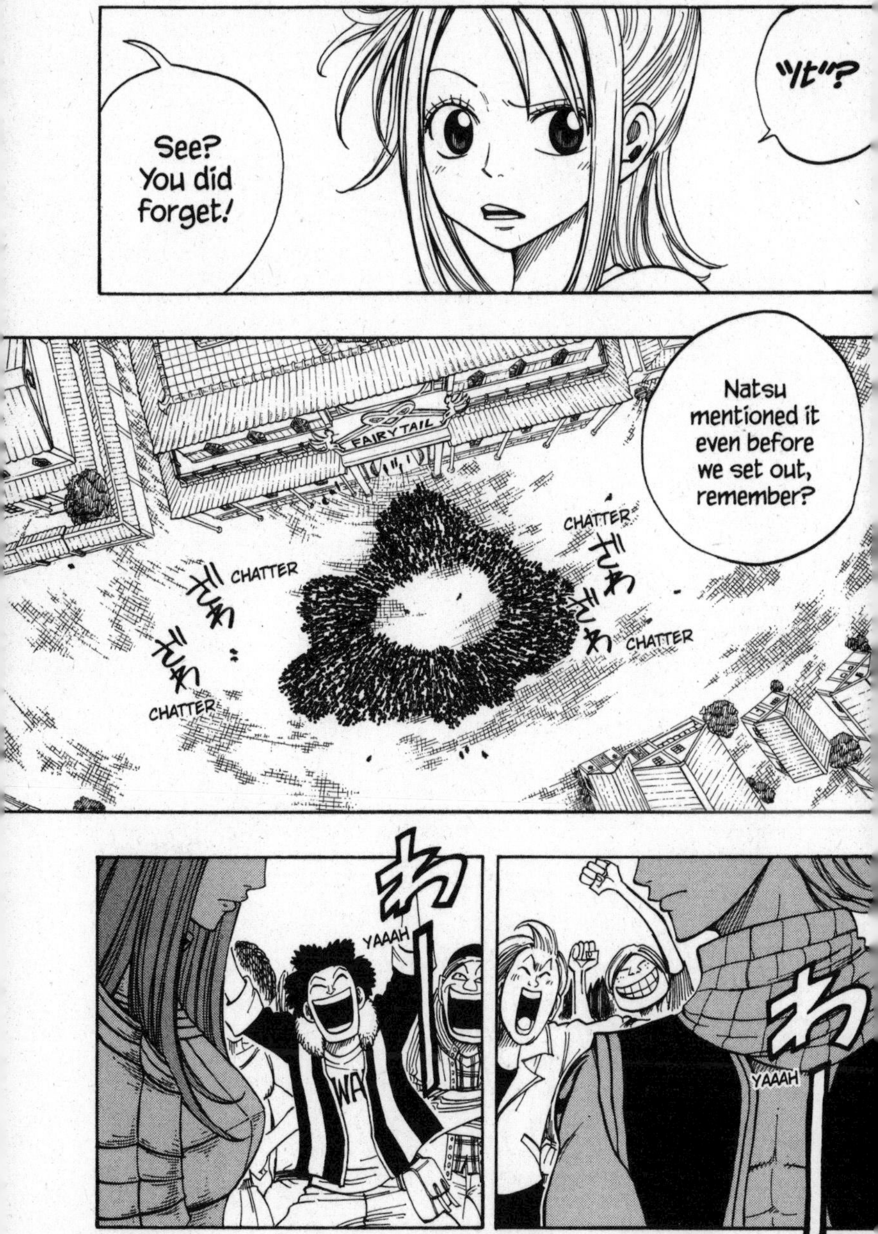
"It"?
See? You did forget!
Natsu mentioned it even before we set out, remember?
ざわ ざわ
CHATTER
CHATTER
ざわ ざわ
CHATTER
CHATTER
わー
YAAAH
わー
YAAAH

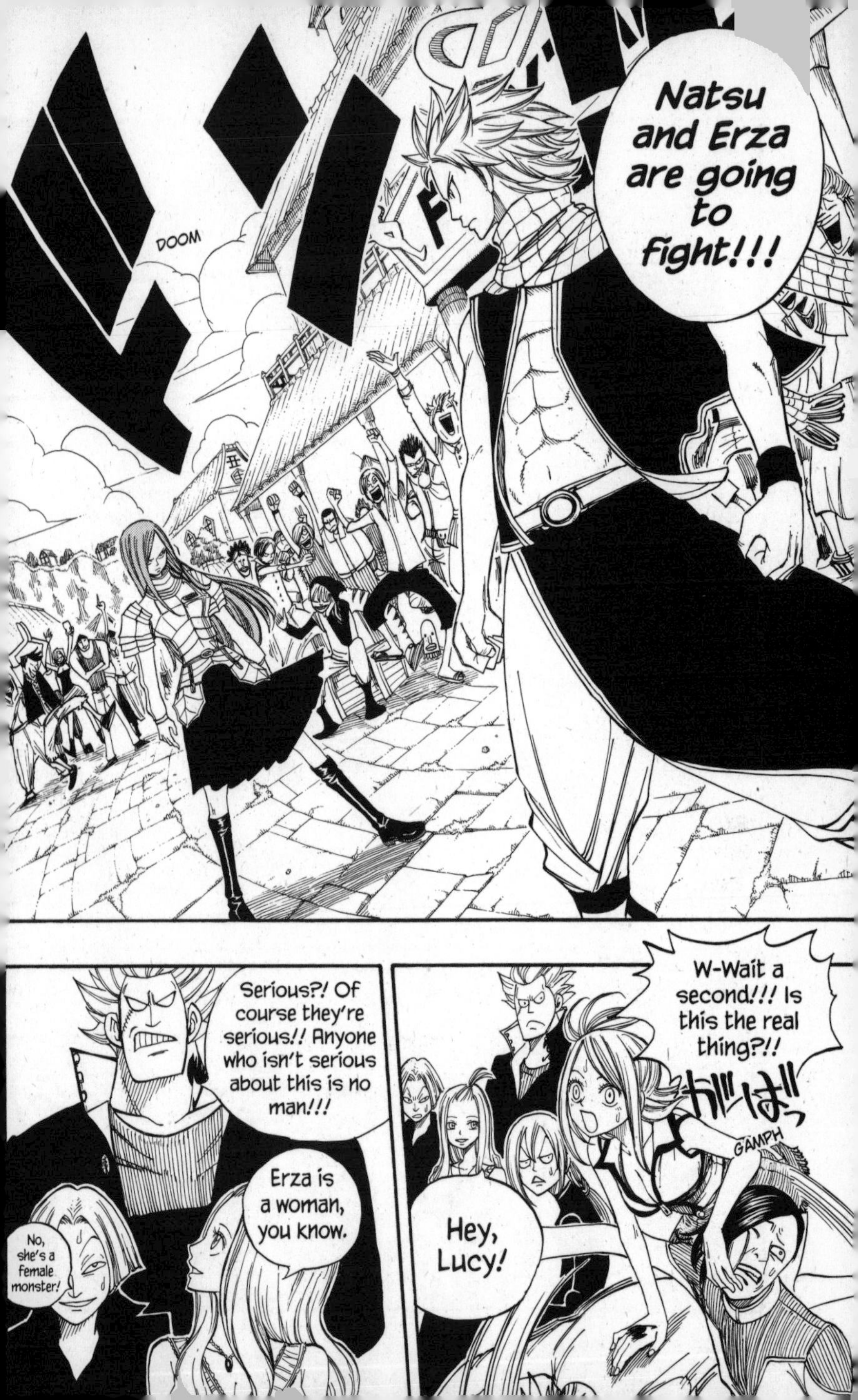
Natsu and Erza are going to fight!!!
DOOM
W-Wait a second!!! Is this the real thing?!!
がばっ
GAMPH
Hey, Lucy!
Serious?! Of course they're serious!! Anyone who isn't serious about this is no man!!!
Erza is a woman, you know.
No, she's a female monster!

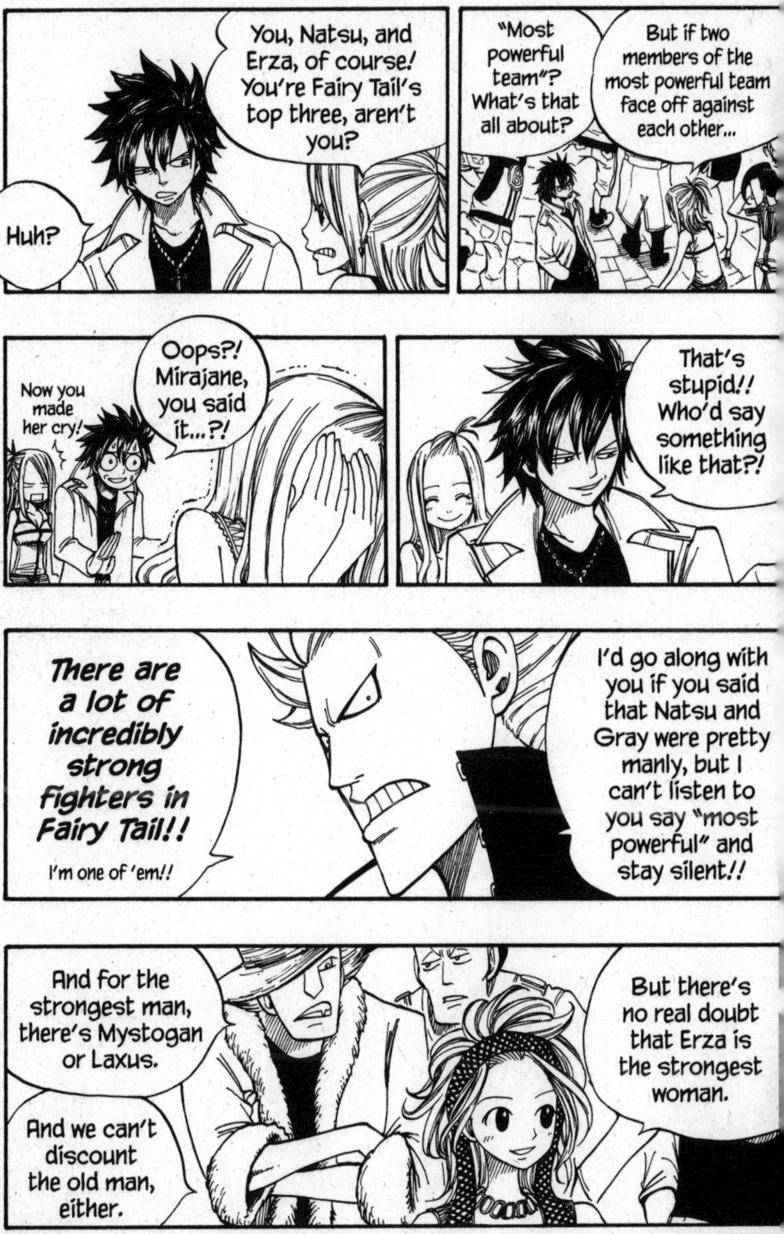
But if two members of the most powerful team face off against each other...
"Most powerful team"? What's that all about?
You, Natsu, and Erza, of course! You're Fairy Tail's top three, aren't you?
Huh?
That's stupid!! Who'd say something like that?!
Oops?! Mirajane, you said it...?!
Now you made her cry!
I'd go along with you if you said that Natsu and Gray were pretty manly, but I can't listen to you say "most powerful" and stay silent!!
There are a lot of incredibly strong fighters in Fairy Tail!!
I'm one of 'em!!
But there's no real doubt that Erza is the strongest woman.
And for the strongest man, there's Mystogan or Laxus.
And we can't discount the old man, either.

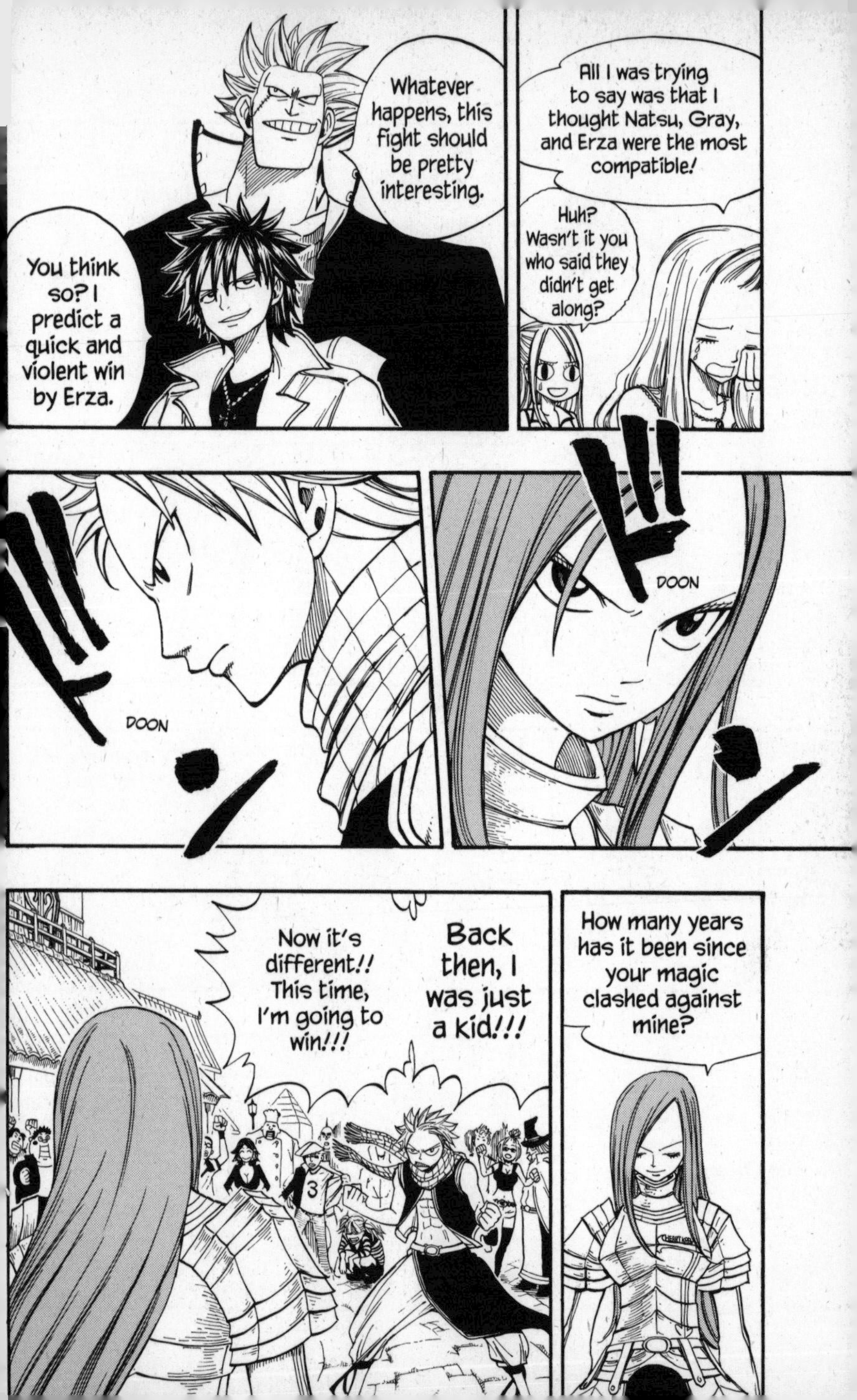
All I was trying to say was that I thought Natsu, Gray, and Erza were the most compatible!
Huh? Wasn't it you who said they didn't get along?
Whatever happens, this fight should be pretty interesting.
You think so? I predict a quick and violent win by Erza.
DOON
DOON
How many years has it been since your magic clashed against mine?
Back then, I was just a kid!!!
Now it's different!! This time, I'm going to win!!!

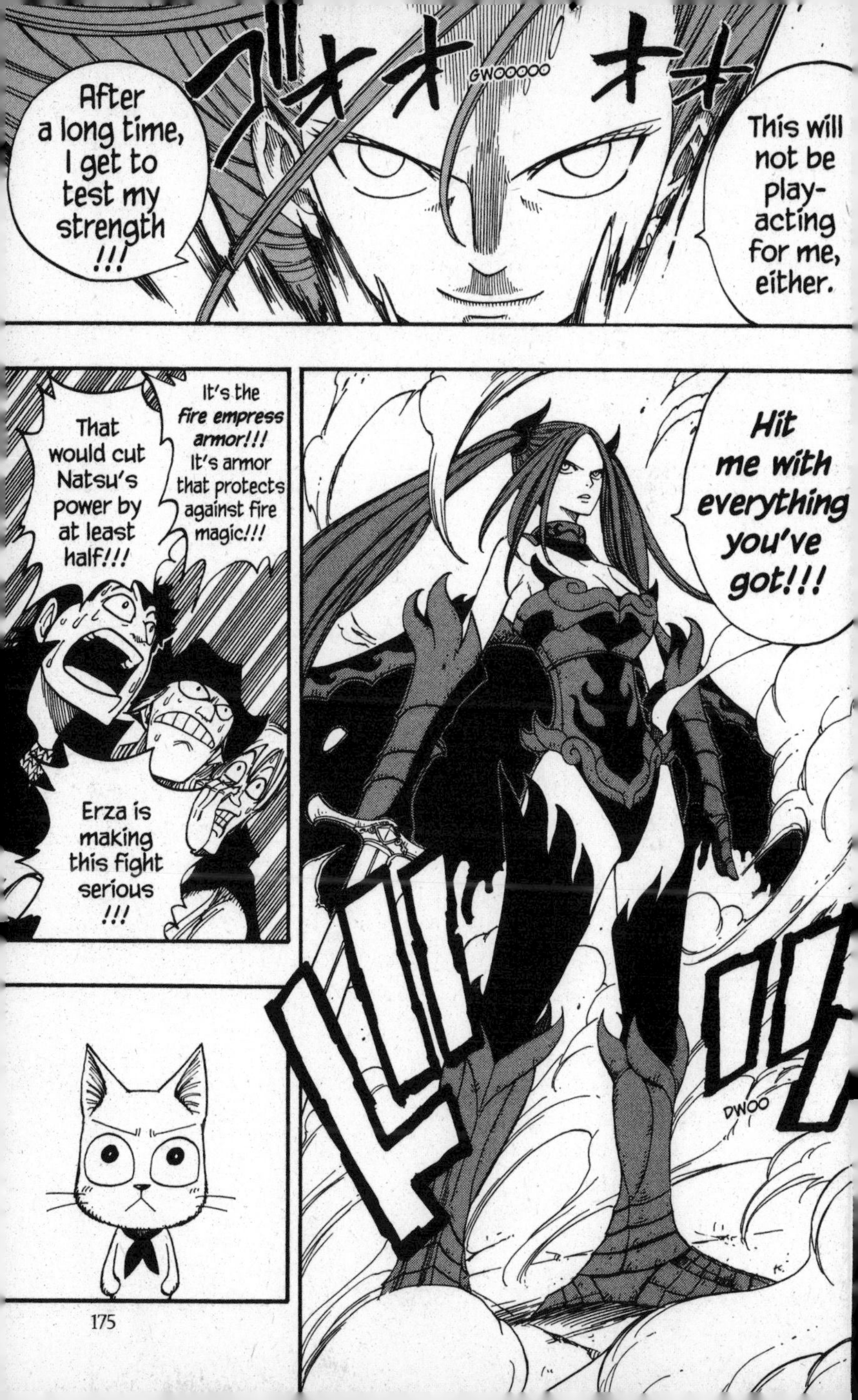
This will not be play-acting for me, either.
GWOOOOO
After a long time, I get to test my strength!!!
Hit me with everything you've got!!!
DWOO
It's the fire empress armor!!! It's armor that protects against fire magic!!!
That would cut Natsu's power by at least half!!!
Erza is making this fight serious!!!

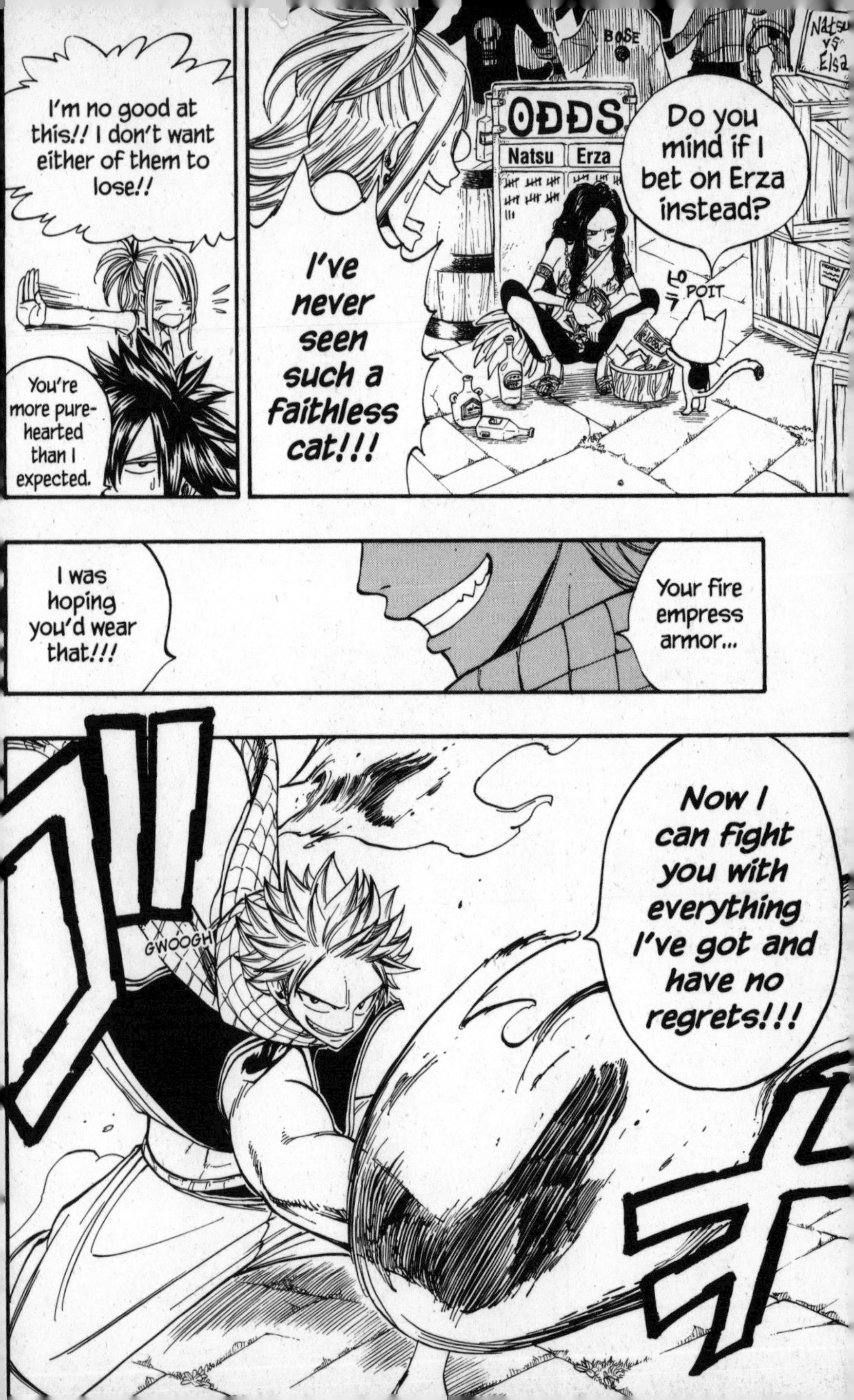

Natsu vs Elsa
ODDS
Natsu
Erza
Do you mind if I bet on Erza instead?
POIT
I've never seen such a faithless cat!!!
I'm no good at this!! I don't want either of them to lose!!
You're more pure-hearted than I expected.
Your fire empress armor...
I was hoping you'd wear that!!!
Now I can fight you with everything I've got and have no regrets!!!
GWOOGH

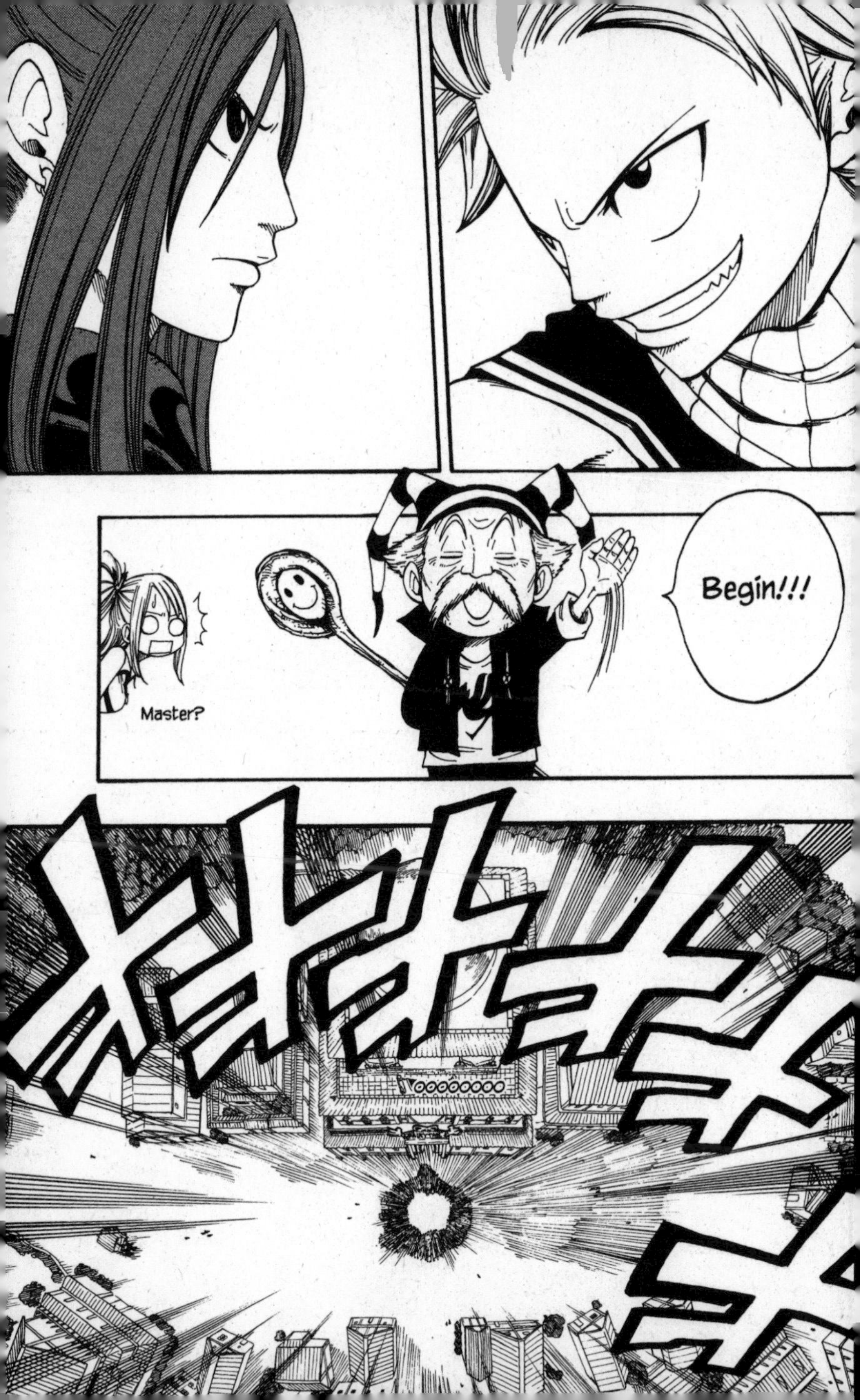
Begin!!!
Master?

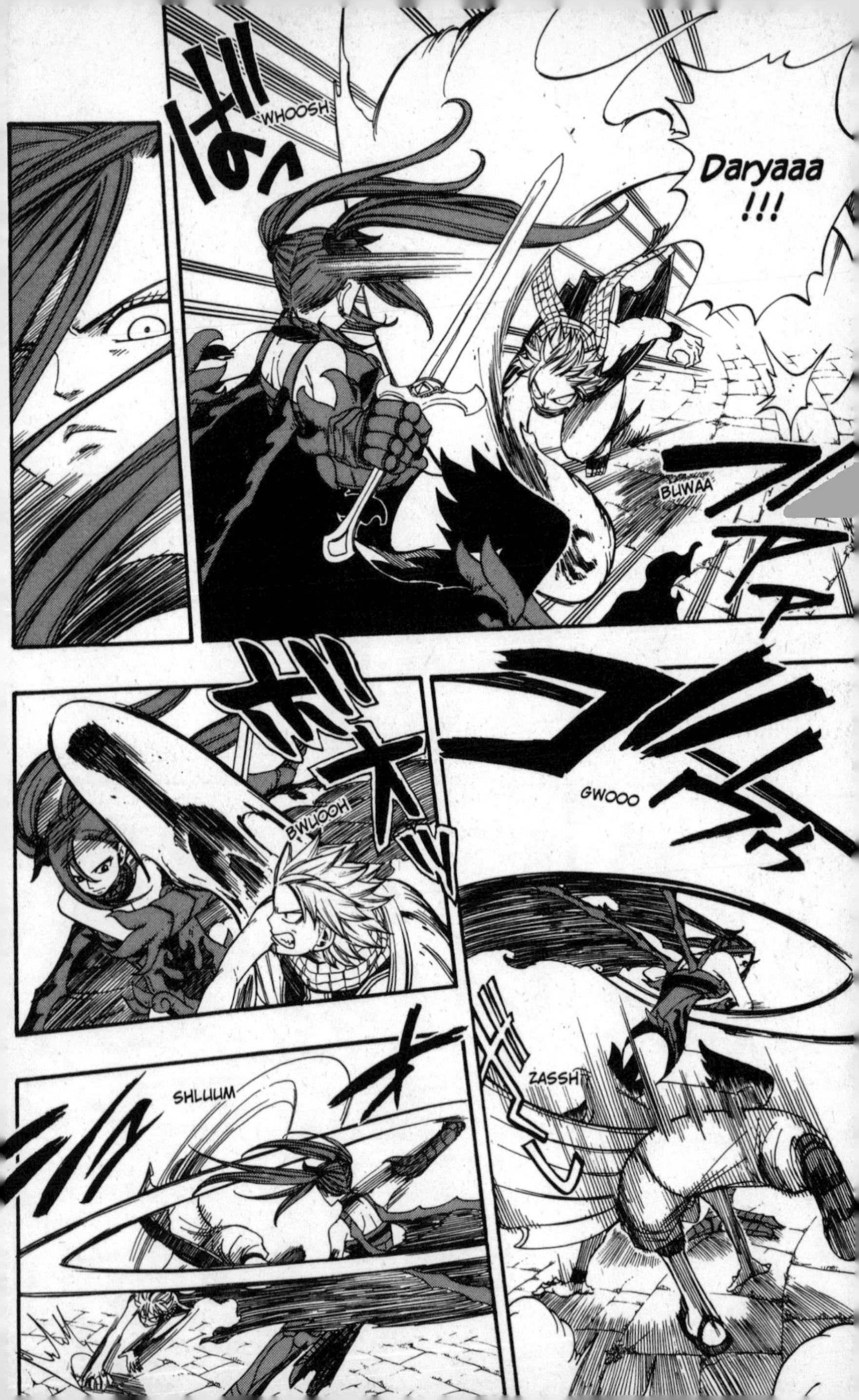
Daryaaa !!!
WHOOSH
BUWAA
GWOOO
BWUOOH
ZASSH
SHLUUM

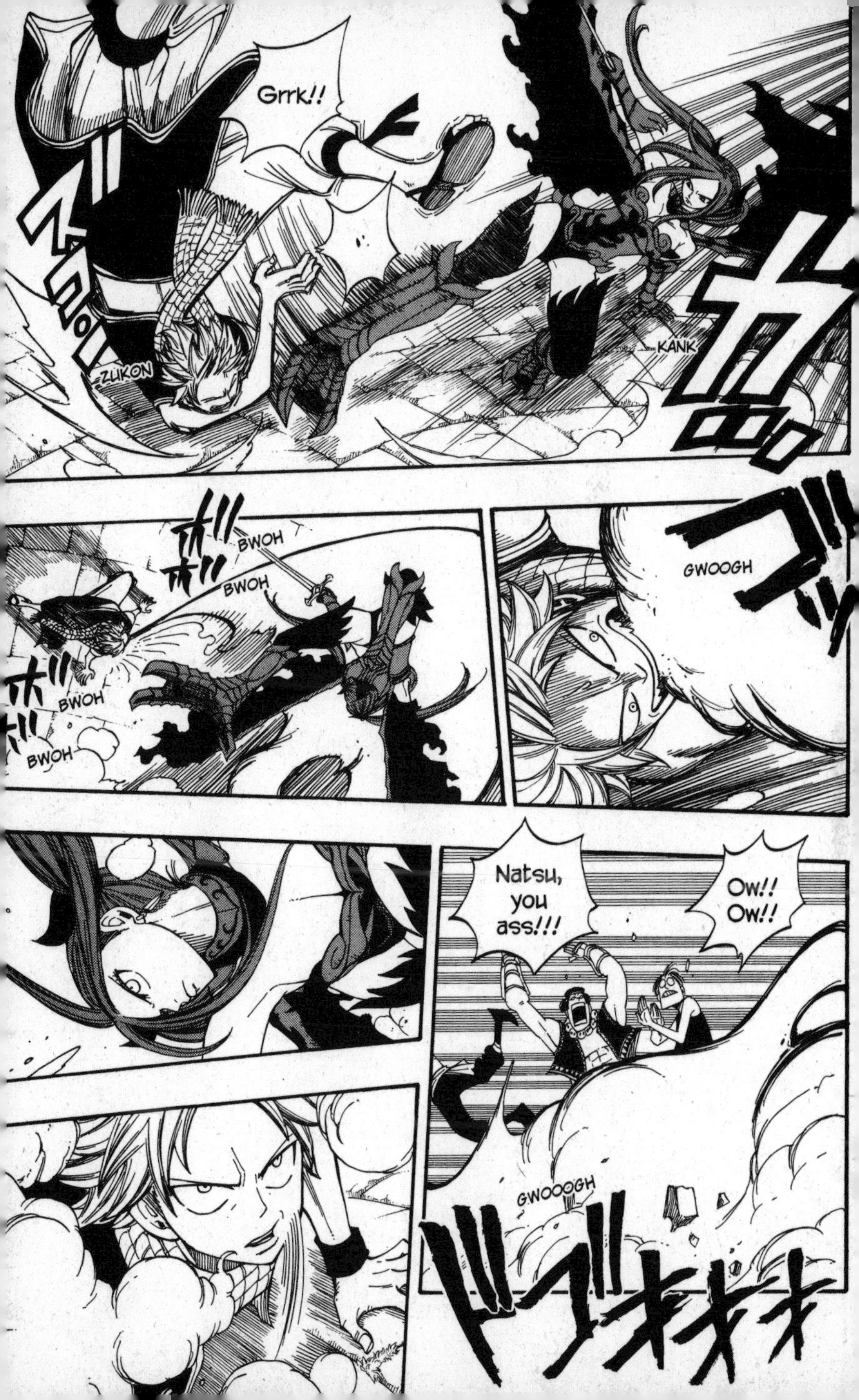
Grrk!!
KANK
ZUKON
GWOOGH
BWOH
BWOH
BWOH
BWOH
Ow!! Ow!!
Natsu, you ass!!!
GWOOOGH

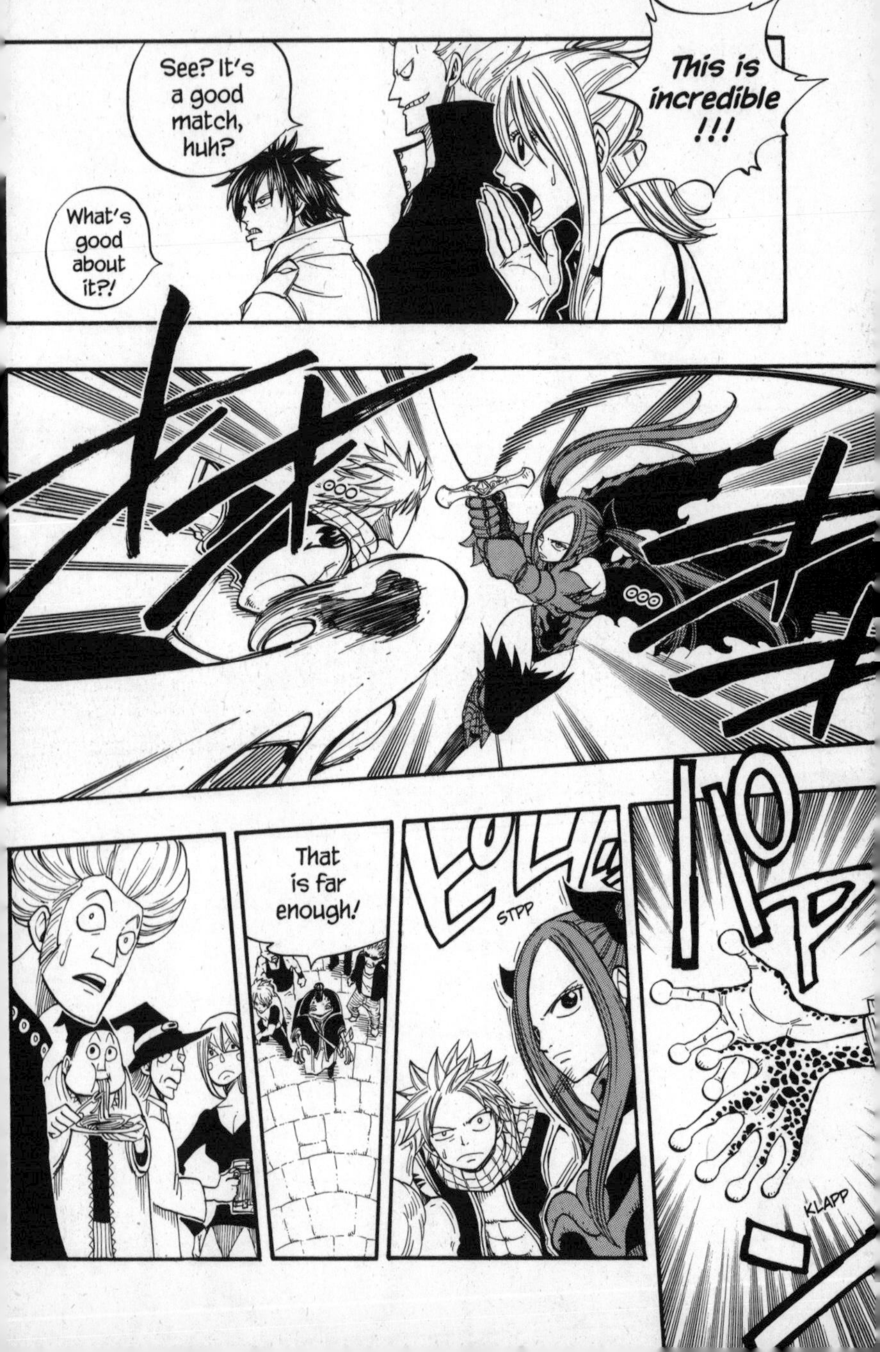
This is incredible!!!
See? It's a good match, huh?
What's good about it?!
KLAPP
STPP
That is far enough!

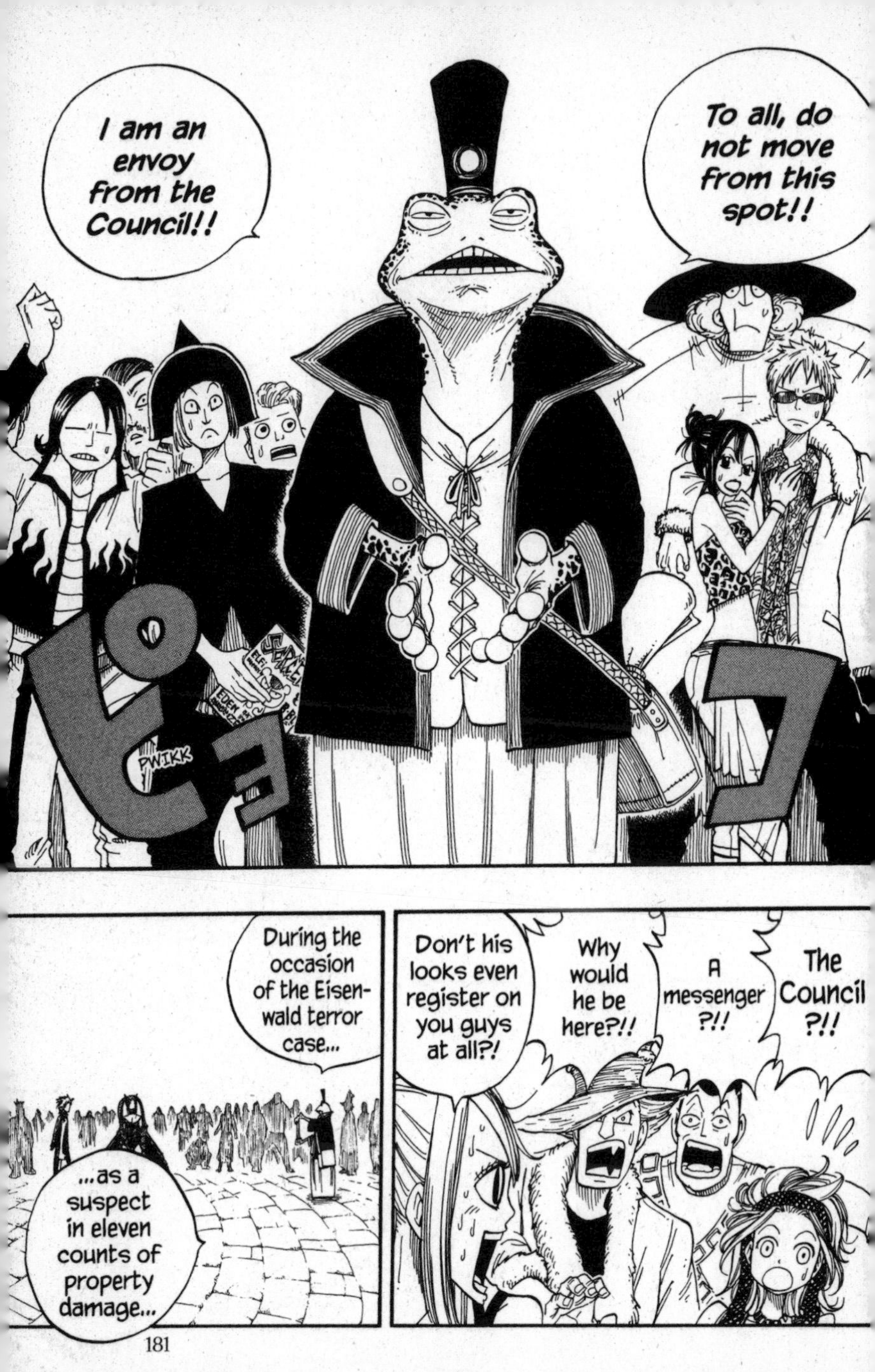
To all, do not move from this spot!!
I am an envoy from the Council!!
PWIKK
The Council ?!!
A messenger ?!!
Why would he be here?!!
Don't his looks even register on you guys at all?!
During the occasion of the Eisen-wald terror case...
...as a suspect in eleven counts of property damage...

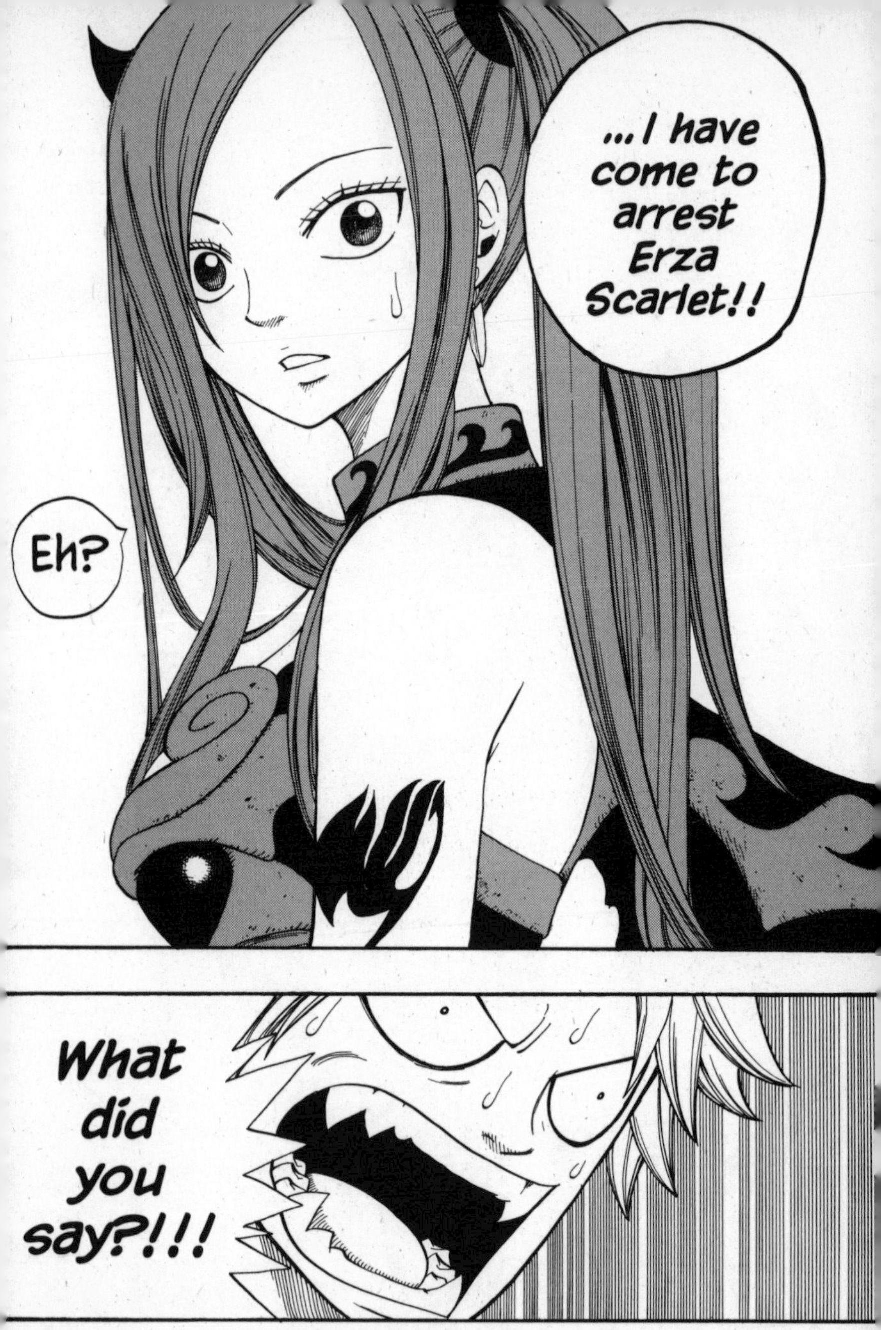
...I have come to arrest Erza Scarlet!!
Eh?
What did you say?!!!

TO BE CONTINUED

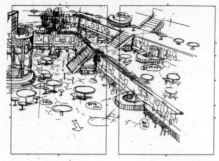

The Early Design Work for the Fairy Tail Bar

We've only been able to fit a small selection onto these pages (and only those that were rejected). Actually, several dozen sketches were drawn for it. As I'm sure you'll see if you look at the manga pages, the interior has gotten much simpler. There are all sorts of odd characters all over the place, so we went with a simple interior so as not to distract from them.

I ANSWER YOUR QUESTIONS!

Among all of the letters that I've received from fans, the question I am asked most often is this:

"What's the relationship between *Siegrain* and *Seig Hart*?"
Yes. *Siegrain* is that guy on the Council, right? And Seig Hart...isn't even in this manga!! He's a character from my previous manga, *Rave Master*! Anyone who hasn't read both wouldn't even understand this question, so I'll explain briefly. Seig Hart has a name similar to Siegrain, and they have similar faces. Moreover, they both use magic. So those who know my previous work well would like to know their relationship. Very well. This is the answer.

They are completely unrelated!! (Utterly)

My previous work, *Rave Master,* and *Fairy Tail* are two unrelated universes. Even if Siegrain seems like a character you may have seen before, he is a completely different character. Basically Siegrain is a character I designed as a bit of fan service for those readers who have also read *Rave Master*. But he's a different character with a different personality. So, if you don't know who Seig Hart is, no problem! It's just that Seig Hart is a cool guy, and a good guy as well. Siegrain, this time, will probably turn out to be a bad guy. I still don't quite know, though...

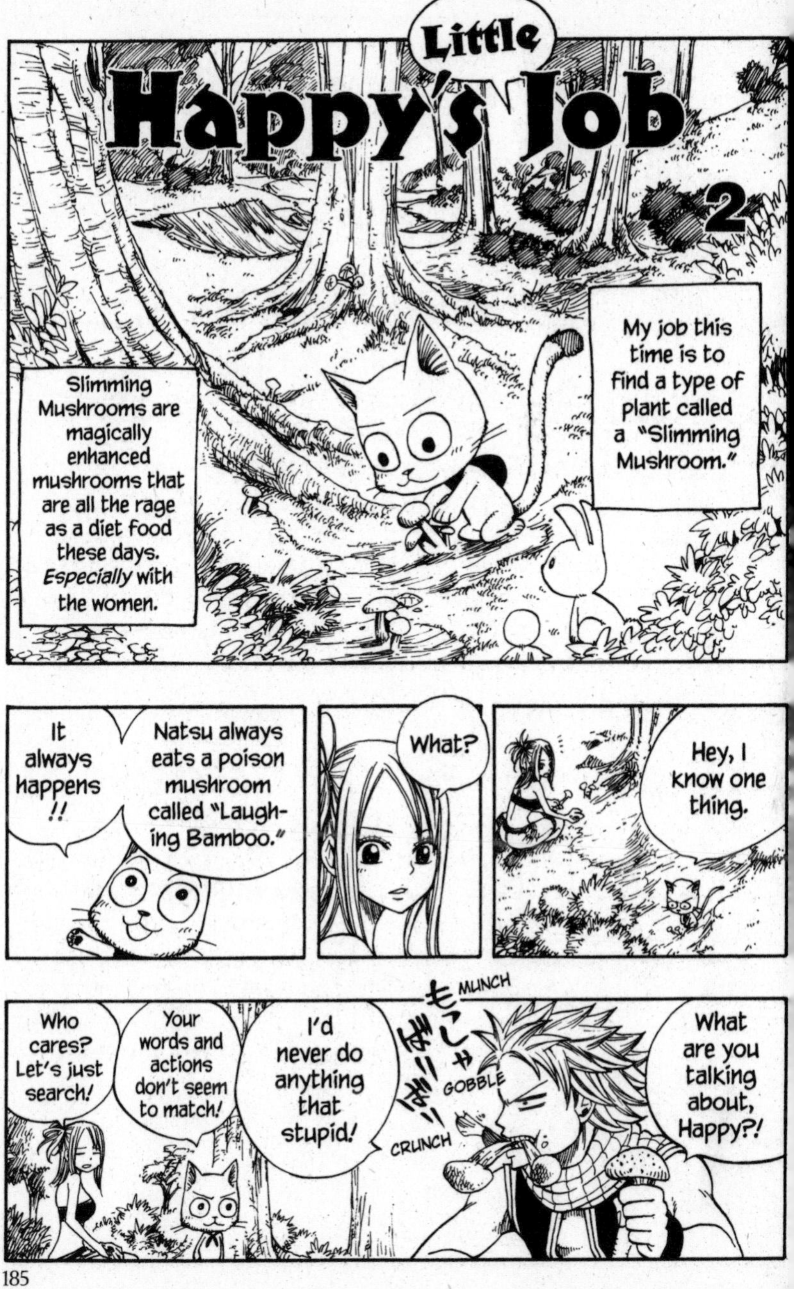
Little
Happy's Job
2
My job this time is to find a type of plant called a "Slimming Mushroom."
Slimming Mushrooms are magically enhanced mushrooms that are all the rage as a diet food these days. *Especially* with the women.
Hey, I know one thing.
What?
Natsu always eats a poison mushroom called "Laughing Bamboo."
It always happens!!
What are you talking about, Happy?!
MUNCH
GOBBLE
CRUNCH
I'd never do anything that stupid!
Your words and actions don't seem to match!
Who cares? Let's just search!

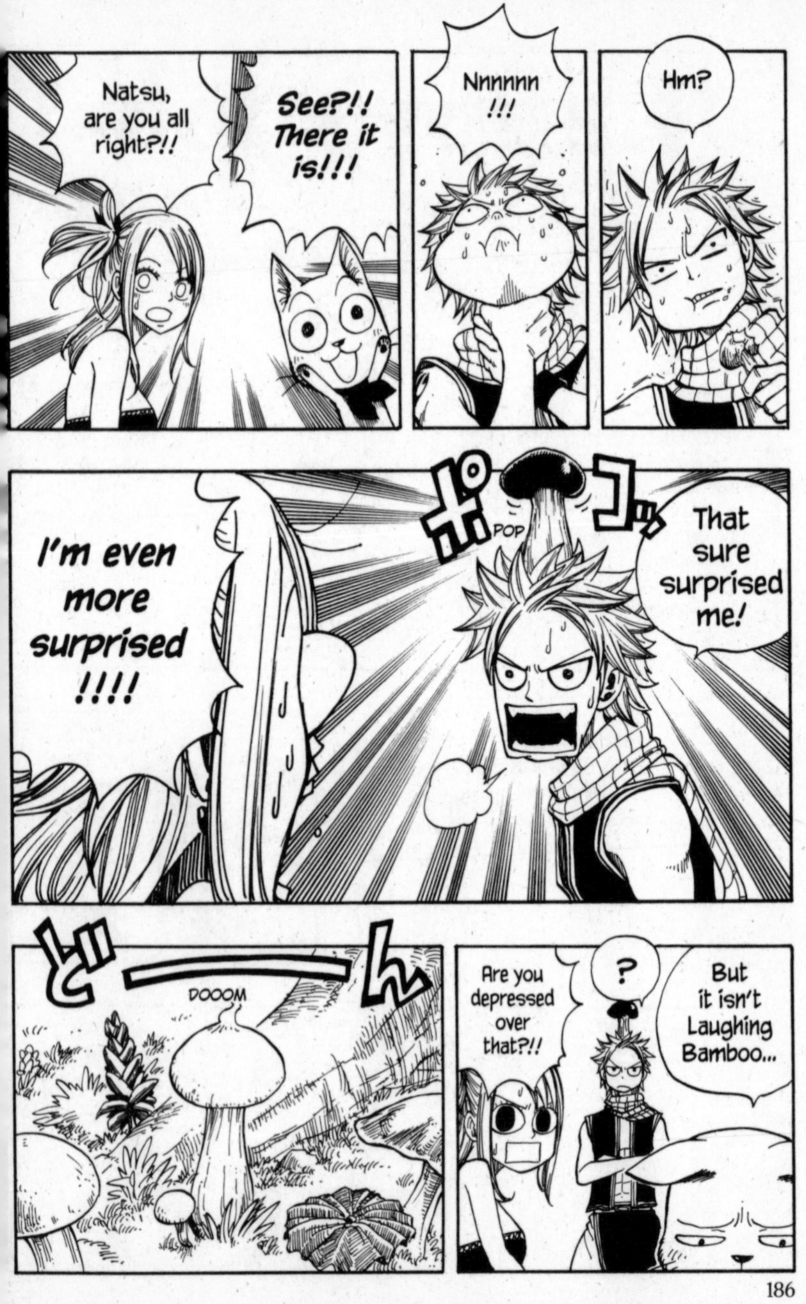
Hm?
Nnnnnn !!!
See?!! There it is!!!
Natsu, are you all right?!!
POP
That sure surprised me!
I'm even more surprised !!!!
But it isn't Laughing Bamboo...
?
Are you depressed over that?!!
DOOOM

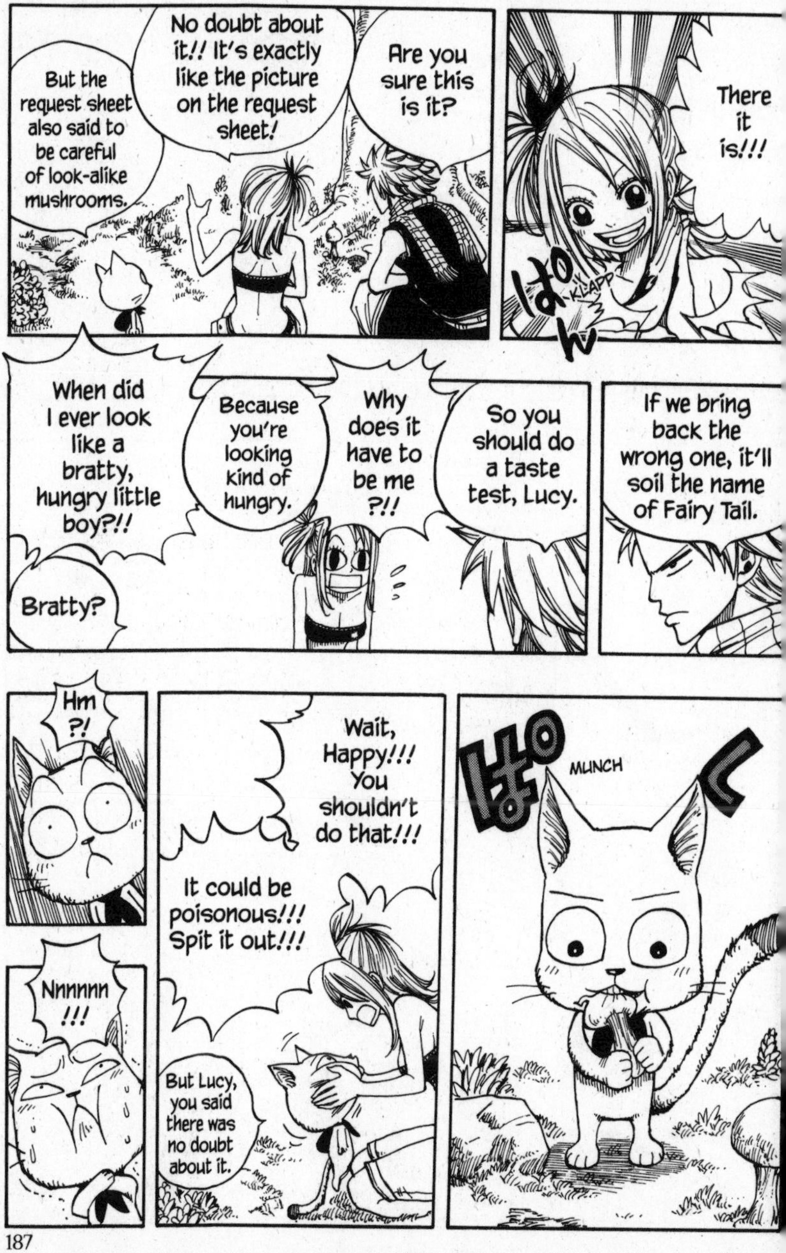
There it is!!!
KLAPP
Are you sure this is it?
No doubt about it!! It's exactly like the picture on the request sheet!
But the request sheet also said to be careful of look-alike mushrooms.
If we bring back the wrong one, it'll soil the name of Fairy Tail.
So you should do a taste test, Lucy.
Why does it have to be me?!!
Because you're looking kind of hungry.
When did I ever look like a bratty, hungry little boy?!!
Bratty?
MUNCH
Wait, Happy!!! You shouldn't do that!!!
It could be poisonous!!! Spit it out!!!
But Lucy, you said there was no doubt about it.
Hm ?!
Nnnnnn !!!

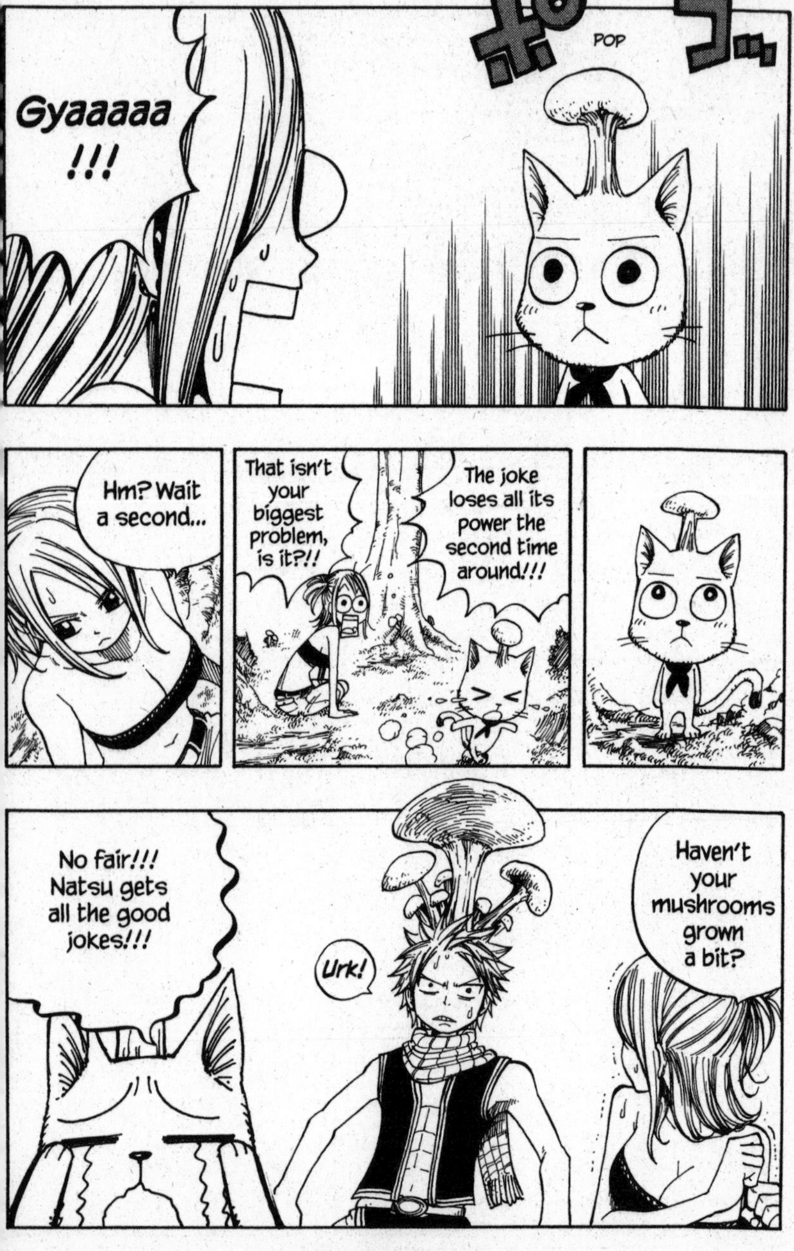
ポコッ
POP
Gyaaaaa!!!
The joke loses all its power the second time around!!!
That isn't your biggest problem, is it?!!
Hm? Wait a second...
Haven't your mushrooms grown a bit?
Urk!
No fair!!! Natsu gets all the good jokes!!!

The End

AFTERWORD

In the afterward of volume 2, I asked what people would like to see in bonus pages, and the most frequent response was "I'd like to see a Fan Art section!" Wow!! You people really love to draw, huh? As someone who likes to draw myself, I'm very happy to hear it! And so, I guess I'll just go ahead and make a Fan Art section!! Clap clap!! Hm... Let's see... As a name for the section, how about, "Fairy Tail d'Art"? Hm... Too long, huh? And I get the feeling that I've heard it somewhere before... Oh! I know!! "Guild d'Art"!! How about that?

The idea is this: Inside Fairy Tail, there's a corkboard, and people post art there instead of requests for missions. What do you think? What's that? You don't care how I package it? Well, anyway, I hope everyone sends drawings into the Guild d'Art. Draw whatever you want, but make sure it's with black pen. Even if you want to shout, "I can't draw!!" send in your drawings anyway. This isn't about good drawings or bad drawings. Guild d'Art is about fun drawings (depressing drawings are good, too). Just bring it!! I'll figure out some kind of present for those lucky few who get into the publication.

Send your art to:

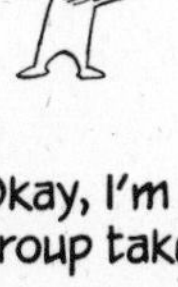

DEL REY MANGA
1745 Broadway
New York, NY 10019
delreymanga@randomhouse.com

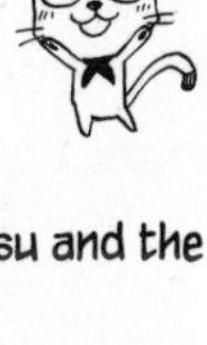

Okay, I'm going to draw, too!! Oh, in the next *Fairy Tail*, Natsu and the group take on a job they really shouldn't take!!

When you send letters, postcards, and other mailings, personal information such as your name, address, postal code, etc., will also be delivered to the author. Please keep that in mind when you send mail.

Also, please keep in mind that while Del Rey Manga will make its best efforts to deliver your fan letters to Mashima-sensei, a reply to your letter cannot be guaranteed.

About the Creator

HIRO MASHIMA was born May 3, 1977, in the Nagano prefecture. His series *Rave Master* has made him one of the most popular manga artists in America. *Fairy Tail,* currently being serialized in *Weekly Shonen Magazine,* is his latest creation.

Translation Notes

Japanese is a tricky language for most Westerners, and translation is often more art than science. For your edification and reading pleasure, here are notes on some of the places where we could have gone in a different direction in our translation of the work, or where a Japanese cultural reference is used.

General Notes:
Wizard

In the original Japanese version of *Fairy Tail*, you'll find panels in which the English word "wizard" is part of the original illustration. So this translation has taken that as its inspiration and translated the word *madôshi* as "wizard." But *madôshi*'s meaning is similar to certain Japanese words that have been borrowed by the English language, such as *judo* (the soft way) and *kendo* (the way of the sword). *Madô* is the way of magic, and *madôshi* are those who follow the way of magic. So although the word "wizard" is used in the original dialogue, a Japanese reader would be likely to think not of traditional Western wizards such as Merlin or Gandalf, but of martial artists.

Names

Hiro Mashima has graciously agreed to provide official English spellings for just about all the characters in *Fairy Tail*. Because this version of *Fairy Tail* is the first publication of most of these spellings, there will inevitably be differences between these spellings and some of the fan interpretations that may have spread throughout the Web or in other fan circles. Rest assured that the spellings contained in this book are the spellings that Mashima-sensei wanted for *Fairy Tail*.

Requip, page 11

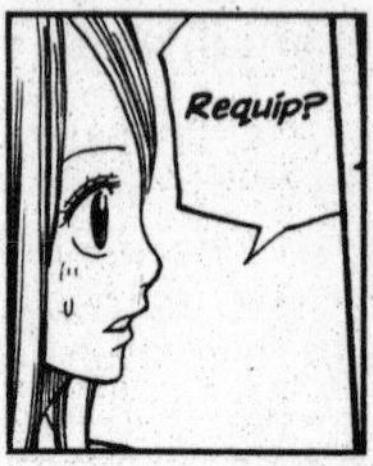
Requip?

The Japanese used a word that isn't standard Japanese, *kansô*, that is made of the kanji that means "change" and another kanji that means "equipment." Since the Japanese word was coined just for *Fairy Tail*, I decided to make up an English word that will convey the same concept.

Titania, page 15

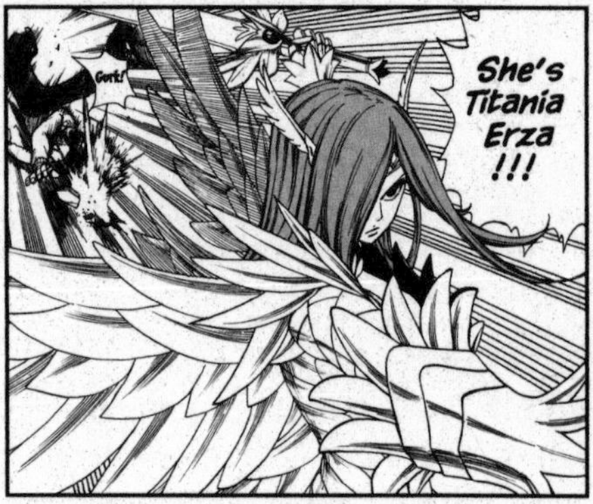
She's Titania Erza !!!
Gurk!

The kanji translates out to "Queen of the Fairies," but the katakana pronunciation guide next to the kanji reads "Taitaania." This seems to be an obvious reference to the queen of the Fairy Kingdom, Titania, who is found in Shakespeare's comedy *A Midsummer Night's Dream*, among other classic fantasies.

WakuWaku Land, page 52

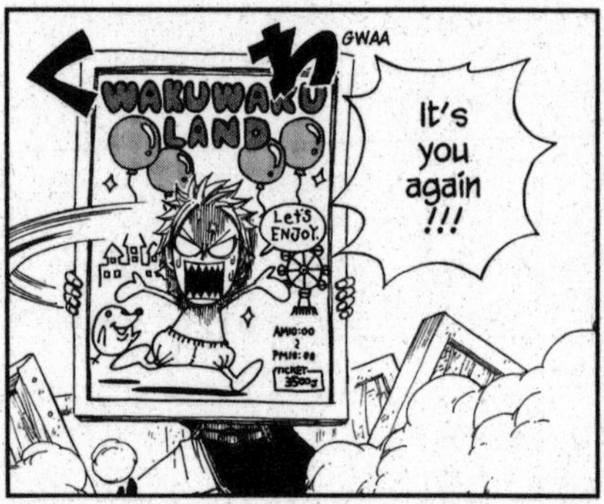
It's you again !!!
GWAA
WAKUWAKU LAND
Let's ENJOY.

The Japanese word *waku waku* means to be excited, and it seems a fitting word for the name of a theme park. Northeast Asia is second only to North America when it comes to the popularity of amusement parks. Japan has about thirty large amusement parks with attendance of more than a million guests per year, and an equal number of medium-sized parks with an annual attendance of 500,000 guests. Overall, the industry accounts for seventy-five million attendees and $1.5 billion in annual revenues—about 30% of U.S. attendance figures in a country that's only as large as California. (Figures circa 1998.)

Orochi, page 53

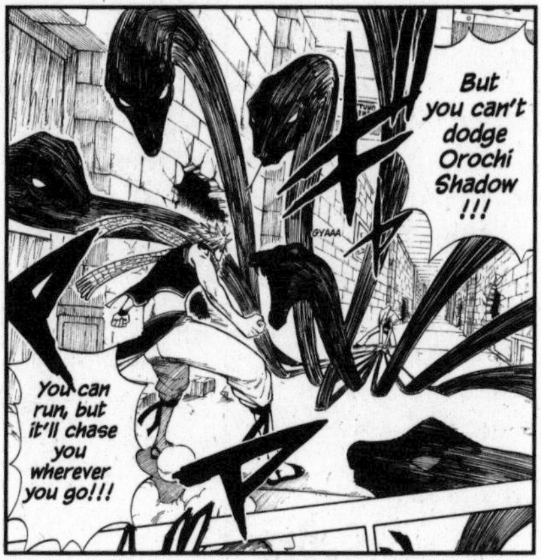
But you can't dodge Orochi Shadow!!!
GYAAA
You can run, but it'll chase you wherever you go!!!

The mythological beast's full name is Yamata no Orochi (the eight-forked serpent), and it comes from the book of Japanese myths, the *Kojiki*. Orochi is said to have eight heads and eight tails. The god Susanoô, who had descended to Earth, helped save the last of the eight daughters of an earthly god from being devoured by the beast. Susanoô had the god brew saké, which had been refined eight times, as bait and place the saké in eight vats. When the serpent was drunk, Susanoô started hacking away.

Meow and not be heard, page 75

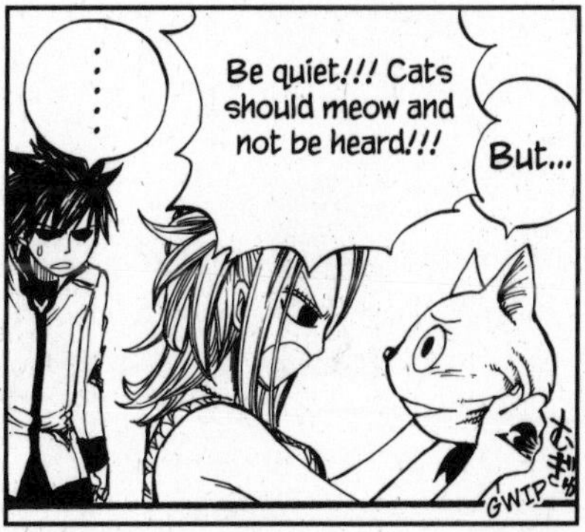
Be quiet!!! Cats should meow and not be heard!!!
But...
......
GWIP

I know Lucy's line doesn't make any sense, but this is very close to a direct word-for-word translation of the Japanese. It doesn't make any logical sense in Japanese, either, and that's probably the reason for Gray's reaction.

Dominatrix, page 77

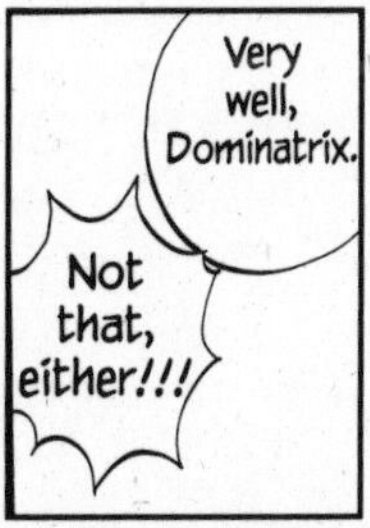
Very well, Dominatrix.
Not that, either!!!

"A woman with a whip" is shorthand for an S&M dominatrix in Japan. In Japanese, they are called *joô-sama*, which is one of the Japanese words that mean "queen." But, although the word "queen" is apparently also used in western S&M circles, it does not immediately conjure up the image of a "dominatrix" to the average English-speaking reader. For that reason, this translation uses a more direct term.

Storm Bringer, page 94

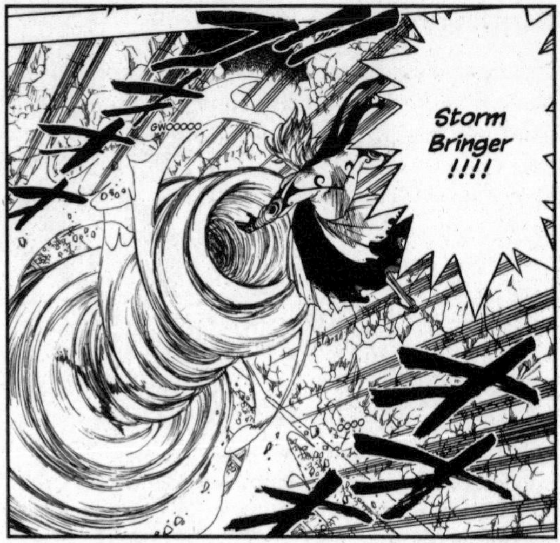
Storm Bringer !!!!
GWOOOOO

Although Erigor's attacks have kanji in the Japanese original, the kanji have a pronunciation guide (*furigana*) that was written in the characters usually reserved for foreign words (katakana). And the pronunciation written was the English words "Storm Bringer." The same holds true for Erigor's later attack names (with the exception of Emera Baram below).

Emera Baram, page 107

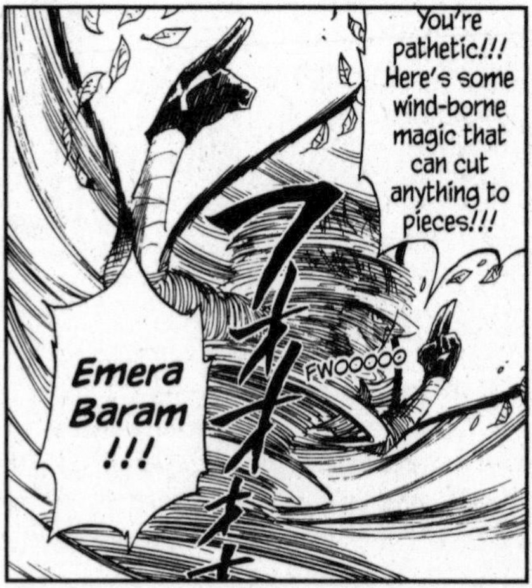
You're pathetic!!! Here's some wind-borne magic that can cut anything to pieces!!!
FWOOOOO
Emera Baram !!!

Most of Erigor's spells are in English, but this one wasn't. Since the pronunciation guide was written in katakana (see the above note), it was obvious that the pronunciation was supposed to be foreign sounding. Unfortunately, I could not find what language it was supposed to be in (if any). If you know, please let us know.

Flaming brat, page 108

It may seem to the readers that I, as translator, am taking advantage of Natsu's fire magic to add in some fire-based puns to the script. Actually, Japanese uses fire-based descriptive language as well, and whenever the dialogue mentions "burning up," being "on fire," "flaming," etc., there was a Japanese reference to fire in the original line of dialogue.

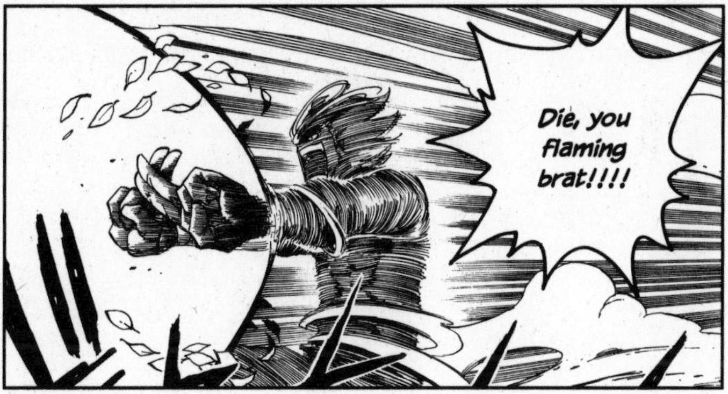
Die, you flaming brat!!!!

Finger in the cheek, page 130

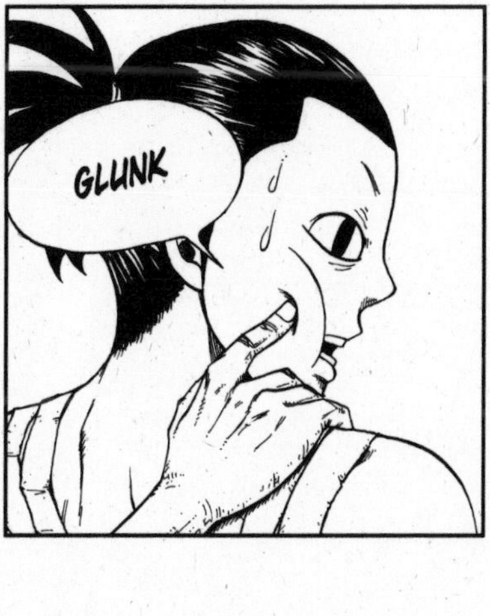
GLUNK

Do you know the practical joke of tapping someone on their right shoulder when you stand on their left side (or vice versa) so that they turn to find no one there? This scene represents a common shoulder-tapping joke for the Japanese. You tap a person on the shoulder and point your index finger at their cheek, so in turning toward the tap, they poke their cheek on your immobile finger.

Preview of Volume 4

We're pleased to present you with a preview from volume 4. Please check our website (www.delreymanga.com) to see when this volume will be available in English. For now you'll have to make do with Japanese!

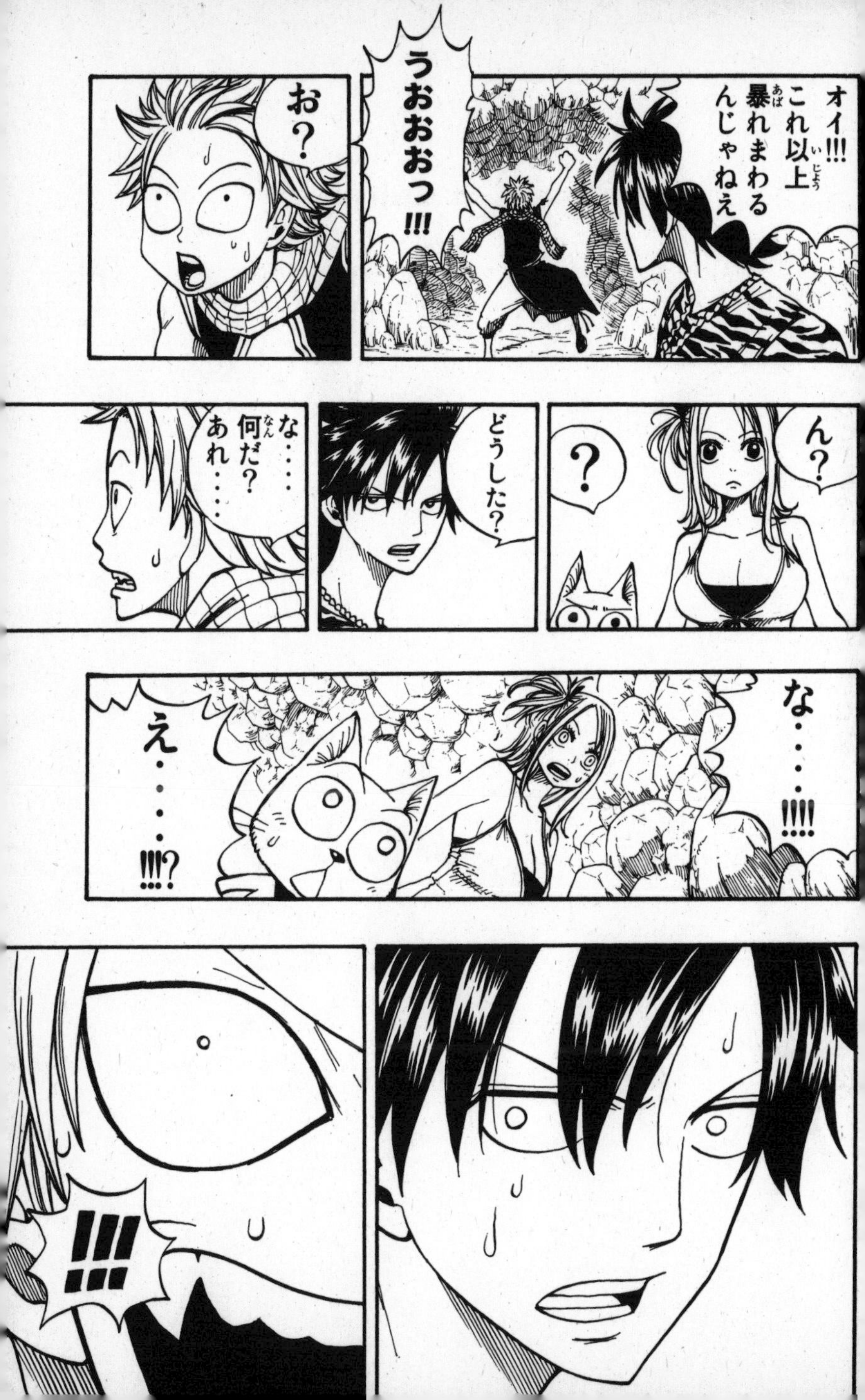
オイ!!! これ以上暴れまわるんじゃねえ
うおおおっ!!!
お?
ん?
?
どうした?
な・・・・何だ?あれ・・・・
な・・・・!!!!
え・・・・!!!?
!!!!!!

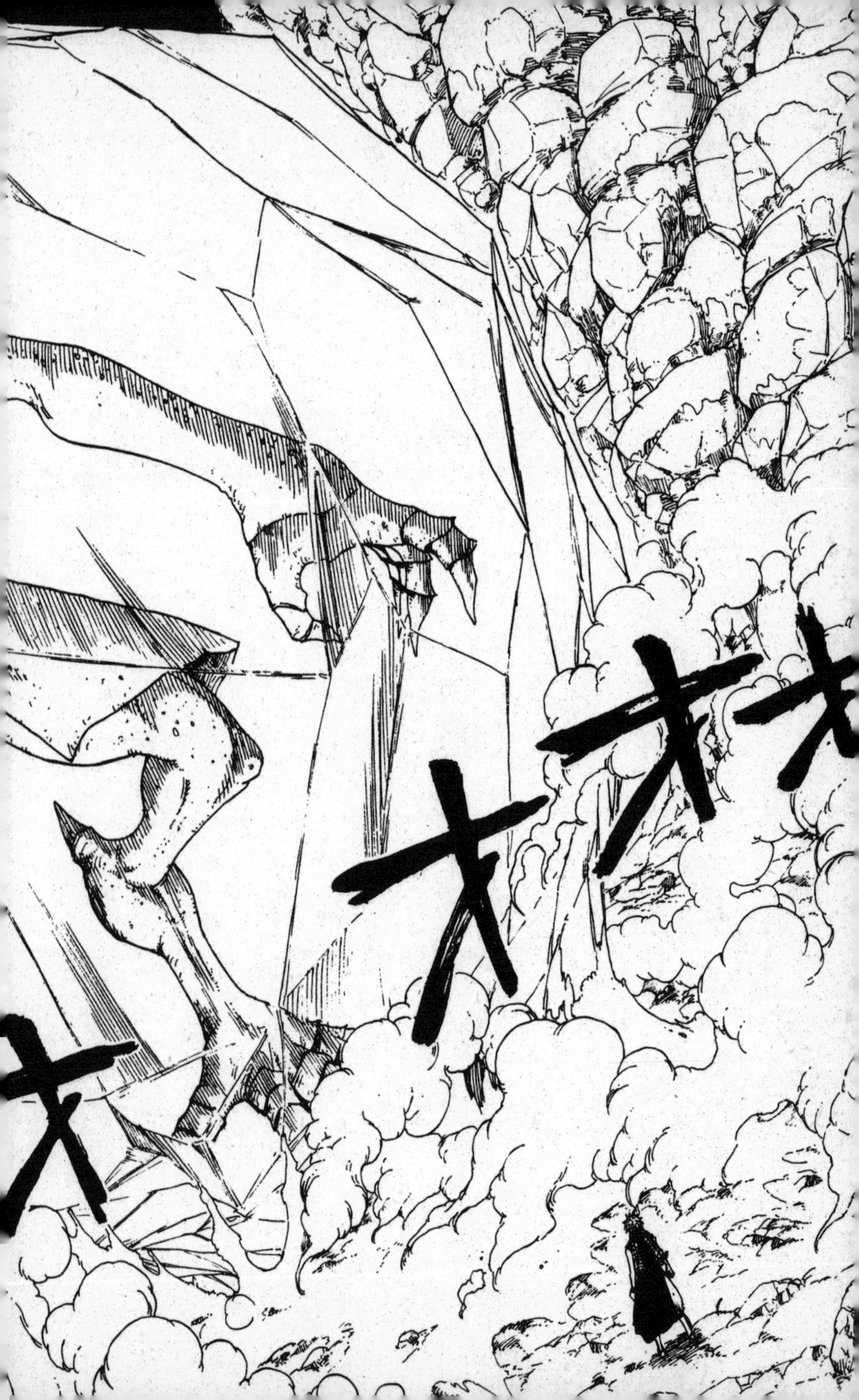
オオオオ

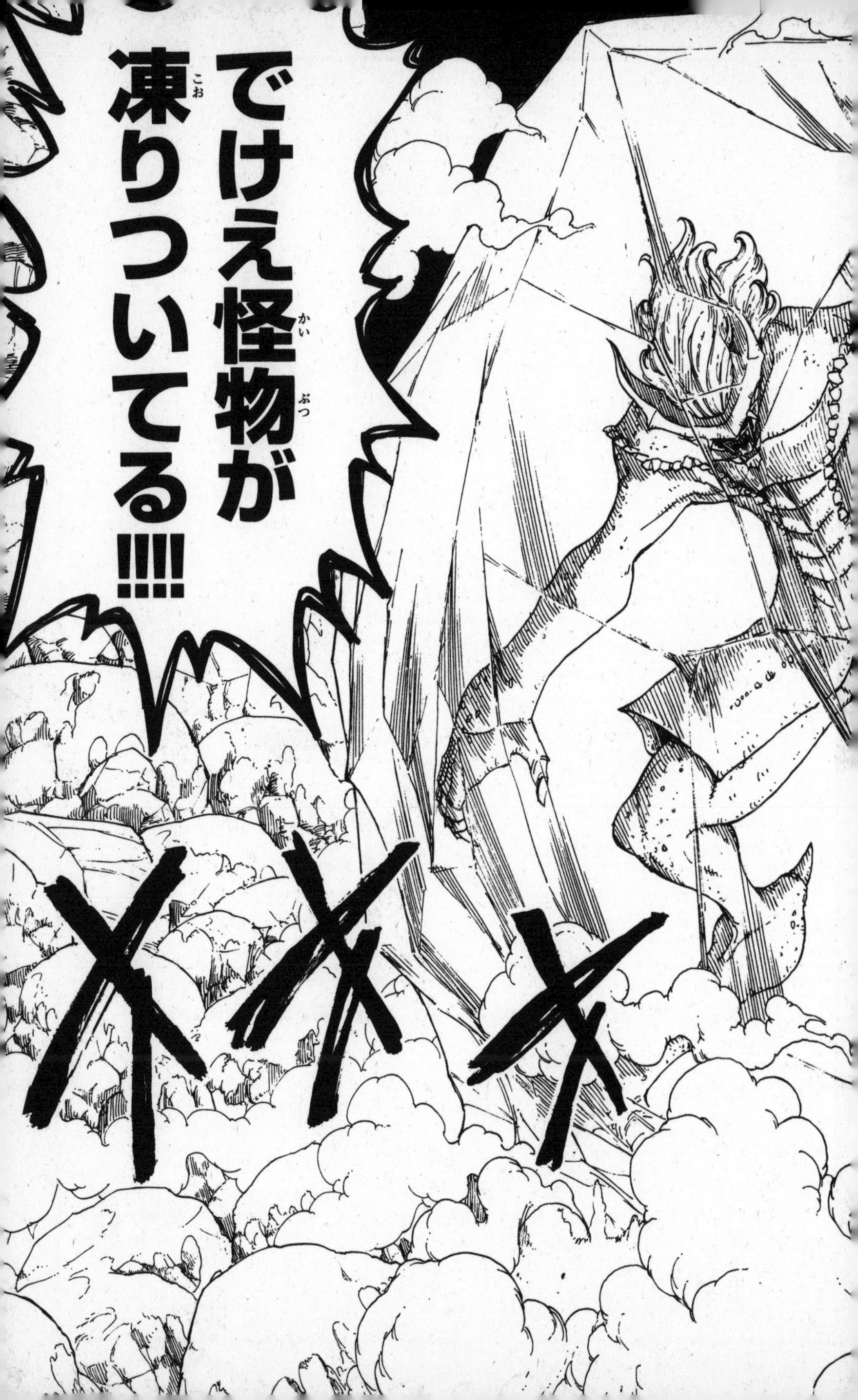
でけえ怪物が凍りついてる!!!!

STORY BY SURT LIM
ART BY HIROFUMI SUGIMOTO

A DEL REY MANGA ORIGINAL

Exploring the woods, young Kasumi encounters an ancient tree god, who bestows upon her the power of invisibility. Together with classmates who have had similar experiences, Kasumi forms the Magic Play Club, dedicated to using their powers for good while avoiding sinister forces that would exploit them.

Special extras in each volume! Read them all!

VISIT WWW.DELREYMANGA.COM TO:
- Read sample pages
- View release date calendars for upcoming volumes
- Sign up for Del Rey's free manga e-newsletter
- Find out the latest about new Del Rey Manga series

RATING | T AGES 13+

DEL REY MANGA

The Otaku's Choice.™

TOMARE!

止まれ

[STOP!]

You're going the wrong way!

Manga is a completely different type of reading experience.

To start at the *beginning*, go to the *end*!

That's right! Authentic manga is read the traditional Japanese way—from right to left, exactly the opposite of how American books are read. It's easy to follow: Just go to the other end of the book and read each page—and each panel—from right side to left side, starting at the top right. Now you're experiencing manga as it was meant to be!